Informix DBA Survival Guide

Second Edition

ISBN 0-13-079623-9

9 780130 796233

90000

PRENTICE HALL PTR INFORMIX SERIES

To See a Complete List of Informix Press Titles, Point to
  http://www.prenhall.com/~informix

Informix DBA Survival Guide

Second Edition

Joe Lumbley

Prentice Hall PTR
Upper Saddle River, New Jersey 07458
http://www.phptr.com

Library of Congress Catologing-in-Publication Data

Lumbley, Joe
   Informix DBA survival guide.—2nd ed./Joe Lumbley
      p.   cm. --(Prentice Hall PTR Informix series)
   Includes index.
   ISBN 0-13-079623-9
   1. Relational database. 2. Informix-SQL. I. Title.
   II. Series.
   QA76.9.D3L859 1999   98-44764
   005.75'65--dc21   CIP

Editorial/Production Supervision: *Kerry Reardon*
Acquisitions Editor: *Miles Williams*
Buyer: *Alexis R. Heydt*
Cover Design: *Design Source*
Cover Design Direction: *Jerry Votta*
Art Director: *Gail Cocker-Bogusz*
Series Design: *Claudia Durrell Design*
Marketing Manager: *Dan Rush*
Manager, Informix Press: *Sandy Emerson*

© 1995, 1999 Prentice Hall PTR
Prentice-Hall, Inc.
A Simon & Schuster Company
Upper Saddle River, NJ 07458

Informix Press
Informix Software, Inc.
4100 Bohannon Drive
Menlo Park, CA 94025

The following are worldwide trademarks of Informix Software, Inc., or its subsidiaries, registered
in the United States of America as indicated by ®, and in numerous other counties worldwide:
INFORMIX®, Informix DataBlade® Module, Informix Dynamic Scalable Architecture™, Informix Illustra™
Server, InformixLink®, INFORMIX®-4GL, INFORMIX®-4GL Compiled,
INFORMIX®-CLI, INFORMIX®-Connect, INFORMIX®-ESQL/C, INFORMIX®-MetaCube™,
INFORMIX®-Mobile, INFORMIX®-NET, INFORMIX®-NewEra™ INFORMIX®-NewEra™ Viewpoint™,
INFORMIX®-NewEra™ Viewpoint™ Pro, INFORMIX®-OnLine, INFORMIX®-OnLine Dynamic Server™,
INFORMIX®-OnLine Workgroup Server, INFORMIX®-OnLine Workstation, INFORMIX®-SE,
INFORMIX®-SQL, INFORMIX-Superview™, INFORMIX®-Universal Server

All other product names mentioned herein are the trademarks or registered trademarks of their
respective owners.

The publisher offers discounts on this book when ordered in bulk quantities. For more
information, call the Corporate Sales Department at 800-382-3419; FAX: 201-236-714,
email corpsales@prenhall.com or write Corporate Sales Department, Prentice Hall PTR,
One Lake Street, Upper Saddle River, NJ 07458

Prentice Hall books are widely used by corporations and government agencies for training,
marketing, and resale.

Printed in the United States of America

10 9 8 7 6 5 4 3 2 1

ISBN 0-13-079623-9

Prentice-Hall International (UK) Limited, *London*
Prentice-Hall of Australia Pty. Limited, *Sydney*
Prentice-Hall Canada Inc., *Toronto*
Prentice-Hall Hispanoamericana, S.A., *Mexico*
Prentice-Hall of India Private Limited, *New Delhi*
Prentice-Hall of Japan, Inc., *Tokyo*
Simon & Schuster Asia Pte. Ltd., *Singapore*
Editora Prentice-Hall do Brasil, Ltda., *Rio de Janeiro*

This book is dedicated to my wife Jayne and my daughter Katherine, who both had to put up with way too many late nights and grumpy mornings during the production of this book.

Chapter 11   Exploring the Sysmaster Database   **289**

Chapter 13   Common DBA Tasks   363

Foreword to the Second Edition

It's really interesting the way a book comes together. I started this project as a completely new book, to be called *The INFORMIX Debugger's Survival Guide*. After about six months of work, I had only about 150 pages completed and was at a total loss for more material. I could have thrown in a lot of technical mumbo-jumbo, code listings, and the like, but it would have just been filler and would have been incredibly boring to write and probably even more boring to read. That's when I decided to incorporate the debugging manuscript into the second edition of the *DBA Survival Guide*.

The first edition was written for Version 5. At the time I didn't feel comfortable enough with Version 7 to write about it, and it took me a couple of years to convince myself that I finally understood the new products enough to write about them. In the meantime, Carlton Doe came out with his excellent Informix Press book, *INFORMIX-OnLine Dynamic Server Handbook*. I recommend Carlton's book highly and intend to "borrow" from it liberally. Some of you may be asking, "What happened to Version 6?" Like the rest of the

Informix community, I think that we'd all be better off forgetting that V6 ever existed. It was the first attempt at multithreading and was quickly replaced by V7. Rest in peace.

When I wrote the first edition, I agonized over the inclusion of what I call "soft" material. This includes such things as the political elements of being a database administrator (DBA), how to deal with things other than computer code, and tricks and tips for maintaining some level of sanity while being a DBA. I wondered whether these items belonged in a technical book. My readers answered that question for me. By far, the most satisfying reviews I received touted the "soft" material. Maybe we're not such computer geeks after all and actually have such things as a sense of humor. My absolute favorite review praised the book's "breezy, blue-collar writing style." For months afterward I signed my Internet postings Joe "Bubba" Lumbley.

After making the decision to abandon the debugging book, the proper way to write a book on debugging was dropped into my lap from a most unexpected source. I had been having trouble with the fuel injection system of my Isuzu Trooper and went to my local auto supply store to buy a motor manual to try to trace down the problem. I've been buying such motor manuals since I was 14 and working on my first Mini Cooper. You know what motor manuals are like. Mine are always covered with grease and grime. You can tell the history of the car problems I've had just by finding the pages with the most grease. With my old Mini, you could just barely see the print in the electrical troubleshooting sections because of all the grease. The carburetion section of my Alfa Romeo manuals are even worse because of the addition of dog-eared pages, margin notes, and lots of big question marks.

Motor manuals are great tools for their intended jobs. They have numbered instruction steps, troubleshooting flowcharts, and plenty of pictures, diagrams, and wiring charts. They're the perfect thing to have when your whole body is crammed into the engine compartment and you have to have that sucker fixed by the end of the day. You're not looking for somebody's master's thesis; what you want is a simple outline that leads you through the process of solving your problem.

Like a lot of other DBAs I've been somewhat resistant to this type of approach. I think I developed a case of "white lab coat syndrome," the same malady that isolated early mainframes into glass houses tended by a cadre of white-coated acolytes who spoke their own language and had special knowledge restricted to their priesthood. While I never went so far as to create a DBA secret handshake, I have been known to assert that "this is DBA stuff and I can't explain it to you in words of fewer than three syllables." Gotta justify that salary, right?

I've come to realize that what we really need is a motor manual for the Informix engine, and I'm trying to restructure this book to meet that need. I'll give you the bare minimum of theory and as much greasy, hands-on techniques as I can. Since I'm having to write this thing, I'll also try to make it fun for me to write, so I'll throw in enough snide comments, semi-off-color humor, and lousy puns to keep it interesting, provided I can slip them by my editors and technical proofreaders.

Being essentially a lazy writer, I've had to struggle to figure out how to gracefully marry the first book's material with the new material without having to totally rewrite the original. While the Version 7 engine is much more complicated and complex than the Version 5 engine, it is very much a superset of the earlier Version 5. That is, most of the material that specifically addressed Version 5 is also applicable to Version 7. As I go through the original material, I'll point out those few instances where Version 5 techniques do not apply to Version 7, and I'll include separate sections for the Version 7 specific material. I had actually considered putting the new material into a distinctive font or printing it in red, but it seemed a little bit too biblical for my style. However, I will try to identify any of the items that apply to Version 7 but not to Version 5.

I'd like to thank several people who have been instrumental in the development of this book. A book is never a solo project, and I have received help from numerous people. First of all, my original acquisitions editor at Prentice Hall, Mark Taub, was instrumental in convincing me to get started on a revision project. I wouldn't have even started on this revision without his enthusiastic support. Mark left for another position at Prentice Hall after this book went into production and I wish him all the best. Many thanks to my new editor, Miles Williams, who has helped me work through the details of producing this book. Thanks to Kerry Reardon, whose thoughtful proofreading has caused me to reopen my freshman English books more than once. Thanks to Anne Trowbridge at Prentice Hall for her efforts in coordinating the production of this book.

Special thanks go to Lester Knutsen, who graciously allowed me to use a paper of his as my chapter on the System Monitoring Tables. He also provided many of the SMI scripts that are included on the CD-ROM. I want to thank Art Kagel for his assistance in proofreading this document and correcting my many fact and conceptual errors. Thanks to David Williams, who gave me permission to use the Frequently Asked Questions (FAQ) file for the USENET newsgroup, comp.databases.informix.

While on the topic of comp.databases.informix, I'd like to thank all of the inhabitants of newsgroup for their patience with some of my technical questions and for the many good ideas that they gave me in their postings. This newsgroup is truly one of the great Informix resources available to Informix users. Thanks to another Informix Press author, Carleton Doe, for his modifications to some of the first edition's scripts and for the many good ideas that his book has given me.

The final set of thanks has to go to my wife Jayne and my daughter Katherine, who put up with this project for almost a year. I want to give them special thanks for not having me institutionalized when I started talking about doing a third book just a few weeks ago.

The Database Administrator: Doing the Job

*T*here are probably as many different descriptions of the database administrator's job function as there are DBAs. Depending upon the complexity and culture of the firm, the database administrator can be anything from a developer who just happens to also wear a DBA hat all the way up to a member of a team of DBAs, all of whom have different responsibilities. Most will fall somewhere in the spectrum between the two extremes.

As a result of the increasing popularity of data warehouses and data marts, we are seeing the emergence of such specialties as data warehouse managers, database analysts, and data managers. Many of these terms are rather loosely defined or are unique to certain corporate cultures. No matter what the job title, an in-depth understanding of the internal operations of the database will be of benefit.

I'm not sure that I've ever seen a proper definition of a database administrator. Perhaps the broadest definition would be: "The person or persons in charge of the database." Oftentimes, though, what this really means is: "The person who's read the DBA manual."

In the hierarchy of database consumers, there's usually an identifiable division between developers and end users. As we move more into empowering the end users, this dividing line becomes less distinct. In many shops, generating reports is strictly an Information Services "glass house" application. The more we move into the client/server model, the more blurred these distinctions become.

Likewise, as more tools become available for managing the database, the line between developer and DBA begins to blur. Developers and systems analysts regularly design database schemas and address application performance questions. They often create their own tables and indexes as well as develop the application code. Database administrators often write application code, especially when they are not full-time DBAs.

Actually, there is a continuum that begins at end users and works up through developers, analysts, DBAs, and Information Service managers. One of the more challenging aspects of working in this field is deciding if and where to draw the lines.

TOWARD A CLIENT/SERVER MODEL

When this book was first published in 1994, Informix's "state of the art" client/server applications were Informix-WingZ and Informix-Viewpoint. Four years later, in 1998, WingZ has been sold to another company and Viewpoint doesn't exist. An entire application development system, NewEra, has been released, upgraded twice, and is losing ground to more modern tools. Informix purchased an online analytical processing systems company and incorporated its product into its MetaCube option, which provides extended summarization and drill-down into Informix-based data warehouses.

In the same four years, the Informix database engine has seen a short-lived Version 6 followed by a continually improving Version 7, now known as Informix Dynamic Server, or IDS. Informix purchased an object-oriented database company, Illustra, and incorporated its object-oriented database into what was originally called Informix Universal Server, and is now called Informix Dynamic Server with Universal Data Option. Informix extended Version 7 into an extended parallel processing system that operates within clusters of UNIX machines. This product has variously been called Extended Parallel Server (XPS), Version 8, and the current Informix Dynamic Server with Parallel Option.

Informix Dynamic Server has been ported to the Microsoft Windows NT environment, and the engine looks almost identical to its older UNIX siblings. Some differences exist at the installation level due to differences between NT's and UNIX's filesystems, but at the database and application levels, the ports look identical. The installation is actually much cleaner and less error prone in the NT port.

The database administration and query tools are also totally revamped for the NT port. The dbaccess program still exists for those who are insistent on using a character-based interface, but Informix has added a graphical query program called SQLEditor   The `tbmonitor/onmonitor` program is completely replaced by a graphical interface very similar to that used on Microsoft SQL Server.

Being the diehard UNIX bigots that most of us DBAs are, Windows NT has still not achieved the respect of a "real operating system," but even the UNIX lovers are beginning to salivate at these graphical tools. From what used to be a total UNIX environment, many are going toward using NT as client platforms and leaving the real work to Informix Dynamic Server on UNIX machines.

Look for this to change, and to change more and more in favor of Windows NT. I know, such sacrilege is grounds for my ejection from the UNIX priesthood. The fact is that four-processor NT systems are becoming available with faster processors than many UNIX machines, and Informix Dynamic Server on such machines can actually be made to perform extremely well. The Parallel Option is now available for clustered NT systems.

The point is that the NT systems are closing in on the UNIX systems in performance and usually have a significant advantage in cost of ownership. Don't discount either their performance or their impact in the market. For those UNIX bigots who still refuse to see the light, at least admit that NT has given us a lot of really neat client tools.

TYPICAL DBA JOB FUNCTIONS

No matter where the lines are drawn, there are certain functions that need to be part of the overall management of any database system. This list is not comprehensive. Every organization will have its own quirks and peculiarities, but these are the basic items.

Keeping the Database Running

This is the primary function of the database administrator in production environments. Especially in mission-critical applications that run 24 hours a day, 7 days a week (24x7), the database administrator is judged first on system downtime. In some situations, the cost of minutes of downtime can be more than the annual salary of the DBA.

This has become more prevalent as Informix-based systems have been developed for transaction processing systems for banks and retailers. These systems are now appearing more and more in such telecom, credit card processing, and Web-based systems. These systems have to be up all of the time or have failover capability that can transfer their duties over to other machines should they fail. There are application requirements in some cases that permit less than an hour of downtime a year. Companies such as Stratus are producing fault-tolerant systems that are capable of less than 15 minutes downtime a year. Obviously, applications that need such hardware dependability will demand a similar dependability from their database operations, which are often the heart of the application.

In most applications, whether mission critical or not, database downtime impacts just about everyone associated with the database. Order entry personnel, service and help line personnel, data-entry staff, and software developers need to have the database up and running to get any work done.

Downtime is not only when the database is completely down. It is perceived downtime that hurts. If the database is running slowly, no matter what the cause, the effect is just about as bad as if it is not running at all. In fact, when the database is running slowly, it is often even worse than when it is not running at all.

Have you ever waited for an elevator that is running slowly? Chances are, you've pushed the button several times, hoping that repeatedly pushing the button will somehow make the elevator get to you faster. Computer users exhibit the same type of superstitious behavior. They will put jobs in the background, use the UNIX `nice` command, open additional terminal windows and database jobs, fill their keyboard buffers with useless keystrokes, or hit a series of breaks, all in the hope that something will make the database go faster. Usually this just makes things worse. What started as a slowdown winds up as a crash. Crashes that occur because of this type of load-related problem are often quite difficult to diagnose, especially when they are at the operating system level. Here, the operating system dies and doesn't give Informix the time to log whatever errors or problem it has.

What this means to the DBA is that you must communicate with your users. If the database is slow, let the users know. Believe me, they already know. What you're doing is telling them that you know there's a problem and you're working on it. If it's possible, plan your downtime in advance. Give everyone lots of notice. If you can negotiate scheduled downtime, do so. The users will get used to it and your life will be easier.

Often, the DBA will be the cause of the slowdowns. This you can almost certainly control. If you're using any of the Informix utilities, be aware of their effects on the database. Certain options in `tb/oncheck` can cause tables to lock. Using `tb/onlog` on an active logfile can freeze up the database. Know your tools.

If the database does inexplicably freeze up, look first for problems with the checkpoints. This is a common cause of database hangs. Often, a checkpoint may hang while it is blocked by some other system activity. The checkpoint hang may very well be a symptom of some other problem. As an example, a checkpoint that is requested while the `tbape` archive is waiting for a new tape in an OnLine system will freeze up until the new tape is inserted. Beware of such interactions between programs. Luckily, this type of tape-change freeze-up is no longer a problem in IDS systems, since the system uses internal temporary tables to help avoid the problem.

Training the Users

The user community can make or break the DBA. If the users are knowledgeable about the database, they'll make fewer demands on the DBA and do more for themselves. The DBA will spend less time fighting fires and more time in more constructive activities if he devotes the necessary time to helping the users get up to speed.

Of course, different users have different needs. If most of your users are using "canned" software, meaning that all of their dealings with the database are through well-tested and well-debugged programs, they'll need a lot less training. As long as they don't engage in impatient or superstitious behavior, they will need little database training. Users of such "canned" programs quite often just view it as a "black box" anyway. They don't realize they're dealing with a database. They just deal with screens and keystrokes.

More sophisticated users need more training. When you begin to give users unstructured access through various access tools, there's more that can go wrong. If they use SQL, they need to be schooled in how to compose their queries, especially in how to compose the WHERE clauses. A *disjoint query* is a query using multiple tables that do not join properly. Rather than restricting the number of rows that the query returns, this type of query often returns a number of rows equal to the product of the number of rows in each table. Thus, a disjoint query on two tables, each with 10 rows, could return 100 rows, which is the Cartesian product of the two tables. Disjoint queries on large tables can quickly overwhelm the database with millions of rows of output. Likewise, queries that join on unindexed tables or that generate unreasonable query plans can take forever to complete. On systems more recent than Version 7, decision support queries can be run that could take a system down to its knees.. The user will often wait for 30 minutes or so, realize that it's taking too long, and then try to kill the job. This often results in long transactions, database rollback, or database crashes if the job is killed incorrectly. This can also leave back-end and front-end processes running, which can eventually overwhelm an operating system If you have these somewhat sophisticated users, get them some training. If you have software developers, try to get *them* to train the ad hoc users. It'll help both of them.

Software developers are often the most challenging training problem for DBAs. Most often, developers are building highly specialized applications. They'll know much more about the applications than you do. They'll probably know a lot more about the logical database structure than you do. These sophisticated developers can be a valuable resource when it comes to going very deep into the database. Quite often, though, developers will be weak on either extreme of the database. They often know the structure of the data, but many times they know a lot less about the contents of the data than the data-entry people do. On the other end of the spectrum, the developers will know a lot about how individual parts of the database behave, but they'll be weak on how it all fits together.

Development environments such as Visual Basic, PowerBuilder, and Forte further isolate the developer from the database itself. With the emergence of ODBC as a database communication standard, such development environments can work with most or all of the databases in the market. Often, the system being developed will try to work with multiple brands of databases for competitive reasons, and the developer may not even know which database his application runs against.

Often, developers are not aware of the effects of long transactions, logfile use, resource contention, and latch contention. They will code their software until it gives them the results they want. They're usually under such time pressures that they don't spend a lot of time trying to optimize the code. Produce, produce, produce! Of course, these are generalizations. No two users are the same. If you're lucky, you'll have developers who can view the overall picture and create finely crafted code that fits in well with the overall system. If you don't have these kinds of developers, it's the DBA's job to try to create them. If you can, get them to develop some code for you. Teach them about the things you need to monitor and let them work on it for a while. You'll get some good tools as well as a better-trained developer community.

There's nothing better for developers than teaching them how to run and interpret the SET EXPLAIN output. If they know how the optimizer is interpreting their queries, they'll write better queries.

As more and more emphasis is placed on individual development projects that access a single database, it becomes more important to balance the requirements of various classes of user against other users' requirements. The best way to do this is to involve the DBA in the development project from day one.

One successful method of guaranteeing the quality of a development project is to require that the DBA approve all SQL that is coded to run against the database. Developers write and test the code and run SET EXPLAIN and submit the EXPLAIN outputs to the DBA for approval. Bad queries can be caught immediately, and the DBA may see an immediate need for changes in the indexes or fragmentation.. This is a little more complicated when the SQL statements are dynamic, as in coding search screens that allow users to search for an item based on multiple search parameters. Here, the DBA can be of great help to the developer in laying out the search screen. For example, a developer will think twice about allowing someone to search a million-member names database for everyone whose state is "TX" after going over the resultant query plan with the DBA.

What I've found that is so neat about this method is that if you make it part of the development process, it becomes a rule and a habit. Especially with contract developers, it's just another requirement that needs to be met, just another milestone. Of course, I've also heard it called a millstone. Actually, even old-time developers can see the value of this approach if you use it to help them, not to dictate how they write code.

A DBA who is really on the ball would then take this approved SQL and put it in a database for later use in maintenance and troubleshooting. A super DBA would use such a database and a set of benchmark tables to track performance. A super DBA with added points for political style would get the developers to write a frontend that managed the benchmark system as a "training exercise."

Although said partly in jest, this last bit is often possible, especially in larger organizations. If you can't get the services of developers working directly with you, see if anyone offers training in a development environment that can talk to your database. Talk to that trainer and see if you can help develop a course that will eventually develop an in-house system that you need. Everybody benefits, and you get a system that you can use and can't buy anywhere. Then go to the graduates of that course and let them further their skills, on your project, of course.

Another area that developers and system analysts often can use help with is developing a concept of a data life cycle. Often, much attention is paid to getting data into a database, with little or none paid to getting rid of the data when it's out of date. If the developers don't develop plans for archiving and removal of obsolete data, guess who finally gets the job? When you suddenly get to 95 percent capacity, you'll start frantically trying to clean out the junk, and you'll be fighting a hopeless battle. If the software specification calls for creating new data or inserting data into tables, the specification should include a plan for the archival or deletion of old data.

Providing Services to Users

The DBA needs to be seen as a resource person for the users. She needs to be aware of the overall structure of the database system and needs to know how the parts fit together. Often, the DBA tends to inherit the job of documenting the database, especially if the organization has been somewhat lax in documentation in the past. Users need to know the structure of the tables and indexes, where source code is located, which utilities are available, and which scripts have been written to make their jobs easier.

If your organization uses a 3GL language such as INFORMIX®-ESQL/C, the DBA will often be the resource person who helps the developers when their programs don't compile. Hint: Look first at their makefiles.

It's usually good procedure to prohibit all but a few of the more sophisticated users from ever killing an SQL job or backend on earlier Version 5 systems. As this is a major cause of system crashes, it's usually better to let the DBA be the "executioner" of runaway jobs. On Versions 7 and up, the fan-in/fan-out architecture means that various virtual processors (VPs) may be performing tasks for a query, and nobody kills the `oninits`. The only way to kill the process is to use an `onmode` command. This should restricted as much as possible to DBAs and other qualified users.

The DBA should also be available to help developers interpret `sqlexplain.out` files to help them tune their queries. Here, the DBA needs to understand in detail the operations of the optimizer.

Often, the DBA needs to be the person who grants access and privileges in the database. Along with this comes the job of providing the correct environmental variables to access the database and to compile ESQL/C code. The DBA often needs to be able to provide synonyms and aliases for the user. It's better if the DBA and system administrator cooperate in this area and that they have scripts or other programs designed for the task. This task is made more complex if the system utilizes a distributed database across a network. Here, the DBA and system administrator need to ensure that all of the above items occur, not only on one computer system, but on many.

Another DBA service consists of setting up database connections from various client machines into the network. This is always in great demand in larger organizations, especially those that tend to use their databases a lot. This is pretty much "cookie cutter" stuff, in that establishing connectivity to Informix is usually just a matter of properly setting up the Informix client-side applications. Since these are usually operating system specific, you need to know only the connectivity quirks of each of the operating systems on your network. Setting up one Windows NT workstation is usually exactly like setting up another NT workstation. It gets more complicated with systems using Open Database Connectivity (ODBC) to communicate between clients and server. Again, once you've done it once, the rest is "cookie cutter". Usually, it's a bit complicated for users, but it's a perfect task for a trainee DBA.

Disaster Recovery

System crashes are an unfortunate fact of life for all those who deal with computer systems. No matter how fault tolerant the system is, no matter how good the database is, no matter how good the DBA plans, the system will crash. Take that as a given. If you're lucky it will be recoverable. If you're unlucky, your entire computer center will disappear into a hole in the earth some night. Even worse, you may *want* your entire computer center to disappear.

We're all subject to the "it can't happen here" syndrome, which says that all bad things happen to someone else. Next time you see a disaster scene on the news, look around and you'll probably find someone's computer system at the bottom of one of the piles of rubble. What would you do if it were yours?

That's the worst of the disaster recovery scenarios. Your more common occurrences will usually be of a less catastrophic nature, simple things like disk errors, hardware failures, and user errors. If you plan for the end-of-the-world scenarios, you'll always be able to handle the simple problems.

Your disaster recovery plan needs to begin with the simple recovery of the database. Usually this means setting up and following a plan for periodic archives of the database. Regular archives, combined with database logging, can be an almost foolproof means of recovering from just about all kinds of errors. The only drawback is the time needed for performing the archives and the time necessary to recover the system from the archives. Crashes are usually chaotic times, and a well-practiced plan is a necessity. This is not the right time to begin reading up on database recovery in the manual!

Although archives and logs will suffice most of the time, you need to keep the catastrophic situation in the back of your mind. Disaster recovery entails recovering from a partial or complete destruction of *everything* in your computer room. Look at your backup tapes right now. Where are they? If they're sitting on top of the computer in the computer room, the airliner that crashes into your computer center will probably take them out, too. What about communications? What'll you do if the phones are down? Or the power? Where are the telephone numbers of your critical staff members? In the computer?

Disaster recovery is often not just a matter of recovery of the database. Many systems create supporting or work files that need to be kept in sync with the database. Any disaster recovery plan has to be sure that these files are also recoverable.

Devising a good disaster recovery plan is an exercise in paranoia. You need to think about these things. Imagine your computer center in the middle of that hole in the ground that used to be an airliner. It may not be practical to devise contingencies that will cover the end of life on earth as we know it, but you'll be surprised how some simple precautions can let you sleep better at night.

Planning for the Future

The DBA is often the person in the organization who has the broadest view of the data management function. Individual developers and project leaders usually view a piece of the overall application, but the DBA's viewpoint must be more global and wide ranging. The DBA must maintain this global view and must participate in planning how to best meet the organization's data management needs.

This planning function is often pretty far down the DBA's list of priorities. The DBA can get into a firefighting mode in which it seems that 90 percent of her time is spent handling emergencies. This is probably due to someone's failure to plan adequately. While firefighting is usually the most visible and often the most exciting part of the DBA's functions, the ideal situation is to avoid the fires.

The DBA needs to participate in planning for such items as hardware and software upgrades, maintenance schedules, facilities management, communications capabilities, and project plans. If the enterprise is of any size at all, most of this planning will be the responsibility of someone else. Even so, the DBA must represent the realities of the database to those who are doing the planning. Failure to do so will result in unworkable plans, unreasonable expectations, and much frustration down the line.

The DBA should also take the lead in planning for the integration of new products and tools. As more third-party tools become available that work with the Informix family of products, the DBA has a wider range of options. It also means that the DBA must be able to support various development environments and tools.

Many of these are graphical tools that allow users to compose their own queries, build their own forms, and write their own reports. These tools can provide a mixed blessing to the DBA. On the one hand, they allow the DBA to shift some of the development out of the MIS department and into the hands of the users. Balancing this benefit is the risk of allowing inexperienced users access to the database.

The DBA needs to assist in plotting a course that will allow these new classes of tools to fit into the existing IS structure. The DBA's perspective is crucial in ensuring that such areas as database security, resource monitoring and controls, and data validity are considered in the integration of new tools.

Tuning the Database

Monitoring and improvement of database system performance are a constant part of the DBA job function. Although we are classifying this as "tuning the database," the function really encompasses:

- Tuning the hardware
- Tuning the operating system
- Tuning the database engine
- Designing the database schema
- Tuning the application, and
- Monitoring daily operations

Of these, tuning of the hardware and operating system is usually considered to be the system administrator's bailiwick. These two functions, though, are absolutely critical if we are to wring the best performance out of the entire system. The DBA should endeavor to become familiar with tuning the UNIX operating system and with the parameters that can affect the speed of the operating system. Of particular interest from the hardware and operating system viewpoints are:

- Disk layout
- Disk striping
- Single versus multiple processors
- Shared memory parameters
- Other resource limitations in the kernel

The same types of issues will arise between the DBA and the NT system administrators for NT-based systems. Often, they will be complicated to some degree by differences between UNIX security and NT security.

Tuning the database engine is usually the sole responsibility of the DBA. If not, it should be. The DBA should be the one point of contact for any parameter changes to the OnLine system. The DBA is constantly monitoring system performance and tweaking the parameters until the system is matched well to the types of tasks it is asked to perform.

The DBA should also be responsible for maintaining the structure and layout of the tables. Although system analysts and developers most often specify the tables and structure, the DBA needs to be the person who actually creates the tables and indexes. If the DBA is attempting to create and maintain an enterprise-wide data dictionary, this is even more important, as the data dictionary needs to know about new tables and indexes.

Maintenance of indexes is a large part of the overall performance of the database system. You will find that most of the time, performance problems can be traced back to improper indexing.

Running a close second to poor indexing as a performance bugaboo is inefficient application design. Often, the queries can be made much more efficient by analyzing them with SET EXPLAIN. It is sometimes advisable to restructure the application to access its data in a completely different way, especially if the old way requires unindexed scans of large tables. There are some types of queries, such as correlated subqueries, that are inherently inefficient. Sometimes it is possible to significantly speed up SQL statements by using temporary tables to force the optimizer to evaluate the SQL statement in a preferred manner.

A final part of the speed enhancement function calls for the DBA to monitor and correct resource hogging and other disruptive activities of the users. The DBA should be alert for instances in which users create disjoint queries or engage in excessive locking or long transactions. Most often, the user is not even aware that his activities are a problem to others. Usually all that the DBA has to do is point out the problem and make the user understand why his activities are causing a problem. Users who continue to create problems usually need a little more prodding.

Maintaining Security

The data in a firm's computer system is often one of the most valuable of the company's assets. Among other things, the database often contains:

- Customer information
- Marketing information
- Vendor information
- Accounting and credit information
- Mailing lists
- Planning data
- Product information
- Source code
- Personnel and salary information

A good way to visualize the value of your database data is to imagine it placed in the hands of your company's biggest competitor. If this thought scares you, your data is probably worth protecting.

Security administration consists of protecting the data from loss and misuse. Your logging and archive plans probably handle the loss contingency, but how well are you protected from theft or misuse? Most databases are being backed up onto DAT, DLT, or other high-capacity tapes. One of these tapes can hold up to 50 gigabytes of data. This means that someone could walk out of your computer room with all of your company's critical data in a shirt pocket.

If your system has connections to the outside world, either through modems, LANs, WANs, or Internet, you have potential security problems. The primary defense against security breaches is your operating system. This is analogous to locking your front door. Once this security is in place, the database itself must be made secure. By granting and limiting access using the GRANT command in SQL, you can further limit data that can be accessed by someone who gets into the operating system.

The primary purpose of the Informix security is provide secure access within an organization. The standard example is salary information. This information is sensitive and is usually available only to a few users. Since Informix SQL allows a table's owner to grant privileges on a table by column, it is possible to restrict access to certain columns for certain users. You can also use views to allow certain users to access only part of the data. Views, which are essentially "canned" queries, can be created by either DBAs or users and look just like tables to the users. In most instances, the user never realizes that he is dealing with data from multiple tables. By creating a view, the DBA has made details of the table layout irrelevant to the user.

An example of using a view to restrict access to certain information often arises when it is necessary for someone to only be able to view a subset of a table:

```
create table salary (name char(30), dept char(5),
salary int);
create view dp_salary as select * from salary where
dept=''DP'';
```

The manager of the data processing department could be granted select privileges on the view dp_salary and be able to view his own employees' salaries, but no others. (Of course, the DP people probably have total access to the system anyway, so you really can't keep anything secret from them!)

Interfacing with your Peers

In any organization in which the DBA is not in total control of the entire computer system (all but the absolutely smallest applications), the DBA will have to work with and become interdependent with other professionals. As the organization becomes larger and more complex, the job functions often become narrower and more specific.

In a small operation, the DBA is often the UNIX system administrator, the development staff, the technician, and the troubleshooter. As the organization gets larger and more complicated, the DBA is forced to wear fewer hats. In the largest organizations, the DBA may be part of a team of DBAs. These DBAs may have their duties divided by function or divided by systems. In these larger organizations, it becomes more important that the DBA communicate and cooperate with many other professionals. The following list is not exclusive, but it includes the major players in the DBA's professional life.

The System Administrator

Both the UNIX and NT system administrator can be a tremendously valuable resources to the DBA. He can be a source of information about the inner workings of the computer system and can help guide the DBA around potential problems and pitfalls. Especially in areas of initial database setup and subsequent performance tuning, the system administrator can be a lifesaver. Often, the only person who really understands the file system and the raw devices is the system administrator. As you begin to design the disk layouts and to make decisions about striping and mirroring of the Informix database chunks and devices, you'll begin to appreciate the value of a good system administrator. If your initial installation requires UNIX kernel modifications, you'll probably have to have the system administrator do it. System administrators are usually quite protective of such things as kernel configuration.

The system administrator is usually conversant with the performance monitoring and tuning tools available with your flavor of the operating system. As you begin to tune for maximum performance, you'll need to be able to differentiate between performance problems at the operating system level and at the Informix level.

The system administrator will often be your best reference for items regarding communications and network protocols. These items can severely harm system performance if they are set up badly, and they're difficult to debug.

Get on and stay on good terms with your system administrator. One good way to work is to cross train with him or her. Let the system administrator learn enough about the database to serve as a backup DBA. Likewise, learn enough about the operating system to be able to serve as a backup system administrator. Together you'll be able to solve problems that neither of you could tackle alone.

Computer Operators

If your organization is large enough to need and afford operators for your computer systems, these people can make your job much easier. Set up well-documented written procedures for such day-to-day activities as doing database archives and handling logging tapes. Give them simple, user-oriented menus for the operational tasks that they can do. You'll appreciate having an operator available when you have a logfile or an archive problem at 3:00 in the morning. It's much easier on the DBA if she can call into an operations center and walk someone through a fix instead of driving into the office.

Operators should know how to start and stop the database, how to start and stop applications, how to handle the archives and logs, and how to detect problems with the system. One of the most important things they need to know is when to call the DBA. It is important to set some guidelines and to make sure everyone knows when the problems need to be escalated to the DBA's attention.

Informix Support

Informix support policies change, so anything you read here may or may not still be in effect, but the general features remain the same.

If you can get access to the Internet or to the USENET UNIX newsgroups, look into becoming a regular on the `comp.databases.informix` newsgroup. If you don't have access, there are several options for getting Internet access. Check with your system administrator or local UNIX gurus. Someone will probably know the best deal in your area. Questions or problems posted to `comp.databases.informix` often get multiple responses with detailed solutions, frequently containing programs or code fragments.

Your primary source of "real person" Informix support will probably be the support 800 number. As support hotlines go, this one is pretty decent. You'll get a voice mail application that will walk you through to a real live person. You'll need your software serial number. It's probably a good idea for the DBA to have the Informix serial numbers tattooed on his arm. They'll get a lot of use. One thing about the hotline that is not immediately obvious is that there's a 911 feature. On dialing in, immediately punch 911 and you'll get to a support person quickly. Informix wants you to use this in emergencies only. They define an emergency as a production system down or seriously impaired. Use some discretion in taking this option. Don't cry "wolf" unless you really have an emergency.

Assuming that you're not taking the 911 option, you'll probably get a support person whose job is to log your call and put you in a queue to talk to another support person. When they give you a problem number, be sure and write it down. It'll make it much easier to follow up later. If you're lucky, you'll get to a technical support person on this call. If not, the technical support person will call you back. At some point in the process, you will probably be requested to rate the severity of your problem. If your system is down or seriously impaired, let the support person know it. The more serious problems are placed at the top of the queue. Don't be shy about requesting faster response or special services. Just about everyone in the support system has the ability to escalate your problem to a higher level. It doesn't hurt to ask, but be nice about it. You will be dealing with these people again. If worse comes to worst, ask to speak to a manager. You'll always have the option to do this.

Your first technical contact may or may not be tremendously helpful. Their usual response is to read sections of the manual to you. These people usually don't have access to the source code and pretty much have to follow the "company line." They do, however, have access to the complete Informix bugs database. If your problem has shown up before, they may have a quick solution for you. It's a good idea to prepare before talking to these first-line technical folks. Think about how you think Informix would classify your problem. The support staff will be looking up keywords in the database. Give them several options. You'll have a better chance of getting an answer. In any questionable situation, they'll often recommend that you either reinstall or restore from your archive tape. If you're not pleased with this, don't be afraid to ask to speak to a manager or to escalate the problem to a higher level.

Your Informix Account Representative

The salespeople who handle your Informix account can be valuable resources as well. They will have access to local technical personnel who can help you solve problems with your systems. Salespeople have a much greater vested interested in keeping you happy as a user, and thus will often knock themselves out to help you out of a problem. If your account is of any significant size, they'll be able to provide evaluation copies of new software in the hope that you'll buy a ton of them. If you have temporary needs for software, such as special tools for conversion, they can often provide "loaner" software to help you out of a bind. Just remember how helpful they were when it comes time to write up purchase orders.

Hardware and Operating System Vendors

These are an often-neglected source of help for Informix-related solutions. Many vendors have close relationships with database vendors such as Informix. If your hardware or operating system vendor has such a relationship, and if you know how to get to the proper people, they can often be the best source of solutions to problems. Inquire about their other installations running Informix. Even if you're a small operation, your vendor may have other, larger accounts running Informix on the same hardware. Piggyback on top of the big guys. It doesn't hurt to check.

Users' Groups

If you have a local Informix users' group, by all means get involved with it. You can usually find out about users' groups through your Informix account reps. If they don't know, check out the users' group sections at http://www.iiug.com. If you can't find a local users group, consider starting one. If you live in an area with many Informix users, this can become a most valuable resource. A users' group is a great tool for networking and providing mutual support and assistance with problems. It's a good source of information on new techniques and new products. It's also a good way to keep your eyes on the Informix job market, whether you're looking for another position for yourself or whether you're looking to hire someone. Don't be too blatant about soliciting employees or employers at users' groups. It's not considered good form to come in and try to hire everyone in sight!

Internet and the General User Community

One of the major untapped resources out there is the collective knowledge of the 60 million or so Internet users. For those of you who are not familiar with the Internet, it is a network of thousands of computer systems tied together with communication lines. The Internet originated as a resource connecting academic and research institutions. As it expanded, it included military, government, and commercial interests. Up until the late 1980's, access to Internet was more or less restricted to those who had access through one of these member sites.

The Internet has now expanded into a more business and commercial role. This vast infrastructure is being opened to businesses and to private individuals as part of the "Information Superhighway" concept. Many of the online services such as America Online®, and NetCom® are offering inexpensive connections to the Internet without your having to go through the time, effort, and expense of actually connecting your computer systems to the network. For most of the reference tasks you'll be needing, this dial-up Internet access will be enough.

One of the best informal sources of Informix information is the World Wide Web. Informix's corporate site at http://www..informix.com is a tremendous resource for the Informix junkie, as is the Web site of the International Informix Users Group. This user group site is http://www.iiug.org. The users group Website includes an archive of public domain software plus links to various Informix resources across the net. This is also the home of the Informix FAQ, or "frequently asked questions," which is a hypertext version of the most asked questions in the newsgroup, `comp.databases.informix`.

One of the big draws of the Internet is access to more than 20,000 newsgroups that are part of the USENET news facility. These newsgroups are essentially bulletin board systems that cater to specific interests. Many of the newsgroups are exercises in anarchy or attempts to see how far the users can push the bounds of bad taste. Ignore them. If you look hard enough, you'll find plenty of hard, useful data.

Most browsers such as Netscape® and Microsoft Internet Explorer® have the capability of accessing newsgroups. If you don't have a news feed into your internet service provider (ISP), you can access newsgroups by using Web-based news servers such as http://www.dejanews.com.

Among the most valuable newsgroups to the Informix DBA is the `comp.databases.informix` newsgroup. You'll find discussions of new and old products, bug reports, workarounds, theoretical discussions, and much peer-to-peer interaction in this newsgroup. No matter what kind of problem or question you have, you can post it to this newsgroup and probably have three or four answers to it within the next day or two. You'll find many Informix employees active in the group, and they are almost all helpful. For the DBA, access to this newsgroup is reason enough to invest the time and energy needed in setting up an Internet connection.

Whenever you connect to the `comp.databases.informix` newsgroup, one of the first documents you need to locate is `informix.faq`. This file is the *frequently asked questions* file. This is a common service that is found in newsgroups on USENET. Reading the *FAQ file* in a newsgroup will give you a feeling for the types of information that is available in the newsgroup and will help you become familiar with the customs and procedures of the group. The `informix.faq` file contains many helpful hints for setting up, maintaining, and troubleshooting your OnLine system.

Inside the Black Box: Engine Architecture

Database administrators need an under-
standing of all of the factors that affect their systems. This includes appropriate operating
system information, general information about Informix OnLine or IDS internal operations,
and specific information regarding the individual site's setup.

This basic knowledge prepares the DBA for effectively managing the operations of an
OnLine or IDS database. These items can be considered the prerequisites for becoming an
effective DBA.

The actual day-to-day operations of Informix databases are straightforward and relatively simple. Keep the system up. Make backups. Kill a few runaway jobs occasionally.
When things are going smoothly, anyone can be the DBA. For the most part, the engine is a
reliable black box. You make requests of it. It gives you back data.

It's when things start to go wrong that the DBA needs to understand what's really
going on inside the black box. When the system crashes, nobody wants to be the DBA. If
you survive the encounter with angry users who've had the database blow up in the middle

19

of **THE MOST IMPORTANT JOB THEY'VE EVER RUN**, you'll have to answer to management types who want to know what went wrong with the system and who to hang for doing it. Unless you are able to get inside the database and avoid the crash in the first place, or at least be able explain what happened, you'll be the most likely candidate for the lynch mob's noose.

I'm making a distinction between understanding the architecture of the database and understanding the data flow. Actually, these two areas of knowledge are so closely associated that they are effectively the same skill set. To understand how the data is managed within Informix, one has to understand the architectural entities that manage this flow. Similarly, to understand the architectural entities, you must know how they are used, what they are used for, and how the data flows through the database architecture.

HOW TO READ THIS CHAPTER

This chapter will discuss the internal architecture of the earlier OnLine 5.XX engines and more advanced architecture of Informix Dynamic Server 7.XX. When the first edition of the book was released, it contained specifics only on the OnLine 5.XX engines. This revision will cover the Informix Dynamic Server 7.XX (IDS) engines as well.

Both engine versions have a lot in common. The major area of differences lies in the multithreaded architecture of IDS as opposed to the two-process architecture of OnLine. Areas such as shared memory and disk structures also differ, but not as drastically as the underlying architecture.

The task of discussing both engines together in somewhat complicated by the differences in naming the utilities. Most of the OnLine utilities began with the prefix "tb," as in tbstat, tblog, and tbmonitor. In IDS, the "tb" was replaced by "on," as in onstat, onlog, and onmonitor. When we are discussing areas where the two engines do not differ significantly, we will refer to the utilities with a "tb/on" prefix, as in tb/onlog, tb/onstat, and tb/onmonitor. In these cases, you should use either "tb" or "on" as a prefix for your actual commands, depending upon your versions. Many UNIX IDS systems include a link from the old name to the new name, and you can enter either the old or new name Scripts included with book will continue to have the "tb" prefix, and a separate series of scripts will be available with the "on" prefixes for IDS systems.

In some cases, the "tb" and "on" programs have different options that are unique to either OnLine or IDS. An example would the onstat -g commands in IDS systems. There is no corresponding tbstat -g command since the -g option is recognized only in IDS. In these cases, we will use the "on" prefixes only.

When I refer to "Informix," "Informix engines" or "Informix products," I'm generalizing across both the OnLine and IDS products. When I'm addressing something that differs between the products, I'll talk about either "OnLine" or "IDS."

We'll also take a UNIX-centric view of the universe and assume that the engines are running on UNIX. Remember that the IDS products also run on Windows NT. There'll be a chapter that later specifically addresses NT, but all of the UNIX concepts are applicable to NT as well.

UNDERSTANDING THE DATA FLOW

We'll look at the data flow first. This will allow us to get an overall view of the needs that are met by the architectural elements. Once the general needs are understood, it is much easier to understand why Informix is doing what it does.

You'll find that the overall Informix system architecture is a tradeoff between multiple factors. Some decisions are made to enhance speed. Others sacrifice speed for security. Still others sacrifice speed and security for memory or disk savings. Like any vendor, the people at Informix have tried to present a product that offers tradeoffs that are reasonable to the largest possible audience. In some cases, the DBA can work around these tradeoffs by tuning the database or the application. Sometimes, though, the DBA just has to admit that the database has some weaknesses that need to be worked around. Although some of the limitations and constraints seem to be arbitrary, most often they make sense when viewed in the context of database operations as a whole.

While IDS was a major rewrite of the engine code from OnLine, one must really look at IDS as a natural progression from OnLine. Most of the concepts from OnLine apply to IDS. IDS starts where OnLine left off.

Informix engines are multiuser relational databases that support transactions. Understanding what these two terms really mean will make understanding the data flow much easier.

Informix Engines: Multiuser RDBMSs

A multiuser relational database management system (RDBMS) must do much more than simply store and retrieve data. It must maintain the integrity of the data and ensure that the user is using the "cleanest" data available.

Most of the finer points of the multiuser design are there to help act as a traffic cop when different users want to work with the same data at once. Informix has implemented a series of locks and isolation levels that manage these multiuser conflicts.

Locks are internal data flags that determine who gets to modify or read data at any particular time. Informix has locks available at many levels, depending upon the user's needs. These locks are available at the database level, locking an entire database. Locks are available at the table level, locking an entire table. They are also available at the page level within a table. Page-level locking is the default in Informix databases. If you don't specify locking levels, you will get page-level locking. For the finest control of locking granularity,

Informix allows locks to be placed at the row level. There are also locks at the index and at the byte level that are used internally by Informix.

Along with locking comes the concept of isolation levels. Isolation levels are transaction level commands that specify the levels of "cleanness" the user will accept. The least clean isolation level is *dirty read*, in which the user really doesn't care if someone is changing the data while the user is working with it. Isolation levels range up to *repeatable read* in which the database has to ensure that a query will return the same rows if it is run twice in a row with no other actions in between. We'll go further into these items in the section on tuning.

Informix Engines: Support Transactions

Informix also supports the concept of transactions. Supporting transactions begins with the admission that lots of things can go wrong in an RDBMS. Most of these things can have disastrous results if the data is left in an inconsistent state.

The textbook example of transactions is designing a database to handle the accounting transactions at a bank. Such transactions consist of two balancing debit and credit transactions to two separate tables. Suppose you have two tables, bank_cash_on_hand and customer_account. To simplify matters, consider that each table has one column, balance. When the customer comes in and withdraws $1,000, the following two SQL statements are generated:

```
update bank_cash_on_hand set balance=balance - 1000;
update customer_account set balance=balance - 1000;
```
(Ignore the credits and debits, DBAs aren't accountants!)

Clearly if one of the above SQL statements completes successfully and the other fails, the bank's books will be out of balance. What kind of failure could cause this?

DBAs are finding new kinds of failures daily. A needed table could be locked. The disk could fill up. The system could crash after completing the first SQL statement. If the database were distributed over two machines, one machine could crash or the network connection between the two could fail. Possible failure modes could fill a book.

What transaction processing does is to consider the separate SQL statements as a single entity. Any changes made to the database while inside a transaction are not made permanent until the transaction is committed with an SQL statement. The database designer and application designers build their systems to assure that both parts of the transaction are completed before the program issues the commit statement. If the transaction is not committed, the changes will be rolled back to the original status.

If the particular database is using transactions, any changes are logged to logfiles as they are made. If, for some reason, the user decides either not to commit or to roll back the work, the logfiles are used to restore the data to its original status. The purposes and uses of these mechanisms will become clearer as we track the flow of data beginning from when the user makes a query.

TRACKING THE FLOW OF DATA

This is a greatly simplified view of the flow of data to, from, and inside an Informix database server. The differences between OnLine and IDS are minimal here. There are some differences in areas such as transport mechanisms for the connectivity tools, but they are not germane to the understanding of the overall architecture.

We are assuming that the query initiates from a client application such as dbaccess, SQL Editor, or ESQL/C. Don't worry too much about the details now. Just get a feel for how the data flows. We're glossing over such items as data concurrency, transactions, and isolation levels for the time being. In this simplified view, we are also glossing over the differences between simply reading data and performing an update or an insert.

The data flows something like this:

- Client program formulates its SQL request. The client generates SQL requests to be presented to the server.
- Client transmits it to the server. The request is transferred through UNIX pipes, in the case of the client and server being on the same machine. When the client and server are on different machines, the transmission is via UNIX pipes and a transport program such as INFORMIX-Net or INFORMIX-Star.
- Server optimizes the query and formulates a plan to retrieve the data. The server process uses its cost-based optimizer to calculate the most effective order in which to access the database tables and which indexes to use.
- Server requests a page from the database. This may be a data page or an index page. The query may need the entire page or only one row. Either way, it still pulls in an entire page.
- Server searches for the page in the shared memory buffer pool.
- If the page is in the buffer pool, server tries to get a lock on the buffer page. If the lock succeeds, server process can read and/or modify the buffer.
- If the page is not in the buffer pool, look for a free buffer. If there is no buffer free, go to the LRU queue and look for a free buffer. If no free buffer is found, flush out the oldest buffer and load the data into it.
- Server writes a copy of the unchanged original page to the physical log buffer.
- If logging is turned on and if data has been modified, the changes are logged to the logical log.

- Server returns data to the client The server returns the data either over UNIX pipes, using INFORMIX-Net or INFORMIX-Star if the client and server are on separate machines.

- Server updates its disk with the new data. At some time, either through a foreground process or through the actions of the page flushers, pages in shared memory that have been modified are flushed to the hard disk. These flushes do not empty the buffer: they just copy it to disk.

To fully understand the flow of data, remember that just about everything is buffered in shared memory and that access to any resource requires obtaining a latch on the resource. A latch is a temporary lock that controls access to a resource. In IDS systems latches are known as mutexes.

UNDERSTANDING ONLINE 'S PHYSICAL ARCHITECTURE

Here, the differences between OnLine and IDS differ significantly. This section speaks to OnLine's physical architecture only.

The DBA's goal is to understand what is going on inside the database. Informix can be an intimidating, complex creation that uses as much shared memory as the disk capacity of some personal computers. Shared memory sizes of 50 to 100 megabytes are not uncommon. All of the files are usually invisible to the computer's operating system and cannot be inspected as ordinary files.

Most of the workings of an OnLine database will show up as `sqlturbo` on a UNIX `ps` listing, yielding very little data about what the process is really doing. On IDS systems, the virtual processors will show up as `oninit` in the `ps` listing. Understanding what's really happening means learning how to use the Informix tools provided for peeking into the database and knowing how to interpret the data provided by these tools.

Processes and Daemons

The OnLine system uses a *two-process* architecture. The database process, or *server* process, does the actual manipulation of data within the system. This manipulation consists of retrieving (querying) and modifying (inserting or updating) the data within the database tables. This process is named `sqlturbo`. The other process is the *client* process. This process is often I-SQL or ESQL/C. The client process is the interface between the user and the database system. It interprets user input and commands, passing the requests to the server process and receiving appropriate responses from the server.

Even when the client process is operating against a single database on a single machine, the client/server model is in effect. When a transport mechanism such as INFORMIX-Star or INFORMIX-Net is added to the OnLine system, the client and server applications can be on different machines connected by a network. Thus, the OnLine database is designed from the beginning as a client/server database.

Although the division of labor between client and server processes is efficient, one of the drawbacks is that each client, or *frontend* process must have a corresponding server, or *backend* process. Since these backend processes can use over a half megabyte of RAM, performance can deteriorate when available RAM begins to get low. This problem is often addressed by third-party "middleware." Middleware, also known as transaction monitors, accepts requests from multiple clients and calls the server only once. IDS systems reduce the need for some middleware, as this new version supports a dynamic server environment that allows the DBA to choose to start a given number of back-ends that will serve the requests of all the frontend processes. IDS is designed using a *multiprocess* architecture, rather than a two-process architecture.

Unlike the Oracle database, which allows the frontends to communicate with the backends using different methods, OnLine uses UNIX pipes to transmit the data from the frontends to the backends.

References to UNIX in general are full of discussions of *daemon* processes. In OnLine these daemon processes run in the background and are responsible for such jobs as handling the checkpoints and maintaining the shared memory. The daemon processes for the OnLine system will show up first in the `tbstat -u` output and can be identified by the trailing "D" (for daemon) or "F" (for page flusher) in the flags field. These daemons will show up in `ps` listings as `tbinit`.

HOW ONLINE MANAGES SHARED MEMORY

Shared memory is an area of the system's memory that is available to all OnLine users. Much of the shared memory is used by buffers. Using shared memory for these buffers enables OnLine to pool its memory resources for multiple servers rather than set aside individual buffer areas for each process.

These buffers are used to buffer pages to and from the physical disk storage on the system. Only the most recently used pages are kept in the shared memory buffers. Thus, if a needed disk page is in the buffers, it will be the latest version and can be accessed quickly. As the buffers begin to fill or as the system detects the need to flush the buffers, buffered pages are written back to disk. When the system needs to read data from the disk, it looks for the page in the buffers first. If it's there, the page is accessed from the buffer, saving on time-consuming disk I/O. If the needed page is not in the buffers, the system chooses a free buffer, if there is one. If there is no free buffer, the system forces the oldest page (the *least recently used*, or *LRU*) to flush to disk freeing up that page.

OnLine shared memory segments are allocated by database instance. Each instance will maintain its own shared memory, and each instance will require adequate resources to be allocated for its use. The DBA has control over many parameters that determine the size and division of the shared memory.

The `tbmonitor` utility allows for the sizing of the shared memory. As different parameters are changed, the program will indicate how much shared memory is needed.

If your UNIX kernel has been configured with adequate shared memory resources, you can alter the amount of shared memory used by changing the parameters in `tbmonitor`. Always add a little "fluff factor" to the suggested shared memory. For instance, if `tbmonitor` indicates that 13 megabytes shared memory is needed, make sure that UNIX is ready to give you an extra megabyte or so. This will allow you to have some flexibility for later tuning of the OnLine parameters without having to rebuild the kernel.

UNDERSTANDING IDS'S PHYSICAL ARCHITECTURE

IDS is officially known as INFORMIX Dynamic Server Version 7.30 at the time of this writing, but we'll refer to it in its various forms simply as IDS. After OnLine Version 5 of the server had been around for several years, Informix undertook a complete rewrite of the product, resulting in a short-lived Version 6 followed by a much more robust IDS Version 7.X At the time, the database market was maturing quickly, and it became obvious to Informix's management that they needed to make several changes to the product in order to ensure its future.

They saw significant future growth in multiprocessor systems that were becoming more and more popular. The first type of multiprocessor system was the symmetric multiprocessor (SMP) model in which additional processors were added in parallel on an existing bus, sharing common resources such as disk drives. This was a relatively simple multiprocessor model that was a logical extension of the UNIX multiprocessing model on which earlier versions of Informix had run. OnLine had limited ability to use multiple processors, and Informix designed Versions 6 and 7 to make much better use of SMP resources.

This entailed several key concepts that are still being refined and changed to respond to hardware developments. The first key concept was *parallelism*, in which jobs such as sorts, queries, and index builds could be divided up into smaller jobs that could be assigned to other processors. As the processors finished their work, their results were combined with the results of other processing jobs into a final result set. Rather than having the entire task running sequentially with only one processor, this parallelism spread the work out over more of the SMP system's resources and took better advantage of the system's resources.

Closely related is the concept of *multithreading*, which is required to effectively implement parallelism. A thread is a defined series of computer instructions that is contained within one UNIX process. A single-threaded process is best illustrated by a non-threaded

UNIX process such as the `sqlturbo` process in OnLine. UNIX achieves its multiprocessing capability by allowing the operating system to manage these single-threaded processes. The operating system schedules and controls the operation of these processes, allowing them to run for a short period of time and then *preempting* the process and allowing the next scheduled process to run. Only one process runs at a time. A multithreaded process takes this paradigm a level deeper and allows the process itself to contain multiple threads that are controlled and scheduled by the process itself, much in the way that UNIX controls the operations of UNIX processes. It is sort of like forcing the processes to behave like mini operating systems.

One of the extensions to the parallel architecture stems from the relatively recent growth of massive parallel processor systems known as MPP systems. In these systems, often referred to as *clusters* individual compute *nodes* are stand-alone systems that include all of the resources they need to operate. Each node is connected to all other nodes. The nodes share only data and sometimes disk storage. Informix refers to this as a *shared-nothing* architecture, and it is the basic principle underlying Informix's premier multiprocessor option, officially known as INFORMIX Dynamic Server with Parallel Data Option. This product was originally known as Extended Parallel Server (XPS) and I'll refer to it as XPS from here on.

COMPONENTS OF THE INFORMIX DYNAMIC SERVER

Informix Dynamic Server is composed of three separate components: the process component, the shared memory component, and the disk component. The disk component is almost identical to that of OnLine. There are some differences in the shared memory component, mainly due to structures that are put into place to handle parallelism. The major differences between the earlier version and the latest version lie in the process component, which was drastically redesigned.

Process Component

OnLine Version 5.X is a two-process architecture, in which a client process communicates with a `sqlturbo` process that did the processing work in a linear, single-threaded manner. Each client process in OnLine had a corresponding `sqlturbo` process, which led to performance limitations as more and more clients attached to the server.

Informix Dynamic Server did away with the one-to-one correspondence between front-end and back-end processors. Instead, IDS is configured with multiple *virtual processors* running multiple threads.

Virtual Processors

A virtual processor (VP) is an operating system program that can manage multiple threads. Each VP is called `oninit` and runs as a separate process within the operating system and can perform tasks for multiple client programs. This allows for a great reduction in the number of operating system processes that run on the system. It also allows a client process to call upon multiple VPs to do its work. Allowing the virtual processors to manage the threads' scheduling and synchronization is more efficient than allowing the operating system to manage the threads. Removing control from the operating system and giving it to the virtual processors allows less conflict between the database processes and other applications running on the machine.

Virtual processors are segmented by function into VP classes. The DBA can control the number of VPs within each class by entries in the $ONCONFIG file. Informix Dynamic Server classes are divided into the following VP classes:

- CPU   All user processing threads. These are the usually the most active virtual processors and handle the lion's share of the database activities. CPUVPs should be kept as active as possible so that they are neither paged out or allowed to sleep. CPUVPs are not allowed to run any tasks that call for built-in wait states such as waiting for disk I/O or any type of messages. These types of tasks are handled by other VP classes.

- AIO   These are asynchronous input/output processes. They perform all disk input and output to the database chunks as well as writes to the message log. If your system is configured to use KAIO (kernel asynchronous input output), disk input and output from raw disk devices is handled by KIO VPs. These virtual processors use operating system calls to access the data and often run faster than AIO VPs. Even with KAIO configured, i/o to operating system files is still handled by the AIO VPs.

- PIO   Virtual processors of this class handle writes to the physical log.

- LIO   Virtual processors of this class handle writes to the logical logfiles.

- MSC   This class has only one VP, and it handles various miscellaneous tasks such as managing licenses and authenticating UNIX users.

- ADT   This class handles auditing tasks if auditing is set up.

- SOC   Runs communication protocols using sockets. Note: An individual system may use SOC VPs or TLI VPs, but not both.

- TLI   Runs TLI communications protocols if TLI networking is in use.

- SHM   Runs shared memory communication threads if one of the shared memory protocols is established and if the NETTYPE ipcshn parameter specifies NET. Otherwise, shared memory listener threads run in CPU VPs.

- ADM   Runs the Informix internal timer.

- OPT   Used to transfer blob data to and from optical disks

Shared Memory Component

Shared memory in both OnLine and IDS is used mainly to cache data pages from disk. Since access to RAM is much faster (by an order of roughly 50 to 1) than access to the hard disk system, performance is greatly enhanced every time the Informix engine is able to read a page from shared memory instead of having to go to the disk. Much of the effort of tuning Informix systems is a quest to improve the cache hit ratio of database reads.

Shared memory in IDS is divided into three separate components: the resident component, the virtual component, and the message component. The major difference between OnLine and IDS lies in the virtual portion of shared memory, as OnLine does not have a virtual component.

Resident Portion of Shared Memory

The resident portion of IDS's shared memory contains the same structures as the earlier, OnLine. The resident portion is static; its sizing does not change unless changes are made in the onconfig file and the engine is shut down and restarted. In most online transaction processing (OLTP) systems, the resident portion of shared memory is the largest portion. In systems that do a lot of decision support (DSS) queries, you may see the virtual portion become the largest part of shared memory.

The main function of the resident function is to handle caching of disk data. In some Informix ports (check your release notes), the onconfig parameter RESIDENT can be set to a value of 1, which guarantees that the resident portion is never paged out. Since this is a very critical portion of shared memory that receives a lot of use, any paging can be detrimental to performance. One of the negatives of setting RESIDENT to 1 is that other applications may be adversely affected if Informix grabs and holds much of the shared memory. For a system that runs only the Informix engine, this may be a good thing, but it may not endear the DBA to other users who are running non-Informix applications on the same machine. Yet another reason to have Informix running on a machine of its own.

For a more detailed explanation of this portion of shared memory, read the chapter on shared memory in the OnLine architecture. The concepts and execution are the same.

Buffer Pools

The buffer pools are usually the largest portion of the resident shared memory. These are the buffers that are established with the BUFFERS configuration parameter in the onconfig file. As in OnLine, the buffers are used to cache data that is read from disk. Each buffer contains one page of data that has been read from disk. Buffers use a least recently used (LRU) algorithm whenever a buffer needs to be recycled. This works exactly as it does in OnLine.

Internal Tables

Internal tables are virtual tables that reside in the resident portion of shared memory. They hold data related to the setup, configuration, and status of the Informix engine. There are internal tables for dbspaces, chunks, tablespaces, locks, and logfile locations. It is these internal tables that are accessed by monitoring utilities such as `onstat`. Since these are virtual tables, they don't really exist as tables. You cannot see them in any way except through the monitoring utilities. These tables are similar across the engine versions, with the exception that the later IDS has more features and thus, more internal tables than OnLine. IDS systems maintain SMI tables for all shared memory data structures.

Physical Log Buffer

There are two physical log buffers in the resident portion. These buffers are configurable in size by the LOGBUFF parameter in the onconfig file. The value of LOGBUFF is the size in kilobytes of each buffer.

Logical Log Buffer

There are three logical log buffers in the resident portion. They are configured through the PHYSBUFF parameter, which represents the size in kilobytes of each of the three buffers.

Virtual Portion of Shared Memory

The virtual portion of shared memory has no analog in the earlier Informix versions. This section of memory can contract or expand according to the needs of the engine and the desires of the DBA. IDS is officially known as Informix Dynamic Server, and it is this portion of memory that gives rise to the "Dynamic" in the name.

Session Data

Information about different users and different connections to an IDS database.

Dictionary Cache

As tables are used in the IDS database, their structural information is stored in this area.

Stored Procedure Cache

As stored procedures are run, their preparsed and precompiled contents are saved in this cache for later access.

Thread Information

Information about various threads running inside of virtual processors.

Sort Space

Used to do in-memory sorts in some ORDER BY, GROUP BY, dynamic hash joins, temporary indexes, and index build operations.

Big Buffers

Big buffers are data areas that are used to perform readaheads in order to maximize the efficiency of sequential scans.

Message Portion of Shared Memory

The message portion of shared memory is used in systems that use one of the shared memory communication protocols that uses shared memory rather than streams or sockets.

Disk Component of Both IDS and OnLine

Both the OnLine and IDS engine series handle the low-level organization, access, and structures of the disks in similar ways. IDS extends some of the concepts of logical and physical layout to embrace a concept known as fragmentation. For many of us, the term fragmentation has a negative connotation, as in "*the disk is highly fragmented and doesn't perform well.*" In the Informix IDS world, though, fragmentation has a much kinder, gentler interpretation. IDS defines fragmentation as intelligently placing data across multiple disks for maximum performance. As the OnLine product matured into IDS, Informix found that by smartening up this concept of fragmentation, it was able to take more advantage of multiple CPU systems. In this way the fragmentation concepts are an extension to the disk component in OnLine. Fragmentation has also been called "horizontal partitioning of data" by C.J. Date.

To understand how the engines deal with the data on the disk, the DBA needs to understand the differences between physical and logical storage. Physical storage refers to the actual devices or files that Informix uses to talk to the hardware by way of the UNIX operating system. Logical storage refers to the method in which the database views the data structure internally.

Units of Disk Storage

Both IDS and OnLine can address the disks directly, bypassing the UNIX filesystem. This results in efficiencies because the Informix disk access routines can be much more specialized than UNIX routines. These processes are designed strictly for database access, while the UNIX routines have to be able to handle everything from disk input and output (i/o) to device i/o. Use of these raw devices by the engine can take advantage of the fact that these raw devices are large, contiguous blocks. This allows Informix database engines to use more efficient i/o methods such as *big reads* and direct memory to disk transfers. The disk subsystem is just another resource to the system.

In IDS versions prior to 7.3 NT systems do not utilize this concept of raw disks. All database chunks in NT are stored as files visible to the operating system. This is one of the major differences between IDS on UNIX and IDS on NT. IDS versions greater than 7.3 allow NT systems to use raw disk devices.

Disk space is made available to either engine through the `tb/onmonitor` or `tb/onspaces` utilities. Using `tb/onmonitor` is somewhat safer for the DBA, as tb/onmonitor will respond with verification prompts on the line of "Do you really want to do something as stupid as this?"

Throughout this book, we will be using the tb/onmonitor command because it is simple and intuitive and because it provides a menuing interface. Most if not all of the functions of tb/onmonitor can be called individually by using the underlying programs and the reader should realize that most of the work can be done directly from the command line should it be necessary.

Don't get too comfortable with tb/onmonitor. When IDS came out on Windows NT, the graphical utilities completely replaced onmonitor. Most of the functions are capable of being done through the graphical user interface (GUI), but in several instances, you have to go to the underlying utilities such as onspaces or onparams.

Tb/onmonitor allows the DBA to assign parts of a raw UNIX device or a UNIX file to a dbspace. It will also allow the DBA to specify offsets into the device to be used. An offset is a certain number of kilobytes that the engine is instructed to skip at the beginning of a device. Informix does not place any data within the offset. In some systems, the formatting of a disk will place system data in the first few tracks of a device. If Informix writes over this, the disk format is blown. Specifying an offset allows the DBA to map around areas such as this.

Using offsets also can allow OnLine to place several chunks within the same UNIX device. If separate data areas are needed, this can be a boon to the DBA, as reformatting a hard disk is often quite a chore. Even if it were easy, the wise DBA will avoid making such UNIX-level changes lightly.

Chunks

The actual unit in which disk storage is made available to overall database access is the *chunk*. Chunks are sections of the hard disk. Chunks can be either actual UNIX files or portions of the disk outside the UNIX file system. Using the non-UNIX, or *raw* chunk is preferable to using UNIX files because the additional overhead of managing the UNIX file system will slow the system down.

Note that both raw and UNIX filesystems will show up in a listing of /dev. The difference is that the raw devices are never mounted and do not show up in a UNIX df output. They also never have a makefs done on them, as it is the makefs command that creates the UNIX file system.

For the most part, an Informix engine is happy with a chunk if it can identify it through a UNIX device. OnLine does not know whether the device is a single disk partition or a virtual device composed of multiple disks, perhaps striped and mirrored. It's all the same to Informix. Anything that the DBA can do to speed up access to the chunk will help Informix. If your UNIX supports striped or mirrored disks or RAID (redundant arrays of inexpensive disks) and if you have the option of using them, they will provide payoffs in the area of fault tolerance. There's seldom any reason not to use the UNIX disk striping, as striping generally provides overall improvements in disk performance. Mirroring and

RAIDs can greatly increase your fault tolerance, but there is often a cost to balance against the improvements. Mirroring will usually slow down disk operations a bit, whether you are using the operating system's or Informix's mirroring. Using a RAID can also slow down writes to a disk. For some areas of high write activity, such as physical and logical logfile spaces, the DBA may want to explore using lower levels of RAID to optimize the write speeds. Most popular for database work is RAID5, which stripes data across all the disks and provides the capability to lose any one disk in a RAID cluster without losing data. RAID5 is usually as fast as or faster in read performance, but can be costly in write performance.

The speed and efficiency of disk access is a powerful indicator of overall database speed. A little effort spent at the time the system is installed will pay you back many times over in better performance.

There are both advantages and drawbacks to using raw devices or operating system files. You need to be aware of these limitations and risks before committing to either type of storage because it can get complicated to have to change from one to the other. Advantages of raw disk over cooked files are:

- Raw supports KAIO (kernel asynchronous i/o) on ports where the operating system uses it. KAIO often represents a significant performance increase.

- Raw devices won't be destroyed when some well-meaning new system adminminstrator decides to clean out some of the "large junk files" that happen to be in your data directory. Raw disks are harder to create, but they are a lot less liable to being destroyed by someone who doesn't know what he's doing.

- Raw disk devices are totally controlled by the Informix processes, so Informix knows their status.

- Raw disk devices do not need the relatively large operating system load as do files in a UNIX filesystem.

On the other hand, there are several advantages to using the cooked files over the raw devices:

- Cooked files are easier to deal with because they can be seen by normal operating system utilities.

- With cooked files, you can let the operating system tell you how much space is free. With raw files, it's hard to see them in the utilities, and it's easy to make mistakes regarding them.

- On NT versions prior to 7.30, for example, you're forced to use the cooked files. There's no choice. IDS versions later than 7.30 give you the option of using raw devices on NT systems.

- With cooked files, you're not likely to have two chunks overlap each other or leave a big hole in the middle of the device that nobody knows is there. These are problems that plague the layout of raw devices.

- Having the data in operating system files also adds other possibilities to database backup, in that normal backup procedures can "see" the data. Be careful, however, to have the database engine completely shut down during such backups. If your backup program locks a file and Informix tries to read it, the chunk will be marked offline. This can range from a mere nuisance in later versions of IDS, to an event requiring a call into the system by Informix Support.

Usually, performance is a deciding factor, and raw spaces are preferable if you have a choice. If you have other factors involved, it may make sense to look at cooked files. The two can coexist, however. Often, creating a database in a hastily created cooked file dbspace is the fastest, cleanest method of solving a problem. There have been reports of cooked filesystems performing as well as raw filesystems in more recent UNIX implementations. The implementation on NT relies solely on Microsoft's NTFS filesystem, and the performance has been shown to match the performance of UNIX systems.

The only real rule here is not to take everything you hear or read at face value. Even though it may go against "conventional wisdom," try out your options if you have the chance and time. Systems are evolving so fast that what may be true one day is hopelessly outdated the next. Don't be afraid to experiment.

The Informix manuals recommend that the actual names of the partitions that comprise a chunk not be used, but that they be linked to a more descriptive name. Thus, you may have a chunk that is physically known to UNIX as /dev/rdisk23h but known to Informix as /dev/chunk1. The DBA has used the UNIX ln command as follows:

```
ln /dev/rdisk23h /dev/chunk1
chown informix /dev/chunk1
chgrp informix /dev/chunk1
chmod 660 /dev/chunk1
```

Using links rather than actual device names serves more than a mnemonic purpose. If you ever lose a disk or have to rearrange your system's disk layout, the links will be much easier to set up than the actual devices. For instance, in the above example suppose you have a disk crash on /dev/rdisk23h. If you have called your chunk /dev/rdisk23h, you will be down until you physically replace /dev/rdisk23h. The chunk name and its path are stored within the chunk reserved page for the OnLine system. When the system comes up, it will always look for chunks and paths found on this reserved page.

If you have used links, you can scrounge around and find another device to link to /dev/chunk1. This is important because disk problems usually lead to the need to restore your system from a tape archive. The tape archive program requires that the device names of the target system match the source system. The sizes of the target system's chunks must be at least as large as those of the corresponding source system's. They can be larger.

The ownership and group ownership are critical. If you have it wrong in OnLine systems, you will often have no problems as long as user `informix` is using the system, but you will get error messages when another user tries to use the system. IDS systems will not even start up if the permissions and ownerships are not correct.

Notice also that the UNIX `/dev/rdisk***` devices are used. These are character-based devices, not the block-based devices such as the `/dev/disk***` devices. If you have accidentally created your raw devices on block devices, you may find that the initial process of disk initialization takes a long time. Subsequent accesses to the disk will take much longer than usual. This is because of the additional overhead of using the UNIX kernel services. Using the block devices will use the UNIX kernel buffer cache, while using the character device will not. To guarantee that writes are flushed to disk in a timely manner, you must use the character device.

Chunks can be further divided into tablespaces and pages. Many chunks can be joined together to form `dbspaces`, which can be joined together to form databases. Lets look at the differences between these terms.

Pages

The smallest, most atomic unit of disk storage is the page. Page sizes are either 2K or 4K, depending upon your architecture. This page size is not changeable. Most of the reports generated by `tbcheck` and the other utilities express size in number of pages. SQL CREATE TABLE statements refer to sizes in kilobytes. Remember the difference.

Extents

Extents are groups of pages that are contiguous on the disk. The first extent is allocated to a tablespace at table creation time. When a table is created in the database, the table creator can specify the FIRST SIZE and NEXT SIZE in the CREATE TABLE statement. The tablespace is initially created with one extent with a size of FIRST SIZE (in kilobytes, not pages) As the table grows, additional extents of size NEXT SIZE (in kilobytes) are allocated. Although the space within an extent is contiguous, when additional extents are allocated they are not necessarily contiguous with the previous extent(s). The Informix engines attempt to allocate subsequent extents contiguously, but if there is not enough available space to add an extent of NEXT SIZE, the database engine will look elsewhere for the space. When two extents are created contiguously, they are merged into a single extent. Informix defaults to four pages FIRST SIZE and four pages NEXT SIZE if the table builder does not specify the sizes.

Tablespaces

A tablespace is a collection of all of the extents that are allocated for a given table. These extents hold the table's data and indexes and any free space that may be in the table. A tablespace can gain extents, but it never loses them unless the table is rebuilt, either as an explicit rebuild or by use of an ALTER INDEX TO CLUSTER statement or by issuing any ALTER TABLE statement that affects the structure of the table. Another way of rebuilding a table to consolidate extents is to use the ALTER FRAGMENT ON TABLE...INIT syntax in IDS. This is often the fastest way of consolidating a table.

Dbspaces

A dbspace is a collection of chunks. Additional chunks can be added to a dbspace at any time if there is adequate disk space and an available UNIX device or file, and provided that there are adequate slots in the chunks pseudotable. Adding chunks can be done without bringing the database down.

The chunks are known as the *primary* chunk for the first chunk in a dbspace and as *secondary* chunks for any additional chunks added. There are also *mirror* chunks if you have chosen to use Informix mirroring. Databases and tables are created in particular dbspaces. Tables cannot span multiple dbspaces, but databases can span multiple dbspaces. If you run out of space in a dbspace, you must add another chunk. In a pinch, create a chunk out of a cooked UNIX file until you can get your system cleaned out.

It is important to note that once added, a chunk cannot be dropped in OnLine systems. The DBA has to drop the entire dbspace to clear up its chunks. IDS allows you to drop un-used chunks from a dbspace.

Blobspaces

A blob is a "binary large object." Blobs are used to store text or binary data. Blob storage can be used for such items as compressed picture files, encoded voice data, word processing documents, and the like. Blob data can be stored either in ordinary tablespaces or in dedicated blobspaces. In most cases, using blobspaces is more efficient, since the blobspace creator can specify the page sizes for the blobspace. Using larger page sizes for blobspaces is a good way to reduce the number of locks required for updating the blobs. This will also allow the engine to handle the large I/O requests that are used to access blobs much more efficiently. Thus, blobspaces can be tailor-made to hold particular types of blob data.

How UNIX Manages Memory

The UNIX operating system is responsible for allocating sufficient memory resources for all processes running on the system. UNIX operating systems allocate three separate areas in memory for each process.

Text Segment

The text segment ontains machine-level instructions for the program or process's operation. These instructions can be used by multiple processes without loading individual copies of the code if the code is written to be *reentrant*. Such reentrant code is code that is written to resolve multiuser conflicts caused by several processes calling the shared code simultaneously.

Programs running under UNIX use shared text segments and therefore share code. This greatly cuts down on memory requirements, as multiple client processes can access the same code without having multiple copies of the code in memory. Multiple server programs also share common code.

Data Segment

The data segment contains global variables, buffers, and other data structures to be accessed by the process. These data segments are private to each `sqlturbo`.

Stack Space

The stack space contains internal storage for individual processes. Largely invisible to the user. OnLine processes maintain individual stack spaces and these areas of memory are not shared.

Contents of OnLine Shared Memory and IDS Resident Shared Memory

The engines differ in the way they refer to these similar sections of shared memory. This section is the complete shared memory of the OnLine systems and the resident portion of the IDS shared memory. With the exception of more structures in IDS, they are similar enough to discuss at the same time. Informix uses its shared memory to store system information as well as to buffer actual pages from the database. This system information keeps track of system resources and their availability to the user.

This data is stored in arrays and other data structures within shared memory. These data structures are created and sized at the time the shared memory is initialized. The parameters come from the $TB/ONCONFIG file for that particular database instance. The tbmonitor utility writes to the $TB/ONCONFIG file as its parameters change. These data structures are accessible to the DBA only through the use of the engine or other utilities, mainly tb/onstat. In IDS systems, many of these structures are also available through tables in the system monitoring interface (SMI) database called sysmaster.

These data structures, or *pseudotables,* contain information that is critical to the DBA. A large portion of the task of understanding what is going on in the database consists of understanding how to use tb/onstat to decipher the contents of the pseudotables. The following are major areas and pseudotables in the shared memory structure.

Latches

An inherent problem with a multiuser database is the situation in which multiple users need concurrent access to a system resource. Shared memory is such a resource, and OnLine needs to consider what happens when there are conflicts in accessing shared memory resources.

Even though a pseudotable itself may contain locks that grant access to a database resource, access to the pseudotable itself must be controlled. Informix does this through *latches*.

A latch is a data mechanism that allows a user to modify a system resource. Before a user or process is allowed to modify a system resource, it must first acquire the latch that is associated with the resource. There is not actually a separate pseudotable for latches because the latch data element is the first item in its respective lock table.

IDS systems refer to latches as mutexes. They are the same thing. Latches can be viewed by using the tb/onstat -s command:

```
joe 53> tbstat -s
RSAM Version 5.01.UC1    -- OnLine-Up 8 days 17:34:19 -- 18704 Kbytes
Latches with lock or user set
name       address   lock wait user
bbf[0]     e075adb8 1    0    e0002770
physlog    e0001670 1    1    e0002e30
physb2     e0001694 1    1    e0002470
bf[3276]   e072dcac 1    0    e00024d0
pt[33]     e067afa0 1    0    e0002590
pt[48]     e067bdec 1    0    e0002a10
bbf[0]     e075adb8 1    0    e0002a10
bh[4749]   e06e9cb0 1    0    e0001e70
bbf[0]     e075adb8 1    0    e0002a10
bbf[0]     e075adb8 1    0    e0002a10
tblsps     e00000f8 1    0    e0001e70
LRU13      e000046c 1    0    e0002230
```

```
(Note:  This is a composite run over several tbstat -s invocations.
The data is not necessarily consistent.  It's just a format sample)
```

Locks

The locks pseudotable is one of the busiest of the pseudotables. The lock table is broken down into a number of linked lists, each controlled by its own latch. The server uses a hashing mechanism based upon the lock requested to control access to the correct linked list. As access to this table is controlled by a small number of latch resources, the locks table can become a bottleneck in active systems. There is one lock for every OnLine resource that is shared or is otherwise in use. Entries in the lock table are cheap because they each use only a small amount of shared memory. Configure your system for as many as you can, within reason. Lock configuration depends on the level of locking that you are using for your tables. If you have a 200,000-row table with row-level locking, you will need 200,000 locks to do an update to every row in that table. If you are using the default page-level locking, you can get by with fewer locks.

One lock space in the lock table is used for each lock, whether that lock is a very high level lock like a database lock or a very low level lock like a row lock. Suppose you were doing an insert of a million rows into a table. The target table is set for row-level locking. Attempting this insert would cause an overflow of the locks table and would cause the job to crash unless you had a million locks table entries. There is a simple rule that helps you avoid this locking problem:

> **Always lock the target table in exclusive mode, if you can.**

The "if you can" is an important caveat here. Locking the target table means that no other users can access the table while the table is locked. If this causes a concurrency problem with your operations, you'll have to split the insert into several separate jobs or, better yet, use the dbload utility to load the rows without having to worry about locks (or long transactions).

Here's an example:

```
insert into new_table (select * from million_row_table);
```

This would use a million locks if new_table had been created or altered to row-level locking, but the following would use just one lock (assuming no indexes):

```
begin work;
lock table new_table in exclusive mode;
insert into new_table (select * from million_row_table);
commit work;
```

Locks can be viewed by using the tb/onstat -k command:

```
joe  42>tbstat -k
RSAM Version 5.01.UC1  -- OnLine—Up 7 days 23:48:24 -- 18704 Kbytes
Locks
address  wtlist   owner    lklist   type    tblsnum  rowid   size

e0058e68 0        e0002230 0          S      1000002  202     0
e0059a28 0        e0002bf0 0          S      1000002  202     0
3 active, 200000 total, 16384 hash buckets
```

Chunks and Dbspaces

The chunk pseudotable is actually two pseudotables, one for the primary and one for the mirrored chunks. The chunk pseudotable keeps track of each chunk that has been allocated in an OnLine system. The total number of allowable chunks is the tunable parameter CHUNKS in tb/onmonitor and in the $TB/ONCONFIG file.

One latch or mutex controls access to the chunk pseudotable. The dbspaces pseudotable registers all dbspaces in the system. Access to this table is also controlled by one latch.

There are two tb/onstat options that can view chunk and dbspace information. To see the space utilization of the database, use the tb/onstat -d command:

```
joe  43>tbstat -d
RSAM Version 5.01.UC1  -- OnLine—Up 7 days 23:48:38 -- 18704 Kbytes
Dbspaces
address  number  flags   fchunk  nchunks  flags   owner     name
e0016e88 1        1       1        3       N       informix  rootdbs
e0016eb8 2        1       4        2       N       informix  logspace
e0016ee8 3        1       5        2       N       informix  dbspace1
e0016f18 4        1       7        2       N       informix  logspace2
e0016f48 5        1       10       1       N       informix  slowdbspace
5 active, 20 total
Chunks
address  chk/dbs offset  size     free     bpages  flags pathname
e0014e78 1    1   0       135000   35718            PO-   /dev/rootdbs3
e0014f10 2    1   0       57000    56997            PO-   /dev/rootdbs1
e0014fa8 3    1   0       75000    74997            PO-   /dev/rootdbs2
e0015040 4    2   0       147500   24542            PO-   /dev/log1
e00150d8 5    3   0       812500   74310            PO-   /dev/chunk1
e0015170 6    3   0       677000   78338            PO-   /dev/chunk2
6 active, 27 total
```

To see read and write information regarding your database's chunks, use the tb/onstat -D command:

```
joe  44>tbstat -D
RSAM Version 5.01.UC1  -- OnLine—Up 7 days 23:48:53 -- 18704 Kbytes
Dbspaces
address  number  flags   fchunk  nchunks  flags   owner     name
e0016e88 1        1       1        3       N       informix  rootdbs
e0016eb8 2        1       4        2       N       informix  logspace
e0016ee8 3        1       5        2       N       informix  dbspace1
e0016f18 4        1       7        2       N       informix  logspace2
```

```
e0016f48 5          1          10         1          N          informix dbspace3
5 active, 20 total
Chunks
address   chk/dbs offset    page Rd    page Wr   pathname
e0014e78 1    1    0         731422     1030390   /dev/rootdbs3
e0014f10 2    1    0         114001     0         /dev/rootdbs1
e0014fa8 3    1    0         150001     0         /dev/rootdbs2
e0015040 4    2    0         233963     120000    /dev/log1
e00150d8 5    3    0         8498773    238186    /dev/chunk1
e0015170 6    3    0         10034058   178169    /dev/chunk2
e0015208 7    4    0         341480     173365    /dev/log3
e00152a0 8    2    0         239961     120000    /dev/log2
e0015338 9    4    0         193767     164848    /dev/log4
e00153d0 10   5    0         1628350    114065    /dev/chunk3
10 active, 27 total
```

Users

Every time a server process starts up, it attaches to the shared memory of the Informix system. When this occurs, the user obtains an entry in the users pseudotable, and certain information, such as process ID and user name, are stored. Besides server processes, some OnLine administrative functions occupy a user slot. This data can be seen using tb/onstat.

You can also see some information about OnLine users by using the UNIX ps command. There is always a tbinit process running. It started up the shared memory in the first place. If your system is using page cleaners, you will see one user tbpgcl for every page cleaner that you have configured. With some versions of UNIX, the page cleaners will be identified as tbinit rather than as tbpgcl.

On IDS systems, the only engine processes that the operating system will see are the onit processes that are the virtual processors.

OnLine has a "trap-door" built into its user table that often saves the DBA when the user table fills. It saves the last user entry for a tbmonitor process, whether there are existing tbmonitor processes running or not. The DBA can always get into the system as a user through tb/onmonitor.

To see the contents of the users pseudotable, use the tb/onstat -u command:

```
joe 46>tbstat -u
RSAM Version 5.01.UC1    -- OnLine-Up 7 days 23:49:06 -- 18704 Kbytes
Users
address   flags   pid    user     tty      wait   tout locks   nreads nwrites
e0001b70 ------D 555    informix console  0      0    0       6746   2607
e0001bd0 ------D 0      informix console  0      0    0       0      0
e0001c30 ------F 556    informix          0      0    0       0      0
e0001c90 ------F 557    informix          0      0    0       0      0
e0001cf0 ------F 558    informix          0      0    0       0      0
e0002890 ------- 4143   dba      -        0      0    1       2907   148
e00028f0 ------- 16460  dba      -        0      0    1       54972  4767
e00029b0 ------- 12247  support  -        0      0    1       100726 6677
e0002b90 ------- 12245  support  -        0      0    1       100554 6651
e0002bf0 --B---- 12246  support  -        0      0    1       101859 6650
```

```
e0002c50 ------- 13547   dba       -      0        0    1    6522    1741
e0002e30 --A---M 2740     informix ttyi02 0        0    0    0       0
42 active, 150 total
```

Transactions

OnLine versions beginning with version 5.0 include transaction information in the
tb/onstat -u output. This is useful in looking at distributed transactions across different databases on different machines. It's not too useful for simple applications, since each
user will have only one transaction going at a time. To see users and their transactions
(OnLine 5.0 and later), use the tb/onstat -u command:

```
joe  27>    tbstat -u
RSAM Version 5.01.UC1   -- OnLine—Up 6 days 06:40:42 -- 12976 Kbytes
Users
address   flags   pid     user     tty     wait     tout locks nreads   nwrites
e0001bbc  ------D 3954    informix ttyp8   0        0    0     1348    16
e0001c28  ------D 0       informix ttyp8   0        0    0     0       0
e0001c94  ------F 3956    informix         0        0    0     0       0
e0001d00  ------F 3957    informix         0        0    0     0       0
e000227c  ------- 16936   dba      -       0        0    1     0       1
e00022e8  ------- 16965   dba      -       0        0    1     0       19
e0002354  ------- 16957   dba      -       0        0    1     0       16
e00023c0  ------- 16948   dba      -       0        0    1     0       1
e000242c  ------- 22832   tony     -       0        0    1     0       0
e0002498  ------- 23247   dba      ttyp1   0        0    1     158     18
e0002504  ------- 23246   dba      ttyp1   0        0    1     510     33
11 active, 110 total
Transactions
address   flags user        locks log begin isolation retrys coordinator
e0004a24 A---- e0001bbc 0        0          NOTRANS   0
e0004c04 A---- e0001c28 0        0          NOTRANS   0
e0004de4 A---- e000242c 1        0          COMMIT    0
e0006464 A---- e000227c 1        0          COMMIT    0
e0006644 A---- e00022e8 1        0          COMMIT    0
e0006824 A---- e0002354 1        0          COMMIT    0
e0006a04 A---- e00023c0 1        0          COMMIT    0
e0006be4 A---- e0001d6c 1        0          COMMIT    0
e0006dc4 A---- e0002498 1        0          COMMIT    0
e0006fa4 A---- e0002504 1        0          COMMIT    0
10 active, 110 total
```

Tblspaces

The tblspace pseudotable tracks open tablespaces in the system. All tables are tracked here,
whether they are permanent or temporary. Temporary tables that are created because of
ORDER BY clauses also receive entries in this table. If multiple processes are accessing the
tablespace, a single entry will be in the pseudotable.

To see the tablespaces in use, use the tb/onstat -t command:

```
joe  30>    tbstat -t
RSAM Version 5.00.UC2    -- OnLine—Up 6 days 06:41:15 -- 12976 Kbytes

Tblspaces
 n address   flgs ucnt tblnum   physaddr npages nused  npdata nrows  nextns
 0 e00b85f4 1    1    1000001  10000e   5405   408    0      0      1
 1 e00b88b8 1    1    2000001  200004   905    2      0      0      1
 2 e00b8b7c 1    1    3000001  300004   10005  940    0      0      1
 3 e00b8e40 1    1    4000001  500004   1355   2      0      0      1
 4 e00b9104 1    19   3000002  300005   64     59     35     627    8

5 active, 1100 total, 512 hash buckets
```

Buffers

The buffers are by far the largest portion of the shared memory in OnLine systems and are a large portion of the shared memory in many IDS systems.. The internal data structure for the buffer is a threefold structure.

First, there is the actual page from the disk itself. The buffer holds the entire page, so another structure is used to track the information about the page itself. This is the buffer header table. The third structure is a hash table to simplify locating an individual buffer.

The tb/onstat command comes in two flavors, depending upon whether you want to see just the buffers in use or whether you want to see all buffer data. To see the status of buffers currently in use by an engine, use the tb/onstat -b command:

```
joe  31> tbstat -b
RSAM Version 4.10.UD4    -- OnLine—Up 8 days 17:26:14 -- 18704 Kbytes
Buffers
address   user    flgs pagenum  memaddr  nslots pgflgs xflgs owner    waitlist
e070976c 0       0    651566   e0937000 29     1      400   e00023b0 0
e06fff6c 0       6    50479c   e0807000 23     1      0     0        0
e07052ac 0       0    504894   e08ad800 77     10     400   e00020b0 0
e071c7ac 0       2    50af71   e0b97800 101    90     100   0        0
e072ae6c 0       0    5047b1   e0d65000 29     1      400   e00020b0 0
e073feac 0       0    50661f   e1005800 1      90     400   e00026b0 0
e072876c 0       0    537ffb   e0d17000 51     90     400   e0002530 0
e072986c 0       2    56c416   e0d39000 48     90     100   0        0
2526 modified, 4750 total, 8192 hash buckets, 2048 buffer size
(NOTE:  this output is a composite output from several runs of tbstat.
There may be inconsistencies because of this.  It's just a sample.)
```

To see the status of *all* the buffers, use the tb/onstat -B command:

```
joe 35> tbstat -B
RSAM Version 4.10.UD4   -- OnLine—Up 7 days 23:51:48 -- 18704 Kbytes
Buffers
address   user    flgs pagenum  memaddr  nslots pgflgs xflgs owner waitlist
e06fa9ac 0       6    69c58b   e075b800 27     1      0     0     0
e06faaac 0       6    57a379   e075d800 144    10     0     0     0
e06faaec 0       6    60f8e3   e075e000 36     90     0     0     0
..
..  (continues for all of your defined buffers)
..
```

```
e06facac 0        6     66d87f   e0761800 82     90     0     0        0
e06facec 0        6     69beac   e0762000 75     90     0     0        0
e06fad2c 0        6     69c49f   e0762800 27     1      0     0        0
284 modified, 4750 total, 8192 hash buckets, 2048 buffer size
```

LRUs

The least recently used (LRU) queues are data structures that track usage of the buffer pool. The queues are allocated in pairs, one for *clean* data and one for *dirty* data. Data is clean if the buffer is not flagged as having been modified. The queues are arranged so that the most recently used buffers are found at the head of the queue.

When a buffer is accessed, it is moved to the beginning of the queue. Buffers at the least recently used end of each queue (dirty queue and clean queue) are the ones that are used first for storing new data from disk or for flushing to disk.

There is one latch for each queue, making two latches for every queue pair. The number of LRU queues is determined by the $TB/ONCONFIG parameter LRUS.

To see the status of the LRU queues use the tb/onstat -R command:

```
joe 57>tbstat -R
RSAM Version 4.10.UD4    -- OnLine—Up 7 days 23:53:44 -- 18704 Kbytes
16 buffer LRU queues
LRU  0:     6 ( 0.9%) modified of  643 total
LRU  1:     6 ( 1.0%) modified of  631 total
LRU  2:     8 ( 1.2%) modified of  674 total
LRU  3:     6 ( 1.1%) modified of  557 total
LRU  4:    13 ( 2.4%) modified of  551 total
LRU  5:     6 ( 1.0%) modified of  601 total
LRU  6:     8 ( 1.4%) modified of  569 total
LRU  7:     4 ( 0.8%) modified of  524 total

57 dirty, 4750 queued, 4750 total, 8192 hash buckets, 2048 buffer size
start clean at 60% dirty, stop at 50%; first pass search 70%
```

Page Cleaners

As the buffer pool fills with data, it becomes necessary for some buffers to be reused to hold new data. It is advantageous for there to always be some clean buffers on the queue. If the database engine needs to bring data in from the disk into a buffer, it is most efficient if the target buffer is a clean buffer, since clean buffers can be overwritten with the new data.

A dirty buffer is another thing. If there are no clean buffers, Informix has to use a dirty buffer. First, the dirty buffer needs to be written out (flushed) to disk. Then the engine brings the new data into the newly clean buffer. This creates more load for the engine, as the engine has to perform the flush. This is known as a foreground (fg) write. If you are getting many foreground writes, the buffers need cleaning more often.

The preferred way of cleaning the buffers is through the actions of the page cleaner daemons. Their actions are controlled by the Informix parameters LRU_MAX_DIRTY and

LRU_MIN_DIRTY. As each LRU queue becomes populated with dirty buffers, it will eventually reach the LRU_MAX_DIRTY percentage. When the buffer reaches this percentage of dirtiness, the page cleaner daemon is awakened and it begins cleaning the buffers. When the dirtiness is down to the LRU_MIN_DIRTY percentage, the page cleaner goes back to sleep.

The defaults are usually 60 percent for MAX and 50 percent for MIN. These parameters are tunable. The object is to reduce the foreground writes to a minimum, as these are engine processes. We'll talk extensively about tuning these parameters in Chapter 8.

To see the status of the page cleaners, use the `tb/onstat -F` command:

```
joe  59>tbstat -F
RSAM Version 5.01.UC1  -- OnLine—Up 7 days 23:53:56 -- 18704 Kbytes
Fg Writes     LRU Writes    Idle Writes   Chunk Writes
0             279744        5142          471793

address  flusher  snooze   state   data
e0001c30 0        60       I       0        = 0
e0001c90 1        60       I       0        = 0
e0001cf0 2        60       I       0        = 0
e0001d50 3        60       I       0        = 0
e0001db0 4        60       I       0        = 0
e0001e10 5        60       I       0        = 0
states: Exit Idle Chunk Lru
```

Logs

There are two types of logs in the Informix engines, physical logs and logical logs. The physical logs store pages of data or indexes from the buffer pool as the pages are modified. The physical log is used primarily in the fast recovery process that accompanies the startup of the database. It also coordinates with the `tbtape` archiving processes when an archive is running.

Access to the physical log is through two physical log buffers, which are periodically flushed to the actual physical log. There is one latch controlling access to each of the two physical log buffers.

The logical logs are areas of the disk (often in their own dbspace) in which Informix stores records of transactions that are in progress or are completed. A newly-installed OnLine engine begins with 3 logs in the root dbspace. IDS systems default to a minimum of 6 logs in the root dbspace. The size of these logs is a tunable parameter in `tb/onmonitor`.

In OnLine systems only, it is very important to give thought to the sizing of your logical logs before you begin to initialize your system. The sizing of the logical logs can be changed only by reinitializing the entire database. This is a major task, so it is important to get the sizing right the first time. Additional logs can be added and become available for use only after an archive is done.

IDS systems have done away with this limitation. Logical logs can be of various sizes, and the size is controlled at the time the logical log is created

Access to the logical logs is through three built-in logical log buffers, each controlled by its own latch or mutex.

To see the status of your logs, use the `tb/onstat -l` command:

```
joe  62>tbstat -l
RSAM Version 5.01.UC1    -- OnLine—Up 7 days 23:54:27 -- 18704 Kbytes
Physical Logging
Buffer bufused  bufsize  numpages numwrits pages/I/O
  P-1  69        128       713655   5901     120.94
      phybegin physize  phypos   phyused  %used
      117202   6000     2999     69       1.15

Logical Logging
Buffer bufused  bufsize  numrecs   numpages numwrits recs/pages pages/I/O
  L-1  8        64        31030148  668262   21047    46.4       31.8

address   number  flags    uniqid  begin    size    used   %used
e06d25d8  1       F------   0       400b8e   30000   0      0.00
e06d25f4  2       F------   0       4080be   30000   0      0.00
e06d2610  3       F------   0       40f5ee   30000   0      0.00
e06d262c  4       F------   0       10126e   30000   0      0.00
e06d2648  5       F------   0       10879e   30000   0      0.00
e06d2664  6       F------   0       10fcce   30000   0      0.00
e06d2680  7       F------   0       416b1e   30000   0      0.00
e06d269c  8       F------   0       800003   30000   0      0.00
e06d26b8  9       F------   0       700a94   30000   0      0.00
```

Profiles

The profile pseudotable contains various items related to the performance of the Informix system. It includes items such as cache hit ratios for reading and writing, number of different types of calls to the database, number of times pseudotables overflowed, and number of times a process had to wait for different resources.

This is one of the most important pseudotables, as this is just about the only source of data about the performance of the database in OnLine systems. IDS has more depth to its database monitoring capabilities because of the SMI database, but you still be using `onstat -p` quite a bit. You'll be doing `tb/onstat -p` in your sleep the more you work on tuning the database.

The last line of this output differs between OnLine and IDS systems. For more detail see Chapter 10. For an overall performance profile, use the `tb/onstat -p` command:

```
joe  63>tbstat -p
RSAM Version 5.01.UC1    -- OnLine—Up 7 days 23:54:38 -- 18704 Kbytes
Profile
dskreads pagreads bufreads %cached dskwrits pagwrits bufwrits %cached
14970755 22166265 498552631 97.00   543747   2139408  49870693 98.91

isamtot    open     start     read      write     rewrite  delete   commit   rollbk
424714409  5813437  23348999  175473799 10989374  5499045  2603325  8699910  101
ovtbls  ovlock  ovuser  ovbuff  usercpu    syscpu    numckpts flushes
0       0       0       0       387006.97  41611.33  294      587
```

```
bufwaits lokwaits lockreqs deadlks  dltouts  lchwaits ckpwaits compress
21748    8046      476500421 9        0        1594907  1664     2220019
```

## CHAPTER 3

Understanding Logging

Both of the Informix engines keep track of changes to its data by the use of logfiles. There are two types of logfiles, physical and logical. Each logfile is accessed through buffers in the shared memory. You need to make the distinction between the log buffers, which are areas of shared memory and the logfiles, which are areas of the disk that receive data from the buffers. The shared memory is by definition transitory. If the system goes down, this data is lost. The logfiles on disk are persistent. Assuming there are no hardware problems with the disk, their contents survive system crashes.

The essential point of difference between the physical and logical logs is really indicated by their names. The physical logs are simply images of the pages as they come in from the disk system. They are essentially reference points to bring the system back to a known state. The logical logs represent a chronological record of data changes that occur within the database. Should the engine receive a ROLLBACK WORK command, it is able to go to the logical logs and undo any transactions that are affected by the ROLLBACK WORK command.

Whenever a data page is needed by a process, the engine first looks in its shared memory. If the data page is not found in shared memory, it is pulled in from the disk into a page buffer in shared memory. As soon as any data on this page is scheduled for modification, the page is copied into the physical log buffer. This occurs only on the first update to the particular pages. This before image data in the physical log buffer is then flushed out to the physical log on disk. This flushing of the physical log buffer to the physical log on disk occurs when the buffer is full, during checkpoints, or when a page in both the shared memory buffers and the physical log buffer is flushed to disk.

The physical log buffer is actually a pair of buffers in shared memory, each of which is the size indicated in the `tb/onconfig` file. This "double buffering" allows the system to switch between the first and second buffers so that no time or data is lost while the other is flushing to the physical log on disk. These buffers are identified as `P-1` and `P-2` in the `tb/onstat -1` output.

Likewise, the logical log buffer is actually three separate buffers in shared memory, each the size indicated in the `tb/onconfig` file. This "triple buffering" allows one buffer to flush while one of the others fills, and provides an additional buffer in case the active buffer fills up before the first buffer is completely flushed.

Flushing the physical log buffer to the physical log on disk occurs in three separate circumstances. In the first instance, the physical log buffer becomes full. When this occurs, the system switches to the other physical log buffer and flushes the full buffer to disk.

The second instance is somewhat more subtle. This flush must occur before any page cleaner activity flushes pages in the page cache buffer back to the disk. Here, it is possible that a page in the page cache buffer pool has been modified, causing its before image to be written to the physical log buffer. If a page cleaner fires up in this case, it is possible for the modified page to be on disk while the original before image is still in the physical log buffer. This gives rise to the rule that flushing a before image of a page to disk must occur before the actual modified page can be flushed to disk.

The third instance in which the physical log buffer is flushed is at a checkpoint. The first step of a checkpoint calls for this flushing of the buffer.

When any data is changed in the shared memory page buffer pool, the engine checks to see whether or not anything needs to be logged to the logical logfile. In addition to changes that are either specifically or implicitly part of a transaction, the engine also logs SQL data definition language (DDL) statements, changes to the database configuration such as changes in chunks, `dbspaces`, and blobspaces, and any checkpoint events. All of these loggable events are first placed into the logical log buffer and then flushed back to disk.

PHYSICAL AND LOGICAL LOGS

The physical and logical logs are used by the engine in three major situations:

Transaction Rollback

If a SQL command or a series of SQL commands is executed within a BEGIN WORK/COMMIT WORK structure, the engine will not commit any of the transactions until it receives the OK to "commit work." If something fails, either in a SQL statement or for outside reasons, the engine uses the information in the logical logfiles to roll back the transaction. This brings the database back to a consistent state as though the transaction had never begun.

Restoring from Tape

In the event that the data is completely lost as the result of mechanical or human error and it is necessary to recover the entire system from tape, the `tb/ontape` program first loads the data from the last archive. This is either one tape from a Level 0 archive, or a combination of Level 0, Level 1, and Level 2 archive tapes. After the last archive tape is loaded, the engine then applies data contained in the logfiles that have been saved to tape. This brings the database up to its condition before the crash. After all of the logged data is back in the system, any transactions that were not yet committed at the time of the crash are rolled back to ensure the consistency of the instance. If the instance was using buffered logging, it is possible that some of the last transaction data will be lost due to the loss of data in the buffer.

Fast Recovery

Most of the time when the system goes down, it is not necessary to recover from tape. Informix has a robust recovery process that is part of its shared memory initialization process. When the shared memory is initialized upon restart after a crash, the engine goes into *fast recovery* mode, which is automatic and not under control of the DBA. In fast recovery, the instance is first brought back into a known good status as evidenced by the condition at the last checkpoint by restoring data from the physical log. After this known status is attained, the engine then goes to the logical logfiles and finds the location of the last checkpoint. From that point onward, the engine applies all of the transactions that it finds in the logical logfiles. Finally, it rolls back any changes that were made inside a transaction and for which it finds no COMMIT WORK entry in the log.

When the system is halted properly, the physical logfile is flushed to disk as part of a final checkpoint that occurs when the system leaves online status and becomes quiescent. When the system crashes, the physical logfile is left with data in it. This is what tells the `tb/oninit` process that the physical recovery is necessary.

Often the fast recovery process is not fast at all. The speed of the fast recovery depends upon many factors, including the length of time from the last checkpoint and the amount of work that has been done since then. This time can often be estimated by checking the number of active logfiles. Whenever you are forced into a fast recovery, it helps to note the number of logs that it has to go through and to note the amount of time it takes to recover. Whenever your system crashes in real life, one of the most pressing questions you'll receive is "How long until the database is up?" Any time you find yourself waiting through a fast recovery, note how many logfiles are involved and time the recovery. Developing such a rule of thumb based on logfiles is better than just answering with an "I dunno."

The IDS engine series provides two entries in the $ONCONFIG file that affect fast recoveries and restores. The OFF_RECVRY_THREADS parameter defines the number of virtual processors that are started when the system is in an off-line mode and goes into recovery after a restart. Due to the parallel nature of IDS, the engine is capable of running its recovery in multiple virtual processes and multiple threads. The ON_RECVRY_THREADS parameter governs the number of recovery threads that are started when the system goes into online mode. If you are experiencing long recovery times after a crash, and if you have sufficient CPU resources, you can try experimenting with these two parameters. Generally the system defaults are adequate, but a system that does heavy transaction processing could possibly benefit from increasing the number of recovery threads.

LOGGING MODES

The OnLine engine provides for three modes of logging operation. The selection of logging mode is important to the issue of data recovery in the event of a system crash.

Until the contents of the logical log buffer are flushed to disk, the transaction log records that the buffer holds are at risk should the system go down. If the system crashes with data in the logical log buffers, any changes to the database held in the buffer will not be recoverable. The three logging modes represent increasing degrees of data survivability.

No Logging

If the database is created with no logging, there is still a small amount of activity directed towards the logical logs and logical log buffers. Any statement that uses data definition language (DDL) statements such as CREATE TABLE or CREATE INDEX will result in entries into the logical logs, as will some internal activities of the engine.

In fast recovery of a database that is not logged, only the physical log records are read back into the system during fast recovery. After these pages are read back into shared memory, the system does an automatic checkpoint as part of the fast recovery process. This brings the database into consistency as of the last checkpoint prior to the crash. In databases that use logging, this checkpoint is followed by rolling forward the transaction data from the time of the last checkpoint, followed by rolling back transactions that have not been committed. These final two steps do not occur in the case of a database created with no logging. The effect of this is that without the use of logging, you can never recover any further than your last checkpoint. Work that occurred between the last checkpoint and the crash will be lost.

In IDS systems, it is possible to specify the clause, "WITH NO LOG" in a table creation DDL statement. In this case, the table is treated as though it were in a no logging database regardless of the logging status of the overall database.

Non-logging databases are useful in cases where the data flow is such that transactions can be recreated in the event of a crash. Often, batch operations against a non-logging database will meet this criteria. Also, non-logging databases are useful for the initial loading of database rows from other sources. Loading tables into a non-logging database will save the overhead of logging and will make the loads go much faster.

Changing of logging modes can occur only when the engine is quiescent. Also, any change from non-logging to any form of logging requires completing an immediate archive. A `tb/ontape` archive to `/dev/null` is a useful tool here.

Buffered Logging

If a database is created with buffered logging, the contents of the logical log buffer are flushed to the disk logfiles only when the buffer is full. This results in more efficient database operations because expensive disk I/O operations are avoided.

Buffered logging also results in more efficient use of logical logfile space on disk. Writes from the logical log buffer to the logical logs on disk occur in page units. Whether there is a full page of transaction entries or only one entry occupying just a small part of a page, the entire page gets written to the disk file. Since no writes occur to the disk logfile until the buffer is full, the logfiles on disk will hold a higher percentage of useful information. The logfile data on disk will thus be more efficiently packed than with unbuffered logging.

All databases in an instance share the same buffers and disk logfiles. Thus, if some of your databases use buffered logging and some use nonbuffered logging, the nonbuffered databases could still force high I/O rates to the disks. When a nonbuffered database completes a transaction, it will force the buffer to flush whether or not the buffer is full. The other databases will just sort of be dragged along.

The cost of buffered logging is the risk of losing data in the case of a crash. Although not as costly as crashing a non-logging database, crashing a buffered-logging database will result in loss of any transactions in the buffer that have not been flushed to disk. Although not as bad as losing all data changed since the last checkpoint, this data loss can still be costly. It's up to the DBA to make the judgment call as to whether the improved performance is worth the risk of data loss.

Unbuffered Logging

In a database created with unbuffered logging, the logical log buffer flushes every time a transaction completes. Note that this includes jobs that are included in a BEGIN WORK/COMMIT WORK section as well as *singleton* transactions that are implicitly considered as transactions. A singleton transaction is any SQL statement that inserts or modifies data. It either completes or fails. It cannot partially complete. You can count on a log flush every time a loggable SQL transaction completes. Even with unbuffered logging, there is some data still at risk. If a crash occurs and leaves uncommitted data in the logical log buffer since the last transaction committed, this data may be lost. There are some pathological instances involving a crash between the START COMMIT record and the COMMIT COMPLETE record that may require that Informix Support call into the system and manually remove the orphaned START COMMIT record.

There is one drawback to using unbuffered logging. Since the logical log buffers flush with essentially every transaction, the buffers often contain only a small amount of data when they flush. Since the flushing occurs in page increments, the empty space is written to the logfiles, causing the logfiles to fill up more rapidly. This can happen if you have only one database set up for unbuffered logging, as every time it flushes, it will flush for all the databases. Log flushing is for the entire instance, not just for particular databases.

Unbuffered logging offers the ultimate in data survivability, at a cost of disk I/O and some bloating of your logfiles. Again, this requires a judgment call by the DBA.

SAVING THE LOG FILES

In the event that the worst happens and the database needs to be recovered from tape, it's essential that the logfiles be regularly copied to tape. They can also be stored on other media. Such saving to disk or optical disk can be kludged together, but the OnLine/IDS archive utilities are really designed to be used with a tape device, preferably two. This changes in the NT port, where archives and logfile backups can both be directed to disk using the Informix Storage Manager (ISM) program in conjunction with onbar/onarchive.

There are really two good reasons to get the logs copied to tape rapidly. The first is the obvious reason of getting them safely stored off-line. The other reason is that once a logfile has filled up with data, it cannot be reused unless it has been marked as "backed up" and copied to tape (or some other medium).

Both engines provide two methods for saving the logfiles to tape, automatic backup and continuous backup. Automatic backup is not really automatic. It just backs up all existing logfiles to tape. It's almost useless except for instances where you need to back up a batch of logs in a one-time situation. After an automatic backup, you need to change tapes in the tape device because tb/ontape will write over them the next time it backs up logfiles. The really useful backup is the continuous backup option. Under continuous backup, whenever a logfile fills up, it is automatically backed up to the tape device and the process waits for the next log to fill up. Continuous backup provides an almost invisible method of assuring that the tape backups get done. Under continuous backup, the tape device is not closed and the backups of the logfiles occur one after another on the tape. The IDS engine also supports an ALARMPROGRAM such as logs_full.sh, that automates the logfile backup. Look in your $INFORMIXBIN directory to see how the ALARMPROGRAM works.

It's recommended that you have two tape devices available for each Informix instance. This can be a major problem if you are running multiple instances. It usually means that it becomes very hard to automate database archives and logfile backups with multiple instances unless you have a lot of tape devices. Consider this if you are considering going to multiple instances of the database.

For a single instance, it is still best to have two tape drives, one for the archives and one for the logfile backups. Working with one drive is possible, but it means that you'll have to do some manual intervention. Actually, this is not all bad. The temptation, especially with large DAT drives, is to just pop in a logfile backup tape, turn on continuous logfile backups, and wait till the end of the tape. This is not advisable for several reasons. First, tb/ontape does not reliably handle end of tape conditions and it's best to avoid getting that far on a tape. Second, if you have gigabytes of logfiles on one tape, you're putting a lot of your eggs in one eight-millimeter basket. If you're on your hundredth logfile and the tape breaks, you've just lost numbers one through ninety-nine.

The most important reason is that if you ever have to apply the logfiles in a restore situation, you'll have to run through the entire logfile backup tape, which may take forever. Suppose you have a logfile backup tape that starts with logfile number 1 and goes through number 100, with each logfile taking 20 megabytes. Your last archive occurred at logfile number 75. If you should have to restore from tape, you'll first have to load the archive tape, then you'll have to apply the logs from number 75 to number 100. Since all of your logfiles are on one tape, you'll have to run through tapes number 1 through number 74 before you get to the first usable logfile. The amount of time that it takes to do this will be magnified greatly if you have users asking you "When will the system be back up?" every five minutes.

It's best to rotate your logfile tapes on a regular basis along with your archive tapes. If you're using one tape drive for both archives and logfile backups, you're forced to do this anyway, since you have to restart the logging after the archive is done.

LONG TRANSACTIONS

One of the most critical things that can happen to an Informix instance is a long transaction. A long transaction occurs when a transaction begins in one logfile and spans multiple logfiles. If it gets to a certain point of logfile usage, the transaction begins to roll back. If there is not enough logfile space available for the rollback, the Informix engine cannot make the database consistent. If this happens, the database needs to be reinitialized and restored from an archive. If you get into this problem, pray that your support contract is up to date because Informix Support may be the only source of help. Otherwise, you'll have to restore from an archive.

    This is almost the worst thing that can happen to the database. You'll certainly lose a lot of time. You'll probably lose data. Before Version 4.1, the situation was much easier to get into. The later versions have several tb/onconfig parameters that are meant to avoid the problem, but their defaults are not conservative enough until later versions of 7.XX, and need to be changed. In versions later than 4.1, the configuration file has two critical parameters.

- LTXHWM: This is the *long transaction high water mark.* The Informix default value is 80 percent. When the total number of filled logs reaches this amount, any transactions that started in the oldest logfile are marked as long transactions and are forced to begin to roll back. This parameter's default is 80 percent, and it is often way too high. Set it at about 60 or 70 percent in most cases. You need to give the transaction enough room to roll back as well as give other jobs room to log.

- LTXEHWM: This is the *long transaction exclusive high water mark.* The Informix default value is 90 percent. When the total number of filled logs reaches this amount, all processes except long transactions that are rolling back are prevented from logging to the logfiles. These processes are effectively frozen. When you reach this stage of fullness, all of the logspace is needed to assure that the long transactions can roll back. It's defaulted at 90 percent and should probably be 75-80 percent.

    The long transaction is the culprit that fills up the logfiles. There are several types of long transactions, most of them easily understood and one that is less obvious. Let's start with the one of the more obvious ones.

    When you are working within a database that supports logging, either explicitly or by virtue of being a MODE ANSI database, the BEGIN WORK statement may precede a series of SQL statements. The BEGIN WORK event is logged in the logfile. This event occurs in a MODE ANSI database when the first SQL statement outside of a transaction is executed and for other logged databases when the BEGIN WORK statement is executed. Until the corresponding COMMIT WORK statement is entered into a logfile, the engine will consider that all of the logfiles beginning with the one holding the BEGIN WORK and ending with the currently active logfile are needed in case the transaction does not complete and the engine needs to roll it back The classic long transaction occurs when a user or a program is performing an update, insert, or delete on a large set of rows from a very large table. Each row affected generates a logfile entry. It is possible that one SQL statement on a table with hundreds of thousands of rows can swamp the logfiles, even if nothing else is being logged within the system. This type of situation often occurs when initially loading the database or when loading or unloading large tables.

The less obvious situation is when a user is doing a short transaction and fails to commit work. In this case, the BEGIN WORK statement is logged. The job does very little work, but the COMMIT WORK statement is not issued. Everything else that is logged into the logfiles then constitutes the long transaction. The engine does not care what is being done between the BEGIN WORK and the COMMIT WORK statements. Until it sees a matching COMMIT WORK statement it thinks it's in a long transaction. The dbaccess program executes a hidden BEGIN WORK statement when you first query a logged non-ANSI database. This is the reason that you sometimes get a "Commit or rollback" prompt inside of dbaccess when you have not actually executed a visible BEGIN WORK statement.

Suppose a user issues a BEGIN WORK statement from within isql/dbaccess for a short transaction and neither issues a COMMIT WORK nor exits from the isql or dbaccess program. That person then goes to lunch, or on a long weekend, or maybe on vacation. You've got a long transaction working. It will continue until the user either commits or exits isql/dbaccess. If the user exits isql/dbaccess, the program will prompt for action on the commit before isql/dbaccess exits memory. As long as that isql/dbaccess instance is running, it will be looking for the COMMIT WORK statement. The lesson here is to train your users to be aware of their transaction usage.

SIZE, NUMBER, AND LOCATION OF LOGICAL LOGS

When either IDS or OnLine is first installed, all logfiles are in the root dbspace. The OnLine engine defaults to three logfiles, so unless changes are made in the tb/onconfig file, you will start out with three logfiles in your root dbspace. The IDS engine creates six logfiles by default. Version 7.30 creates 10. Informix does not allow you to change the size of the logfiles, although it does allow you to change the number and location of the logfiles. In OnLine systems all logfiles will be the same size.

IDS systems give the DBA the option of specifying the size of each logfile at the time of creation. In these systems, the logfiles can be of different sizes. The big advantage to this LOGSIZE parameter in IDS is to allow the DBA to increase or decrease the size of logical logs without having to completely rebuild the instance. Another advantage may be when the DBA desperately needs more logfiles and has to scrounge around finding bits and pieces of disk real estate to use for the logfiles. Here, the different logfile sizes may allow the DBA to extract the most logfile space from his available space.

In the initial configuration, the engine will calculate the total size requested for the logfiles (number times size of each logfile) and will assume that all of these logfiles go into the root dbspace. If this space is larger than the size of the root dbspace, the engine will not initialize. This is a common cause of problems during installation because the DBA will often specify his maximum number of desired logfiles in the tbmonitor process, and the initialization program will try to actually allocate space for all the requested logfiles in the root dbspace.

One of the major questions in the original setup of the OnLine system concerns the anticipated size and number of logfiles. Generally, you need to have sufficient logfiles to allow logging of a transaction in your largest table. If you do not have adequate logs for this, you will get long transaction errors and will not be able to complete your maximum size transaction.

Adding additional logfiles is a simple procedure. Changing the size of logfiles is a complex undertaking in OnLine and a simple one in IDS. To increase the size of logfiles the entire OnLine system must be reinitialized and your data must be rebuilt from an export or from other flatfiles. Changing the logfile size, reinitializing, and then restoring from an archive does not work. The RESTORE command in tb/onmonitor performs an initialization itself. It initializes the system to the parameters that were in effect at the time of the ARCHIVE. If you try to use the RESTORE in this manner, you will end up with the same size logfiles that you started with.

The Informix manual recommends a total logfile allocation of approximately 20 percent of total database space. Depending upon the nature of your transactions, this may or may not be enough. Note that a maximum size transaction by definition takes quite a bit of time to complete. If other loggable transactions are occurring at the same time, the logging requirements must take into account *all* of the logging load simultaneously, not just the largest. Since both the number and the location of the logfiles can be changed, only the size represents an unalterable (without reinitializing the disk) decision. There is only one constraint to consider, and that is the maximum number of logfiles allowed. An OnLine system using a 2-kilobyte page size can have about 60 logical logfiles. IDS removes the limit on the number of logfiles. Size the logfiles such that a total of 60 logfiles will take up about 20 to 25 percent of the maximum anticipated database size. If your database grows to such a size that you reach the maximum number of logfiles, you'll probably be reinstalling on bigger hardware before then anyway. Don't worry too much about trying to predict years into the future. Get the system tuned for now with a little bit of room to expand.

One factor to consider in deciding on logfile size is the speed of your tape backup device. Keep the logfile size down if you have a slow backup device. The real solution is, as usual, hardware. Get a faster tape device. As a system gets larger, the capacity of the archive tape device and the logging tape device often become the limiting factor in how large the database can grow. When your archive devices are running constantly in an attempt to archive your system, you are reaching the limit of manageable size. IDS systems have more flexibility in this regard, as the onbar/onarchive programs can allow parallel logging and archiving to multiple tape devices. Taking advantage of these capabilities requires that the DBA use onbar rather than ontape.

New logical logs do not come into use until after an archive is done. The level of the archive does not matter. If the DBA is just adding or moving logfiles, the trick here is to do the archive to /dev/null.

The location of logical logs is also important. Logfiles usually have a relatively heavy write activity. This usually consists of efficient sequential writes. Still, Informix recommends that logfiles be optimized for writing. If you have a preferred disk location that allows more efficient writes, this is a good place to place your logs. An example would be in a UNIX-mirrored rather than a RAID 5 disk partition. RAID 5 is optimized for reading. Depending upon your implementation, writing to a RAID 5 partition can be significantly slower that writing to a mirrored partition. The DBA should also look at placing the logfiles on a separate disk to minimize disk contention.

One thing to consider is moving the initial three logfiles out of the root dbspace. If there is a lot of temporary table creation, and if the temp tables are created in the root dbspace (the default) relocating the logfiles is often a good idea. Since OnLine requires a minimum of three logfiles at all times, moving the initial three is more complicated than simply dropping the old ones and adding the new ones. You must always have three logfiles available at all times.

To move the logfiles, you need to be logged in as user informix or root. The informix login is preferred because all activities as root need to be done through the command line rather than through tb/onmonitor. First, you have to create at least three more logfiles in another dbspace. To activate them, do an ARCHIVE to /dev/null. The /dev/null archive occurs very quickly, as OnLine handles archiving to /dev/null differently from the way it handles archiving to a real device. This dummy archive convinces OnLine that a real archive has been done and activates the new logfiles for use.

Now, using tb/onstat -l, see which logfile is currently in use. You can use the tb/onmode -l command from the command line to cause the current log to advance to one of the new, non-rootdbs logfiles. You may need to execute the tb/onmode command several times until the current logfile is one of the newly created ones. You then need to do a backup of any of the logfiles you want to drop. Even if you skipped over them with the tb/onmode command, they need to be backed up to a real tape device, not to /dev/null. After the logs are backed up, go to quiescent mode and drop the three logfiles that are in the root dbspace. If you are using tb/onstat -c to force continuous backup of logfiles, these logfile backups will be happening automatically and you won't have to do them manually. Finally, do an actual Level 0 archive to tape to establish a baseline for future recoveries.

If you already have an Informix system running, it is very informative to watch your disk I/O statistics to see exactly how your application reads and writes to disk. This simple c-shell script called watch_hot will do the job:

```
#!/bin/csh
while ( 1 == 1 )
tbstat -D
tbstat -z
sleep 5
end
```

Since this script reinitializes the `tbstat` statistics every five seconds, make sure that it does not interfere with any long-term `tbstat` statistics collection that you or someone else may be doing. The script will output numbers representing the incremental reads and writes to database chunks every five seconds.

The above script will work with both engines. You can accomplish the same function by running queries against the SMI database tables on IDS systems. We'll go into more detail in the chapter on SMI system tables

One thing that you'll find with this script is that your highest rate of writing is probably to your physical logs. This is where you need to watch your disk placement to optimize for writing speed. The physical log can be a bottleneck for the entire system, so place it carefully.

Another thing that this script can show you is where you are in completing an archive. If you run it while an archive is running, you'll see a running bulge of heavy read activity in your chunks as the archive program walks through your database structure

Understanding Archives

One of the main duties of the database administrator is ensuring the safety of the data. Although each of the Informix engines is a very robust product, a number of factors can cause the system to go down. In OnLine systems, these problems often arise from user errors such as killing engine processes with a UNIX `kill -9` command. Other things that can crash the system are hardware problems and UNIX problems that crash the entire computer. IDS's multithreaded architecture and its strict prohibition against killing *oninit* jobs make it less likely that a UNIX kill command will crash your database, but there are many other things that can crash your system.

In most instances, the database will recover from the error during the fast recovery process that occurs automatically when the shared memory is first started. In most cases, user errors and software problems cause no physical damage to the data, and this fast recovery is adequate to bring the system back up. It is the hardware crashes that most often cause the database administrator to have to recover the database from the archives. When this happens, the DBA quickly realizes that the only thing between him and the deep blue sea is a flimsy length of recording tape. It behooves the DBA to be absolutely certain of the Informix archive and recovery system. This chapter will explain the archive and recovery system and point out some of the ways that the DBA can assure the integrity of this system.

LIMITATIONS OF THE tb/ontape PROGRAM

In addition to the UNIX filesize limits noted in the previous section, there are several more items that can cause serious problems with the archiving process.

The Informix manuals recommend that a terminal be dedicated to the tb/ontape program and that someone watch that terminal for instructions to change the tape. If you do this, the terminal should actually be in the same room as the tape drive, so that the operator can visually check the status of the drive and change the tapes quickly. Although this looks good on paper, it is not always the best method from an operational standpoint. Sometimes, the DBA needs to have these processes working in the background or as a part of a management script. This can be done as in the following script:

```
#!/bin/csh
tbtape -s << EOF
0
^M     (note, this is a control M
EOF
```

This script runs the tb/ontape program and answers "0" to the Level? prompt and then enters a carriage return when prompted to hit enter when the tape is mounted. Please note that running tb/ontape from a script or in the background is *definitely not recommended* by Informix. You're doing it at your own risk, but the risk is manageable.

What's so risky about this? Problems arise if you exceed the capacity of your tape archive device. This capacity is set with the tb/onmonitor program. This tape size parameter, as well as the names of the archive and log devices, are changeable without having to restart the engine. When tb/ontape thinks you've reached the end of your tape, it will send a prompt to the standard output requesting you to change tapes and hit ENTER. If tb/ontape is running in the background or as part of a script, you cannot hit ENTER, and tb/ontape continues to wait for you to change tapes.

This creates a problem when your system needs to perform a checkpoint. Whether the checkpoint is needed because the checkpoint interval has elapsed or because the physical logs have reached 75 percent full, the checkpoint program will try to write out data to the archive tape. (Remember, the archives, logs, and checkpoints all work together and know of one other's status.) This write cannot occur when the archive is waiting for a tape change, so the checkpoint cannot occur. This causes the engine to freeze up and allows processes to perform nothing but data reads. The only way out is to kill the tb/ontape process. (Kill it with a UNIX `kill -15` command, not with the very dangerous `kill -9 command.`) This problem has been corrected in the IDS engine. In the IDS engine the physical log before images are constantly copied to temp tables instead of to the archive.

You can feel relatively comfortable with running `tb/ontape` either in a script or in the background as long as you are *absolutely sure* that your entire archive will fit within a single archive tape.

Another thing to do if you're running `tb/ontape` in this way is to redirect the standard error and standard output to a file. Since `tb/onmonitor` and `tb/ontape` both use UNIX standard input and standard output, standard UNIX redirection methods work. If you redirect the output into a file, you can then access this file and check on the status of the archive without having to be at a dedicated terminal. You can also use the file output in other scripts. This is done in the `status` script included with this book. Note that `tb/ontape` uses the UNIX curses library and that it addresses the screen directly. The output file is difficult to read with the `vi` editor, as `vi` thinks it is all one line. Use the UNIX `cat` command and pipe it to `more` and you'll be able to see the output better. The `status` script runs a UNIX `tail` command on this output file to print the progress messages from `tb/ontape`.

GENERAL ARCHIVE CONCEPTS

Archiving in OnLine is done with the `tbtape` program. This program performs both the data archiving when invoked as `tbtape -s` and the logfile archiving when invoked as `tbtape -c` or `tbtape -a`. The `tbmonitor` Archive menu options invoke the `tbtape` program.

IDS systems can use either `ontape` or the newer `onbar` program to backup and archive data. The `ontape` program is almost identical to `tbtape` because `ontape` is the natural progression of concepts found in `tbtape`. The extensions to `tbtape` that are embodied in `ontape` relate to restores for replicated systems and to restores of individual dbspaces.

This ability to archive and restore at the dbspace level gives the IDS administrator more flexibility in performing partial archives and restores. Indeed, it is conceivable that an IDS database administrator can achieve table-level archives and restores simply by placing each table in its own dbspace.

This book will not cover the `onbar` program in any depth. Informix includes a 300 page manual devoted to archiving and restoring the database, and most of it deals with the `onbar` program. Whereas the `tb/ontape` and `onbar` programs were written by Informix, the `onarchive` program was purchased from a third party and thus differs significantly from `tb/ontape/onbar`.

Like many other Informix database administrators, I have personally adopted the stance of being very slow to adopt the "latest and greatest" programs from any vendor, Informix included. I prefer to monitor the USENET newsgroups for six months to a year following introduction of a new product before using it for any mission-critical application. There is almost nothing more mission-critical in the database world than regular, reliable archives. If you are not certain of this yet, you will become certain the first time that you realize that your system has crashed and the only thing between you and the deep blue sea is a few hundred meters of flimsy magnetic tape.

Based on the feedback that I have been seeing on the Internet, avoiding onbar may have been a good decision, as the newsgroups are full of DBAs with problems or questions about onbar. I believe that the root cause of most of these problems is improper initial setup of the utility. This setup is complicated and error-prone, and many DBAs tend to approach it with a cavalier manner. I believe that onbar can be a workable and even necessary archive solution in certain cases because there are several things that onbar can do that tb/ontape cannot do, and if you fall into one of these categories, you may find yourself forced to use onbar. One of these areas is with extremely large databases in which the time to archive the system begins to cut into your window of time needed for other activities. One of the more important improvements to onbar is its capability to parallelize archives and restores and to use multiple tape drives simultaneously. If you decide to use onbar, I highly recommend attending the Informix class on the subject. Some day you will find yourself absolutely depending upon your archive and you need to be 100 percent confident in your archiving hardware, in your software, and in your operating procedures.

One of the more compelling features of the OnLine database is that archives can be run without shutting down the database. In an environment such as a large transaction processing system, this becomes a critical point. There is just no time available to take the database off-line for long enough to complete an archive.

When you consider exactly what is happening in backing up a database that is being accessed and modified at the same time, you will better understand some of the limitations of the archive process. At the same time the archive process is trying to take a snapshot of the database, users and batch jobs are trying their best to make that snapshot out of date. The archive process has to cooperate with checkpoints and logging processes to maintain the integrity and consistency of the data.

Do you Really Need to Archive?

There's a time that I would have considered such a question asinine, but there are applications that do not call for doing an Informix archive. One case may be with transient data working from batch loads that are frequently performed. The DBA and other system administration personnel need to evaluate the value, longevity, and time and cost needed to rebuild the data. In a system that is fed by batch jobs and is used for query processing, it may be that it will be faster and cheaper to rebuild the database and reload it from your source data in the event of a crash.

Note that I said "need to archive" and not "need to backup". If you are on an NT system or are only using cooked files in UNIX, you may have a non-Informix solution available that makes more sense than using the Informix archive and restore programs. There are three things that the Informix utilities give you that a non-Informix solution might not:

- Ability to do a "hot" backup with the database up and running during the backup
- Ability of the Informix utilities to allow you to recover from a disk crash by using the archives in conjunction with the logical logs to restore data up to the instant before the crash
- Ability to do incremental backups or backups by dbspace

If you do not need any of these capabilities and if you are using cooked files on NT or UNIX, it will be much faster to use native operating system or third party backup and restore programs to backup your system. In a rare case like this, it is absolutely critical the database be shut down for the duration of the archive. Shutting the database down will ensure that the backup is totally consistent and that there are no data changes to parts of the database that have already been backed up during the course of the backup. Another reason that the database must be shut down is that many operating system backup programs will place a lock on files that are being backed up. If database activity were occurring during a backup, it is possible that Informix will try to read from a locked data file. If Informix cannot read a chunk, it assumes that the chunk is physically bad and internally marks the chunk as down and unavailable for use. This can range from a major inconvenience in later IDS engines to an emergency in earlier engine versions that requires Informix Support to call into your system and mark the chunks available. The IDS onspaces command supports a flag that will mark the chunk as online and available and in many cases the IDS DBA can avoid a support call-in by bringing the chunk online herself.

When considering your archive and restore options, do not limit yourself to consideration of the database alone. If your application generates any output files, critical logfiles, or temporary work files, an Informix archive may not be sufficient to restore your system to operation after an incident. The perfect example to this is a large data warehouse that does some of its summarization and aggregation work in operating system files not controlled by the database. If these files need to be kept in sync with the database data, restoring the database after a disk crash may not be enough to make the system operable. Unless the database and the aggregation files are consistent with each other, all of the data would be suspect.

Don't take this section as carte blanche to run without doing Informix archives. Indeed, in all probability you need to do regular Informix archives. Just be aware that there may be some situations that call for breaking the normal rules.

ARCHIVE DEVICES

Informix has somewhat of a split personality with regard to archive devices. The tb/ontape program can use any UNIX device as an archive destination, but it's really designed to archive to tape. Actually, tape is the only option that makes sense in many cases, especially if your disk space is limited. Archiving to tape reduces your exposure to catastrophic disk crashes. If you are archiving to disk and crash a raw disk because of hardware problems, you may well also crash the disk device you are using for the archive. With tape, you spread your exposure to mechanical problems across two totally separate types of devices, most often controlled by different controller boards. In a pinch, you can archive to a UNIX file, but it takes some manual intervention, especially if the archive is larger than one file.

For a system of any size, you can't beat a large DAT or DLT drive. These drives, although expensive, can give you tremendous data capacity and a high transfer speed. Most large tape drives can also use data compression to cram even more data onto an archive tape. The combination of fast reading and writing speeds and tremendous storage capabilities is hard to beat. Given the difference in price between large tape drives and drives of lesser capacity, one can often justify going to DAT or DLT simply by calculating the differences in media cost.

If you are using logging with your OnLine engine, it is preferable to have two separate tape drives, one for the archives and one for the logs. That way, your log tapes can continue their continuous backups to tape while the archive is going on. It's possible to get by on one tape drive if you are willing to do a lot of tape swapping. Tape drives seem to have a higher failure rate than other components, so having at least two drives available for OnLine makes sense.

If you plan on using multiple instances of Informix, remember that their archiving and logging needs should also be considered. The preferred but costly solution is to have two separate tape drives per instance, if the multiple instances will both be doing a lot of archiving and logging.

Archiving to Disk

If you do need to archive to disk on OnLine systems, it is very important to have enough disk space available for the archive. One thing to watch out for is the filesize limits that many UNIX operating systems impose on the user. Many UNIXes have a filesize maximum of 2 gigabytes. If your archive goes over this size, the archive will fail. To create an archive to disk on OnLine systems, create an empty file owned by the informix user with proper permissions. Then set the TAPESIZE parameter in the ON/TBCONFIG file to be less than the amount of free space available on disk. Then run the tb/ontape program. Informix thinks it is writing to a nonrewinding tape and does not realize that the archive is going to disk. Informix is very trusting with tape issues. If you are archiving to disk and reach the tape size limit specified in your `tb/onconfig` file, Informix will prompt you to swap tapes and hit ENTER. When you hit ENTER, Informix will assume that you really did swap the tape and will proceed to merrily write to the same disk file. For this reason, if you go over one "tape," you need to do a little bit of manual intervention to "change the tape". First of all, Informix looks only at the definition of the tape device at the beginning of the archive. You can't just change the tape device in the config file when it comes time to swap tapes. There are two ways to do it. One way is to make the archive device a link. When the archive program wants you to change tapes, change the link to point to another file. A second way is to rename the first "tape" file to another name and re-create the old-named file for the second tape, continuing until the archive is completed. Once the disk archives are created, move them off to tape using operating system utilities. Restoring the database is essentially the reverse of this procedure. If you decide to use this technique, don't depend upon it until you have archived and successfully restored several times. Also be aware that if you get into trouble with this, Informix will probably not support you, since you are not following their archive recommendations.

Again, note that IDS on Windows NT does support archiving to disk and this is fully supported by Informix in an NT environment.

ARCHIVE SCHEDULES

The `tb/ontape` program provides a three-level archive schema. A full archive is a Level 0 archive, and it corresponds to an `epoch` level UNIX `dump`. Everything is dumped to tape. A Level 1 archive will back up any database pages that have changed since the last Level 0 archive. Likewise, a Level 2 archive will back up any changes since the last Level 1 archive.

In deciding on an archive schedule, the DBA needs to balance several factors. Obviously, if the DBA has two fast extended capacity tape drives available, he will handle the archives differently than he will if he is backing up to one smaller tape drive. How volatile is the data? Does it change often, or are some of the tables very large and relatively static? How valuable is the data? Can it be easily re-created from other sources? How much time is available to do the archives? Are there people available to change tapes? Can you dedicate a terminal just for archiving?

For a system that has large-capacity tape drives with the entire archive being well below the UNIX filesystem size unit, the answer is easy. Simply do Level 0 archives daily. As the database gets larger, the archive process must become more complicated. At some point it becomes necessary to begin to do Level 1 and maybe Level 2 archives.

One of the major factors to consider when deciding on an archive schedule is what will happen in the event that you actually have to use the archives to recover the database. Archive tapes are sort of like atomic bombs. You keep them around but hope you never have to use them. If you are doing only Level 0 archives, the recovery process consists of loading the Level 0 tape and then applying any subsequent log tapes. Systems using Level 1 and Level 2 archives require loading the Level 0 tape first, followed by any Level 1 tape, followed by any Level 2 tape, then followed by any log tapes.

The process of applying the log tapes after restoring the archive is the most time-consuming part of the process. For this reason, it is best to schedule your archives so that you do not allow an excessive number of logs to accumulate between archives. For example, on a Pyramid multiprocessor system using 60-megabyte logs, it takes about 15 to 20 minutes to apply each log tape. At a TAPESIZE of about 2 gigabytes per tape, a full tape could take close to 10 hours to apply all of the logs if the tape were totally full and if all logfiles were used. Faster DAT and DLT tapes reduce the times needed.

Problems with an archive usually do not show up until you try to recover the data. The fact that tb/ontape completed an archive without errors and without complaint does not mean that the archive has completed properly. When setting up your system, at some point you need to schedule a test of your recovery process. The test should be as realistic as possible. If you are using multiple levels of archives, create them and try to recover from them. Let several logfiles accumulate after the last archive. When you recover, time the process, note the size of the database, note the size of the archives, and note how long it takes for each activity of the recovery. This data will help you to fine-tune your procedures.

Having to recover from an archive is usually a traumatic event, accompanied by confusion, angry users and managers, and much finger-crossing by the DBA. Recoveries also seem to occur after midnight on holidays. You want to make the process as simple and as fast as possible. Remember, though, that the most important part is actually getting the data back.

The archecker Program

The Informix User Group archives at www.iiug.org contain several versions of a program called archecker. This program can inspect an Informix archive tape and verify that it is indeed readable and consistent. This program was written by an Informix employee and is "unofficially supported" by Informix for IDS versions prior to 7.24. This means that Informix may help you acquire the program but that anything you do with it is your business and your responsibility. Archecker is included with IDS 7.30 releases with minimal documentation in the release notes. With IDS 7.31, it will be fully supported and documented.

Principles of Debugging

*I*f Sherlock Holmes were alive today, he'd probably be in the computer troubleshooting business. With the avowed knowledge that it could be very easy to take this analogy way too far, we'll attempt to outline a method for the common-sense debugging of Informix problems.

The person who's attempting to solve a difficult system problem is in much the same position as someone who's trying to solve a mystery. The perpetrators of the problem are probably gone, all that's left are the clues (some real, some red herrings), and there may or may not be witnesses who are helpful.

OBSTACLES TO DEBUGGING

The Unreliability of Witnesses

In the real world, witnesses have ulterior motives, they forget things and embellish others, they make unwarranted assumptions, and they misidentify suspects. Why should it surprise us that humans who cannot or will not get it straight in a life-or-death murder mystery should automatically turn into paragons of the scientific method when reporting computer problems? Of course they don't.

Anything reported to you needs to receive the same critical treatment that the mystery sleuth gives his prime witnesses. Of course you cross-examine them! You usually don't need bright lights and rubber hoses, although there have been times when I wished for them. Question everything. "What do you mean it's too slow? Too slow compared to what? How are you measuring *slow*? Was it ever fast?".

Questioning everything can be a very useful tool in dealing with an irate customer/user, also. Occasionally reflect back to them what they just said, "So, you believe that the posting process is now taking three times as long as it used to, did I get you right?" Don't be afraid to say, "Slow down, I don't understand." Take your time in getting this information from your customer. Don't rush, and pay attention if the customer starts off down another track. You may gain some good data. In addition to helping you get the complaint straight, this type of questioning lets the customer know that you're listening.

Don't be shy about wanting to see the evidence for yourself. If possible, try to see everything yourself. Don't be happy just getting some logfiles and core dumps. Can the customer replicate the problem? Have them try to show you the whole process. An interesting example of this occurred after a 6 a.m. emergency flight to Tampa to fix a customer's problem

A business-critical system that had worked for a year was suddenly getting overloaded and crashing in most un-business-critical ways. Since this system costs the customer over $20,000 an hour when it's down, I got a five a.m. call from my CEO telling me to get on the nearest airplane and go solve the problem. When I got there, I was totally stymied. I did my usual snooping around in logfiles. They showed abrupt crashes with no warnings in the logs. I did my usual poking around for about an hour. By then I was certain that nothing "normal" was happening. I asked the users to really crank up their use of the system so that I could see it crash. The users in this case were about 40 keyers keying financial data into the system. Sitting back in a cubicle, I could not see any indications that the system was under stress. Finally, I heard one of the keyers say to the group at large, "This status job is frozen up again. Should I kill it?" The manager was just ready to answer "yes" when I yelled out, "Don't touch it!" and went to find out what was going on.

It turns out that there was a script that gave work status to the keyers. It was home-grown, and was not part of the supported product. This script had just been modified to give more information, and the SQL had some problems. It was doing sequential scans on big tables. What happened was that the majority of the info needed by the keyers popped up in the fast part of the query. Rather than waiting for the query to complete, the users learned that they could "control-c" out of the process. In fact, the first one who learned it sent e-mail to all the other keyers. What was happening was that exiting with a `control-c` was leaving database backends strewn all about the landscape, eventually exhausting system resources and causing a crash.

This problem would never have been solved without getting out there with the keyers and watching what they were doing. Pay attention to everything. Sometimes even the most insignificant item will lead to cracking the mystery.

Red Herrings

Red herrings are little false clues that mystery writers love to leave scattered about their work just to throw the readers off the track. The same dark beings that write good mysteries must also be in the bug-generating business because the red herring is one of the most common inhabitants in the bug universe.

Maybe a few examples of red herrings will clarify how they behave. I've had an instance where we replaced a SCSI tape drive several times due to hardware failures. We'd get the drive running, and a day or so later, it would turn itself into a smoking mass of aluminum and plastic. Two replacements, two tape drives dead on arrival. Finally, we got it running and surprise, the next day the database archive failed with a hardware error. We immediately got onto the line with the vendor, arranging to have another one shipped. Once it came in, it had the same problem. After a lot of debugging, we determined that the tape drive was not part of the problem. The archive had just reached a 2-gig size, and the operating system wasn't able to write a file that big. We were so primed to find a hardware problem that we were blind to the real nature of the problem.

Everyone who deals with multiuser systems is probably aware of the next red herring. Have you ever been in the middle of doing something on a UNIX machine, only to have the system either freeze up or crash? What's the first thing you think? Of course, it's "What did I do to crash/freeze up the system?" You start looking at what you were doing just prior to the problem, looking for excuses to use when the sysadmin comes calling. Actually, you probably had nothing to do with the problem. You were just a victim just like all the other users.

There's probably a good psychological reason why computer types are so prone to falling into red herring traps. We're judged by others based upon how fast we can come up with a solution to a problem. As a group, we're pretty sure of ourselves and usually have pretty big egos. If a red herring presents itself as a quick, easy answer to a problem, we tend to seize it as the answer.

GATHERING THE EVIDENCE

The Scene of the Crime

Very seldom will you have the luxury of investigating a problem where the perpetrators are still on the scene of the crime. Most business systems must continue running whenever possible, and it is rare for the customer/user to be able to hold off on everything else while you are poking around in the database. You'll be lucky to even be able to get access to the system, much less have access to it by yourself. Most often, you'll need to reconstruct what happened from the user's reports, from the logfiles, and from operating system utilities.

Usually, you're really trying to do two things, fix the problem, getting the customer back online, and correct the problem, making sure that the problem doesn't happen again. These are often at cross purposes. Many times, patching the problem destroys the symptoms. You'll have the choice of trying to fix or trying to patch, all under the constraint that the customer absolutely must be back up and running within an hour.

The point here is, no matter how much pressure you are under to get the customer up and running again, you absolutely must get to the root cause of the problem. If possible, save off the bad environment so that you can come back to it later for further postmortems. If you have the luxury of time, before starting any debugging would be a very good time to do a database archive.

We often overlook the operating system's utilities when reconstructing a problem. Especially in UNIX, there's a lot of information available to you. For example, if the user is using the Korn shell (ksh), there'll be a file in his home directory called ".sh_history," containing the last hundred or so commands that the user ran. I've actually used this to solve problems that involved a developer who was "sanitizing" the logfiles to hide his errors.

Determining the Nature of the Problem

The user will probably have already told you where the problem is. Their view of the problem is: "The computer system's not working. Fix it." That's probably as fine a point as they'll put on it. From the user's view, everything from the terminal to the database engine is part and parcel of the same thing, "the computer system," You'll probably need to refine the problem definition a little further. Working from the top down, you will find your problem lurking at one of these levels.

Application

Problems here include logic problems, code problems, data problems, and operational problems. Check the program's logs for any hints of the problem. Most processes that die will leave some trace or some error messages in the logs.

I'll throw in a common red herring here, since it seems to invariably catch up with us. I don't know what it is about software types, but we're awfully anxious to find problems in others' code. Maybe it's the "not invented here" syndrome, maybe it's just that we've seen lots of lousy code, but we are always quick to accept the premise that it's a code problem and we'll need to make a patch. I think we should be a little more cautious here. In my experience, many database problems will be data related. Those that aren't strictly data-related will probably be of a conceptual nature. We don't understand exactly how something either does work or is supposed to work. Thinking about going in and modifying code should be the last trick in our arsenal of debugging techniques.

Database and Connectivity Problems

Examples of potential problems here include poor table design, poor table layout, inadequate Informix tuning, inadequate resources for the database operations, and poor or inefficient communication between client and server.

While this book will concentrate on the Informix side, a tuner cannot ignore the items either higher or lower in this hierarchy. Unless the application is efficiently designed and the operating system is set up properly and all of the hardware is working properly, you'll never realize the full potential of the system. If you as a tuner are not familiar with the application, the operating system, and the hardware find someone who is and cooperate closely with her.

Operating System Problems

The operating system is the underlying platform on which the Informix database depends for CPU cycles and operating system services. If the OS is not functioning properly, the Informix engines will be hamstrung from the beginning.

Common operating system problems are:

- Inadequate kernel resources to support the Informix engine and applications
- Swapping in the operating system
- Random crashes of the OS
- Load balancing problems due to heavy processing loads from other processes
- Informix-specific requirements not supported such as kernel async i/o
- Improper or noninstalled patches applied to the OS
- Problems with process priorities

When approaching a debugging session on a new system, always check the kernel parameters. Read all of the text files in the $INFORMIXDIR/release directory tree and be sure that all required kernel parameters, operating system patches, and environmental variables have been correctly set.

Once you are familiar with the system, it may be possible to become a little more lax in this area, but don't get complacent. If a new problem arises on an older system, look first to see if someone has changed something at the OS level. Pay attention to OS upgrades, patches, and new programs that have been added to the system. If the OS is upgraded, be sure that your version of Informix is certified on that version of the OS. Sometimes an OS upgrade will require a corresponding upgrade of Informix.

Hardware

Everything depends upon the hardware. If it is not working optimally or if it has intermittent problems, the whole system will have problems. Be sure that you know where hardware error messages can be found on your system. Know whom to contact to have the hardware checked out for problems. Have alternative methods of checking out the hardware. For example, on a UNIX system you can verify the readability of a hard disk partition by using the UNIX dd command. It won't tell you whether or not the data is correct, but it will allow you to verify that it is readable.

A SCIENTIFIC APPROACH TO DEBUGGING

Students go to classes for years to learn how to design computer systems and to learn how to write programs, but they usually have exactly zero hours of instruction in techniques of debugging. It is expected that their ability to debug system problems will somehow magically develop as they learn how to write code. To an extent, this is a reasonable expectation. Most computer professionals develop debugging skills as a side effect of their programming, but the results vary wildly, running the gamut from little or no debugging ability to bonfire guru status.

The problem with this "learning by osmosis" approach is that debugging becomes more black art than science. It depends heavily upon past experience with systems in general as well as with specific experience with the program being debugged.

We've all had the experience of wrestling with a difficult bug for days and finally going to the person who wrote the code, only to have him spot the problem immediately. Are they geniuses and we bozos? While this may be the case, it's more likely that the person who wrote the code knows where the bugs are already. If the original coder hasn't actually seen the bug yet, he probably knows where the program is weak. He knows where he's cut corners in the coding and is probably not too surprised to see the bug appear.

If the code is old and poorly documented (and most of it is), even the original coder may have a problem chasing down problems. I know that I've gone back and tried to debug code I wrote several years ago, only to ask myself, "Who wrote this junk?"

Most of the time the original coder is not available. Computer professionals are a very mobile lot. It's not unusual to see coders staying for two years at a company and then moving along. It's even more pronounced when the code is written by contractors who may be gone in two or three months, leaving the debugging to be done by someone trying to support the system.

WHAT IS DEBUGGING?

The term *debugging* is a holdover from the earliest days of computing. According to popular lore, one of the early systems crashed and nobody could find the source of the problem until someone found that an insect had immolated itself inside one of the crude switches in the system. From then on, the process of fixing software problems became known as debugging. For the purposes of this book, we will be using a very broad definition of debugging Informix applications.

Debugging Informix Applications: The process of identifying and correcting portions of Informix applications that are either not working at all, not working according to specifications, or not working at optimal efficiency.

This definition can cover:

- Coding errors in ESQL/C, 4GL, NewEra, or other Informix application development tools
- Coding errors in SQL statements
- Tuning problems with Informix engines
- Database design errors
- Physical database layout problems
- Design problems with custom applications

Most of the coding examples will utilize ESQL/C, not because of any inherent superiority of the language, but because of the fact that it is the language with which I am most familiar. For specific debugging techniques for 4GL or NewEra, the reader is directed to the other Informix Press titles on these subjects.

This chapter will take a global approach to the process of debugging. These principles can be applied to any type of troubleshooting or debugging and is most definitely not limited to Informix issues. We'll cover the Informix-specific material later in the book. For now, we need to develop an overall strategy and mindset that will put us in a position to later apply these techniques to debugging Informix systems.

OBJECTIVES OF DEBUGGING

Effective debugging requires that you have a goal in mind and that you know where you're going. Equally important is knowing why you are doing it and whether you should even be doing it at all.

Computer people sometimes fall into the trap of believing that everything can be solved by coding. That's the way we are trained, recognized, and rewarded. Many of us have gone into the computer business to avoid having to deal with people. You get the attitude of "just give me the source code and I'll fix it."

Sometimes, though, someone needs to step back a bit and decide if it really needs fixing. Maybe the system is old and outmoded and really should be replaced with more current technology. Maybe the system itself is the main problem. Maybe the users need more training. There are a lot of different problems not related to code that can be the real underlying cause of system difficulties. Only by having definite objectives in mind can you be effective in debugging not just individual lines of code but entire computer systems.

Fix the Problem

This is the most immediate and the most simplistic objective that most of us have when beginning to debug a problem. It's broken. Fix it.

Different people and different organizations may have wildly varying definitions of this, ranging anywhere from applying a quick-and-dirty fix to going through the full ISO 9000 quality process. In some cases, this definition of "fix it" includes such approaches as:

- Deny that it exists.
- Blame it on another vendor.
- Blame it on the operating system.
- Blame it on the user.
- Find someone else to do it.
- If all else fails, try to patch it up enough to just get by.

While the items listed here are very much tongue-in-cheek, the reader will probably recognize times when she has either used one of these approaches or had it used on her. It's important to remember how you felt when someone used such a tactic on you. This is exactly how your customers or users feel when they get it from you. Not a very productive approach, and certainly not a way to build long-term respect. Each of these approaches is likely to cause you more trouble and take more time than doing it right in the first place.

A real fix will:

- Solve the immediate problem as soon as possible. In a production system governed by time constraints, this may entail a quick fix or workaround that stays in place until a permanent fix is made. In this case, be sure that the process doesn't end with the quick and dirty solution.
- Be a long-term solution.
- Ensure that the problem stays fixed. All systems go through a life cycle of releases and upgrades. Unless the problem is corrected both at the source and onsite, the next upgrade or revision of the software will contain the same problem, and either you or someone else will have to solve it again. Make sure that you fix a problem only once.
- Correct similar problems in the system. If you're debugging a program and find that there is an error in the logic or in the code, the odds are that there will be similar errors either in the piece of code you are working with or with other code written by the same programmer or programming team. The first time you see an error is the best time to poke around and see if it exists in other places. Doing this will allow you to leverage your time.

Placate Angry Users

There are three major times that you will be presented with a debugging problem. You may recognize a bug while developing code yourself. You may discover a bug during the testing and validation process. Finally, you may find a bug after the code has been deployed. In the first two cases, you probably won't have to deal with angry users. In these cases, the debugging process is simply an extension of the coding and testing process, and you'll probably be working on code that you wrote yourself. If anybody's angry, it will probably be you being angry with yourself for making a stupid mistake.

If the bug is discovered after the product is deployed, you're facing an entirely different set of circumstances. Dealing with end users requires at least as much skill in psychology as in debugging. You will find yourself debugging more than just software. You'll be debugging problems with attitude, with respect, and with confidence. You really need to expand the concept of debugging to cover these intangibles because these intangibles are ultimately more important to success than any code problem.

Knowledge Transfer

This is not a first-level objective in most debugging tasks, but it should always be an eventual objective. Every time you discover and fix a problem with a system, it presents you with an opportunity to teach others and to teach your organization how to avoid similar problems in the future. This requires some sort of formal or informal process for feedback within an organization. This is where bug-tracking databases and knowledge bases can be useful.

DEFINE THE PROBLEM

Assuming that you have determined the need for a debugging effort, it's important to approach the effort with a plan rather than with a hit-or-miss, haphazard approach. This chapter will lay out a methodology that you can apply to any type of debugging or troubleshooting effort.

Following a plan or method is often viewed as taking too long or being too involved by software professionals. Most often, they'd rather just jump in and fix the problem rather than take the time to go through a lot of useless steps. Sometimes this is actually the case in simple, straightforward problems. The problem is that it is not always possible to identify the simple cases. Problems that appear simple may in fact be quite complicated, and problems that appear intractable may indeed be simple.

It is overkill to go through complex debugging procedures when a single, acute error occurs. If you do something that generates an obvious, "Jeez what a stupid mistake" type of error message, just go ahead and correct it and go about your business. There will be times when you'll be fooled by this, however, and find out that your "simple" problem is really a symptom of something else. Knowing the difference between when to do the quick fix and when to dig deeper is the part of debugging that falls more into the art of debugging as opposed to the science of debugging. If you're doing quick fix, view it as the first step in the debugging process and don't claim that its fixed until other problems have had time to manifest themselves or work themselves out.

Understand the Specifications

In order to troubleshoot a system adequately, the debugger must first be sure she understands the way the system is actually supposed to behave. In the case of the OnLine engine, the higher-level specifications are pretty simple and straightforward. The user makes a request and the engine executes it. If it doesn't execute the request, there's a probably a problem somewhere.

Where this gets more complex is when the troubleshooter is expecting one type of behavior and receives something totally different. For example, you may be trying to achieve parallelism by tuning the engine's PDQ priorities. When you make a database request, you'll usually get some sort of response from the engine, but the path that the engine takes to get the response will differ based on your PDQ settings. Unless the person trying to tune the system knows exactly what to expect in the way of number of threads, priorities, and response times, he will have a hard time determining whether the system is behaving correctly.

The same situation arises in debugging custom-written code. If you don't know exactly what the code is supposed to do and how it is supposed to do it, you will be at a marked disadvantage in your troubleshooting efforts.

Get First Hand Reports

Make sure that you fully understand the problems that are presented to you. Don't ever try to debug a system without a clear, unambiguous description of the problem. Try to deal with the people who actually discovered the problem. If you get into a situation of "John said that Mary said that such-and-such a process took too long," you need to be talking to Mary, not John. Actually you need to be sitting beside Mary while she duplicates the problem herself.

Poor communications are the bane of the software debugger. We've all probably played the old party game of "rumors" in which someone starts out by telling a story to one person, who then tells it to another and so on until the story gets back to the originator. This final story often bears little resemblance to the original story. The same principles apply to troubleshooting and debugging. By the time that the report goes through several interpreters, much of it will be either incomplete or totally wrong. Human communication is an imperfect process, and this imperfection is magnified by every person in the chain. Go to the source.

ISOLATE THE PROBLEM

A main principle of debugging is "divide and conquer." It's impossible to address problems when their domain is the entire system. Certainly, you need to be able to take a global view at times, but you will seldom if ever find a system that is totally messed up. If you do find such a system, the best recommendation is usually to scrap it and start over. In most systems, the problems will most likely be restricted to one program or one function or one functional error. Until you can narrow down your search, you'll be searching for the proverbial needle in a haystack.

One time when you need to be able to take an overall or global view of the system is when you are trying to visualize the logical layout of your system. You have to be able to understand all of the components and to understand how they fit together. If you don't know this, you'll never be able to tear the pieces apart and decide exactly where to look for your problem. Once you understand the functions and roles of all of the various components, you're ready to begin to focus in and try to isolate which functions are failing and where the problem may be found.

Duplicate the Problem

The first step is always to duplicate the problem. This is often the hardest step, especially if the problem is intermittent or load-related. Unless you can reliably duplicate a problem or error, you are basically shooting in the dark. Often, just the process of duplicating the problem will point you toward the solution.

Duplicating the problem can be a frustrating exercise, especially if you are working on a system that is not the same one that is experiencing the problem. It is usually preferable to have a development system and a production system so that you can do your debugging on the development system without fouling up the production system. Even if your development system is identical to the production system, it is sometimes difficult to put the same amount of user and data loading on a development system as you see on the production system.

There will be times when you have to perform your investigations on the production system if you cannot duplicate the error on a development system. This sometimes leaves the debugger with a difficult decision. When you are finally able to duplicate a problem on the production system, do you try for a quick workaround to get production back up or do you let the production system stay fouled up or even worse, down, until you can track down the problem?

The ivory tower answer is never to debug on the production system. This is good in theory and can sometimes be the best solution, given that you can maintain the development environment as an exact duplicate of the production environment. Oftentimes, though, this is impossible and you'll find yourself debugging on the production system. In this case, follow one of the same principles as medical doctors must follow. "First of all, do no harm." If your debugging efforts on a production system make the problem worse or introduce new problems, you can expect a few angry phone calls from users and managers.

Check it in Different Environments

The very fact that you cannot duplicate an error on a development system can allow you to eliminate some potential dead ends in your search for a solution. If an error occurs on one system but not on another, you must determine where the systems differ. Assuming that the systems are supposed to be alike, you will have several possibilities for the differences:

- Hardware: Are there hardware differences between the systems? Look at things like disk capacity and memory. Are there potential hardware errors? Check operating system error logs to see if you may have a hardware problem.

- Operating system: Are the OS versions the same? Are the patch levels the same? Has something been changed on one of the systems? Are the swap spaces the same for UNIX? How about paging files on NT? What about temp space?

- Users: Are you running the jobs under the same user ID? Are their environments the same? Are their permissions the same?

- Applications: Are you sure that the applications on both systems are exactly the same? Were they compiled the same way, with the same compile options? Are all of the setup variables identical between the two systems?

- Load factors: Is the production system under an especially heavy load? Are there more users than normal? Is the mix of jobs running on the system different? Is there something new running that hasn't been running before?

- Database engine: Are you using exactly the same versions of Informix? Are there differences in tuning? Are there differences in PDQ tuning?

- Network: Are there network slowdowns in the production system? Can you ping all of the parts of the system? Can you connect to Informix from various components?

- User factors: Are there new users running on the production system? Could they be doing something different? Could you be running the program differently from the way the users are running it?

Each of these potential areas of difference can be viewed not only as areas of difference between a test and a production system but also as differences within the malfunctioning system itself. Have any of these items changed in the system?

If you find differences, either between test and production or between an earlier version of the production system and the current version, this may very well point you in the direction of the solution.

LOOK AT THE HISTORY

There are a lot of analogies that you can use in debugging computer systems. One is a trip to the doctor's office. When you first go to a doctor, the first thing that happens is that he takes your medical history. You need to do the same thing with your database system. It is very rare that a problem just comes out of the blue. Something usually has to happen; something needs to change in the system to cause a new problem to occur. It's your job to evaluate whether or not one of these changes has caused your system to begin generating errors.

Keep a System Log

If you want to evaluate the effects of past system changes on your database system, it helps to have one place where all changes to the system are tracked. Various parts of your system will automatically generate logfiles, but they will probably be scattered across the landscape. For example:

- Informix configuration changes will be logged in your `online.log`.
- Operating system changes may be logged in various OS logfiles.
- Your application may generate their own logfiles.
- Hardware components may generate their own logfiles

Be sure and differentiate between *operational* logfiles and *setup* logfiles. An operational logfile is generated as part of the daily operation of the system. This type of logfile will list the normal types of tracking information that your system generates. An example would be the Informix online.log, which notes such things as checkpoints beginning and ending, Informix errors, login errors, and the like. A setup logfile will note changes in the operating parameters of the system. The Informix online.log also serves this purpose, as it logs any changes made in the Informix tuning and configuration parameters.

Good applications should always generate useful logfiles. What's useful in a logfile? First, everything should have a time and date stamp. Most applications do this, but some do not do it very well. The Informix online.log is an example of a logfile that could be more convenient to use. It registers dates in one section of the log, and it registers times alongside each of the individual events. It would be much more useful if every timestamp included the date. That way, it makes scanning through the logfiles with such utilities as `grep` or `awk` much easier for the debugger.

If you are dealing with a system of programs and cannot change or influence how the logfiles are generated, you can at least try to enforce a policy of keeping a manual operational log. This log should contain changes in setup parameters, operational incidents such as system restarts or crashes, hardware and software additions, deletions, updates, and bug fixes applied or attempted on the system.

You could probably make a pretty good argument that this system log should be a manual affair kept in a hard-copy logbook. After all, if the entire system were to go down or if you were to lose the hard disk that holds the electronic copy, you would not have access to the logbook.

Keep an Incident Log

Just as it is most important to maintain an operational log, it is also important to log error reports or other incidents. Try to have the user log any problems immediately and to note the exact times that the problem occurred. Usually a reportable problem will occur when other personnel are running jobs on the computer. Most often the troubleshooting and debugging experts will be called later, after the problem has been cleared up. It will be your job to find out why it happened and how to keep it from happening in the future.

Sometimes you may be called in to fix a production problem while the problem is actually going on. This can either be an ideal situation for debugging or the world's worst situation for debugging, depending upon the needs and priorities of the users. It'll be the debugger's hell if the system is mission-critical and high-use. Here, the most important thing is clearing out the problem and restoring functionality. Everything else is secondary to getting back online.

The situation can be ideal if the system is either not mission-critical or is low-use. If the users can stand to give you an hour or so to dig around when an error is reported, you'll be able to avoid many of the difficulties associated with trying to duplicate an error. The error will already be staring you in the face.

Unfortunately, we don't usually see the ideal situations. The best we can do is to anticipate the types of investigations that we would do when confronted with various types of errors. Knowing that, have the users record the data that you'll need for those investigations at the time the problem occurs.

The general idea is to be able to take a snapshot of the system at the instant the error occurs. The more information you can get, the better off you'll be when it comes time to duplicate and correct the problem later.

Has it Ever Worked Before?

This question is a key one for your debugging effort. If it has never worked before or if you are testing something for the first time, it will be relatively simple to determine if the database engine is working satisfactorily. If it is running properly, then the error is probably with the new program or process. If you are the one developing the new program or process, then you will already know how to continue to develop and debug your program. If it's being developed by someone else, let her know what you know about the problem and let her solve it. She is probably better equipped for the task.

Has Anything Changed?

If the system has worked correctly in the past, then something must have changed to make it not work now. Go back through all of your system and configuration logfiles and see if any changes have occurred on the malfunctioning system. Try to include all changes to the system, whether they appear to be database-related or not. Some things that are notorious for breaking Informix systems are:

- Operating system upgrades
- Network reconfiguration

- Adding or removing other software (did it change the services file?)
- Changing kernel parameters
- Adding new Informix third-party programs or applications
- Adding new Informix programs (did you mess up the TEN installation order?)

Has the System Load Changed?

There will be times when you absolutely cannot find any changes that have been made to a system, and yet it has suddenly broken. If you're sure that there have been no overt changes made to the system, you have several areas that you should investigate:

- Number of users on the system. (Has it recently increased?)
- Number of Informix jobs running on the system.
- Number of other jobs running on the system.
- Jobs running from cron.
- Change in the types of jobs that run.
- Change in timing of when jobs are run. You see this a lot when someone decides to run a database archive during the day instead of running it at night as they usually do.
- Amount of data being processed in batch jobs.
- Differences in the data.
- Changes in operational or functional staff. Maybe a new person is doing something differently, or maybe the usual person is on vacation.

Hardware Problems

If it's not a change in configuration and it's not a change in load, look to a hardware problem as a potential culprit. No matter how capricious we think databases are, they usually don't break without reason.

Note that a hardware problem may not be catstrophic. In fact, it may be subtle and not really noticeable except in the context of your error. An example would be a hard disk that is going bad or that has developed media defects. Depending on where the problem is on the disk, the problem may become evident only when you try to access the one table or one data record that is in the bad spot. Another example could be a slowdown or other intermittent problem in the network. Certain jobs, or only certain jobs that have to pass through a network switch or router, may be the only hint of network problems.

Software Bugs

If all else fails, you could be running into a latent bug either in Informix or in the operating system. I've met a lot of people who, the instant they have a problem with a product, are on the phone to their product support trying to report a bug in the product. Certainly, there are more than enough software bugs out there that could be causing a problem, and you cannot totally eliminate them from consideration. The odds are, though, that you have changed something else or that you are doing something wrong.

I've mentioned before that we software types are awfully eager to find bugs in other people's work, but in the 15 years I've dealt with Informix products, I've probably reported only three or four new bugs to Informix. True, I've run across other known bugs and short-comings, but the new bug is a rare find. To be truthful, I've always had the fear that Informix treats bugs like astronomers treat stars. You find it; it's named after you. Actually, this may grant you more immortality than having a new star named after you. The star will probably explode within a couple of million years, but Informix bugs seem to be somewhat more persistent.

One of the things that you should do occasionally is go through the bug reports for your particular hardware and software configuration. The release notes in $INFORMIXDIR/release will contain information about bugs that have been fixed or that are known to be outstanding for your particular version. A much better source is the full bug list found at the Informix home page: http://www.informix/com. You'll need a special password to get to the actual bug list. Get it through your friendly Informix salesperson.

Have you Seen This Before?

If you have gotten this far and still have not zeroed in a little more on the source of the problem, you have a few more possibilities before you have to start tracing your way through code. Check to see if you or anyone else in your organization has ever run across this type of problem or a similar problem before. Hopefully, your system logs will have notations when others have solved problems. If you can't find anyone internally who has seen the problem, try posting a message on the Internet newsgroup favored by Informix cognoscenti; `comp.databases.informix`.

Just because this is at the bottom of the list does not mean that is the last thing to do. When you approach a new problem, your mind automatically places this item pretty close to the top of the list. After all, if you've already solved the problem once, why go through all the rigmarole of working your way through it again?

Just beware of the red herring effect. Don't allow yourself to develop the mindset of "knowing" where the problem lies just because you've solved it this way before. Invariably, there will be some twist or permutation that makes it almost like a previous problem but different enough that the same old solution won't work again. Even worse, the old solution might actually make the problem worse.

Track the Logic Flow

Assuming that you've been able to duplicate the problem, either on a development or on a production system, you still need to be able to zero in on a potential cause. If you've been able to spot differences in the system that can generate the error, you've been lucky and you are well on you way to fixing the problem. If not, it's time to go to a deeper level of debugging, which is tracing the logic of the system. Here's where understanding the specifications and flow of the system comes in handy.

Formulate a Hypothesis

By now, you should have developed an idea about the underlying cause of the problem you're trying to fix. Since we're espousing a scientific approach to debugging, we may as well go all the way and give this idea its proper scientific name, a hypothesis.
    Your hypothesis should be as specific as possible. Examples of good hypotheses are:

- The system is too slow because of too-frequent checkpoints.
- The system is too slow because the table have too many extents.
- The system is crashing because of a defect on the disk.
- Archives are failing because the TAPESIZE is set too high.

Your hypothesis should be both specific and testable.

Test the Hypothesis

With your new hypothesis in hand, develop a way to test it and see if it is correct. You should be able to make a guess at what should happen in certain situations if your hypothesis is correct. It's important to formalize this and to make the guess before you start testing. Otherwise, no matter how right your eventual answer may be, you're really just guessing and taking a haphazard approach to the analysis.
    Once you've worked out an organized method of testing the hypothesis, you need to determine some criteria for scoring the results. If you're trying to speed something up, measure the speed before the change, make the change, and then remeasure the performance after making the change. Determine in advance how you will decide if the differences are really significant. Determine how to be sure that your changes are indeed the factor that is affecting the performance.
    Try as much as possible to control the user load and system load during the before and after stage of testing. Only by controlling the environment to the greatest possible degree will you be able to attribute any performance changes to your work and not just to the phase of the moon.

Change One Thing at a Tme

Inherent to the concept of controlling the environment is the idea of making only one change at a time. If you throw in five or six changes to the system at one time, you are not doing a methodical, scientific job of debugging. True, you may fix your problem, but you can never be sure exactly what you did to fix it.

Sometimes you will have to deviate from the structured, scientific debugging method because of expediency. You may have a system that does not allow much downtime, thus limiting your opportunity to experiment. You may be under the gun to fix all the problems at once. You may just not have enough time to do it right, and "almost right" may be good enough.

In these cases, you may be forced to make multiple changes at once. If possible, phase in the changes so that multiple changes at one time don't interact with one another. I'd feel better having to throw in multiple changes if the individual changes were to different areas of the system that probably don't interact with one another. This is often a hard call, as sometimes things that you don't think affect one another actually do have an effect. Here's where all of your rigorous scientific method in the past can come to your aid. If you follow a method for most of your debugging, in the rare case when you have to shoot from the hip, you'll have more to go on and it won't be random shooting.

FORMULATE A PLAN FOR FIXING THE PROBLEM

In many cases, you will go through several hypotheses before coming up with a solution. These may be sequential hypotheses, in which you make a guess that turns out to be wrong, you make another somewhat better hypothesis that turns out to be closer, and so on until you finally come to one good answer.

They may be parallel hypotheses, in which you make one guess that turns out to be right and it leads to another hypothesis about something else that's affecting your problem, and so on. The final solution may be to make many changes to different areas. Once you've tested your hypotheses and think you know what's happening, it is time to plan how to roll out the changes to production.

TEST THE SOLUTION

If you have only one system, your process of sequential changes automatically ends up with the proper changes made to the system. If you have multiple systems or if you're dealing with a product that you have in multiple locations, you can then make the changes all at once to all of the other systems. Be aware, though, that systems that are supposed to be alike are not necessarily alike. Monitor the performance after the changes just to be sure that somebody's unique configuration does not interfere with the success of your changes. There are several questions to ask.

Does it Solve the Immediate Problem?

This should be fairly simple to determine. You've been focusing on this problem for a while, and you shouldn't have any problems deciding when it's fixed. Go to your bencmarks for performance problems and to your logs or other diagnostics for other problems.

Try not to want your solution to work so much that anything that it does looks like success to you. Try to be objective and look at it from the user's perspective.

Does it Create Other Problems?

This question is more difficult. If your fix causes problems in other areas, it may not be apparent immediately. It may be a month before the program that broke with this fix gets run again, and by then everyone may have forgotten that you did something that caused it to break.

Continually fixing one thing while breaking another is not usually conducive to advancing your career path. If anyone relates the fix to subsequent problems, you come out looking like an idiot. After you make any type of change, make sure that the system undergoes more strenuous monitoring than usual for the next few weeks, at least. Let your users and other administrators know that you've made changes, and alert them to possible symptoms or indications that may be caused by possible side effects of other interactions. If you do this and actually do see subsequent problems, you end up looking more like a guru than an idiot, since you've anticipated potential problems. Of course, if the subsequent problems entail completely destroying the database or bringing it down for days, you're back to being an idiot again.

IMPLEMENT AND PROPAGATE THE FIX

If you have multiple systems or if you're dealing with a product, roll out the tested fixes to your other sites. Make sure that any code changes are placed into your source code control system and into any archives that you use to prepare and stage your software for distribution. There's nothing more embarrassing than having to fix the same problem again because subsequent software releases lost the changes you've made. If you're really unlucky, this will happen a year after the first fix, and the person who made the first fix is gone Then you'll actually have to go through the process again. If you are not using source code control, start using it!

Document All Changes

In addition to placing changes into your source code control system and making sure that these changes get propagated to other or later systems, always come up with some sort of a written document that explains exactly what you have done and why you have done it. This will be of immense help later if you are trying to work through someone else's fixes, if someone is trying to figure out your fixes, or even if you are trying to figure out why you did something yourself a year ago. These changes should also be reflected in your system and application logs.

Informix Dynamic Server on Windows NT

*I*nformix has had database products running in the Windows environment for several years, ranging from its entry-level Informix SE database up through application programs such as WingZ, NewEra, and I-4GL for Windows. Most of Informix's Windows development has previously been limited to client-side tool. Informix has recently made a corporate commitment to the Windows environment, and promises to make its entire product line available on Windows NT. Until recently, the only database engine available for Windows was Informix SE.

INFORMIX SE

Informix SE is a decent desktop database and has the advantage of being very compatible with its larger UNIX brothers and requiring much less administration. There have been several fairly large systems built around SE, and it always surprises me to see how far people have managed to take these very inexpensive SE systems. On the surface, SE resembles its UNIX brethren. It has a dbaccess program almost identical to the UNIX versions. Installing an SE system on a laptop has long been one of my favorite methods of getting a copy of dbaccess that can work with any of the Informix engines. I've also used SE as part of a demo version of a client/server system. This demo version was used by salespeople, so they were interested in the flashy GUI, and SE served very well in place of the normally-required Online Dynamic Server engine.

INFORMIX DYNAMIC SERVER, PERSONAL EDITION

This product is the only version of IDS that will run on Windows 95. The regular version of IDS for NT requires an NTFS filesystem, which is not supported in Windows 95. IDS-PE was introduced as a beta test through the Informix International Users Group and was available for free downloading from their Web site:

The product was derived from IDS 7.22 on NT and has all of 7.22's features with the exception of:

- ONPLOAD the parallel data loader and Parallel Data Query (PDQ)
- ONBAR the online archive tool
- XA the XA transaction manager support
- Security Auditing feature
- Multiprocessor support
- Fragmentation
- Continuous Data Replication (CDR)
- Informix Optical optical disk support
- Informix Storage Manager (ISM)
- Mirroring

There are also significant changes to the security subsystem due to lack of operating system security in Windows 95.

IDS-PE is a viable alternative to Informix-SE for Windows 95 and Windows NT. Since it is derived from IDS 7.22, all of the utilities work against it in much the same manner as IDS. For a development or a demonstration system, IDS-PE is hard to beat.

INFORMIX DYNAMIC SERVER-WORKGROUP EDITION

IDS Workgroup Edition is very similar to IDS-NT, with the exception that some of the parallel features have been removed. It was aimed at production environments at the workgroup level, with relatively small numbers of users and not a heavy production load.

Other than that, this product is identical to IDS-NT. It was made available in one incarnation as part of a package that included a Netscape server and tools for accessing the data over the Web. This product was also made available in several UNIX versions, including SCO and HP/UX.

INFORMIX DYNAMIC SERVER FOR WINDOWS NT

One of the first results of Informix's newly found commitment to Windows NT is the port of its workhorse database engine, Informix Dynamic Server to Windows NT 3.51 and Windows NT 4.00. This will prove to be a very good business decision on Informix's part as NT increases its market share in midrange computing applications. Currently, a large portion of Informix's customer base are running on various flavors of UNIX systems. Informix seems to have realized that they must support the upstart Windows NT operating system as it becomes more popular in their target markets.

Please note that this doesn't mean that diehard UNIX types are going to be eager to embrace the new NT systems. From some of the spirited exchanges going on in the Internet news groups, the only embracing the UNIX diehards will be doing will be for the purposes of strangling the NT contingent. This type of "religious war" always seems to be going on in our techie-oriented community. If it's not UNIX versus NT, it will be `vi` versus `emacs` or page level locking versus row-level locking. Usually, these wars provide a lot more heat than light.

Areas of Similarity to UNIX

Same Code Stream in the Engine

IDS for Windows NT is almost identical to its UNIX counterparts, down to compatible model numbers. Version 7.23 will look the same whether it runs on UNIX or NT. Parallelism is the same. Multithreading is the same. They're essentially the same products.

Blasphemous as it may be to fellow UNIX bigots, the Windows NT systems may soon outperform our big-iron UNIX boxes, if for no other reason than faster and faster hardware. The PC market is famous both for its rapid rate of change and its constantly decreasing cost. Minicomputer systems seem to evolve at a much slower pace.

Due to its ubiquitous nature, Windows NT can run on just about any piece of new hardware. This means that when 300-MHz processors become generally available, they'll run on NT before they show up on UNIX systems, especially the more popular and proprietary ones. Multiprocessor Windows NT systems are becoming popular, and they perform on a par with their minicomputer brethren with like numbers of processors. Any time some budding entrepreneur develops a new whiz-bang speed trick for personal computers, it will show up first on Windows NT systems.

This means that running your IDS server on an NT system will allow you to work as close to the cutting edge as you either dare or have the funding for.

Areas of Difference from UNIX

In an attempt to avoid becoming a casualty in the NT versus UNIX holy war, I would like to first remind fellow UNIX bigots that I personally played no part in the development of any Windows product and that, basically, it's not my fault.

That is why I won't be reciting the scriptures of either side of the war. I'll even restrain myself from making proclamations that either side is better than the other. Suffice it to say that NT and UNIX are different in a lot of ways and that it pays to understand the differences. Whether NT is as good as UNIX is actually a moot point. While we were all making technical points, the market has made its financial point, and that is that NT is going to become a fixture in our computing environments. Like it or not, deal with it.

Use of the Windows Registry

One of the first things you notice about IDS on NT is that there's no `sqlhosts` file. If you've experienced some of the recent 32-bit client offerings from Informix, you'll already be familiar with this. In these tools such as INFORMIX-Connect, the information that was once part of the `sqlhosts` file is now kept in the registry of NT systems.

Use of Cooked File Systems

Informix OnLine for NT requires the use of NTFS filesystems. In the UNIX implementations, OnLine can either use the UNIX filesystem (*cooked files*), in which UNIX handles I/O to the data files, or *raw* data storage, in which OnLine manages the buffering to and from the disks. The user does not have this option on NT systems in IDS versions prior to 7.30, but the native NT filesystem (NTFS) performs very well. I have not been able to identify any performance degradation due to using NTFS.

NT systems are often configured using the FAT (file allocation table) filesystem that is compatible with earlier Windows 3.1 systems. This is done to provide a bit of recoverability to the system. In order to have the ability to boot up into MSDOS rather than Windows NT, the C drive needs to be a FAT filesystem rather than NTFS. Being able to boot into DOS can be a lifesaver if the operating system get corrupted, so it is usually a good idea to set a system up with a relatively small FAT partition (about 30 to 50 megabytes) and the rest of the system as NTFS.

If you have a system that has nothing but FAT filesystems, you can alter it to use NTFS by using the `convert` utility that comes with NT. When using this utility, you will often find that some of the files on the FAT filesystem that you're converting may be in use. If this is the case, NT buffers up the request to convert the filesystem and executes the request at reboot time. Be sure that you really want to convert from FAT to NTFS. It's not undo-able.

There are really only a couple of reasons why you would not want to use NTFS. One reason would be if you had some program that requires FAT rather than NTFS. I can't think of any such program, but they probably exist. Another reason would be if you are building a system that dual-boots between Windows NT and Windows 95. Windows 95 cannot see NTFS filesystems. Windows NT can see both types.

Permissions

Getting the file access permissions for data files or chunks is part of the rite of passage for new DBA's on UNIX systems. This is not needed on Windows NT systems. The NTFS filesystems handle the permissions automatically, and you don't need to manually change anything.

Multiuser

One of the major differences between NT and UNIX is that NT is not truly multiuser. NT systems do allow the sharing of files and other system resources, but unlike UNIX, it is not possible for more than one user to be logged in and executing commands that will execute on the NT's processor. Users are often confused by this. They can mount NT network drives on their systems and execute commands that reside on these shared resources, so they believe that they are working on a truly multiuser system. The difference is that when users do this, they are executing these programs on their own CPUs, not on the host computer's.

There are several ways to work around this problem. There are third-party firms that provide `telnet` server programs for NT. This will allow you log into an NT system and run non-graphical utilities just as you do on UNIX systems. For the diehard UNIX lovers out there, this type of access can be greatly enhanced by providing UNIX-like utilities on the NT system.

UNIX-like Utilities on NT

Most if not all Informix OnLine users and administrators come from UNIX environments, and for most of us, Windows NT does not include many of the utility programs that we have grown to love and hate in the UNIX environment. Fortunately, there are several third-party or shareware options that will allow us to run our favorite UNIX utilities and scripts in an NT environment.

Many of the data manipulation activities that we perform at the operating system level have to do with text manipulation, and it is here that UNIX historically excels. We are quite often called upon to deal with large ASCII files in association with such tasks as analysis of logfiles, preparation of data input files, and other database administration function.

For these purposes, it is hard to beat such UNIX utilities such as:

- `grep`
- `awk`
- `split`
- `join`
- `sed`
- `vi`
- `perl`
- `shell`

A good source that I've found for providing all of this and more in one package is the Mortice Kern Systems MKS toolkit. This has become one of my "can't live without" packages for any systems running Windows NT.

The Graphical Client Utilities on Windows

*A*nother option for managing remote Informix systems is to use client/server utilities that can operate on the distant servers. This is the approach that Informix is taking for its NT products. This is a good solution, provided that you can do all of the functions you need to do remotely through the client/server GUIs. Informix is providing their first cut at providing this functionality with the release of their Relational Object Manager (ROM) and Informix Enterprise Control Center(IECC) software. This software will make the job of remotely administering both NT and UNIX servers much easier.

The target for most of these Informix utilities was Microsoft SQL Server. You'll see an immediate resemblance to the graphical programs used to administer the SQL Server products. Although SQL Server has long been considered a "lightweight" player in the database power wars, almost everyone who has used it has developed a somewhat grudging admiration for its graphical user interface.

The new utilities are actually targeted to two separate groups of Informix users. The end user has the ability to create queries in a very nice graphical editor and run them against remote databases, receiving the results in a nicely formatted graphical screen. The administrator can monitor and administer some aspects of the database, such as disk layout, table and index structures, constraints and stored procedures. The DBA can also administer the backup and archiving utilities via the remote GUIs.

These utilities are still lacking in some areas such as monitoring of threads and other internal database processes. They also do not monitor database performance in any but a trivial manner.

Relational Object Manager

As of July 1998, Informix is still making many of the graphical utilities available at no cost to their customers through the Informix Web site. The tools are:

- Table Editor
- SQL Editor
- Database Explorer

These three tools, along with the INFORMIX-Connect connectivity package, have been grouped together and called Remote Object Manager. They were first made available in late 1997 through the Informix Web site, www.informix.com, and have also been incorporated into the NT server product distributions as well.

These tools will change somewhat in format beginning with Version 7.3, but it is believed that these changes will not alter the general concepts. This book is written as 7.2 versions are available, but 7.3 is not yet available.

Missing tools

With the introduction of the graphical tools, Informix discontinued support for the *onmonitor* character-based utility which has been available on both UNIX and NT systems for several versions of Informix products. Its functions have been taken over in a large part by two NT GUIs, *Command Center* and *Space Explorer*.

Onmonitor actually made calls to other character-based programs that still remain with current NT Informix systems, but onmonitor was a very good frontend for them. Since these underlying programs such as onspaces, onparams, oninit, and ontape still exist in the NT world, any functionality lost with onmonitor can be accomplished by using the underlying programs.

The only noticeable loss that I've found to date has been the inability to create chunks with temporary attributes with Space Explorer. In the UNIX environment, the DBA will put his temporary data in dataspaces created as temporary spaces in onmonitor. In order to do this with the latest NT release (7.23), the DBA must run `onspaces` manually with a "-t" parameter that will create the databases properly as temp spaces. As this book goes to press, Informix has announced that `onmonitor` will again become available for NT systems, beginning with Version 7.24.

INFORMIX ENTERPRISE COMMAND CENTER

Beginning with Informix OnLine 7.22, Informix has included the Command Center application with its Windows servers. This is a graphical user interface that allows the DBA to start and stop the database and monitor the status of multiple Informix databases, both NT and UNIX, located across a network. As the product marketing shifted a bit, the name was changed to Informix Enterprise Command Center, and that is the name by which it is currently known.

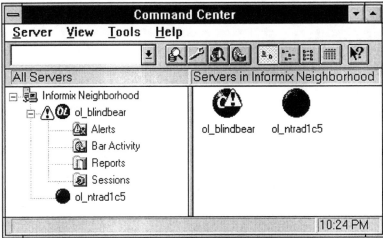

Command Center also contains an extensive mechanism for generating alerts and other types of notification that are triggered by predefined conditions within the database. When Command Center is first started, the user is given a graphical screen that shows the available servers.

Populating the Informix Neighborhood

The available servers in Command Center must be defined using the wrench (setup) icon of Command Center. These servers are not automatically located, and simply setting up the servers in `setnet32` will not make them available in the Informix Neighborhood. Clicking on the wrench icon brings up the following screen.

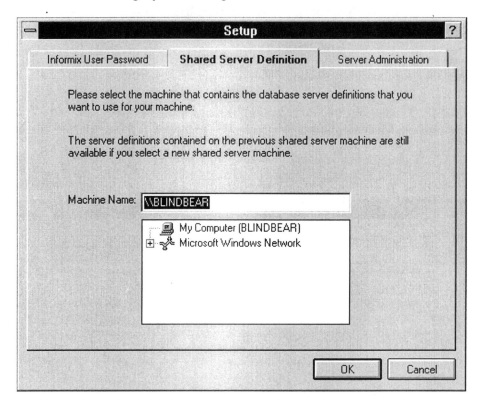

The Shared Server Definition screen shows one of the more handy aspects of the Windows administration tools, the ability to designate a single system as the master system for containing sqlhosts information. This has always been one of the little arcane things that DBAs have had to do in order to ensure that Informix databases on different machines can talk to one another. With one or two servers, it's no great task, but with tens or hundreds of servers, it becomes a challenge to keep all of their sqlhosts files in sync, especially with systems that are constantly changing.

Since the NT port has effectively done away with the sqlhosts file and has stored this information in the Windows registry, this opens up the capability of sharing this information with other systems on the network. This screen allows the DBA to designate one NT machine as the master source of sqlhosts data. Other systems can use the same registry information simply by choosing the proper machine from the system tree. Now the DBA can make connectivity changes in one place and not have to worry about propagating those changes in other NT systems.

Since UNIX systems do not have the concept of a registry, any Informix databases running on UNIX will continue to need a local sqlhosts file and cannot use this feature.

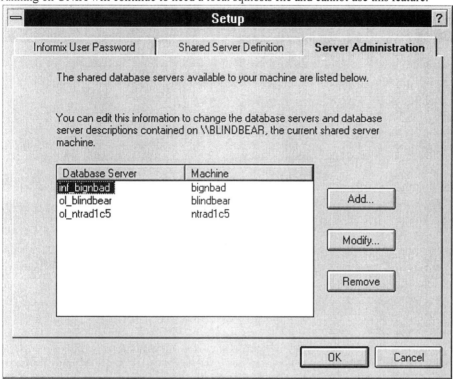

The Server Administration tab is where the servers are actually defined. This definition must be done from this screen, even if the servers are already listed in the registry from a previous run of setnet32. Clicking the Modify or Add buttons will bring up a screen that allows the DBA to enter information about the server

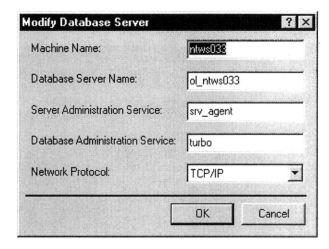

The systems need to have an entry in the registry for each server and this entry is most often entered using the `setnet32` utility. It can be done manually using the Windows program `regedit` or `regedt32` (depending upon Windows version), but doing it manually is somewhat more hazardous than allowing `setnet32` to do the work. As in `setnet32`, the database server name needs to be the name of the Informix server, not the name of the computer itself.

The Server Administration Service needs to be running on any system that is to be controlled by Command Center. Making these connections is somewhat easier with NT systems than with UNIX systems. In order to control a UNIX server with Command Center, the UNIX server needs to have a TCP service such as "srv_agent" running with a defined TCP port, much the same way as the Database Administration Service has always been needed for Informix-to-Informix communication. The Database Administration Service is the same service that is listed in the sqlhosts file. The Server Administration Service is new to Informix, and needs to be defined on both UNIX and NT systems. If you need to control UNIX machines with Command Center, contact your Informix representative to obtain the necessary software to establish and run the Server Administration Service on the UNIX machine.

Going back to the initial screen of the Command Center application, drilling down on a particular server will open four folders in the right-hand panel, in which the user can get information about alerts, backup (bar) activity, reports about database status, and session information about the database.

Alerts

Alerts are a new feature with the NT port. UNIX IDS ports have long included the ALARMPROGRAM feature which monitored the `online.log` and allowed the user to set up actions based upon what was happening in the database. The alerts feature is an extension of that concept, with a prettier interface and a more intuitive approach to the whole matter.

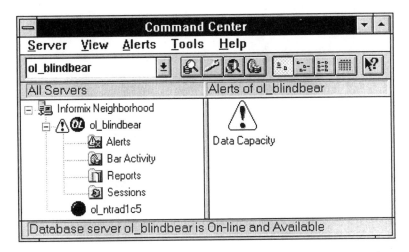

Clicking on an active alert reveals another ease-of-use feature of Command Center. Informix has created an alert resolution wizard that walks the DBA through the tasks of responding to an alert. Whereas this may not be terribly impressive to a jaded DBA who knows all of this stuff anyway, it can be a lifesaver to an inexperienced DBA or someone who is filling in while the real DBA is away on vacation.

Just the fact that an alert shows up on a graphical screen is an improvement for the neophyte DBA, who probably would not have identified and corrected the problem until after the fact without the use of Command Center.

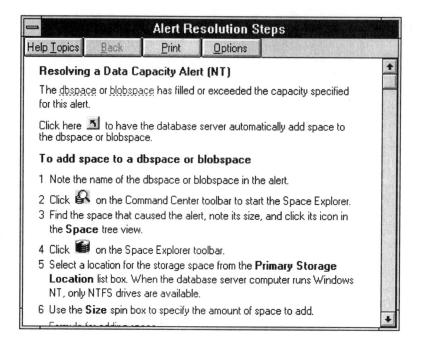

Bar Activity

Contrary to what many DBAs may believe, the Bar Activity screen has nothing to do with libations or tall tales. This is the interface with the latest backup, recovery, and logfile archiving program, `onbar`.

Reports

This screen shows the reports that are available in the Command Center for each server defined. The alert log is a listing of any alerts that have been generated by Command Center. These alerts cover such items as disk full, logfiles full, out of operating system resources, and other system-level problems.

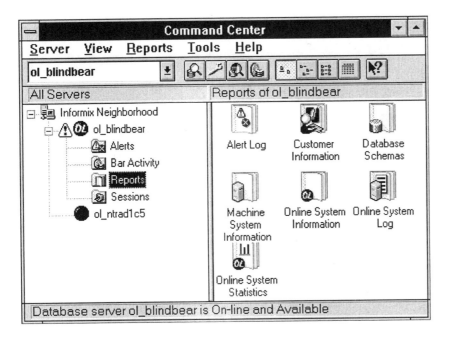

The Customer Information icon contains licensing information and a mechanism for faxing this information directly to Informix Support. The Database Schemas icon creates a schema for a database whose name you select from a window of available databases on the server. The Machine System Information icon shows basic information about the hardware and operating system of the database computer. It also shows memory information and gives a listing of the environmental variables for the computer. The Online System Information runs `onstat -c` and provides a listing of the $ONCONFIG file. The Online System Log icon shows the contents of the online.log. finally, the Online System Statistics runs an `onstat -a` against the database.

All seven of these report icons first generate a "save as" screen, with the default filename set to "report.txt." Be sure and change the name to something more meaningful to assure that the output is not overwritten the next time that one of the reports is generated.

All of the reports are pretty simplistic and cannot approach the quality of reports that you can generate by running the dbschema and `onstat` commands from the command line, with the myriad of options that are available. The most useful aspect of these reports is that it will allow Informix Support to gather decent information about a system even if the DBA is not available. Any of the users could just click on the appropriate icon and generate information that will be helpful in a support call.

Sessions

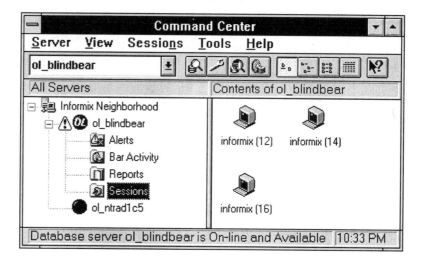

The Sessions folder gives a subset of the information that is available with the `onstat` utilities. It shows an icon for every database session, identified by the user name of the user running the session. Clicking on a session icon gives an output similar to the `onstat -g sql` command, showing the SQL statement that the session has most recently run.

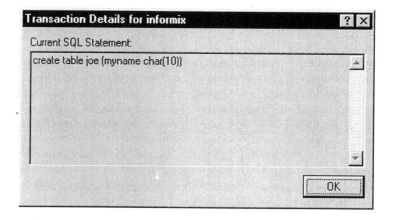

The session information is information that the DBA always seems to need. Quite a bit of a DBA's time is spent trying to track down rogue SQL statements that are either doing sequential scans or taking up too many resources in the system. Often, these statements are embedded in programs written either in ESQL/C or in 4GL, and it is quite often difficult to actually find the statements that are running.

IDS made substantial improvements to the process of identifying these statements with the advent of the `onstat -g sql` command. While this Sessions screen does not provide the in-depth information that the `onstat` commands give, it does provide a quick and dirty way for a DBA to identify what is going on. She can then do further research to track down offending statements.

Much of the chapter on optimizing and tuning applications will concentrate on methods of using the SMI tables and the character-based utilities to further ferret out these rogue SQL statements.

Command Center Summary

The Command Center application, while no substitute for understanding the underlying, character-based utilities, does provide ease of use for smaller installations as well as a method of graphically monitoring more complex systems. As usual, there are tradeoffs to the concept of making a database easier to use and understand.

Informix is neither easy to use nor easy to understand. It is a large, complicated product that requires in-depth knowledge to use correctly and safely. Don't let the flashiness and apparent simplicity of the GUIs lull you or your management into believing that this is a simple desktop application. The GUI is a simple desktop application, but the IDS engine is not.

Command Center could potentially allow a naïve user to set up and maintain an IDS database. As long as data volumes are small, the user count is low, and system loads are not excessive, an IDS database can be treated almost like a low-end desktop database, with all of the simplicity of operation that such a database entails. With low loads it is not necessary to extract the last bit of performance out of the engine. Tuning and setup errors probably won't be fatal and the system will run, although not at peak performance. A user can perform the basic database administration functions using the GUI without understanding the underlying complexity and without having to learn all of the commands, options, and switches necessary to use the character-based utilities.

The problems will occur when the load gets heavier and it becomes necessary to tune the database in order to extract more performance. Suddenly, the "DBA" who was competent doing the simple things with the GUI will be faced with more complicated decisions. Unless the DBA is trained well enough to appreciate the complexities and subtleties of the engine, the GUI may lull him and his management into believing that he understands something that he really understands only superficially.

This is one of the risks that we face as we move into a Windows-based environment. There is a basic difference between UNIX and NT applications. Windows applications tend to be more "shrink-wrapped" and more user friendly than UNIX applications. If the users and management see the shrink-wrapped GUI running on Windows, there is the risk that they will view the database as a typical PC application, rather than the complex engine that it really is. This expectation has ramifications in how the community views hardware requirements, training requirements, hardware and software costs, personnel costs, and support costs. It's up to the DBA to make sure that the expectations are set correctly and that management understands that this is really a very complex, capable product masquerading as desktop software.

SPACE EXPLORER

The Space Explorer graphical utility is used to create, modify, delete, and manage the dbspaces and chunks that comprise the database. It has the capability of adding or dropping dbspaces, creating mirrored dbspaces, and adding or deleting storage to existing dbspaces. One of the things that it does not do is create temporary dbspaces. You can create a dbspace to be used for temporary space in this GUI, but it will not be a proper, nonlogging tempspace. To create it properly, you need to create the space using the onspaces utility. You can then add chunks to it through the GUI.

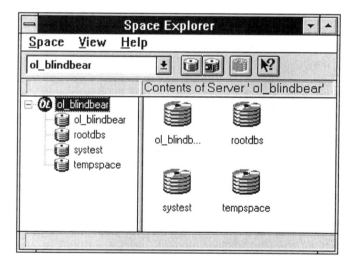

When you first enter the utility, you can choose your server either from the drop-down list box underneath the menu or by clicking on the appropriate icon in the left-hand frame. Once you've chosen the server, you can then click on any of the dbspaces listed.

This will open a screen that shows you the number of chunks in that dbspace and the size of each one. By using the menu, you can change the view from large icons to medium-sized icons to a text list, in standard Windows 95 fashion.

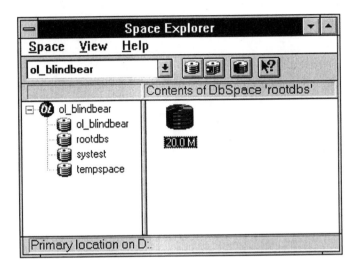

Space Explorer, like the Command Center application, uses the srv_agent socket defined in the setup icon of Command Center. If the server agent is not running on the server, Space Explorer cannot see that server,

The first button on the toolbar creates a new dbspace and gives you the opportunity to either mirror or not mirror the space. Unlike UNIX, the space for a new chunk does not have to be predefined before adding it. You can simply give it a name, a primary storage location, a size, and any mirroring information. The GUI will check for enough disk space, create the file housing the chunk, and initialize it for you. By the way, this process is immensely faster than under UNIX. Creating a 2-gigabyte dbspace under UNIX may take 5 or 10 minutes. On NT, it is done in a matter of seconds.

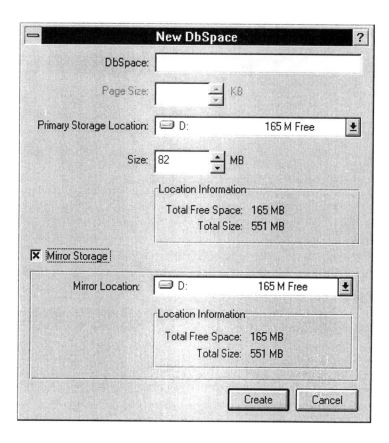

When the user clicks on one of the drop-down list boxes for either primary or mirror storage locations, only those disks which have an NTFS filesystem will be listed. This is a cause of frequent confusion when the user knows he has multiple disk drives and can see only one or two.

The second button creates a blobspace for the storage of blob data. Blobspaces are specialized dbspaces that can hold binary or other nontraditional data. Blob usage is a somewhat specialized area and will not be covered in this book.

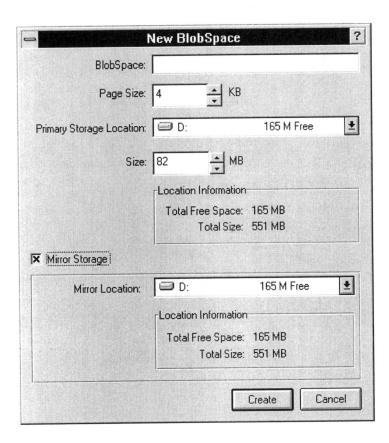

The third button allows the user to add storage to an existing dbspace. There is a maximum size for any chunk of 2 gigabytes. Informix cannot address any file directly that is larger than 2 gigabytes. This size limit also includes any file offsets that the user may specify in creating the chunks. The total of offset + chunksize needs to be less than 2 gigabytes. Note also that the GUI does not handle file offsets. If you need to specify an offset for the chunk, you'll need to use the character-based onspaces utility and create the chunks manually.

In the initial dbspace creation, the user has the option of specifying mirroring. If the user decides later to mirror the chunk, it can be done with the GUI, but there is no toolbar button for it. It's done by choosing Space from the menu and then choosing Enable Mirroring. The following screen comes up and allows the user to specify the name, location, and size of the mirror dbspace.

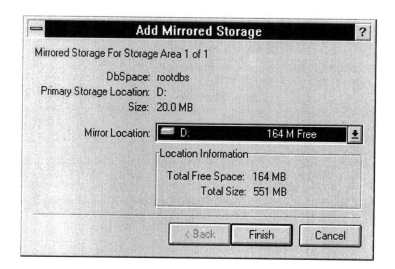

DATABASE EXPLORER

When the Database Explorer program first starts, it gives you a list of the known servers in the left-hand panel. Clicking on any server then shows the user the databases available on the server. Only the user databases are shown. The sysmaster database is not shown.

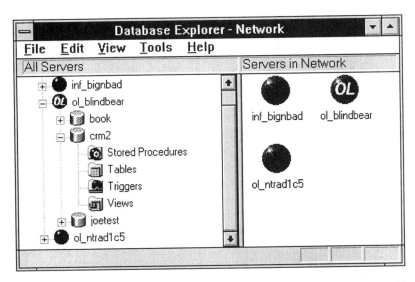

Clicking on any of the databases opens four folders in the right-hand panel. Folders show stored procedures, tables, triggers, and views.

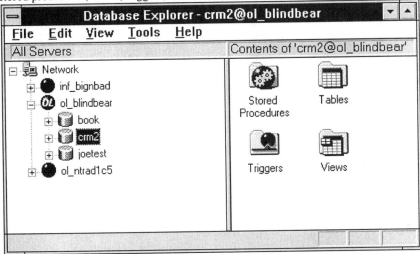

Clicking on any of these folders will generate a list of any stored procedures, tables, triggers, or views in the chosen database, depending upon which folder was entered. In the example below, the user has clicked on the Stored Procedures icon and has generated a list of stored   procedures.

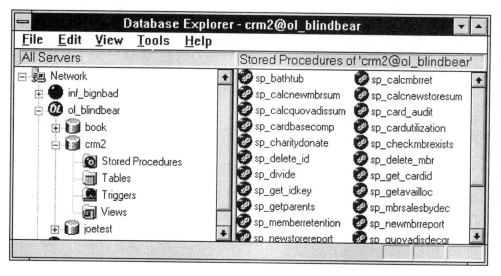

If the user clicks on any of the objects in the right-hand panel, an editor will open that allows the user to see or modify the listed objects. These editors are of two types. If the object is a table, the Table Editor program will be called as the editor. This is the same program that can be called as a stand alone program. If the user chooses stored procedures, triggers, or views, an instance of the SQL Editor program is called.

In the example below, the Views folder was clicked and the SQL script for creating a view was automatically placed in the editor. The same procedure works for the other applications that use the SQL Editor. If you click on the Stored Procedure folder, the SQL Editor will come up with that stored procedure already loaded.

This GUI view, especially of stored procedures and triggers, is much more useful than those obtainable from the character-based interfaces. In the older interfaces, the only way to see the stored procedures was to run a series of SQL statements, and even then the formatting made the output all but unreadable. For someone using lots of stored procedures or triggers, this feature alone is reason to obtain the GUI.

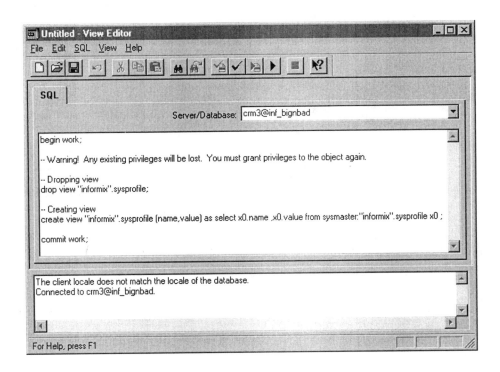

TABLE EDITOR

The Table Editor application provides a graphical method of creating, inspecting, and modifying table structures in Informix databases. When the utility is first entered, the user
chooses a server, then a database on that server, and finally a table within that database. This
choice of server/database/table can also be made directly from the toolbar or from the menu
using the Table→Open menu choice or the Open Folder toolbar button.

The Table Editor has three main tabbed pages, Columns, Indexes, and Foreign Keys.
Much of the useful information is in the Columns tab. From the Table→Properties menu,
the user sees a screen listing several items of interest regarding the table. The Status tab
shows name, owner, modification date, row size, and number of rows, columns, and indexes. Under the General tab is information about extent sizing and locking levels. The
Constraints tab shows any constraints defined in the table. Finally, the Location tab shows
information about how the table is physically laid out. It allows the user to place the table in
a default database, in its own dbspace, or partitioned across multiple dbspaces.

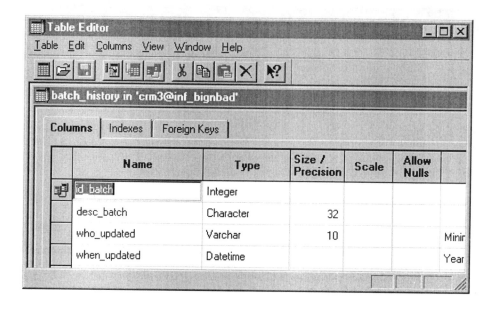

Under the Columns tab, the user can name or rename columns or attributes. Clicking on any of the column type entries produces a drop-down box that gives the user a choice of all Informix data types.

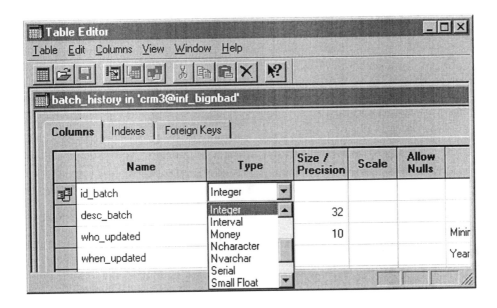

Using either the toolbar or the Columns menu option from the menu, the user can in-sert or delete columns as well as declare a column part of the primary key and define its properties. These properties include the column name, data type, size or precision, default values, and whether or not the column can be null. Clicking on the size/precision or allow nulls cell in the Columns tab will open listboxes allowing the user use the mouse to select the desired information.

The Indexes tab shows index name and columns as graphical icons that also indicate whether or not the value is indexed as ascending or descending. When on the index tabbed page, the user can create a new index using the menu choice Indexes→ New Index. This calls the Index Wizard, which walks the user through creating a new index. This wizard allows the user to specify:

- Index name
- Columns used
- Order of the columns in the index
- Whether the columns are sorted ascending or descending
- Whether the index is unique
- Whether the index is clustered

- Whether the index is stored with the table, in its own dbspace, or across multiple dbspaces

Clicking on the Foreign Key tab, the user sees any defined foreign key constraints in the database. By using the menu or the toolbar, the user can use the Foreign Key Wizard to define these relationships This wizard allows the user to:

- Name the foreign key
- Select a table to relate to the current table
- Choose a primary key or constraint for the foreign key constraint
- Define the join between the two tables for the foreign key
- Choose whether or not to use cascading deletes on the foreign key table

Both of these wizards greatly simplify the creation and modifications of indexes and foreign keys. While most DBAs are proficient with creating indexes using the character-based tools, they often miss some of the fine points such as location of the indexes. Foreign keys may or may not be used often. If used infrequently, the DBA usually has to dig into the documentation for the correct syntax. These two wizards can make either of these functions much easier and much less error prone.

As in all of the other GUI tools, the Table Editor provides cut and paste capability with other Windows applications.

SQL Editor

Graphical Versus Character-Based Utilities

The SQL Editor application is a graphical program equivalent to the ISQL and dbaccess programs in the character-based world. For a while it seemed that Informix was intending to completely replace the character-based utilities with these new graphical utilities, but an outcry from the users convinced Informix to retain the character-based utilities. There are still many things that can be done from the character-based utilities that cannot (yet) be done with the graphical utilities, and the character-based utilities still are the main method of database access and manipulation on UNIX systems, since the Microsoft Windows-based graphical utilities will not run on UNIX. To date, one of the main limitations of all of the GUI utilities is the lack of a scripting language. Until there is a workable scripting language, even Windows systems will need to retain the character-based utilities.

Advantages of SQL Editor

SQL Editor provides a much more user friendly environment on Windows 95 and Windows NT systems than dbaccess. One of the big improvements is a much more sophisticated editor that supports cut-and-paste, undo, toolbars, find and replace, and a useful help system. It supports multiple SQL statements that send results to separate tabbed output pages. It also allows the user to highlight and run individual SQL statements from the editor.

SQL Editor Operations

When entering SQL Editor, the user is presented with the now-familiar drop-down list box that allows the user to navigate through multiple servers and drill down to individual databases on each server.

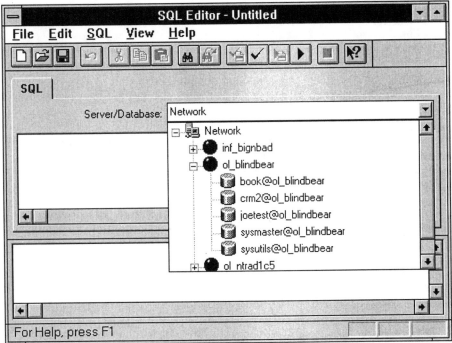

SQL Editor allows the user to work with the sysmaster database, but each time it generates a warning that can be somewhat annoying. A way to do this is to choose any database but sysmaster and to access the sysmaster database with a statement like:

```
SELECT * from sysmaster:sysprofile
```

This syntax has the advantage of allowing the user to work with the sysmaster (or any other database, for that matter) from any database on the system.

After choosing a database, the user can use either the toolbar or the menu to either open an existing SQL script or create a new one. Hitting the open-folder icon or using the menu opens a familiar (to Windows users) window that allows the user to choose a script.

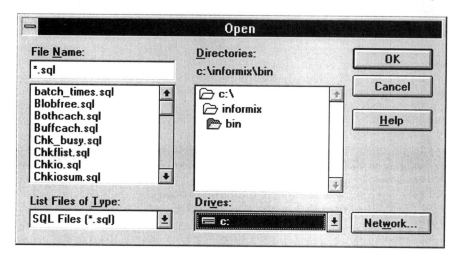

Clicking on the diskette icon or using the File→Save menu option pops up a similar screen to allow the user to save a new or modified script. After choosing an existing script or creating a new script, the script is brought up in the top window of SQL Editor.

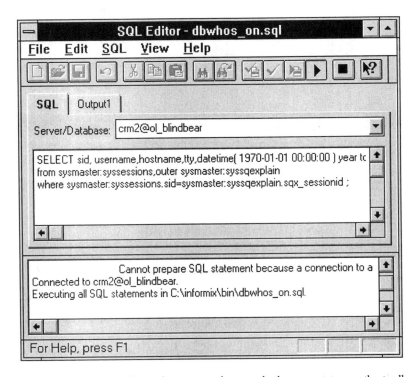

The View menu item allows the user to choose whether or not to see the toolbar, the status bar (at the very bottom of the screen), and the SQL result history (the bottom box), which gives feedback about the execution status of the SQL statements. Error messages appear in both the result history box and in a separate pop-up window, so not making the result history box viewable does not interfere with receiving error messages from the Informix database engine.

Several new toolbar icons become available when there is an SQL script resident in the editor window (they are grayed-out if not available). These icons are the find button, the check button, and the execute button (the triangle, VCR-like button). The checkmark button checks the syntax of the SQL statement(s), and the execute button opens an output tab and displays the result of the SQL statement. If there are multiple SQL statements separated by semicolons, multiple tabbed output pages are generated, one for each SQL statement. If any of the SQL statements is highlighted with the mouse, two additional toolbar buttons are activated that allow the user to either check the syntax of the highlighted statement or to execute the statement.

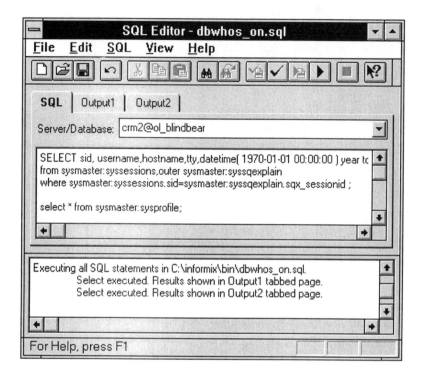

When there is a script in the window, the SQL→Set Explain option becomes usable. This has the same effect as inserting a SET EXPLAIN ON statement at the beginning of the script. When a script is actually running, the little square box icon will allow the user to interrupt the script in the same manner as hitting a control-c in dbaccess.

When the user clicks on one of the output tabs, a grid is displayed giving the data retrieved by the query. This also makes a few more options active from the menu. The Save menu now has an option to Save As Data. This allows you to highlight some or all of the data on the screen and save it into a text file with the extension .txt. This has the data delimited by tab characters. A very useful upgrade to the program would allow the data to be saved in multiple formats, such as pipe-delimited for imports and exports or spreadsheet format for importing directly into a spreadsheet.

The grid output has a few other shortcomings that could benefit from further development. First, the titles for the tabbed pages are simply Output1, Output2, etc. It would be much more user friendly if these tabs could be user-defined.

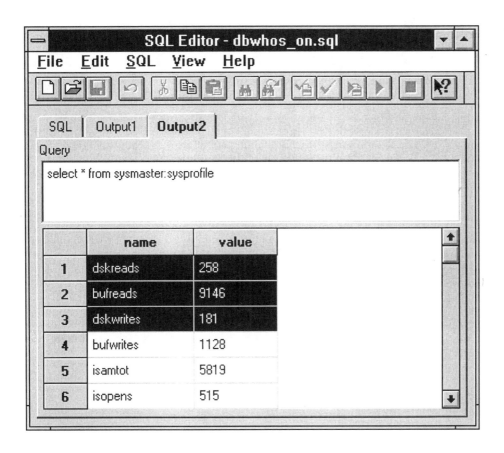

There's one little quirk in the SQL Editor that is not immediately obvious and can cause a lot of confusion if the user is not aware of it. If there is an active query in the editor that has been run and if it has generated one or more output pages, minimizing the SQL Editor and then maximizing it causes the SQL tab to disappear. When this happens, a little arrow appears to the right of the tabs. Clicking on the left-hand arrow causes the editor window to reappear.

Informix Connectivity Products

In earlier chapters we have looked at both the database servers and the GUI clients. In this chapter, we will investigate the connection between the client and server components of the client/server applications and will look at the tools provided by Informix to connect these two applications. These Informix tools are currently called Informix-Connect and Informix-CLI. In OnLine (pre version 6) systems, Informix-Connect was called I-Net or I-Star. Whatever the name, these programs are the glue that holds the clients and servers together. This chapter was written with Informix Dynamic Server (IDS) as its primary inspiration. Older OnLine engines can be connected to in much the same way as can IDS engines, with the exception that connections to OnLine systems lack many of the more advanced options and complexities of IDS. Read this entire chapter with IDS in mind, but refer to your manuals for specific OnLine information.

Informix engines operate as a client/server system no matter whether the client and server are running on the same physical computer system or on separate systems connected over a network. The client application formulates a request and sends it to the server, and the server delivers the result back to the client over the connecting link.

CLIENT AND SERVER ON THE SAME SYSTEM

When the components are on the same physical machine, there are several different mechanisms that may be used for this connecting link. They include:

- Shared memory connections: These are usually the fastest and most reliable connections between co-located clients and servers. Both client and server attach to the same shared memory segment and communicate with each other by leaving and retrieving messages in shared memory. If you are setting up or tuning a large UNIX system in which all or most of the client activity occurs on the single UNIX computer, there are significant performance gains in using shared memory connections, assuming you have enough shared memory to go around. The major drawback of shared memory connections is that since shared memory must be readable and writable by all users, they are less secure than TCP/IP or stream pipe connections. It is theoretically possible for a hacker to write code that will read the contents of shared memory and eavesdrop on client/server communications. It is also possible for a rogue program to write to the shared memory area, crashing the database engine.

- Network connections: These connections use the either the TLI (transport-level interface), IPX/SPX protocols, or the sockets interface which forms the basis of Internet communications. Network connections are the only type of communications for clients and servers on separate host machines and is set up by default in most cases where the client and server co-reside on the same host. In this case, Informix uses a local loopback communication and doesn't actually send packets out onto the network. This is both the most common communications method and the most difficult to set up because of the necessary interrelation between Informix and the networking system. Because of this, we will concentrate on TCP/IP and sockets in this chapter.

- Streams connections: These connections became available with IDS 7.1 and are available on some UNIX systems. Check your release notes to see if they are supported in your environment. Streams connections use UNIX pipes to provide interprocess communication between client and server. They are good performers and have the advantage of being somewhat more secure than shared memory connections.

Different ports of the OnLine and IDS engines support different combinations of these transport mechanisms. To find out which mechanisms are supported in any particular port, look at the files in the release notes. These release notes will be found in the $INFORMIXDIR/release directory structure. In OnLine systems, the notes will be found in the release directory. In later IDS engines, the release notes will be buried deeper in this directory structure, in subdirectories based on the language chosen (GLS) for the application. Just drill deeper into the directory until you find a subdirectory with several text files in it. If your system actually supports multiple languages, search until you can find notes in a language you can read. These different communication mechanism are not mutually exclusive. If your system supports the connection method, you can use one or all of the mechanisms for connecting local clients to local servers. This will be illustrated later in this chapter.

CLIENTS AND SERVERS ON SEPARATE HOSTS

This is the commonly understood meaning of client/server computing where the server resides on one host system and clients can reside on one or multiple additional computer systems. If all of the clients connect to the same server, this is known *as a two-tier architecture*. If there are multiple servers that do different types of work and can each one can connect to multiple clients, this is known as a *multi-tier architecture*. A common type of *three-tier architecture* (a subset of multi-tier) is a case in which one server holds data, one holds business rules, and the clients connect transparently to both servers. These types of connections are referred to a *remote connections*.

There are two network protocols over which Informix can talk to connect remote clients and servers:

- TCP/IP (Transmission Control Protocol/Internet Protocol): This is the most common protocol and is the protocol used for all Internet connectivity. This chapter will concentrate on TCP/IP connections for remote connections.
- IPX/SPX: This protocol is only used for NetWare networks. If there is a UNIX machine involved, it must have IPX/SPX software installed.

REMOTE CONNECTIONS OVER TCP/IP

On UNIX systems, the task of connecting the client and server together was strictly a manual task. The DBA had to manually edit two ASCII files, one of which needed system administrator privileges to modify (/etc/services). The manual editing usually occurred only on the UNIX system, with the GUIs making the setup on Windows machines a little bit more automated. Since most UNIX machines support some type of Windows clients, most DBAs have worked with the GUIs.

In order to understand the relationships between all of the files used for TCP/IP communications, refer to the following diagram.

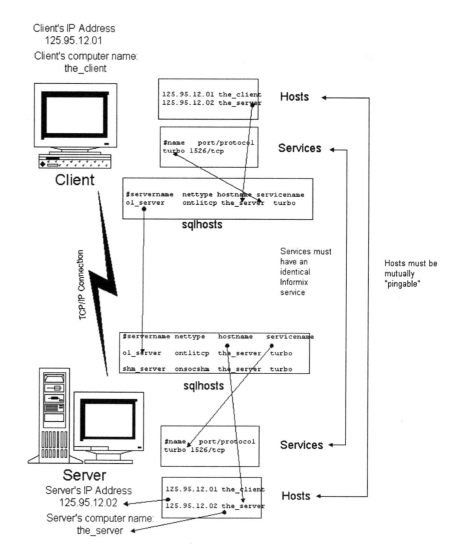

Files Used in TCP/IP Remote Connections

There are several ASCII files that must have proper entries to allow the clients and servers to communicate. If any of the entries are wrong, the client and server will not communicate correctly.

Onconfig

The onconfig file is located at $INFORMIXDIR/etc/$ONCONFIG if $ONCONFIG is set in UNIX system or $INFORMIXDIR/etc/onconfig if the $ONCONFIG environmental variable is not set. Onconfig is the default filename unless overridden by $ONCONFIG. The onconfig file (by whatever name it is called) is the file used to store all of the instance's tuning and configuration parameters, so it should be quite familiar to DBAs. There are a few lines of interest from the communications viewpoint:

```
# System Configuration
DBSERVERNAME      ol_server     #Name of default server
DBSERVERALIASES   ol_localhost  #List of alternate servernames
NETTYPE  onsoctcp,1,10,NET      #Override sqlhosts nettype
```

The DBSERVERNAME parameter is the name by which the server is identified. This name is not the name of the host machine. It is the name of the actual Informix server. The DBSERVERALIASES is used to provide different server names for different connectivity methods.

Services

In both UNIX and NT systems, the services file is an operating system-owned file called /etc/services on UNIX systems and %WINDOWS%\system32\drivers\etc\services on pre-WindowsNT 4.0 systems and %WINDOWS%\services on NT4.0 systems.

The services file is located in /etc/services on most UNIX systems. It may or may not be found on WindowsNT systems depending upon whether or not another application has used it. Its location also seems more variable on Windows systems, as there does not seem to be a standard with file locations in third-party TCP stacks. If you do not find a services file on NT, look for the sample file, services.sam, and copy it to a file named services in the same directory.

The services file is a TCP/IP file that provides information about how and where commonly used TCP/IP communication functions are handled. Don't confuse this with the concept of services that run on Windows NT systems. NT systems may provide both a TCP/IP service and an NT service that work together. An example would be the NT ftp service, which monitors and communicates over the TCP/IP port reserved for ftp. A port is simply an area of memory which that connections will connect to. Ports are also known as *sockets* or services. Actually, socket communication is more complicated than just talking over one port, but that's only interesting to people who are programming the sockets programs. You'll be safe enough if you just understand the basics. TCP/IP provides built-in ports for such things as:

- telnet
- ftp
- finger
- nameservers
- time servers
- talk

Each of these services is assigned a port. For example, the telnet program usually connects over port 23 and ftp usually connects over port 21. Informix needs ports to allow the clients to communicate with the servers. These ports are not included in the "standard" ports that come with TCP/IP, so they have to be inserted. On the server end, the services file is usually modified as part of the Informix install process. Here's a sample from an NT services file:

```
sta7_sfs_jx2     3616/tcp     # Informix on HP/UX system
svc_crm2_tli     1599/tcp     # Informix on UNIXWare system
turbo            1526/tcp     # IDS - Personal Edition
turbo2           1527/tcp     # second port for local connect
srv_agent        1530/tcp     # INFORMIX-OnLine Server Agent
infconn          4000/tcp     # Informix on Stratus Polo
```

The format is service_name, white_space, port number/tcp. Anything after the hash symbol (#) is a comment. You will see services in the services file that use "/udp" instead of "/tcp." These are datagram ports. They are useful to somebody, but I don't think I know anybody who really understands (or cares) what they are. All of the ports we are interested in are "/tcp" ports.

You can set up as many services for Informix as you want. Windows NT Informix installs usually default to the "turbo" service on port 1526/tcp. The "turbo" is a holdover from early (4.X) Informix engines that went by the name of "Informix Turbo." As an aside, this is the source of the "tb" prefix in the OnLine utilities. There are three limitations:

- The port numbers must be unique.
- The port numbers must be greater than 1000. Ports numbered less than 1000 are reserved for "standard" TCP/IP services.

- The last line of the services file should be blank. This last item is purely super-stitious behavior on my part. There are several systems that have problems with the last line of the file, and if you make it blank, it will never cause you prob-lems.

In the example file above, the first four entries are different services for different ma-chines. The last entry is a service for the GUI administration tools on NT, which needs its own unique service port to connect with the engine for maintenance activities.

Why would you want to have different services for different host systems? For one thing, systems that have more than one ethernet card can control which card to use for par-ticular remote connections by assigning them different IP addresses and giving them differ-ent service names and ports for each connection. This would allow the DBA or the system administrator to balance the loads across multiple cards. Another reason to do this would be to simplify the monitoring of network communications. The database administrator can use the netstat command to view TCP/IP communications at the operating system level. Differ-ent options to netstat can show the port number over which the TCP/IP conversation is tak-ing place. If different machines use different ports, it will be easier to decipher the entries and it will be easier to tell which TCP/IP sessions are talking to which systems. There could also be some performance gains in a heavily loaded system by spreading the work across multiple ports, but the system would have to be pretty heavily loaded to make significant gains.

The services file is an indexed lookup file. Given a service name, the system internally performs a lookup into this file in order to find which port number to use. IDS engines be-ginning with 7.10UD1 allow you to completely bypass the services file by including the port number rather than the name in the Informix configuration files. This saves the time needed for the lookup and can make it easier to understand what is going on. This can also be a use-ful debugging trick if you having problems getting the services name to match to the right port. If the connection works with the port number but not with the port name, you know that you must have a problem somewhere in the services file.

Hosts

The hosts file is used by TCP/IP to associate a computer's system name to an IP ad-dress used by the ethernet board that provides the networking connection. In UNIX systems, the hosts file in usually found at /etc/hosts. In Windows NT systems, it is an ASCII file located at %WINDOWS%\system32\drivers\etc\hosts. In Windows 95 systems, it is located at %WINDOWS\hosts. The format of the file is simple. An IP address followed by a hostname followed by an optional alias, all separated by white space.

```
#  IP Address      Hostname        Alias
#
125.95.12.01      the_client
125.95.12.02      the_server
```

TCP/IP uses the host file to allow a user to communicate with a system by name rather than IP address. This is the only thing that Informix uses it for. As with the services file, IDS systems beginning with 7.10UD1 can bypass the hosts file by using the actual numeric IP address rather than the hostname.

The best way to test whether the hosts file is set up properly is to use the ping command. In many UNIX systems, the ping command is not in a typical user's path. If you get a "ping not found" error, try using the full pathname for ping. This is usually /etc/ping in UNIX systems. First, try pinging the host with the following command:

```
ping the_server (using the appropriate name, of course)
```

If you don't get a response from this command, try pinging the server using its numeric IP address:

```
ping 125.95.12.02   (using the correct IP address)
```

If both ping commands fail, you'll never establish connectivity until you make it work. See your system administrator or network administrator and fix your networking before going any further. If the ping by number works but the ping by name doesn't, you have a problem with your hosts file. Either fix the file or simply use the IP numbers rather than the name if your are on an IDS system later than 7.10UD1.

This pinging needs to work both from client to server and from server to client. Make sure that both sides of the communication are able to ping each other. The following flowchart illustrates the process of testing your underlying network communications using the ping command:

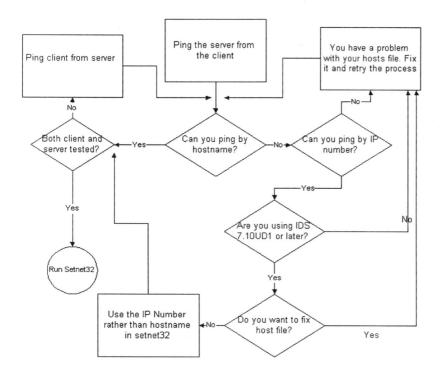

Validating network
communications with ping

Sqlhosts

The sqlhosts file is the linchpin of Informix connectivity. It is in this file that we tie together the data from the onconfig, services, and hosts files. It is here that we instruct the engine how to connect to the servers in various ways, what transport mechanisms to use, and how to behave in specific instances by using options in the file.

We will refer to this as the sqlhosts *file,* although on NT systems and on Windows-based clients there is no actual sqlhosts file. On these systems, the sqlhosts information is stored in the Windows registry, where it can be shared with other systems on the network. It is set up using the Informix program setnet32 (or setnet for the older 16-bit Informix-Net systems).

IDS 7.30 for NT has an interesting program in %INFORMIXDIR%\demo. This program is called "ershed.exe," and it may be helpful if you are more comfortable dealing with the UNIX-style sqlhosts file. Ershed can read the registry from any machine you designate and presents you with a UNIX-style sqlhosts file. You can make your changes in this file and save it back to the registry of the original or different machine. This can be a valuable utility if you prefer the UNIX-style sqlhosts manipulation.

In UNIX systems, this the sqlhosts file resides in $INFORMIXDIR/etc. Here is a sample from a 7.22 version of IDS:

```
#server         nettype       hostname          service
#-------------------------------------------------------

crm2            ontlitcp      s2radC3           svc_crm2_tli
ol_server       ontlitcp      the_server        turbo
ol_localhost    onipcshm      the_server        turbo2
ol_ipnumber     ontlitcp      125.95.12.02      turbo
ol_bothnumber   ontlitcp      125.95.12.02      1527
```

The first field is the name of the IDS or OnLine instance. If you are using an NT system, the IDS install program suggests an instance name by prepending "ol_" to the hostname of the system. Be sure that you differentiate between the servername and the hostname. The second field is an eight-character code called the nettype. This code identifies the server type, interface type, and network or IPC protocol in use. Codes are:

- First two characters: Database server type
    - on = OnLine
    - ol = OnLine (equal to on)
    - se = Informix SE
    - dr = Informix Gateway (with DRDA)
- Chars 3,4,5: Network interface
    - ipc = IPC (interprocess communications or streams)
    - soc = sockets
    - tli = TLI (transport level interface)
- Chars 6,7: IPC mechanism or network protocol
    - shm = shared memory connection
    - tcp = TCP/IP protocol
    - spx = IPX/SPX protocol
    - str = Stream Pipe

In the sqlhosts sample file above, the first two servers, crm2 and ol_server, use the same nettype, ontlitcp. This decodes to OnLine systems communicating over TCP/IP protocol using the TLI interface. The third server, ol_localhost, has a nettype of "onipcshm," meaning an OnLine system communicating via shared memory locally using interprocess communications. This is the same physical database as ol_server, only with a different means of communication between the client and the server (both client and server are local to the machine, the_server).

Note that this is one time in which the term "OnLine" does not strictly apply to versions 5.X. When Informix changed the name from "OnLine" to "Informix Dynamic Server," it did not change the server types in nettype. To be totally consistent, it probably should create a fourth server type, "id," for IDS systems, just to alleviate confusion. Here, the "OnLine" term refers to versions 5.X, 6.X, 7.X, 8.X, and 9.X. If it's not an Informix SE engine, it will be "OnLine" in this area only.

The third field in the sqlhosts file is the hostname of the target system. This must correspond either to a hostname in the hosts file or for versions later than 7.10.UD1, to the actual IP address of the server. The final field is the service to be used for the connection. This entry must correspond to a valid service name in the services file. Both the client and the server must be using the same ports for the service, although the names do not necessarily have to be the same, although not having them the same seems needlessly complicated. For engines after 7.10.UD1, the services file may be bypassed by placing a service number rather than a service name in this field. The last two entries in our sample sqlhosts file illustrate doing this.

MANAGING SQLHOSTS WITH SETNET

On UNIX systems. ensuring that the correct entries are placed in the sqlhosts file is strictly a manual job. Informix has simplified this greatly with the inclusion of the `setnet` utility on NT systems. Actually, `setnet` originally saw light as part of Informix-Net for OnLine 5.X clients running on Windows 3.1. In the time since then, Informix-Net went from being a 16-bit application to being a 32-bit application called Informix-Connect. `Setnet` became `setnet32`.

It is possible to run both the 16-bit and the 32-bit connectivity packages on the same machine if this is needed. Install the 16-bit I-Net first. Go into %INFORMIXDIR%\bin and rename `setnet.exe` to `setnet16.exe`. Rename ilogin.exe to ilogin16.exe. Then go ahead and install the 32-bit Informix-Connect product in the same directory tree. The 16-bit connectivity should be used with 16-bit clients, and the 32-bit connectivity should be used with 32-bit clients. Trying to run a 16-bit connectivity package with a 32-bit application package will not succeed.

When you run `setnet32`, you get the following screen:

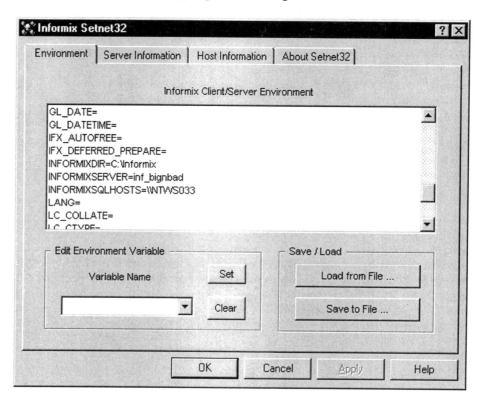

You will see four tabbed pages:

- Environment: Holds the environmental variables for the instance. This is a definite improvement over having to set the variables in startup scripts ala UNIX.
- Server Information: This tabbed page is where the information that UNIX machines keeps in the sqlhosts file goes on Windows systems.
- Host Information: Includes the hostname, the user to log in as, whether or not to ask explicitly for a password, and an encrypted version of the password.
- About `Setnet32`: Just a standard "about" page. There's a help button at the bottom of the form.

Let's look at the salient pages, one by one.

Environment

In the example on the previous page you will see that the list of environment variables has been scrolled down about two-thirds of the way, down to the area that most often gets used. These three variables are usually filled in automatically, but if their values are wrong, the communications will fail:

```
INFORMIXDIR              =  c:\informix
INFORMIXSERVER           = inf_bignbad
INFORMIXSQLHOSTS         = \\ntws033
```

For those of you who are not familiar with the "\\ntws033" nomenclature, this is the way that NT identifies names of servers on the network. If you have troubles with this variable, try using the fully qualified name, like this:

```
INFORMIXSQLHOSTS         = \\ntws033.mydomain.com
```

To change a variable on this screen, highlight it in the left-hand panel. The name appears in the lower-left panel, just above the drop-down list box. To change the value, type the new value in the list box and hit the "Set" button. The information is not actually committed to the registry until you hit either the "OK" or the "Apply" button at the bottom. Unless you use the set button followed by either "OK" or "Apply," the value will not be committed to the registry.

This list of environmental variables is taken directly from the help system of setnet32 for IDS 7.3 on NT:

```
CC8BITLEVEL     Specifies how the C-language compiler proc-
esses non-ASCII (8-bit and multibyte) characters. ESQL/C
only

CLIENT_LOCALE   Specifies the locales that the ESQL/C appli-
cation uses to perform read/write operations that involve
the keyboard, display, file, or printer on the client com-
puter.     Any valid locale specifier.

COLLCHAR  Specifies that existing ESQL/C applications take
advantage of the NLS collation feature without requiring a
change in their code. You must also set DBNLS to 1 or 2.
Provided for backward compatibility with NLS products.
```

CONRETRY Specifies the maximum number of additional connection attempts made to a database server in the time limit
that CONTIME specifies. Same as INFORMIXCONRETRY.

CONTIME   Specifies the number of seconds an SQL CONNECT
statement continues to try establishing a connection before
it generates an error. Same as INFORMIXCONTIME.

DB_LOCALE Specifies the locale of all the databases that an
ESQL/C application accesses in a single connection (the database locale). Any valid locale name.

DBALSBC   When set to 1, enables compatibility with ALS
products. 0 or 1.

DBANSIWARN   When turned on (y), causes the ESQL/C pre-
processor to check for Informix extensions to ANSI-standard
SQL syntax at compile time, and causes an ESQL/C application
to check for Informix extensions at runtime.

DBAPICODE allows pre-7.2 systems that use nonstandard or
rare code sets to access databases that store data in a
standard code set. Maximum size = 23 characters. Provided
for backward compatibility with NLS and ALS product. Usage
and values depend on language system.

DBASCIIBC When set to 1, enables compatibility with Ascii
Cop. Products. 0 or 1

DBCENTURY Specifies how to expand values of two-digit-year
DATE and DATETIME values.

P = past century,
R = present century,
C = closest century.
F = future century

DBCODESET Specifies an Asian-locale code set. Overrides the
code set that DB_LOCALE specifies. Provided for backward
compatibility with Version 4.x and 5.x ALS products. Same
value as ALS DBAPICODE.(8859-1) unless the informix.rc file
specifies another system-wide default.

DBCONNECT Specifies whether or not connections are restricted. 1 or 3.

DBCSCONV Controls code-set conversion initialization. Maximum size is 8 characters. Provided for backward compatibility with ALS products.   1 or 2:<codesetname>.

DBCSOVERRIDE   Forces the user-specified DB_LOCALE to override default restrictions on accessing databases with locales different from DB_LOCALE. Provided for backward
compatibility with Version 6.0 ALS database servers.   0
or 1.

DBCSWIDTH   Maximum number of display bytes (1-2) and
storage bytes (1-4) for the characters in up to three code
sets. Display and storage widths are separated by commas.
Code sets are separated by colons. Maximum size of this
field is, therefore, 11 characters. Provided for backward
compatibility with ALS products.   Example:1,1:2,3 means a
display and storage width of 1 byte for character set 1; a
display width of 2 bytes and a storage width of 3 bytes for
code set 2.

DBDATE   Specifies the end-user format for DATE values so
that they can conform with various international date conventions. Provided for backward compatibility with pre-7.2
products. Informix recommends GL_DATE for new applications.
MDY4 unless NLS variable LC_TIME is activated).

DBFLTMSK Specifies the number of decimal digits to use when
storing a DECIMAL, SMALLFLOAT, or FLOAT data type in a character buffer.   0-16

DBLANG   Specifies the subdirectory of the %INFORMIXDIR%
directory that contains the product -specific message (.iem)
files.   (%INFORMIXDIR%\msg)

DBMONEY   Specifies the end-user format for MONEY values so
that they can conform with various international and local
monetary conventions. ($.,)

DBMONEYSCALE   Specifies the total number of digits and
number of of decimal digits for monetary values. Provided
for backward compatibility with NLS products.

DBNLS   Specifies whether an ESQL/C application can access
NLS features. Provided for backward compatibility with NLS
products.

DBPATH   Identifies the database severs (online) or directories that contain databases that the ESQL/C application
accesses.

DBSS2   Maximum size is 4 characters. Provided for backward compatibility with ALS products.   0x00-0xff or 0-255

DBSS3   Maximum size 4 characters. Provided for backward
compatiblity with ALS products.   0x00-0xff or 0-255

DBTEMP   Specifies the directory on the client computer
that the ESQL/C processor uses to store temporary files
(also called swap files).   (\tmp)

DBTIME   Specifies the end-user format for DATETIME values
so that the user can conform with various international date
conventions. Provided for backward compatibility with pre-
7.2 products. Informix recommends GL_DATETIME for new ESQL/C
applications.   (%Y-%m-%d%H:%M:%S)

DELIMIDENT   Indicates whether (y) or not (n) to interpret strings in double quotes as delimited identifiers.

ESQLMF   Indicates whether the ESQL/C processor automatically invokes the ESQL/C multibyte filter (value=1 and
CC8BITLEVEL<3, or not value=0). ESQL/C only.

FET_BUF_SIZE   Allows you to override the default size of
the fetch buffer.   Any valid buffer size, in
bytes.(Default value depends on row size.)

GL_DATE   Specifies a customized end-user format for DATE
values.

GL_DATETIME   Specifies a customized end-user format for
DATETIME values.

INFORMIXDIR   Identifies the location of the ESQL/C processor as well as the location of library files, message
files, header files, and other executables.

INFORMIXSERVER   Identifies the default database server.

INFORMIXSQLHOSTS   Specifies the name of the computer on
which the central registry resides.

LANG   Specifies the language environment (called a locale) for an NLS database that the ESQL/C application accesses. Provided for backward compatibility with Informix
NLS products.

LC_COLLATE   Specifies a collation or sort sequence for
data in NCHAR and NVARCHAR columns of an NLS database. Provided for backward compatibility

LC_CTYPE Specifies character attributes such as character
classification and case conversion of regular expressions
for data in NCHAR and NVARCHAR columns of an NLS database.
Provided for backward compatibility.

LC_MONETARY   Specifies the end-user format for MONEY values in an NLS database. Provided for backward compatibility.

LC_NUMERIC   Specifies the end-user format for numeric
values in an NLS database. Provided for backward compatibility with NLS products.

LC_TIME   Specifies the end-user format for DATE and
DATETIME values in an NLS database. Provided for backward
compatibility with NLS products.

For more information about these environment variables, their syntax, and acceptable
values, see Chapter 4 of the Informix Guide to SQL: Reference. Remember that the NT
products store all of these values in the registry, not as conventional environment variables.
Keeping the environmental variables along with the connection information simplifies the
task of administering multiple client/server systems.

Another feature of setnet that simplifies these administrative duties is the ability to save these settings to a file and to retrieve them from a file. To save the connectivity portions of the Informix registry to a file, hit the "Save to File" button.

Setnet files have the default suffix of ".nfx." These files are simple ASCII files that contain the relevant connectivity and environmental variables. You can move these files from system to system   These files do not contain any information about the available protocols on each individual system. The available protocols that populate the "protocols" list box in the Server Information page are placed there by the Informix setup program.

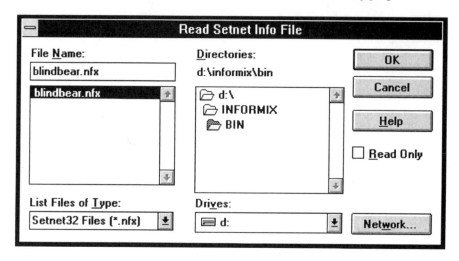

The save and load programs perform a complete replacement of the registry data. There is currently no provision for merging the output files rather than totally replacing them. This could probably be done fairly easily by hand, but it is really easier to designate one machine as the master SQLHOSTS machine. You can then make all of your changes on that machine, and either point all the other clients to that machine for SQLHOSTS or create an ".nfx" file from that machine and export the file to other clients for loading.

Server Information

The server information screen is where the "traditional" sqlhosts data is stored, that is, the same information that is included in the Informix sqlhosts file on UNIX. Both the Informix Server and HostName listboxes are populated from already-defined systems in your registry. The Protocol name information is placed there by the Informix install.

Beginning with IDS 7.30, there is a fifth edit box entitled "Options," in which special options to the server are included. Click on the "Make Default Server" to designate the currently-chosen server as the default server. In conjunction with setting the INFORMIX-SERVER variable, this will allow easier access to your most commonly used server.

As an aside, several of the third-party tools that communicate with Informix systems prefer to talk only to the default server. This is the case with the 5.X versions of PowerBuilder. To talk to any other servers in this environment, you also have to write code to change the default server registry entry. This is supposedly fixed in PowerBuilder 6.0, but if you have an application that can't seem to connect to your Informix database, try making that database the default. It can't hurt.

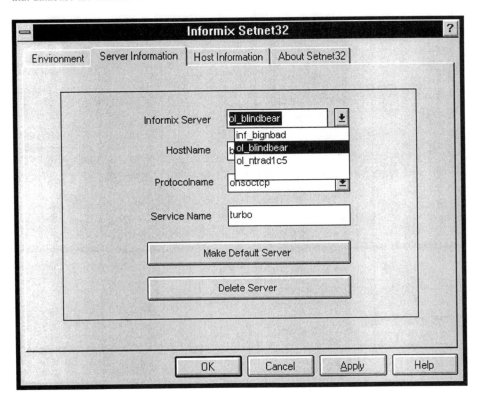

Host Information

The Host Information screen allows the user to include information about logins and pass-words for the host. If you are adding a server into `setnet` and if you do not have a previ-ous host information entry for it, you will need to enter the host information here.

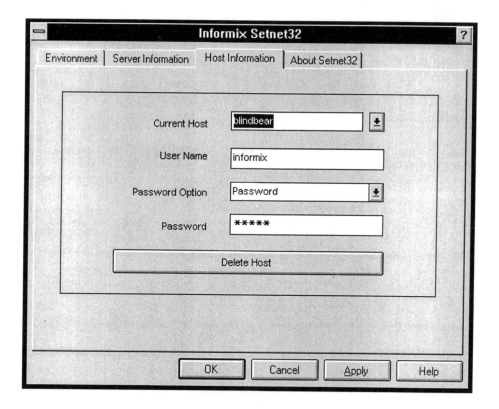

The Password Option box allows three options:

- Ask password at runtime
- Password
- No Password

- Using the "Ask password at runtime" can sometimes be of help when testing connectivity. Sometimes it is difficult to determine exactly which server you're talking to, and if your servers have different passwords, sometimes this will help you be certain you're talking to the right machine

NETWORK SECURITY AND TRUST RELATIONSHIPS

Since the Informix database products stem from a UNIX environment, it is not surprising that the model for security is the UNIX model. In a UNIX environment it is required that a user have a valid entry in the /etc/passwd (or /etc/shadow) files. Informix uses the UNIX security to decide whether or not to let the user into the system, and Informix takes the security a step further by specifying access to tables and other data objects within the database itself. For now, we are just interested in the ability for a user to get into the system, that is, get past the UNIX security.

The dbaccess program is a good example of the nature of this security. When dbaccess starts up on a remote (client) machine, the user can choose databases in one of two ways. The first way is to simply select the database using either the "Query" or the "Database" option. The user is then presented with a listing of databases available on the server identified by the $INFORMIXSERVER variable. This server can either be a local server on the same machine as the dbaccess program or a remote machine. If the connectivity is set up properly, the user can access this server without needing to enter a password. The second method is to use the "Connect" menu option to choose a server. The user is then prompted to enter a login name and password. If these are correct, the user is then presented a list of databases on the remote machine, and from then on the remote server is treated just like a local database.

If the user can set the $INFORMIXSERVER variable to a server and log on without a password, then the connectivity is set up properly. If this doesn't work, but the user can use the "Connect" option to log on by entering a name and password, then there is a problem with the security or trust relationship between the two machines.

We're referring to the failure to connect without a password as a "failure." There could be valid reasons for this to be correct behavior depending upon the security needs and requirements of the system. In most development applications, though, the system needs to be set up to allow users and DBAs convenient, unfettered access to all the servers on the system, and this requires that they be able to connect without a password.

An analogous UNIX concept is the use of the rlogin command to login from one machine to the other. For rlogin to work properly, there must be matching usernames and passwords on each machine, as well as a *trusted* relationship between the two systems. A trust relationship between two machines and/or users means that the user on one machine is *equivalent* to the user on the other. This trusted relationship can be enforced by two UNIX level files.

/etc/hosts.equiv

The /etc/hosts.equiv file allows a user from one server to log into a target server without a password as long as the sending server's username is a valid username on the target server. For example, suppose the system administrator wants to give user joe on machine the_client to be able to access the_server as user joe without a password. He would place the following entry in the /etc/hosts.equiv file:

```
the_client        joe
```

The format is servername, whitespace, username. Alternatively, entering a "+" as the only field on a line would give unlimited access to all users on all known servers. Note that there may be differences in the use of both the /etc/hosts.equiv and .rhosts files depending upon your version of UNIX. Check your manpages if you are not sure.

This file can also be placed on a Windows NT system, where it serves the same function for Informix. Put in the same directory as your hosts file.

~/.rhosts

The .rhosts file is located in the home directory of the user name you wish to use on the server. For example, if you wanted a user on client the_client named joe to be able to log into server the_server as user john, in john's home directory on server the_server, john would place an .rhosts file containing the following:

```
the_client            joe
```

If user john wanted to allow unrestricted logins by anybody, anywhere (in blatant violation of just about every security rule in the book), he would enter

```
*    *
```

The general format for the .rhosts file is server_name followed by white space followed by username. The asterisks indicate wildcards for server and login.

This file can also be placed in a user's home directory on a Window NT system. To do this, though, the user must be set up with a home directory in the user manager program. Put the .rhosts file there and it will behave just like it does in UNIX.

Security Implications of /etc/hosts.equiv and ~/.rhosts

These two files affect more than just Informix. They allow remote logins from foreign machines and can have adverse UNIX security implications. For example if you made the root accounts equivalent on two machines, if the root account was compromised on one machine, it would also be compromised on the other. In fact, if you have a complicated trust relationship between multiple machines, a security failure on any one of the machines can affect security on all of the systems.

The ~/.netrc File

As an attempt to partially alleviate some of the security issues, Informix can also use a third UNIX file, the .netrc file in the user's home directory. This file contains information about alternative usernames and passwords that can be used to connect with a machine that is not trusted and does not have a ~/.rhosts file. This file is used in UNIX for allowing ftp access between systems, and Informix has expanded its use to include access to the database. Be aware that entries in this file may open you up to some ftp security issues.

The format of the file is different from both the .rhosts and /etc/hosts.equiv files in that it requires the use of three tokens followed by the values of the tokens. These tokens are:

- machine: Use this token followed by whitespace followed by another machine's name
- login: Use this token followed by whitespace followed by the login name you want to use
- password: Use this token followed by whitespace followed by the password to be used on the other machine

As an example, if you are user joe on machine the_client and want to be able to log into machine the_server as user fake_user with password fake_password, you would put the following line into your .netrc in the joe home directory on the_client:

```
machine the_server  login  fake_user password fake_password
```

Again, realize that there are some security implications here also. Most noticeable is the fact that the password for the user fake_user is written in plaintext as fake_password. In most development environments, security is of little concern, since everyone wants unfettered access to everything. Be aware, though, that as you move into a production environment, you will need to be much more critical of security. Before using any of these three UNIX files to relax security, be sure that your system administrator knows what you are doing and why.

There is no analogue to the .netrc file on Windows NT systems. If you want to be able to access another server with a different login name, you must do it through `setnet32`.

REGISTRY USE WITH WINDOWS NT CLIENTS

For many users, the Windows NT registry is a bit of a mystery, enough so that when users experience problems with their registry setup, often the only solution they are comfortable with is to completely reinstall the products. While this is usually the safest solution, it is often not the solution of choice.

The NT registry is divided into a series of *hives*, which is the term for the tree structure in which the data is organized. The registry is actually kept in two hidden flat files in the operating system directory. Each Windows system that supports the registry uses a differently named program to view and edit the registry:

- Windows 3.51:   Use regedt32
- Windows 4.0:   Use either regedt32 or regedit
- Windows 95:   Use regedit

As an example, we'll look at the listing of root-level hives on a Windows 95 system using regedit:

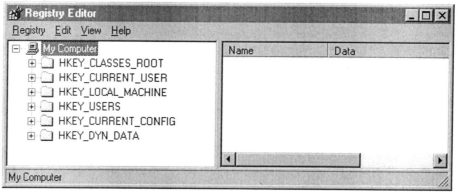

Informix Windows client and server products use two of the six main registry hives:

- \\HKEY_CURRENT_USER\Software\Informix: Holds user-level profile information.
- \\HKEY_LOCAL_MACHINE\Software\Informix: Holds Informix global information for all users.

Each of the registry editing programs gives you the option of saving either the entire registry or parts of it to a file. By default these files end in the suffix *.reg. It is a good idea on all Windows 95 and Windows NT systems to occasionally take a copy of the registry files and keep this copy with your backups. Also, be sure that your backup program is capable of and actually does take a copy of the registry with backups. If the registry becomes corrupted, your entire system may be unusable.

For those who do many client installs, sometimes it is handy to place the install files on the network and do the install over the network. This can be done in one of two ways. Either place the "raw" install disk data on a hard disk and run the setup program for each install, or copy from an existing, running system. Using the install program is the recommended solution from Informix, but that entails a lot of duplicate work and is very difficult or impossible to totally automate via a script.

On the other hand, just taking a copy of the %INFORMIXDIR directory will not save the registry data, and your new system will not be usable without the registry information. Fortunately, it is possible to use the regedit program to get around this. First, on an installed and correctly operating machine, save off a copy of the \Software\Informix subtrees on the two hives, \\HKEY_CURRENT\USER and \\HKEY\LOCAL\MACHINE. Save each hive with a unique name. Then copy the entire directory tree of the Informix products you want to copy to the new machine, being sure that the directory tree and disk naming conventions are the same. Then go into regedit and load the copies of each of the two hives you saved. Finally, allow the new user to go into `setnet32` and supply her own passwords. This a simple solution that can easily be incorporated into a script.

As an educational exercise, the user can go into the regedit program and browse through the hives and subhives in order to see exactly what Informix is doing with your registry. As long as you do not make any modifications to the registry, this is a safe procedure and can give you a much better understanding of what is happening under the covers.

Another source of registry information is in the help file for the `setnet32` program. As a general rule, the help files of all of the Informix products for Windows contains a lot of good, useful information. The screen shot on the next page comes from the `setnet32` help file system. Go through the help files and explore all of the little nooks and crannies. Click on all of the hyperlinks. Who knows what you'll find?

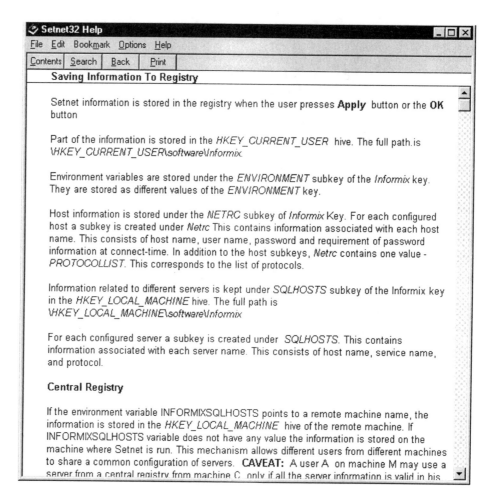

CONNECTION OPTIONS

IDS on both Windows NT and UNIX systems have a relatively recent option (beginning with 7.10) to the sqlhosts file (or registry) that provides security and maintenance information to Informix-Connect. These options are placed in the sqlhosts file as the last field, as follows:

```
ol_theserver   onsoctcp   the_server  turbo    k=1,s=1,b=4000
```

Everything to the right of the "turbo" is options, separated by commas. These options have the following meanings. On later NT systems (IDS 7.3+), the `setnet32` program has a separate listbox for options. On earlier NT systems it may be possible to set or change these options by manually editing the registry. Back it up first.

Keep-Alive Options (k)

These options determine what happens when the networking system detects that the client and server are not communicating. Keep-alive can be enabled on the client end, the server end, or both. These keep-alive options are used for networking protocols over TCP/IP or IPX/SFX. If keep-alive is enabled from the client side, the networking service will periodically poll the engine to see if it is still alive. If keep-alive is enabled from the engine side, the networking service will periodically poll the clients to see if they are still alive. If the polling side does not contact the polled side within a certain time limit (usually determined by an operating system kernel parameter), the polling system's resources are released when the connection fails.

The problem here is that the networking system expects a return communication within a certain amount of time. If the connection is still active, but response time is slowed significantly because of network traffic, the system can be fooled into thinking that the connection is broken, when in fact it is only slow.

The default value is k=1, which enables keep-alive. Having keep-alive active does impose an additional load on both the system and the network, but unless your network is horribly saturated to the state that the additional networking load is significant and you are getting frequent false disconnects because of network latency, keep it enabled.

```
k=0, Disables the keep-alive feature.
k=1, Enables the keep-alive feature.
```

Security Options (r, s)

These options control whether or not the networking service allows usage of the various UNIX security files listed on previous pages.

```
r=0, Disables the ~/.netrc lookup from the client side.
r=1, Enables the ~/.netrc lookup from the client side default setting for the client side).
s=0, Disables both /etc/hosts.equiv and ~/.rhosts lookup from the server side.
s=1, Enables only the /etc/hosts.equiv lookup from the server side.
s=2, Enables only the ~/.rhosts lookup from the server side.
s=3, Enables both /etc/hosts.equiv and ~/.rhosts lookup on the server side (Default setting
for the server side).
```

Buffer Options (b)

Unless specified with this option, the operating system will determine how large the buffers should be for the communications between systems. If you find yourself consistently transferring very large buffers, you may gain some speed improvements by adjusting the buffer sizes. The buffer sizes should be identical on both client and server. This parameter can be useful in handling the transfer of large blobs.

    `b=n, Specify the space (in bytes) reserved for the communications buffer.`

When these Options Become Effective

Options from the client side become effective as soon as you change the parameters either in the `setnet32` program or in the sqlhosts file. The next connection made will reflect these new options. For server-side parameters, the options can be changed at any time but will not become effective until the server is shut down and restarted.

TESTING CONNECTIVITY WITH ILOGIN

Once you have set up all of the sqlhosts, hosts, and services information, the final step is to try to actually connect up to that machine. Informix provides a program called "ilogin," which will attempt to log into a remote system and provide some information that is included in the demo "stores" database. Running ilogin brings up the following screen (resized smaller for this book):

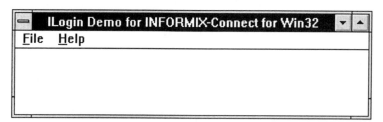

The ilogin program was actually a demo program for one of the earlier versions of ESQL/C for Windows. If you can find an earlier version (around 7.1 - 7.2) with ESQL/C installed, you can view the source code. Reading through this source code is a good exercise if you want to see how Informix handles setting communications variables internally.

When you choose the "File" menu from ilogin, you get the following screen:

```
┌─────────────────────────────────────────────┐
│ ⊟            Login Parameters                │
├─────────────────────────────────────────────┤
│  Server          ┌───────────────────────┐  │
│                  └───────────────────────┘  │
│  Hostname        ┌───────────────────────┐  │
│                  └───────────────────────┘  │
│  Servicename     ┌───────────────────────┐  │
│                  └───────────────────────┘  │
│  Protocolname    ┌───────────────────────┐  │
│                  └───────────────────────┘  │
│  Username        ┌───────────────────────┐  │
│                  └───────────────────────┘  │
│  Password        ┌───────────────────────┐  │
│                  └───────────────────────┘  │
│  Stores Database │stores7                │  │
│                  └───────────────────────┘  │
│              Fill in desired values.        │
│  Server, Host, Service, Protocol, User and Password │
│      fields will be read from Registry if left blank. │
│   Stores7 will be used if Database field is left blank. │
│        ┌──────────┐    ┌──────────┐         │
│        │   OK     │    │  Cancel  │         │
│        └──────────┘    └──────────┘         │
└─────────────────────────────────────────────┘
```

If you do not fill any of the blanks and just hit the "OK" button, ilogin will try to access the server that you have specified as "default" in `setnet`. It tries to read a customer table from the stores7 demonstration database. This database is not installed automatically during Informix installs and is quite often not installed on production machines. You can change the "Stores Database" to a database that is on the machine if you wish. If the stores database is not installed on the target server, hitting OK in ilogin gives you the following error screen:

This is a case in which getting an error message indicates success. Ilogin was able to log onto the default system and did not find stores7, so it told you so. This means that the connectivity is established and verified from your client to your target server.

If you do have the "stores7" database installed on your server, you will get a screen like the following:

```
┌─────────────────────────────────────────────┐
│ ▬          Customer Records Found            │
├─────────────────────────────────────────────┤
│                                              │
│   Number  First Name    Last Name            │
│  ┌─────────────────────────────────────┬──┐  │
│  │ 101    Ludwig         Pauli         │ ♦ │ │
│  │ 102    Carole         Sadler        │ ▓ │ │
│  │ 103    Philip         Currie        │ ▓ │ │
│  │ 104    Anthony        Higgins       │   │ │
│  │ 105    Raymond        Vector        │   │ │
│  │ 106    George         Watson        │   │ │
│  │ 107    Charles        Ream          │   │ │
│  │ 108    Donald         Quinn         │   │ │
│  │ 109    Jane           Miller        │   │ │
│  │ 110    Roy            Jaeger        │   │ │
│  │ 111    Frances        Keyes         │   │ │
│  │ 112    Margaret       Lawson        │   │ │
│  │ 113    Lana           Beatty        │ ♦ │ │
│  └─────────────────────────────────────┴──┘  │
│                                              │
│                ┌──────────┐                  │
│                │    Ok    │                  │
│                └──────────┘                  │
└─────────────────────────────────────────────┘
```

This is also a success, since ilogin was able to log onto the target server and extract information. I mentioned earlier that sometimes it is a challenge to verify exactly which Informix server you are talking to, especially in environments where you have multiple servers and multiple hosts. There's a little trick that I use that makes it simpler. If you have stores7 installed, go into the database and delete all of the rows from the customer table. Then enter one row that has the name of the server that holds the database as the "lname" or "fname" variable. Since this is the data pulled back in ilogin, when you connect you'll get a screen that looks like this:

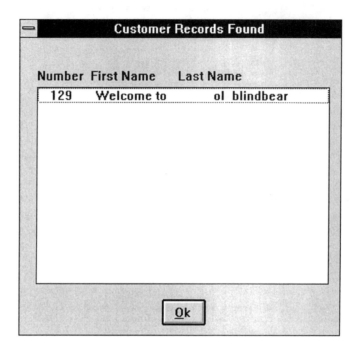

You now have proof positive that you are connected to the system you think you are connected to. You can also accomplish a similar task by entering the name of another unique database in the "Stores Database" edit box on the ilogin Run screen. It will go out to the chosen database and display an empty customer screen, thus showing that you have connected to a machine that contains the proper database name.

If you wish to test connectivity to other systems that are in the sqlhosts file (or registry) but are not the default database, you can enter the Server Name, Host Name, and other sqlhosts information directly into the ilogin Run screen. These systems must be available either in setnet or sqlhosts. Just entering the names in ilogin does not create the sqlhosts information. Being able to enter the parameters manually can be a useful tool for debugging Informix connectivity, as you can try overriding the sqlhosts information. For example, you could enter "1526" instead of "turbo." If it worked with "1526" but not with "turbo," you would look at your services file to see why the translation is not working correctly.

COMMON INFORMIX-CONNECT ERRORS

908 Error: Mismatched Client/Server Port Numbers

This is a common, but quite cryptic error message. Finderr gives the following detail for IDS systems:

```
-908
Attempt to connect to database server (servername, con-
err=connection-error-number, oserr=system-error-number)
failed.

The program or application is trying to access another data-
base server but has failed. Note the server name in the cur-
rent statement. Note also the connection error number and/or
system error number that is shown in the message.

The desired database server is unavailable, or the network
is down or is congested. Ask your DBA and system administra-
tor to verify that the server and network are operational.
If the network is congested, use the environment variables
INFORMIXCONTIME and INFORMIXCONRETRY to tune connection tim-
ing. See Chapter 4 in the Informix Guide to SQL: Reference
for information on setting these environment variables.
```

This really doesn't tell you a lot about the problem. What the message says is that there's some problem with network connectivity. Most of the time the problem will be a difference in the listening ports in use by the client and the server. Check the sqlhosts files on each or use setnet on Windows systems and make sure that both client and server are using the same port numbers.

One common mistake is to not realize that the chosen service on the host for an instance does not change when it is changed in setnet. Actual use of the server does not start until you shut down the engine and restart it. The best procedure is to shut the server down, change the sqlhosts information, and then restart the engine.

If you're getting this error on IDS systems later than 7.10UD1, try using the actual port number rather than its name in setnet. If this works, there is a problem in the services file. Look for a conflict with an existing port number.

Of course, don't rule out the possibility that you're getting this error message and that it's telling exactly what's happening. You're having network problems. If you suspect this, try pinging the host system.

931 Error: Can't Find the Proper Servicename

```
-931
Cannot locate servicename service/tcp service in
/etc/services.
```

The service servicename is not listed in the network configuration file /etc/services (UNIX) or (DOS). Check the
$INFORMIXDIR/etc/sqlhosts file, and check that the service
name for the desired server is correct. If so, contact your
network administrator to find out why the service is not
known. If you are using INFORMIX-OnLine for NetWare, check
the file on the client for the required entries.

    This is a somewhat more specific error message that indicates that the service name
you entered in setnet is not found in the services file. If possible try switching the name
with the actual service number in post IDS 7.10UD1 systems.

951 & -956 Errors: Problems with Trust

```
-951
User username is not known on the database server.
```

The database server that you tried to access does not accept
either your user ID, the login name that is specified for
the desired server host in your ~/.netrc file, or the user
name that is specified in the USER clause of a CONNECT
statement. If you are explicitly specifying your user name
in the ~/.netrc file or in a CONNECT statement, check that
the name is correct. If you do not have a valid user ID on
the server machine, see your system administrator.

```
-956
Client client-name is not in /etc/hosts.equiv on the remote
host.
```

This operation cannot be completed because the specified remote machine does not recognize the name of the client machine (the local host, whose name the hostname command
returns). Client names are normally recorded in the configuration file /etc/hosts.equiv. The rhosts file on the remote
machine might also need modification. For more information
on these files and the relation between them, try man rhosts
on a UNIX system. See the remote host administrator to ensure that the client host name is specified in
/etc/hosts.equiv file for the remote host.

INFORMIX-CLI: ODBC FOR INFORMIX

The type of connectivity provided by the I-Net and I-Connect products is known as *native* connectivity. It is driven by, written by, and proprietary to the Informix Corporation. The other type of connectivity is known as *open* connectivity, and is driven by adherence to standards and to free interoperability between vendors. In order to open the Informix data-base engines to the rest of the non-Informix world, Informix provides ODBC communications with the Informix-CLI (Call Level Interface) product.

Informix-CLI is an ODBC (Open DataBase Connectivity) driver that communicates using the Informix-Connect native database drivers. There are third-party ODBC drivers available that include their own connectivity mechanisms, which claim to be faster than an ODBC driver piggybacking on top of a native driver. One drawback with such drivers is that it is usually necessary to run a special server process on the server host that handles the host's end of the data communications. ODBC is almost strictly a client-side operation. All IDS and most OnLine systems will support ODBC connections with no modifications.

Many third-party reporting and data manipulation programs use ODBC to be able to connect to many databases. Once you set up ODBC on a client system, you can usually use a plethora of tools from various vendors against the same Informix database. We'll concentrate on setting up the Informix-CLI product on Windows NT systems. Most tools using ODBC are Windows-based, so most of your ODBC setups will be on NT systems.

Configure Informix-Connect First

The ODBC services provided by Informix-CLI are transported over the existing communications links provided by Informix-Connect. No ODBC communications will work unless the underlying communication methods are in place. Thus, before you set up ODBC, you have to have gone through the processes listed earlier in this chapter for setting up and testing Informix-Connect connections.

Installing Informix-CLI

Informix-CLI is available in several forms from Informix. At lease with CD distributions of IDS 7.24 for NT, both I-Connect and I-CLI were included on the CD distribution. I have heard that later versions of the engine do not include them. The IDS Developer 7.30 distribution does not include Informix-CLI, although it includes ESQL/C. Informix has a software development kit (SDK) that allows programmers to write and execute ODBC compliant code.

The install scripts for various versions all contain an Informix-Connect version. Before you attempt to install Informix-CLI, check whether there is already an Informix-Connect installed on your client. If there is one installed already, consider doing a test install of Informix-CLI that does not replace your current Informix-Connect. At the very least, realize that installing the Informix-Connect included with CLI may be dangerous to existing communications-dependent programs, and monitor them carefully for error after installing CLI.

Configuring Informix-CLI

This configuration example uses Informix-CLI Version 2.5. At press time, the latest available CLI was Version 3.1, which has a different interface from Version 2.5. The later version makes use of a tabbed user interface much like that of `setnet32`. The concepts will be the same no matter what version you are using.

The ODBC administrator program controls the setup of ODBC connections. This program can usually be found in the folder or program group that is created during the CLI install process. It can also be found as an icon in the Windows Control Panel. The one administrator program can control ODBC connections to multiple databases from multiple vendors. There are two terms in ODBC that are often confused:

- Data Source: A data source is information about the data that is to be retrieved via ODBC as well as information about how to access the data, such as database name, Informix-Connect parameters, hostname, and the like.

- ODBC Driver: A driver is a dynamic-link library (DLL) that a client application can use to insert, retrieve, and manipulate data in a database. Drivers are specific for various brands of databases.

The program starts and gives you a display of existing data sources. You may select one of the existing data sources for modification through the "Setup" button or for deletion using the "Delete" button.

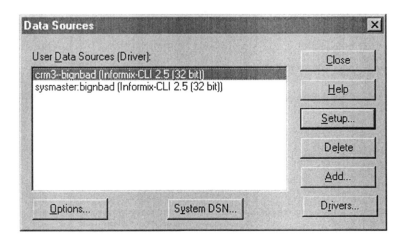

The "Options" button opens a screen that can be very handy in debugging an ODBC connection. If the "Trace ODBC Calls" box is checked, the system will log every ODBC request to a log file that the user can select. Although this tracing process may slow the ODBC connection down considerably, the logfile records the entire communication between client and server.

Be aware, though, that this logfile can not only slow access; it can also consume lots and lots of disk space as the logfile grows. If you're making the decision to turn ODBC tracing on, be careful to shut it off as soon as you have the information you need. If you are debugging a problem with an existing ODBC installation, check to be sure that someone hasn't left the tracing on inadvertently.

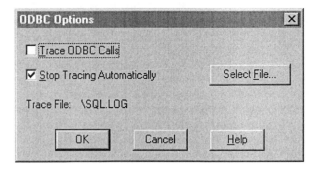

Going back to the "Data Sources" screen, hitting the "Add" button will add a data source to the ODBC system. A list of installed ODBC drivers is shown. Choose the ODBC driver that you want to use for this data source, in our case Informix-CLI 2.5 (32 bit).

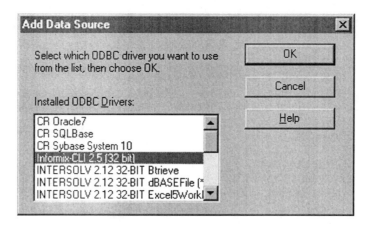

Once you've chosen your ODBC driver, you will get a screen allowing you to enter the specific information for your ODBC setup.

Both the data source name and the description boxes are informative in nature and can be just about anything you want them to be. The database name should be in the "databasename@servername" format. The information under the "Advanced" tab is automatically filled in and contains information from the sqlhosts registry entries.

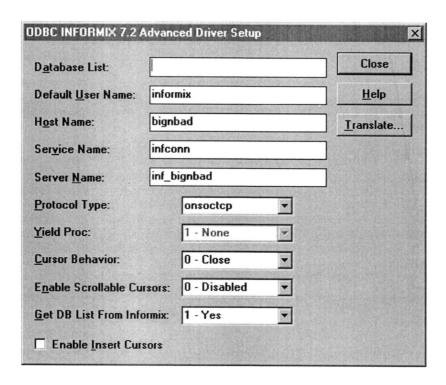

This information is optional, but you can activate such features as management of open cursors, use of scroll cursors, and use of insert cursors from this screen. There's also a "Translate" option that is designed to allow ODBC to handle translation between different character sets. This button allows the user to choose various DLLs that translate the data. This could also be used for encryption/decryption and compression/decompression of data. Unless you really know what you're doing, you don't even need to go into the advanced setup.

The ODBC administrator then returns to its initial screen and shows your new data source. If it gets this far, it has successfully set up the ODBC communications. You can test this by going to any of your client programs that use ODBC and trying to use your new data source.

## CHAPTER 9

Understanding the OnLine Utilities

*T*he discussion of the Informix utilities will be split over this and the next chapter. The IDS engine, while an order of magnitude more capabable than the earlier OnLine engines, still stems from an OnLine code base. Since the IDS engine was to be backwardly compatible to the earlier OnLine engines, much remained the same from OnLine to IDS. In fact, for the most part, the OnLine utilities are a subset of the same utilities for IDS. Since IDS does more, its utilities are more extensive, but just about everything that works in OnLine works the same, to a certain extent, in IDS.

This entire chapter is mostly unchanged from the first edition of the book. This chapter applies specifically to the OnLine engines. We will duplicate much of this chapter in the next chapter on IDS utilities, but there are enough differences between the two that it will be less confusing if we consider them separately. Chapter 10 will specifically cover the onstat utility in IDS.

The tb/onstat utility is the most important of the entire suite of OnLine utilities. It is used to inspect the pseudotables that are held in shared memory structures. In OnLine systems, this information cannot be determined without using the tb/onstat utility. Beginning with OnLine 6.0, Informix included the SMI (System Monitoring Interface) tables, which provide much of the same information as provided in tb/onstat in pseudotable form that is accessible by SQL statements. The SMI tables will be discussed in detail in Chapter 11.

Why is this information important? The main reason is that this is where the operations of the OnLine "black box" are recorded and controlled. For a regular user, the engine is simply the mechanism that translates his SQL statements into actual data returned from the database. This level of detail is enough for most users. The database administrator needs much more detailed information to troubleshoot problems, improve performance, and generally know what is going on inside the engine itself. For the same reasons that it is important for the DBA to understand the architecture and internal operations of the engine, the database administrator needs to understand all of the options, output codes, and interrelations of the tbstat program. The tbstat program is well documented in the *Informix OnLine Administrator's Guide*, and the reader is urged to become familiar with the relevant sections of the Guide. What the Guide doesn't cover, however, is the "why" and "how does this relate to my problem" type of question. The guide's information needs to be assimilated and used, but in order for the DBA to use the tool effectively, the administrator needs to know how the pieces fit together.

THE TBSTAT UTILITY

The tbstat program gives you instantaneous data about the contents of the shared memory structures. It takes very little CPU time, and locks no tables and creates no latches. As such, you can consider that tbstat is essentially "free"; that is, it has a minuscule effect on database performance. You can let it run continuously in the background if you wish, collecting performance data and usage data with little or no performance cost.

There is only one option that could possibly cause you any problems, and that is the tbstat -o filename option. This option places the *entire* contents of shared memory into a file specified by filename. If you have a large shared memory, be sure that you have sufficient room in your UNIX file system to save the file. This option will also cause significant I/O in the system if you have it saving a large shared memory file to disk.

The tbstat utility is often used as a troubleshooting tool. When you encounter problems in the engine such as unexpected freeze-ups, long transactions, deadlocks, and the like, you will turn to the tbstat utility to tell you what's happening in the engine. Usually, this is an effective technique, but sometimes your problem will be transient.

Since tbstat gives you an instantaneous snapshot, by the time you enter the correct tbstat command, the problem may be gone. If you are looking for solutions to these transient problems, you may need to use the tbstat -o filename option. The trick is to catch the database in the act of doing whatever it is doing and save the shared memory to a file.

If you can get the output file saved before the problem goes away, you can then inspect the output file at your leisure and run any or all of the `tbstat` options against the file without worrying about the transient problem going away. To do this you would use the following series of `tbstat` commands:

```
tbstat -o any_filename                           (takes the snapshot)
tbstat -"any_options" "filename"         (reports from snapshot file)
```

The first step in fully understanding the `tbstat` utility is understanding what all of the options mean. This is the help screen for `tbstat` (commonly used items are marked with an asterisk):

```
joe  60>tbstat --
usage: tbstat [-abcdklmpstuzBDFPRX] [-r secs][-o file][infile]
*     --     print this help screen
      -      print just the tbstat header (undocumented feature)
      a      print all info (options: bcdklmpstu)
      b      print buffers
      c      print configuration file
*     d      print dbspaces and chunks
*     k      print locks
*     l      print logging
      m      print message log
*     p      print profile
*     s      print latches
*     t      print tblspaces
*     u      print users
      z      zero profile counts
      B      print all buffers
      D      print dbspaces and detailed chunk stats
      F      print page flushers
      P      print profile, including BIGreads
      R      print LRU queues
      X      print entire list of sharers and waiters for buffers
*     r      repeat options every n seconds (default: 5)
      o      put shared memory into file (default: tbstat.out)
infile use infile to obtain shared memory information
```

Tbstat - -

Using this option displays the help screen for the `tbstat` command. This is actually the "minus" option, not the "minus minus" option. The first minus sign indicates that a command options follows; the second minus is the actual option.

This convention is followed by most of the OnLine utilities. Just enter `commandname   --` and you'll see the help text.

Tbstat -

Using just the first minus and a null option will show just the header of the `tbstat` series of commands. This header looks like:

```
RSAM Version 5.01.UC1   -- On-Line -- Up 7 days 23:54:27 -- 18704 Kbytes
```

This header includes five important sections. The first section gives the version number of the OnLine engine. The second section shows the current operating mode. Possible values of the mode are:

Offline:	Engine not running.
Quiescent:	No user can start a server process. User `informix` can use administrative options of `tbmonitor`. Any user can use `tbstat` or view options of `tbmonitor`.
Online:	Fully usable by all users.
Shutdown:	System is in transition from online to quiescent or from quiescent to offline. Cannot be canceled.
Recovery:	Moving from offline to quiescent. Fast recovery is performed here.

The third section is the (checkpoint) indicator. If applicable, this section can contain:

(CKPT REQ)	Some process has requested a checkpoint, and the engine is trying to initiate the checkpoint. This flag is often seen if the database is hung waiting for a checkpoint.

(CHKT INP)   Checkpoint is in progress. Users have read-only access to the database. No changes to data are allowed until the checkpoint ends.

The fourth section shows the real time that the database has been running, that is, the time since the last database startup. The fifth and final section shows the amount of shared memory in use by OnLine in kilobytes. This is roughly the size of the output file generated by the `tbstat -o` command.

Tbstat -d

The `tbstat -d` command provides several important pieces of information, the most important being the disk and chunk usage for the database. The output is divided into two sections, Dbspaces and Chunks.

```
joe  43>tbstat -d
RSAM Version 5.01.UC1   -- On-Line -- Up 7 days 23:48:38 -- 18704 Kbytes
Dbspaces
address   number   flags    fchunk   nchunks   flags    owner      name
e0016e88  1        1        1        3         N        informix  rootdbs
e0016eb8  2        1        4        2         N        informix  logspace
e0016ee8  3        1        5        2         N        informix  dbspace1
e0016f18  4        1        7        2         N        informix  logspace2
e0016f48  5        1        10       1         N        informix  slowdbspace
5 active, 20 total
```

address	Dbspace's address in the shared memory table.
number	Dspace's unique ID number. Dependent upon the order in which the dbspaces were created.
Flags	First series of flags describes mirroring, status, and/or blobspace status: 1 0x0001 Not mirrored 2 0x0002 Mirrored 3 0x0004 Dbspace is down 4 0x0008 Newly mirrored dbspace 5 0x0010 Blobspace
	Unique identifying number of the first chunk in the dbspace.
nchunks	Total number of chunks in this dbspace.

flags	Second series of flags gives essentially the same information as the first only using alphabetic codes:
	First position: M Mirrored
	N Not mirrored
	Second position: X Newly mirrored
	Third Position: B Blobspace
owner	User name of the owner of the dbspace.
name	Name of the dbspace.

tbstat -d output (dbspace section)

```
Chunks
address   chk/dbs offset    size      free      bpages    flags pathname
e0014e78 1   1    0         135000    35718               PO-   /dev/rootdbs3
e0014f10 2   1    0         57000     56997               PO-   /dev/rootdbs1
e0014fa8 3   1    0         75000     74997               PO-   /dev/rootdbs2
e0015040 4   2    0         147500    24542               PO-   /dev/log1
4 active, 27 total
```

address	Address of the chunk.
chk	Unique ID number of the chunk.
dbs	Number of the dbspace containing this chunk. Corresponds to the `number` field in the `dbspaces` output of this command.
Offset	Number of pages that this chunk is offset into the device, if any.
Size	Size of the chunk in pages.
free	Number of free pages in this chunk. This is the number of pages that are not part of any allocated tablespace. It does not take into account any unused pages within extents that are allocated to tablespaces.
Bpages	Number of free blobpages. Blobpages can have their own page sizes. Don't confuse this number with free pages. They don't necessarily correspond.

Flags	Status flags for the chunk, using the following codes:
	Position 1: P Primary chunk
	M Mirror chunk
	Position 2: O Chunk Online *
	D Chunk Down *
	R Recovering
	X Newly mirrored
	Position 3: B Blobspace
	- Dbspace
pathname	Either the device name or the path name of the UNIX cooked file that contains this chunk.

`tbstat -d` output (chunks section)

On most terminals, the screen displays for the O and the D letters are easily confused. It's often hard to tell from the screen whether a chunk is up or down. Versions prior to 5.0 can run with a chunk down, so it's important to watch your status.

Usage Tips

If you're like most DBAs, you'll spend a lot of time fighting the database "battle of the bulge." Murphy's Law says that any database will expand to fill the amount of space available. OnLine does not bother to warn you when you're beginning to fill up your disks.

The first sign of a problem will be when users get messages saying that OnLine cannot allocate more extents for a table. Especially when you're using raw devices, there is no easy way to tell how much disk space you are using.

The `tbstat -d` program is your most powerful tool for monitoring the usage of your disks. This invocation of `tbstat` is used to develop percentage full statistics for various `dbspaces` in the `status` script that we develop later. You'll probably develop various scripts on your own to massage the output of all the utilities. With `tbstat -d`, you'll find yourself writing scripts to answer such questions as "How much space is there left in dbspace X?"

Here it becomes important to have some naming conventions for your chunks and dbspaces. If all of the chunks contained in dbspace `dbs1` begin with the letters `dbs1`; for example, it will be a simple matter to `grep` for `dbs1` followed by the UNIX command, `awk '{print $6}'` to get the free space in `dbs1`. If you have the luxury of creating your databases from scratch, keep in mind this consistency in naming. Do the same with the names of your `dbspaces` dedicated to logfiles and with the names of your tables too if possible.

You may notice that the examples in this book do not always exhibit this level of fore-sight. I don't have the excuse of having inherited the databases. I developed many of these databases before I began developing DBA scripts to manage them. If you follow these recommendations, you'll do a better job. I know that doing so would have made my life as a scriptwriter a lot easier.

If you're not familiar with the capabilities of the UNIX commands `grep`, `sed`, and `awk` and with the operations of UNIX regular expressions, it may make some sense to learn them early in the game. Using these UNIX tools on the outputs of OnLine utilities can allow you to generate just about any sort of reports and data

Tbstat -D

This is a useful variant of the tbstat -d command. It provides exactly the same output as the tbstat -d command, with the exception that in the Chunks section the size and free statistics are replaced by page Rd and page Wr numbers representing the numbers of pages read from and written to in each of the chunks.

This option provides a very useful tool for locating "hotspots" in your databases, areas that have abnormally high I/O activity. Since disk I/O is most often the slowest activity your computer system will perform, the elimination or minimization of these hotspots can go a long way toward improving the performance of your databases.

One minor drawback to tbstat -D is that it reports cumulative data rather than instantaneous data. The statistics shown cover the time period beginning when OnLine was either last started or when the statistics were zeroed out. While it would be easy to write a script that subtracts out the last totals and only shows you the differences from the last time the script was run, there is an even easier way to do this. Write a short c-shell script and name it hotspot:

```
joe 51>  cat hotspot
#!/bin/csh
tbstat -D
tbstat -z
```

Every time you run the `hotspot` script, it will zero out the `tbstat` statistics when you finish. Each subsequent run will show the actual activity that has occurred since the last run. This is suitable for running hotspot repeatedly in one sitting or over a short period of time. It could be modified to save the date and statistics of the last run, but why get complicated? Just remember that running hotspot will zero out *all* of the `tbstat` statistics. If you (or any other user) are running cumulative statistics monitoring, the `tbstat -z`'s will interfere with this statistics gathering.

The most important thing I've discovered by running `hotspot` is the tremendous amount of activity that occurs to the physical logfile. Conventional wisdom says to locate the logfiles in an area that is optimized for heavy write activity. I had taken this advice to mean the logical logfiles. Study of hotspot output will show that it's the physical logfile that needs to be optimized. It is relatively easy to relocate and/or resize the physical logfile (the database does need to come down however). Watch your hotspots for a while and then experiment with relocating and resizing the physical log. You'll see how much activity it gets. It is also possible to experiment with the size of the physical log buffers as a way to optimize the writing activity.

Tbstat -z

Since we just used `tbmode -z` in a script, this may be a good time to talk about this command option. There's not much to say. It just zero's out everything. This does not affect anything in the database. You can zero it out all day long if you wish. Don't confuse these statistics with the statistics kept by the OnLine UPDATE STATISTICS command. That's a completely different subject. Just be aware of the fact that you may interfere with other statistics-gathering programs. I discourage my users from using any of the OnLine utilities, preferring to give them access through scripts that I control. That way, they won't be stepping on my toes.

If your OnLine system stays up for long periods of time without zeroing out the `tbstat` statistics, you'll eventually reach your UNIX limits on integer sizes and some of the numbers will roll over, showing negative numbers. To correct this, just run the `tbstat -z` program.

Tbstat -u

This option gives you an overview of the database processes that exist at any particular time. This option gives you data from the user pseudotable in the shared memory. It is useful as a debugging tool when the system has inexplicably frozen up and the DBA is attempting to find out what is going on. In the case where everything is frozen, you will need to compare information from this option with data from other `tbstat` options to trace down the offending process. This usually takes some time because you have to track the transactions through several invocations of the utility. If the database is hung up, probably nothing in the user table is changing and you can run multiple `tbstats` against the shared memory and get the same data. If the database is not frozen, you often run into a problem because the data in the user table is changing. In this instance it is often useful to take a snapshot of the shared memory by running the `tbstat -o file` command and then running your `tbstat` options against `file`.

With a hung database in a production environment, it is often tempting to simply restart the database and hope the problem goes away. While this is often a viable solution to the problem, there are instances when the recovery time would be excessive and when it would be better to try to track down the specific problem.

You can expect such excessively long recovery times in recovery from such problems as long transactions interrupted while in rollback or other occasions in which much logfile data has not been released. Whether to try to debug or restart the database is a judgment call. Even if you decide to shut down the database, do a `tbstat -o debug.filename` so that you can later try to find out what caused the problem.

If you learn nothing else of `tbstat`, learn how to read the `tbstat -u` output. OnLine is a black box and `tbstat` is the main way of looking into this black box. This data is impossible to decipher from a UNIX `ps` output. It just shows up as `sqlturbo`. You'll note that many of the flags correspond with the invocation flags for `tbstat`. Keep working with it. Soon you'll be reading these outputs in your sleep.

The output of `tbstat -u` changed from OnLine Version 4.11 to Version 5.0. Both 4.11 and 5.0 have the same first section. OnLine 5.0 gives you a second section, `Transactions`, that applies to the X/A environment and to transactions that are running under INFORMIX-Star.

Here is a greatly abbreviated sample of the output from the `tbstat -u` utility:

```
 joe   46>tbstat -u

address  flags   pid    user      tty     wait      tout locks nreads  nwrites


e0001b70 ------D 555    informix console 0          0    0     6746    2607
e0001f30 ------- 21059  dba       -       0          0    1     31538   3813
```

| address | Address of user in user table in shared memory. This is the only point of contact between user addresses found from other `tbstat` command forms. As you trace a problem using the -s output (latches), the -b -B and -X outputs (buffer status), and the -k output (locks held), you will eventually trace it to a user address. Then match the address with a PID or user name. |

Flags	Probably the most important output of this command. Tells you what the process is doing. Has a four-position alpha output:		
	Position 1:	B	Waiting for Buffer
		C	Waiting for a Checkpoint
		L	Waiting for a Lock
		S	Waiting for a Latch
		X	Long trans. Awaiting rollback
		G	Waiting for loG buffer
		T*	Waiting for transaction*
	Position 2:	B	Transaction w/ Begin work
		T	In trans. Logging occurred
		R	In Rollback
		A	Archive process
		C*	Committed or is committing*
		H*	Heuristically aborted or aborting*
		P*	Prepare state. Precommitted*
		X*	X/A prepared or is doing so*
	Position 3:	R	Reading from the database
		X	Inside a CRITICAL section
	Position 4:	M	Running tbmonitor program
		D	Running a Daemon
		C	Corpse. Dead process awaiting cleanup
		F	Page Flusher daemon
pid	UNIX process identification number.		
user	Name of the user running the process.		
tty	TTY associated with the process, if any.		
wait	Latch or lock ID being waited for, if any.		
tout	How many times a lock timeout has occurred for the process.		
locks	Number of locks held by this process.		
nreads	Number of read calls executed by this process.		
nwrites	Number of write calls executed by this process.		

* NOTE: Items marked with * used in Online V.5.0 and above only

Versions 5.0 and above include this `Transactions` section in the output of the `tbstat -u` command:

```
Transactions
address  flags user       locks log begin isolation retrys coordinator
e0004a24 A---- e0001bbc 0      0                NOTRANS   0
e0004c04 A---- e0001c28 0      0                NOTRANS   0
e0005384 A---- e0001eb0 1      0                COMMIT    0
e0005564 A---- e0001f1c 1      0                COMMIT    0
```

address	Address of the transaction in transaction pseudotable.
flags	A five-position alpha flag of which #1, #3 & #5 are used:
	Position 1: A Attached to a server process.
	C Cleanup. Probably crashed.
	Position 3: B Begin. Work has been logged.
	Writable operation has occurred. Not the same as a BEGIN WORK.
	C Transaction being committed.
	H Heuristic rollback in progress.
	P Prepared to commit.
	R Rollback in progress.
	Position 5: C This transaction is Coordinator.
	G Global transaction.
	P Participant transaction.
user	Address of the user process that owns the transaction
locks	Locks owned by the transaction and thus by its owner process
log begin	ID of the logical log where this transaction begins
isolation	Transaction Isolation Level:
	COMMIT Committed Read
	CURSOR Cursor Stability
	DIRTY Dirty Read
	REPEAT Repeatable Read
	NO TRANS Processes that don't own transaction, or Databases with no logging
retrys	Number of times this transaction has exceeded the timeout (TXTIMEOUT)
coordinator	Name of the transaction coordinator

Tbstat -t

This invocation of the `tbstat` utility provides information from the `tblspace` pseudo-table in shared memory. These may be regular database tables currently in use, temporary tables created by users, or temporary tables created implicitly by the OnLine system for such tasks as SORT or ORDER BY. Each table in use will have only one entry.

```
joe:/devel/usr/joe> tbstat -t

RSAM Version 5.00.UC3    -- On-Line -- Up 2 days 08:09:41 -- 16080 Kbytes
Tblspaces

n address  flgs ucnt tblnum    physaddr npages nused  npdata nrows nextns
  0 c0095c98 1    1    1000001  10000e   2214   2214   0      0     3
  1 c0095da8 1    1    2000001  200004   1285   71     0      0     1
  2 c0095eb8 1    1    3000001  300004   245    245    0      0     1
  3 c0095fc8 1    1    4000001  400004   115    2      0      0     1
  4 c00960d8 1    1    5000001  500004   285    2      0      0     1
  5 c00961e8 1    2    6000001  700004   15     2      0      0     1
  6 c00962f8 1    2    7000001  800004   15     2      0      0     1


7 active, 1500 total, 512 hash buckets
```

n	Counter of the number of open tablespaces.
address	Address of the tablespace in the tblspace pseudotable.
flgs	Status of the tablespace: 0x1 1 Busy 0x2 2 Dirty, needs to be written
ucnt	Usage count. How many users are using the tablespace?
Tblnum	Tablespace number (hexadecimal). Corresponds to hex(partnum) from the system table, `systables`, for the database. The first digit (leftmost 8 bits) of the tblnum will always tell you the dbspace that contains the table (cross-reference to the `tbstat -d` output). The remaining portion gives you the order in which the tables were created in the dbspace. The internal table known as `tablespace tablespace` will always be X000001, where X is the number of the dbspace.
Physaddr	Physical address on disk of the tablespace.

npages	Total number of pages allocated to the tablespace. This includes data and index pages as well as empty space that is left over in any allocated extents.
Nused	The number of pages in the tablespace that have been used.
Npdata	Number of data pages used. Does not necessarily correspond with npages because an extent may have empty pages. This does not differentiate between data and index pages, although the heading (npdata) may seem to indicate so. This refers to DATA + INDEX pages.
Nrows	Number of rows in the tablespace.
nextns	Number of noncontiguous extents allotted. Even though the table grows larger and new extents may be added, if these extents can be created contiguous to the last extent, this number does not get bigger. This is a good indicator of the level of fragmentation of a tablespace.

Explanation of the fields in the `tbstat -t` output.

The final line of the `tbstat -t` output is

```
2 active, 1100 total, 512 hash buckets
```

The `active` represents the number of tablespaces that are currently active, while the total figure is the configuration parameter found in the `$TBCONFIG` table.

A *hash bucket* is part of an algorithm to speed up access to the tblspace table. It's a method of dividing up all of the possible values and cross-referencing them to values in the *hash table*. The cross referencing is done by an internal mathematical algorithm that takes each entry in the `tblspace` table, performs some math on it, and relates it to an entry in the hash table. Each entry in the hash table is called a hash bucket.

Tbstat -s

The `tbstat -s` invocation provides information on the active latches in the OnLine system memory. An active latch represents a user process that is modifying a shared memory structure. In normal operations, latches are granted and released rapidly. At any particular time, a run of `tbstat -s` will most often reveal no latches held.

A latch is a type of lock that is placed on shared memory. Most often, latches are placed on the pseudotables in shared memory. When a user needs to access one of these pseudotables, he first must acquire a latch on the table, then make his changes, and then release the latch. If the user cannot obtain the latch, the user process will wait for that latch to be freed. If for some reason it can never obtain the latch, the user process will hang.

When the database is hung, the DBA usually runs `tbstat -s` to see if someone is frozen on a latch. If anything is found, this is usually a good place to start looking for the bottleneck.

```
joe 53> tbstat -s

Latches with lock or user set

name       address   lock wait user
bbf[0]     e075adb8 1     0    e0002770
bf[2070]   e071af2c 1     0    e0002a10
pt[33]     e067afa0 1     0    e0002590
bh[4749]   e06e9cb0 1     0    e0001e70
```

name	The name of the structure that is being latched by this latch.	
	`locks`	Lock table latch
	`tblsps`	Tblspace table latch
	`ckpt`	Checkpoint latch
	`archive`	Archive latch
	`chunks`	Chunk table latch
	`loglog`	Logical log buffers latch
	`physlog`	Physical log latch
	`users`	Users table latch
	`trans`	Transaction table latch
	`flushctl`	Flush table latches
	`flush%d`	Flush process control latches
	`flushr`	Page cleaners
	`LRU%d`	LRU queue latch
	`pt[%d]`	Partition latch
	`pt`	Tablespace tablespace latch
	`bh[%d]`	Buffer hash latch
	`bf[%d]`	Buffer latch
	`bbf[%d]`	Big buffer latch
	`altlatch`	Alter table count latch
	`physb1`	Physical log buffer 1 latch
	`physb2`	Physical log buffer 2 latch
	NOTE: The `%d` in the above codes will be an integer representing a subscripted value of the structure.	
Address	The address of the latch in shared memory. This address corresponds to the `wait` field in `tbstat -u` output if the process is waiting for this latch.	
Lock	Machine-dependent flag indicates if the latch is locked and set.	
Wait	Indicates if any other processes are waiting for this lock.	
User	The address in shared memory of the owner of the latch. This corresponds to the address in the `tbstat -u` output.	

`tbstat -u` output codes.

Tips on Using the `Tbstat -s` Output:

Should a persistent latch be found in the `tbstat -s` output, it is a straightforward job to track down the culprit. A definite sign of a problem is a persistent latch that has many other users waiting for the latch. If the database is frozen, you can expect to see quite a few users stacked up waiting for this latch to release. The information given in the name field will provide detailed information about what kind of latch is giving the problem. Knowing the type of latch that is hung up can point to the underlying problem in the database.

Once the latch is identified and the fact noted that several users are waiting on the latch, you can run `tbstat -u` and note which users have this latch address in their `wait` field. If these users and processes are the ones that are hung up, you've found your problem. Going back to the `tbstat -s` output for the offending latch, you can check its `user` field and get the address of the user process that is blocking everything. Going back to `tbstat -u` will identify the process and give you a UNIX process ID number. You can then decide whether or not to kill the offending process.

This process is the heart of troubleshooting with `tbstat`. You usually poke around until you find something that is out of place or just doesn't seem right. Then you backtrack using the `tbstat -u` command along with specific commands that seem to be related to the problem. The eventual goal is to find a user process of a job that can be killed to clear up the problem.

Of course, the DBA should be certain that the user process is neither holding a latch nor in a critical part of the code before killing a `sqlturbo` process, as either case will cause OnLine to abort, crashing the system.

The `tbstat -s` output can also alert you to possible bottlenecks and resource limitations in your OnLine system. If you find yourself with an abnormally high percentage of jobs waiting for a short time to get latches, you may be able to improve your performance by increasing the numbers of the structures that are controlled by the latch. You cannot alter the number of latches themselves, because they are set based upon the size of the resource's parameters.

There are several statistics in the `tbstat -p` output that can point to problems with inadequate resources. When we get to that section, I'll point out several ratios that are listed and several ratios that you can derive from the statistics that can give you an early warning to some resource inadequacies.

The `status` script presented in Chapter 6 makes use of several of these ratios and will give you a central place to look to evaluate the performance of your OnLine database engine.

Tbstat -k

The `tbstat -k` invocation of `tbstat` provides information about the state of the locks in the shared memory lock table. The lock table is accessed through a lock hash table in much the same way as the `tblspace` table. Access to the lock table itself is controlled by a single latch.

Before a process can modify the lock table, it must first acquire the latch. Once the modification is complete, the latch is released. Likewise, each entry in the lock hash table is also guarded by one latch that much be acquired before modifications can be made to any particular hash bucket.

Locks are on tablespaces. Their types and scope (table lock, page lock, row lock, key lock, or byte lock) can be deciphered by using the data and a few rules.

```
INFORMIX  206>tbstat -k
RSAM Version 5.01.UC1   -- On-Line -- Up 5 days 04:09:22 -- 18752 Kbytes
Locks
address  wtlist    owner    lklist    type      tblsnum  rowid   size
11056e48 0         110024b0 0            S       1000002  206     0
11056ea8 0         1100243c 0            S       1000002  206     0
11056f08 0         1100209c 11057548 HDR+IX      200035a  0       0
11056f28 0         11002354 110572c8 HDR+IX      200035f  0       0
11056f48 0         11002768 110574c8 HDR+IX      2000354  0       0
11056fc8 0         11002184 110577a8 HDR+IX      200035e  0       0
11057008 0         11002524 0            S       1000002  206     0
110571c8 0         110026f4 0            S       1000002  206     0
110571e8 0         110023c8 110570c8 HDR+IX      2000360  0       0
11057208 0         110027dc 0            S       1000002  206     0
11057288 0         1100243c 11056ea8 HDR+IX      200035c  0       0
110572c8 0         11002354 0            S       1000002  206     0
11057308 0         11002028 0            S       1000002  206     0
11057388 0         11002524 11057008 HDR+IX      2000356  0       0
28 active, 200000 total, 16384 hash buckets
```

address	Address of the lock in the lock table. Corresponds to the `wait` field in the `tbstat -u` output if a process is waiting on this lock.
Wtlist	Address of first process that is waiting for this lock.
Owner	Shared memory address of the owner of the lock. If this value is zero, it means that the server process that owned the transaction is dead but that it continues to hold a lock. In this case, the lock will be almost impossible to clear up and if it's in the way, you'll probably have to restart the database. A valid entry (other than zero) corresponds to the owner's address in the `tbstat -u` output.
Lklist	If the owner of this lock holds other locks, the address of the owner's next lock.

Type	HDR	Header lock (lock hash table)
	B	Bytes lock (for VARCHARS)
	S	Shared lock
	X	Exclusive lock
	U	Update lock
	IX	Intent Exclusive
	IS	Intent Shared
	SIX	Shared, intent exclusive
	A lock can be any combination of the above, its elements are joined by a "+."	
Tblsnum	The tablespace number for the locked resource. The name can be derived by comparing this number with the `tblnum` in the `tbstat -t` output. The first digit represents the dbspace that the tablespace occupies.	
Rowid	The `rowid` identifies the row being locked. The `rowid` can be used to identify the scope of the lock by using the following rules:	
	Table Lock	`rowid = 0`
	Page Lock	`rowid` ends in 00
	Row Lock	`rowid` is six digits or less and does not end in 00
	Key Lock	hex number with more than six digits
	Byte Lock	`rowid` ends in 00, and the "size" field is not zero
size	Number of bytes locked for VARCHAR locking (see Byte Lock).	

Explanation of the `tbstat -k` output.

`Tbstat -b` and `Tbstat -B`

These two options will print information about buffer utilization by the OnLine engine. The difference between the two is that the lowercase `tbstat -b` will list information only about buffers that are in use by engine processes, while the uppercase `tbstat -B` will print out information about all buffers provided for in the configuration file, whether in use or not. Buffers may and probably will contain data even though they are not currently being accessed by an engine process. The fields reported by both commands are identical. An OnLine buffer structure is actually composed of three separate components:

Buffer pool   Contains copies of pages from disk exactly as they come from
                               disk. These pages can be the contents of any disk structure such
                               as data pages, index pages, system data, etc. Each page in this

buffer pool is exactly one page in size, so there is no room left to
put housekeeping information.

Buffer header table   This header table is where the housekeeping information is kept.
                             This header table includes information that OnLine needs to
                             manage the related buffer pool entry. It contains entries for the
                             address of the user using the buffer, the state of the buffer (dirty
                             or clean), and the address of the buffer.

Buffer hash table   Used to facilitate faster access to the buffer pool.

Each of the three elements of the buffer has latches that must be acquired before the
buffer can be modified. These latches will show up in the `tbstat -s` output. Each buffer
has an individual latch. The buffer header table has a single latch that controls access to the
table. Each hash bucket has an individual latch.

```
joe  31> tbstat -b


RSAM Version 4.10.UD4  -- On-Line --Up 8 days 17:26:14 - 18704 Kbytes

Buffers
address   user      flgs pagenum  memaddr  nslots pgflgs xflgs owner waitlist


e070976c 0         0    651566   e0937000 29     1      400   e00023b0 0
e06fff6c 0         6    50479c   e0807000 23     1      0     0        0
2526 modified, 4750 total, 8192 hash buckets, 2048 buffer size
```

address	Address of the buffer header in the buffer table.	
user	Address of the current user or the most recent user to access the buffer.	
Flgs	0x01	Buffer contains modified data.
	0x02	Buffer contains data.
	0x04	Buffer on LRU list.
	0x08	I/O error on this page.
	0x10	Buffer is in near table.
	0x20	Buffer is being flushed.
pagenum	Physical page number the page comes from.	
memaddr	Address of the buffer page in memory.	
nslots	Number of slots on the page. The number of rows stored on this page.	
pgflgs	Flag that indicates the type of data held on the page.	
	0x0001	Data page
	0x0002	Partition page (`tablespace tablespace`)
	0x0004	Free list page
	0x0008	Chunk free list page
	0x0009	Remainder data page
	0x000b	Partition resident blob page
	0x000c	Blobspace resident blob page
	0x000d	Blob chunk free list bit page
	0x000e	Blob chunk blob map page
	0x0010	B-tree node page (index)
	0x0020	B-tree root node page (index)
	0x0040	B-tree branch node page (index)
	0x0080	B-tree leaf node page (index)
	0x0100	Logical log page
	0x0200	Last page of logical log
	0x0400	Lync page of logical log
	0x0800	Physical log page
	0x1000	Reserved root pages

xflgs	Access flags showing how the buffer can be accessed:
	0x0100 Access buffer in share mode.
	0x0200 Access buffer in update mode.
	0x0400 Access buffer in exclusive mode.
	0x0600 Process is waiting for all other users to finish.
owner	User process that locked the buffer with above xflgs.
waitlist	First of the list of users waiting to access the buffer.

Explanation of `tbstat -b` output, continued.

Tbstat -R

This invocation mode is used to display information about OnLine's Least Recently Used (LRU) queue structures. These queues are a means that OnLine uses to distribute the allocation of the buffer pool in as even a method as possible. When OnLine determines that it needs to place a page into the buffer pool from disk, it needs to be able to find a free buffer in which to place the page.

Since OnLine tries to keep pages in shared memory that may be useful, it uses an LRU algorithm to determine which pages to flush to disk. Depending on the OnLine configuration parameters, there are between 3 and 32 pairs of LRU queues. These queues are in pairs, consisting of a clean queue and a dirty queue. When a page is initially brought into shared memory, it is on a clean queue. When it is modified, it is moved to a dirty queue. Every time a buffer is accessed, it is moved to the head of its queue, called the MRU (most recently used) end.

This movement from the LRU end to the MRU end is done in two steps. First, a latch on the queue is acquired and the buffer is removed from the queue. The latch is then released. Now, OnLine attempts to reobtain the latch. If the latch is reobtained, the buffer is placed on the MRU end of the queue. If OnLine cannot obtain the latch for the second time, it tries the next available queue (either clean or dirty as the case may be). It keeps trying to obtain latches on subsequent queues until it gets one, at which time it places the buffer on the MRU end of the queue.

The effect of this queue dance is that buffers may move from queue to queue in an attempt to balance the load between the queues. The `tbstat -R` command lets the DBA see how often the queues are being accessed and how their cleaning is going on. This is more of a tuning tool than a debugging tool. The DBA will use this command to decide whether or not he has enough queues allocated and to decide threshold points for the page cleaner daemons. See the section on tuning in Chapter 8 for more details.

```
joe 58> tbstat -R
LRU  0:    6 ( 0.9%) modified of  643 total
.... (several lines deleted)
57 dirty, 4750 queued, 4750 total, 8192 hash buckets, 2048 buffer size
start clean at 60% dirty, stop at 50%; first pass search 70%
```

The first line of the output gives the total number of queues allocated by the LRUS parameter in $TBCONFIG. For each pair, the output gives you a raw number of modified buffers, its percentage of the whole, and the total number of buffers on each queue. In the last line, the start clean is the $TBCONFIG LRU_MAX_DIRTY parameter and the stop at is the LRU_MIN_DIRTY parameter. Notice that the "total" buffer counts are not necessarily equal for each queue pair. This is because of the "queue dance" just discussed in which the buffers move from queue to queue to balance the load.

Tbstat -F

The tbstat -F invocation provides information about the page cleaners or *page flushers* allocated to your OnLine system. It gives you historical data on the different types of writes that have been used to flush your buffers off to disk. It also tells you instantaneous status on the page cleaners currently allocated for your engine.

Different types of writes are more or less efficient than others. By noting the types of writes that your system is performing, you may be able to affect your overall throughput by minimizing some and maximizing others.

```
joe  59>tbstat -F
Fg Writes     LRU Writes    Idle Writes   Chunk Writes
0             279744        5142          471793

address  flusher  snooze   state   data
e0001c30 0        60       I       0       = 0
e0001c90 1        60       I       0       = 0
states: Exit Idle Chunk Lru
```

Fg Writes	Writes performed by the server process itself. If your system is doing a lot of these writes, your server is constantly having to interrupt itself and go off and do the page cleaner's job. Either increase the number of page cleaners or start them working earlier by lowering LRU_MAX_DIRTY .

LRU Writes	Writes performed by the page cleaners when woken up by the engine, not during the normal operations of the page cleaners. The page cleaners can have their sleep time overridden by the engine in two ways. First, if 16 fg writes occur the engine will assume that the page cleaners need to have their sleep interrupted and will wake them up. The other reason is when the percentage of dirty buffers on the LRU queue goes above LRU_MAX_DIRTY before the cleaner's snooze time is up, the engine will awaken the page cleaners and have them begin cleaning the buffers. In this example, this is the case, as LRU_MAX_DIRTY is set at 60%.
Idle Writes	Writes performed by the page cleaners as part of their normal operations as they wake up at the expiration of their snooze time.
Chunk Writes	Writes that happen during checkpoints. Chunk writes are the most efficient writes performed by OnLine because they are performed as sorted writes. They are also performed when no other writes are allowed and thus can receive more CPU time.

Explanation of types of writes in `tbstat -F` output.

Address	Memory address of the cleaner in the page cleaner table. Although the number of page cleaners is allocated according to the CLEANERS parameter in $TBCONFIG, the table will always have 32 slots, which is the maximum number of page cleaners.
Flusher	Sequential ID number assigned to this page cleaner.
snooze	Current sleep time for this cleaner. This value is set by the page cleaners based upon the amount of activity it is getting, but is a maximum of 60 seconds.

State	Code indicating what the page cleaner is doing at this instant:
	
	 I Idle (sleeping).
	 C Checkpoint (chunk) write in progress.
	 L LRU write in progress.
	 E Exiting. Either the system is shutting down or
	      the page cleaner timed out on its last run,
	      often due to a heavy workload. If it timed out,
	      you'll get a note in your online message logfile.

Data	Used in conjunction with the state field above, this code is written in decimal, followed by an equals sign, then in hex:
	
	 If state=C Data is chunk number where buffers are
	                being written to.
	 If state=L Data is LRU queue from which the page
	                cleaner is writing.

Explanation of page cleaner data in `tbstat -F` output.

The `tbstat -F` command is often used in conjunction with `tbstat -R` to tune the page cleaner system. We'll get into more detail in the section on tuning in Chapter 11, but one point needs to be made now.

Different OnLine applications have different tuning needs, and you have to be sensitive to what your system requires. This is one area where the DBA needs to make tradeoffs. Most of the early information on tuning OnLine emphasized the efficiency of Chunk Writes, and a lot of effort was expended to cause systems to do most of their writes during checkpoints to maximize throughput.

The only problem with that technique is that users started screaming. Even though the throughput may have been much better, the users would have frequent interruptions because writes are prevented during checkpoints. The system would appear to freeze up every few minutes. This would be OK in a batch processing environment, but not in an OLTP environment. Here, the perceived utility of the system was enhanced by forcing the less efficient LRU writes to carry the page-cleaning load while minimizing interruptions to the users when the checkpoints were doing their admittedly more efficient but more intrusive work. The lesson: Know your system. Know your users. Don't follow rules slavishly.

Tbstat -1

This option will give the DBA information about the physical and logical logging of the OnLine instance. There's a lot of information in this invocation, and it is used for both tuning and troubleshooting. We'll break it up into three sections. The first section contains physical logging statistics.

```
joe  62>tbstat -1
Physical Logging
Buffer bufused  bufsize  numpages numwrits pages/I/O
  P-1   69        128      713655    5901     120.94
        phybegin physize  phypos   phyused  %used
        117202   6000     2999     69       1.15
```

Buffer	Which of the two physical logs is being used, P-1 or P-2?
Bufused	Number of buffer pages used.
bufsize	Size of the buffer in pages.
numpages	Number of pages written to the physical log.
numwrits	Number of writes to the disk.
pages/I/O	numpages/numwrits. This statistic is used to tune buffers..
Phybegin	Page number of the beginning of the physical logfile.
physize	Size of the physical log in pages.
phypos	Current offset into the physical log. Where the next page write will occur.
Phyused	Number of pages used in the physical log.
%used	Percentage of pages used (phyused/physize). This statistic is often used for tuning the size of the physical log buffers.

Explanation of tbstat -1 (physical log section) output.

```
Logical Logging
Buffer bufused  bufsize  numrecs  numpages numwrits recs/pages pages/I/O
```

```
L-1   8        64        31030148 668262   21047    46.4       31.8
```

Buffer	Which of the three logical log buffers is used? L-1, L-2, L-3?
Bufused	Number of pages in the buffer that have been used.
bufsize	Size of the buffer in pages.
numrecs	Number of records written to logical logfiles.
numpages	Number of pages written to logical logfiles.
numwrits	Number of disk writes to logical logfiles.
recs/pages	numrecs/numpages. Dependent upon types of transactions logged.
Pages/io	numpages/numwrites. Another tuning statistic. You can alter it by changing the LOGBUFF (buffer size).

Explanation of tbstat -l (logical logging section) output.

```
address   number   flags    uniqid   begin      size     used    %used
e06d26f0  1        F------   0        70f4f4     30000    0       0.00
e06d270c  2        F------   0        716a24     30000    0       0.00
e06d2744  3        U---C-L   2296     907533     30000    14897   49.65
```

address	Address of the logfile descriptor.
number	Logfile number.
flags	Status of each logfile: F Free, available for use. B Backed up. C Current logfile, now receiving transactions. U In use, still contains active transactions. A Newly added. Will become available for use after the next archive. L Contains last completed checkpoint .
uniqid	Unique ID number of the logfile.
Begin	Location of beginning page of the logfile.
size	Size of the logfile in pages.
used	Number of pages currently used.
%used	Used/Size. How full is this logfile?

Explanation of `tbstat -l` (actual logfile status) output

The first two sections of this output see most use as a tuning tool. There are more specifics in the section on tuning, but basically the concept is to try to keep the pages per I/O statistics pretty close to the actual number of pages in the buffers, to ensure that your writes are doing the most possible work each time they are done. This is logical, since the write will have to look at all of the data anyway. You may as well have the data it sees as full as possible to wring the most work out of each of your writes.

The last section will become one of your most familiar friends (or enemies) as a DBA. Since the logfiles are so important to recovery and since the consequences of filling them up are so disastrous, you need to keep a close eye on your logs. First , you need to have continuous backup going on your logs at all times. If you forget and don't turn it on, you'll have problems when they get full. Next, you're looking for incipient long transactions. If you see that you have many logfiles that show a B for backed up and do not show an F for free, you know that some sort of a transaction is still pending. If you have lots of logs, you can probably just let it go and wait for the transaction to complete. If you begin to get short of logs, you need to think about killing the runaway transaction. Do it early enough that you'll have ample logfiles to log all of the activities that accompany a rollback. If you allow the logfiles to reach the percentage full specified in the LTX_HWM parameter, the engine will lock all other users out of the system, causing their jobs to freeze up.

Tbstat -p and Tbstat -P

These two invocations of the tbstat utility provide the closest thing to a dashboard for the OnLine engine that Informix provides. It reports on statistics kept in shared memory that relate to the performance of the OnLine engine. This is probably the number one tuning and monitoring tool available to the DBA. The statistics are useful in evaluating the overall efficiency of your database system and in measuring the effects of changes in parameters upon your database operations.

The outputs for both the uppercase and lowercase invocations are the same except that the tbstat -P output includes an additional field, BIGReads as the first element in the report. Everything else is identical. The output is divided into four lines of data with headings above each line. We'll look at each line individually:

```
  joe  63>tbstat -P

Profile

BIGReads dskreads pagreads bufreads %cached dskwrits pagwrits bufwrits %cached
235 14970755 22166265 498552631 97.00    543747   2139408  49870693 98.91
```

BIGReads	In `tbstat -P` output only, the number of big buffer reads.
dskreads	Number of actual reads from disk.
pagreads	Number of pages read from disk.
bufreads	Number of reads from the buffer cache.
%cached	Percentage of reads cached 100*`(bufreads-dskreads)/bufreads` If this figure is above 95%, your system is performing very well..
Dskwrits	Number of actual physical writes to disk.
pagwrits	Number of pages written to disk.
bufwrits	Number of writes to the buffers.
%cached	Percentage of writes cached 100*`(bufwrits-dskwrits)/bufwrits` If this number is above about 85%, you're doing well..

Explanation of `tbstat -P` (buffer activity) output.

```
isamtot     open      start      read      write     rewrite   delete   commit rollbk
424714409 5813437   23348999 175473799 10989374 5499045   2603325  8699910   101
```

isamtot	Total number of ISAM (Indexed Sequential Access Method) calls. Does not necessarily correspond to queries, as a query may make many ISAM calls.
Open	Calls that open a tablespace.
start	Increments by one when positioning within an index.
read	Increments when the read function is called.
write	Increments when the write function is called.
rewrite	Increments when an update occurs.

delete	Increments when a row is deleted.
commit	Increments when a transaction is successfully committed.
rollbk	Increments when a transaction is rolled back.

Explanation of `tbstat -p` (ISAM statistics section) output.

```
ovtbls   ovlock   ovuser   ovbuff    usercpu     syscpu  numckpts flushes
0        0        0        0         387006.97 41611.33 294         587
```

ovtbls	Number of times the `tblspace` table has overflowed. In the `ovrXXXX` statistics that follow, a small number of occurrences is not necessarily critical. If the numbers are large or keep increasing, increase the parameter.
Ovlock	Number of times attempted to exceed LOCKS parameter.
ovuser	Number of times attempted to exceed USERS parameter.
ovbuff	Number of times attempted to exceed BUFFERS parameter.
usercpu	Cumulative total CPU time by OnLine processes, in seconds.
syscpu	Total system CPU time (UNIX system calls).
numckpts	Number of checkpoints since last boot.
flushes	Number of times the buffer pool has been flushed to disk.

Explanation of `tbstat -p` (other statistics) output.

```
bufwaits lokwaits lockreqs deadlks  dltouts  lchwaits ckpwaits compress
 21748    8046    476500421 9          0      1594907  1664     2220019
```

bufwaits	Increments when a process has to wait for a buffer.
lokwaits	Increments when a process has to wait for a lock.
lokreqs	Increments when a request for a lock occurs.
deadlks	Increments when potential deadlock situation is automatically prevented by the engine. (It kills one of the processes.)
dltouts	Increments when a distributed deadlock timeout occurs.
lchwaits	Increments when a process is forced to wait for a latch on a resource.
chkpwaits	Increments when a process is forced to wait for a checkpoint.
compress	Increments whenever a data page is compressed.

Explanation of `tbstat  -l` (wait states) output.

The first section concerning buffers and cache percentages is most useful in tuning your OnLine parameters for performance. You are looking mostly at the `%cached` fields for reading and writing. If these numbers are low, it is possible that you can increase your performance by tuning the buffer parameters. Be cautious about reading these figures immediately after starting the database. Until the database has "warmed up" and has representative data in the buffer pool, these `%cached` statistics will be low. One good method is to let the database run for a while, and then do a `tbstat  -z` to zero out all of the statistics. The statistics gathered from then on will not be tainted by the initial loading of the caches that occur when the system is initially started up.

The second section will give you an idea of the types of activities that your system is performing. These statistics are meaningful only if you have something to compare them to. As you gather your performance statistics, you will begin to develop a feel for the patterns you can expect.

The `ovrXXXX` sections of the next line are an early warning of a need to increase the value of their respective parameters in `$TBCONFIG` file. For example, if you are getting high numbers for `ovlock`, increase the LOCKS parameter in your `$TBCONFIG` file. If you're regularly going over the parameters, your users are probably already complaining about jobs that don't complete.

The `lokwaits` and `lchwaits` statistics on the last line can tip you off to a need to increase the value of some of your `$TBCONFIG` parameters. They can also tip you off to poorly designed programs that may be hogging resources or causing contention between themselves and other programs.

The `status` script included in Chapter 6 makes extensive use of these statistics in preparing a more complete "dashboard" for monitoring the activity of your database engine.

Tbstat - r and Stacking Tbstat Options

The `tbstat` command can run with any combination of options. You can stack the options like

```
tbstat -lsp
```

You can also use `tbstat -r` with an optional integer `number`. This option runs `tbstat` in a loop with a `number` second pause between loops. This can be quite useful if you are trying to establish trends or are just anxious to find out when something happens. With no `number`, it runs with a 5-second pause. For example, the following command runs the tables option every 15 seconds:

```
tbstat -tr 15
```

Tbstat -a

The `tbstat -a` command gives you one output that includes the following options:

b	buffers
c	configuration
d	dbspaces
k	locks
l	logs
m	message file
p	profile
s	latches
t	tablespaces
u	users

Tbstat -m

Runs the UNIX `tail` command on your online message log.

Tbstat -c

Prints your $TBCONFIG file.

Tbstat (no options)

Gives you a short combined output of:
  u   users
  p   profile

THE Tbcheck UTILITY

The `tbcheck` utility is used to inspect the actual data on the disks. This is an important utility because this data is stored as binary data broken into pages. Short of writing specialized code to decode this binary data, `tbcheck` is the only way of accessing the actual data and index pages on the disk. In fact, in most UNIX installations, it is the only way to even *see* the data. This is because most UNIX installations will use *raw* disk devices to hold the OnLine chunks. Since these devices are not mounted in the UNIX file system, they never appear in most UNIX outputs. Even if the system were using UNIX *cooked* files for data storage, the data is stored in a binary format that cannot be viewed by normal UNIX commands.

UNIX commands such as dd can be used to relocate these chunks, but instances when this would be necessary are rare. Such instances could be the result of replacing a physical disk device. In such instances, the system needs to be down during the operations, as the UNIX commands have no concept of data integrity or consistency.

Commands such as od (octal dump) or hd (hex dump) could be used to inspect the data on the raw partitions, but these commands do not decipher the data layout of the OnLine chunks.

The Informix Customer Support engineers have access to additional tools to inspect and modify the data. They use an internal tool called `tbdump` to dump pages from disk and one called `tbpatch` to modify the pages. When the engineers call into your system to make repairs, they place these tools in the $INFORMIXDIR/astools directory. These tools are often left in the directory at the end of the service call.

The tbdump utility can provide some insights into the layout of the chunks if you have time to poke around in the chunks. The tbpatch utility can be very dangerous. Don't use it unless you are willing to risk losing all of your data.

If you ever get into a situation where things are totally bollixed up, check with Informix Technical Support. Some of their wizards may be able to twiddle the bits and get you back online.

One thing that they do quite often is change the online/offline bits that determine whether a chunk is usable or not. If you ever have a chunk that is down and you cannot get it to come back online, it's time to either restore from tape or call Informix Technical Support. IDS systems allow you to bring a chunk back online yourself without assistance.

Many of the miracles that Informix Technical Support perform are brought about by some of the software tools that they have available to them. Short of having these specialized tools, tbcheck should be your tool of choice.

This utility can have serious side effects, though, and the DBA should be careful when using it. In many instances, tbcheck will place a shared lock on the tables it is addressing. This prevents others from updating the table during its use. This is most visible using the -pt and -pT options. Since these options look at every data (and index for -pT) page in the table, this shared lock can last for a long time. Use these options only during times when your users will not be bothered by your locking the tables. It's best to reserve these options for system downtime.

The other options that inspect data or index pages for specific tables may have similar effects. These include the -ci, -cI, -ck, -cK, -cL, and -cl options, along with their -p counterparts. Use them carefully.

Of the other useful options, -pe is one of the most useful. It does not have any harmful effects on the database and can be used freely without worrying about interfering with your users. The same command, with the check option -cc is also safe to use. The -pc and -cc options are also relatively innocuous. We'll note these side effects as we talk about each option.

The full invocation options of tbcheck are:

```
joe 26> thcheck --
TBCHECK
Usage:  tbcheck [-clist] [-plist] [-qny]
[ { database[:[owner.]table] | TBLSpace number | Chunk number }
{ rowid | page number } ]
    c     - check
    r     - reserved pages
    e     - TBLSpace extents and chunk extents
    c     - database catalogs
    i     - table indexes
    I     - table indexes and rowids in index
    d     - TBLSpace data rows including bitmaps
    D     - TBLSpace data rows including bitmaps, remainder pages and blobs
    p     - print
```

```
r    - reserved pages (-cr)
e    - extents report (-ce)
c    - catalog report (-cc)
k    - keys in index (-ci)
K    - keys and rowids in index (-cI)
l    - leaf node keys only (-ci)
L    - leaf node keys and rowids (-cI)
d    - TBLSpace data rows (-cd)
D    - TBLSpace data rows including bitmaps,remainder pages and blobs (-cD)
t    - TBLSpace report    (CAUTION:  Locks the table!)
T    - TBLSpace disk utilization report   (CAUTION:  Locks the table!!)
p    - dump page for the given [table and rowid | TBLSpace and page number]
P    - dump page for the given chunk number and page number
B    - BLOBSpace utilization for given table(s) [database:[owner.]]table
q    - quiet mode - print only error messages
n    - answer NO to all questions
y    - answer YES to all questions
--   - print this help text
```

DANGEROUS OPTIONS: due to locking problems, be careful with the "i", "k", "l" (ell), and "t" options, along with their capitalized counterparts.

We will cover only a few of the more commonly used options here. If you need further detail, go to the tbcheck sections of the Informix DBA manuals for more detail. We'll try to cover the options that you will use in normal operations here. The other options are usually used for debugging specific problems. If you are sophisticated enough to be doing this level of debugging, you can certainly handle the manual. The items that we will gloss over will be the sections that allow you to check and/or print specific data and index pages. If you're using these options, you are probably looking to correct specific data or index problems. Most of the time this is academic, because you'll have to restore or rebuild your data or indexes if your data is this corrupted.

Tbcheck -ce and Tbcheck -pe

These two options are options that can safely be used at any time to dump information about the extent usage of your OnLine databases. These options check the chunk free list and tablespace extents. The -ce option just does the checks. The -pe option checks the data and prints the extent and table information.

Both options first give you a check of any tablespaces that occupy more than eight extents. This number of extents is important. When a tablespace goes over eight extents, an additional disk access is needed to retrieve data. This is due to the sizing of the data structures that hold the disk access pointers. As a general rule, your tables should be sized such that they and all their related indexes occupy eight or fewer extents. This is not always possible, but it's a good thing to strive for. Oddly enough, some of the most common tables that you find with more than eight extents in larger databases are the system catalogue tables, notably systables, syscolumns, and sysindexes. If you are expecting to deal with a large number of tables and indexes, it is advisable to increase the NEXT EXTENT parameter of the system tables before you begin to build the regular tables. This can be done with the following SQL statement:

```
ALTER TABLE systables MODIFY NEXT EXTENT 32;
```

The table name and actual extent size will vary with your applications. You can alter the NEXT EXTENT, but not the initial extent.

The printing option (-pe) gives you a report in the following format:

```
WARNING:TBLSpace joe:informix.queries has more than 8 extents.
WARNING:TBLSpace joe:informix.performance has more than 8 extents.

DBSpace Usage Report:  rootdbs        Owner:  informix  Created: 06/24/92

    Chunk: 1   /dev/rootdbs3                   Size     Used     Free
                                              135000    99713    35287

        Disk usage for Chunk 1                Start   Length
        ------------------------------------ --------- ---------
        ROOT DBSpace RESERVED Pages                0       12
        CHUNK FREE LIST PAGE                      12        1
        PARTITION PARTITION                       13     2705
        dba:joe.test                            2718        8
        dba:informix.syscolumns                 2726        8
        dba:joe.dummy                           2734        8
        dba:informix.sysreferences              2742        8
        dba:informix.extent_sizes               2750       50
        FREE                                    2800   132200
```

This report will go on to cover every chunk, every extent, and every tablespace in your OnLine system, giving you useful information about the space utilization, fragmentation, and free space.

Practical Uses for Tbcheck -pe

Of all the information available from tbcheck, this report is the most useful. In addition to being safe to run no matter what users are doing, it runs relatively quickly and efficiently. It covers all data in the instance, spanning all databases.

One of the things that I do with my database is have the UNIX cron command run the following script every morning before users log into the system:

```
tbcheck -pe >& /u2/informix/last_tbcheckpe
```

The output file last_tbcheckpe is useful for many things. First, it is a good reference to have around if you just want to locate data about a chunk or tablespace. This file can be compressed and saved in an archive on a regular basis to give you a sense of exactly how your databases are growing or changing.

A third very important use is to provide data for a table size tracking and reporting system. If you've looked at the data in the system tables, it is not always clear just exactly how much space is being taken up by a table's extents. Since the output of this daily report shows exactly how the extents are being used, it is worth the effort to massage the data a little more.

One of the more important things that the output of this command gives you is a picture of exactly how fragmented your tables have become. As a table grows in size, it attempts to allocate additional extents that are contiguous to the last extent. As you add tables, drop tables, add chunks, and generally fill up your dbspaces, it becomes harder for the OnLine engine to keep your extents contiguous. As the tables become more fragmented, the I/O system has to do more work to find all of the pieces of the tables.

This results in a generalized slowdown of access and increased cost in resources to do the work. If you begin to experience a general slowdown of operations, watch the fragmentation of the tables. It may be necessary to occasionally rebuild the tables in another dbspace to collect all of the extents and make them contiguous again. This shows up most emphatically when the engine needs to do long sequential scans of the data.

Tbcheck -pt

This invocation of `tbcheck` generates a report that gives more detailed information about specific tables. It is invoked as

```
tbcheck -pt admin:system
TBLSpace Report for admin:dba.system
     Physical Address           300220
     Creation date              06/05/92 05:09:47
     TBLSpace Flags             1              Page Locking
     Maximum row size           64
     Number of special columns  0
     Number of keys             1
     Number of extents          3
     Current serial value       1
     First extent size          6
     Next extent size           4
     Number of pages allocated  18
     Number of pages used       17
     Number of data pages       15
     Number of data bytes       13952
     Number of rows             218
Extents
        Logical Page   Physical Page      Size
                   0         3030d4          6
......<several lines deleted>.......
```

In the output of this command the columns for `number of pages used` and `number of data pages used` represent maximums for the table as currently configured. It does not break down the number of pages into allocated versus currently used. Note that all of the numbers are in pages

Tbcheck -pT

This command gives more detailed information about the use and allocation of extents for tablespaces and also includes information about index usage. It is invoked as

```
tbcheck -pT admin:system
TBLSpace Report for admin:dba.system

        Physical Address            300220
        Creation date               06/05/92 05:09:47
        TBLSpace Flags              1          Page Locking
        Maximum row size            64
        Number of special columns   0
        Number of keys              1
        Number of extents           3
        Current serial value        1
        First extent size           6
        Next extent size            4
        Number of pages allocated   18
        Number of pages used        17
        Number of data pages        15
        Number of data bytes        13952
        Number of rows              218

Extents
        Logical Page   Physical Page        Size
                0           3030d4             6
                6           303192             4

TBLSpace Usage Report for admin:dba.system
Type                    Pages      Empty   Semi-Full  Full  Very-Full
----------------    ----------  ----------  -------  ------  ----
    Free                          6
    Bit-Map                       1
    Index                         3
    Data (Home)                   8
                             ----------
Total Pages                18
Unused Space Summary
        Unused data slots                                14
        Unused bytes per data page                       48
        Total unused bytes in data pages                384

Index Usage Report for index system_ci on admin:dba.system
                    Average    Average
    Level    Total No. Keys Free Bytes
    -----  -------- -------- ----------
        1        1        2       2002
        2        2      109        930
    -----  -------- -------- ----------
Total        3       73       1287
```

The output from the tbcheck -pT command contains all of the information that is in the tbcheck -pt command, with the additional information about unused space and index usage. Note that both the tbcheck -pT and tbcheck -pt place locks on the target tables, making it impossible for others to update, delete, or insert into these tables while the utilities are running.

This locking is unfortunate in that it limits the usability of tbcheck and makes it difficult to get detailed information about actual space utilization without locking tables. Some of the information can be gleaned from the innocuous options such as the tbcheck -pe option. None of the other options allows you to see what you need, which is the number of pages free in a tablespace. One way of working around this while the database is running is to compute some of the information from tbstat -t. This only works if the target table you want to check is currently open. The following script shows a way of opening the table and running a tbstat at the same time Create this script and name it tstat:

```
#!/bin/csh
(sleep 1; tbstat -t > tstat.out &
isql $1 << EOF
select * from $2;
EOF
```

In all of the scripts in this book, we are assuming that you are using isql as a data retrieval client. If you are using dbaccess rather than isql, simply change the isql to dbaccess in all of the scripts.

This script creates an output file called tstat.out. The program is invoked as:

```
tstat database_name table_name
```

For this sample run, the invocation was:

```
tstat admin test_table
joe 61> cat tstat.out
RSAM Version 5.00.UC2    -- On-Line -- Up 29 days 00:04:50 -- 12976 Kbytes
Tblspaces
 n address   flgs ucnt tblnum   physaddr npages nused  npdata nrows  nextns
 0 e00b85f4 1    1    1000001  10000e   5405   408    0      0      1
 3 e00b8e40 1    1    4000001  500004   1355   2      0      0      1
 4 e00b9104 1    11   3000002  300005   64     63     38     659    8
31 e00bdbb0 1    1    300021d  300220   18     17     15     218    3

4 active, 1100 total, 512 hash buckets
```

Looking at the tstat.out output file, we see that the last table is tblnum 300021d. By using the table script from Chapter 6, we can confirm that tblnum 300021d is indeed test_table.

The difference between the npages and the nused column is the pages free output of the tbcheck -pT program. The only problem with this script is that it outputs all of the target table's rows to standard output. If the table is large, this could take a while. You can run it for a second and then hit a CONTROL-C to exit and still get the output without danger of crashing the system. It's not as good as tbcheck, but it doesn't lock the tables.

Tbcheck - ci and Tbcheck -cI

The options for checking and repairing indexes with tbcheck are similar. The uppercase version is more complete and encompassing than the lowercase version. The tbcheck - ci utility just checks the key values of the indexes. The tbcheck -cI version adds to that a check of the rowids of the keys. If the indexes are consistent, there is no output. If there are problems, they are reported.

Both of these options include the capability of attempting to repair the indexes. You will be given these options only if the system is quiescent when the tbcheck is run. You can give the -y or -n flags to indicate that you either do or don't want tbcheck to try to repair the indexes.

The option to repair the indexes looks good on paper, but it's really pretty useless. Repairing an index requires your system to be quiescent. It is much slower than simply dropping and recreating the index. As a bonus, dropping and re-creating the index does not require you to bring down the instance. About the only time that there is an advantage to attempting an index repair is if the index is on a system table and you think that dropping the system table's index might hurt your performance or integrity. In that case, it might be worthwhile to attempt a repair.

Tbcheck -cc and Tbcheck -pc

These options will check and print the contents of the system catalog tables. The check option will often complain about missing synonym and authorization records. I have yet to see any instances where these complaints are valid.

The printing options are somewhat useful in that they not only provide the same checks as does the -cc options, but they also print extent information ala tbcheck -pt. Again, on all of these options, watch for locking.

Tbcheck -pr database_name

This option is another option that may be useful to the DBA. It provides the following output of data that is contained in the root dbspace reserved pages:

```
joe 71> tbcheck -pr
Validating INFORMIX-OnLine reserved pages - PAGE_PZERO
    Identity                        INFORMIX-OnLine
    Database system state           0
    Database system flags           0
    Page Size                       2048
    Date/Time created               06/04/92 13:24:33
    Version number of creator       2048
```

```
     Last modified time stamp          1
Validating INFORMIX-OnLine reserved pages - PAGE_CONFIG
     ROOTNAME                       rootdbs
     ROOTPATH                       /dev/root_dbs
     ROOTOFFSET                     128
     ROOTSIZE                       540000
     PHYSDBS                        rootdbs
     PHYSFILE                       4000
     LOGFILES                       3
     LOGSIZE                        60000
     MSGPATH                        /u2/informix/online.log
     CONSOLE                        /u2/informix/online.sys
     TAPEDEV                        /dev/rmt1
     TAPEBLK                        16
     TAPESIZE                       3950000
     LTAPEDEV                       /dev/null
     LTAPEBLK                       16
     LTAPESIZE                      13107200
     DBSERVERNAME                   robin
     SERVERNUM                      1
     DEADLOCK_TIMEOUT               60
     RESIDENT                       0
     USERS                          110
     LOCKS                          20000
     BUFFERS                        4750
     TBLSPACES                      1100
     CHUNKS                         27
     DBSPACES                       8
     PHYSBUFF                       128
     LOGBUFF                        128
     LOGSMAX                        35
     CLEANERS                       2
     BUFFSIZE                       2048
     CKPTINTVL                      1200

Validating INFORMIX-OnLine reserved pages - PAGE_1CKPT & PAGE_2CKPT
Using check point page PAGE_1CKPT.
     Time stamp of checkpoint       528303532
     Time of checkpoint             01/13/94 17:47:12
     Physical log begin address     10152a
     Physical log size              2000
Physical log position at Ckpt   208
Logical log unique identifier   349
     Logical log position at Ckpt   1f9c760
     DBSpace descriptor page        100004
     Chunk descriptor page          100007
     Mirror chunk descriptor page   100009
     Log file number                1
     Log file flags                 13              Log file in use
                                                    Current log file
                                                    Log written to archive tape

     Time stamp                     0
     Date/Time file filled          12/31/69 18:00:00
     Unique identifier              349
     Physical location              101cfa
     Log size                       30000
     Number pages used              8093

     Log file number                2
     Log file flags                 0
```

```
        Time stamp                    521789106
        Date/Time file filled         11/18/93 15:06:51
        Unique identifier             0
        Physical location             10922a
        Log size                      30000
        Number pages used             0


Validating INFORMIX-OnLine reserved pages - PAGE_1DBSP & PAGE_2DBSP
Using dbspace page PAGE_1DBSP.
        DBSpace number                1
        Flags                         1            No mirror chunks
        First chunk                   1
        Number of chunks              1
        Date/Time created             06/04/92 13:24:33
        DBSpace name                  rootdbs
        DBSpace owner                 informix
        DBSpace number                2
        Flags                         1            No mirror chunks
        First chunk                   2
        Number of chunks              1
        Date/Time created             06/04/92 13:31:44
        DBSpace name                  log_dbspace2
        DBSpace owner                 informix

        DBSpace number                3
        Flags                         1            No mirror chunks
        First chunk                   3
        Number of chunks              2
        Date/Time created             06/04/92 13:32:42
        DBSpace name                  dbspace1
        DBSpace owner                 informix

        DBSpace number                4
        Flags                         1            No mirror chunks
        First chunk                   5
        Number of chunks              1
        Date/Time created             06/04/92 13:33:42
        DBSpace name                  log_dbspace
        DBSpace owner                 informix
```

```
Validating INFORMIX-OnLine reserved pages - PAGE_1PCHUNK & PAGE_2PCHUNK
Using primary chunk page PAGE_2PCHUNK.
        Chunk number                  1
        Next chunk in DBSpace         0
        Chunk offset                  64
        Chunk size                    270000
        Number of free pages          70645
        DBSpace number                1
        Overhead                      0
        Flags                         2041      Chunk resides on RAW device
                                                Chunk is online

        Chunk name length             13
        Chunk path                    /dev/root_dbs

        Chunk number                  2
        Next chunk in DBSpace         0
        Chunk offset                  16
        Chunk size                    45000
        Number of free pages          14092
        DBSpace number                2
        Overhead                      0
        Flags                         2041      Chunk resides on RAW device
                                                Chunk is online

        Chunk name length             10
        Chunk path                    /dev/logs2

        Chunk number                  3
        Next chunk in DBSpace         4
        Chunk offset                  16
        Chunk size                    500000
        Number of free pages          18527
        DBSpace number                3
        Overhead                      0
        Flags                         2041      Chunk resides on RAW device
                                                Chunk is online

        Chunk name length             11
        Chunk path                    /dev/chunk2

        Chunk number                  4
        Next chunk in DBSpace         0
        Chunk offset                  16
        Chunk size                    500000
        Number of free pages          88404
        DBSpace number                3
        Overhead                      0
        Flags                         2041      Chunk resides on RAW device
                                                Chunk is online
        Chunk name length             11
        Chunk path                    /dev/chunk3
```

```
Chunk number                    5
    Next chunk in DBSpace       0
    Chunk offset                16
    Chunk size                  67500
    Number of free pages        6142
    DBSpace number              4
    Overhead                    0
    Flags                       2041        Chunk resides on RAW device
                                            Chunk is online

    Chunk name length           9
    Chunk path                  /dev/logs

Validating INFORMIX-OnLine reserved pages - PAGE_1MCHUNK & PAGE_2MCHUNK
Using mirror chunk page PAGE_2MCHUNK.

Validating INFORMIX-OnLine reserved pages - PAGE_1ARCH & PAGE_2ARCH
Using archive page PAGE_2ARCH.
    Archive Level               0
    Real Time Archive Began     01/12/94 09:18:23
    Time Stamp Archive Began    527989114
    Logical Log Unique Id       349
    Logical Log Position        a9c224
```

There's a lot of information available from the `tbcheck -pr` utility, and some of it is available nowhere else. It provides a good snapshot of the condition of your database at any particular time. It would be wise to occasionally run this option and save it in an archive file. If this is accompanied by running `newschema` for the entire database, it would provide useful disaster recovery capabilities for the DBA. The `newschema` script is presented in Chapter 6. It allows you to generate a correct, detailed database schema that contains more detail than the Informix `dbschema` program.

The logfile and checkpoint information presented is also unique to this program. I know of no other way to get access to this data other than by using the `tbcheck` utility. Of course, all of this data can be massaged by UNIX scripts, should the DBA have some more specific needs in mind.

DATA MOVEMENT UTILITIES

Before a database becomes useful for real work, it has to have data. Initially, this sounds like a really stupid statement, but it is really the place where we have to start in working with OnLine. The data does not just magically appear in the tables ready to be used in our applications. It has to be put there, most often by being imported from other non-OnLine sources.

Maybe your system is well established and the tables are already populated. You may be tempted to believe that data movement utilities are no longer of use to you. Wrong. You will have many instances in which these utilities will be used. You may need to upgrade your hardware to another machine. You may need to provide data dumps that can be read by another database system on another machine. Your users may want data that they can use in their PC programs. Maybe they want files that they can read into their spreadsheets or word processors. Maybe you need to move large tables from one instance to another or from one dbspace to another. Maybe you need to provide extra archive protection for a few tables. The data movement utilities are essential for all of these applications.

General Concepts

There are some concepts that apply to moving data within OnLine or to and from other systems no matter what methods you choose to use. Data migration requires a knowledge of your particular OnLine setup and of the contents of your data tables. For the most part, unloading data from your OnLine system is fairly simple. It is when you need to load data from another source into OnLine that complications may arise. Choosing the proper tools for data migration depends upon several factors:

- Requirements of the other system
- Contents of the data
- Logging status of your OnLine system
- Indexing requirements
- Degree of logical consistency required between tables
- Time frame
- UNIX resources
- OnLine resources

Requirements of the Other System

Whether the other system is providing data to OnLine or whether OnLine is providing data to the other system, each has to be aware of the other's needs. A basic need is that they both use the same character representations. If you output data in ASCII and the other system wants it in EBCDIC, you will need to use the proper UNIX utilities to translate the data.

Contents of the Data

You need to know how the data is currently formatted and how it needs to be formatted for the other system. If the other system wants multiline records or is sending you multiline records, you will use different tools than if all records are single lines. For the methods that use ASCII dumps, you need to be able to choose a delimiter character. Your data will be junk if you try to use a UNIX pipe "|" symbol to separate your fields and your data actually contains the pipe symbol. Some of the means of unloading data are smart enough to watch out for this, but you need to double-check. For example, the UNLOAD TO xxxx SQL statement will escape a delimiter character if it finds one in a character field. You also need to be aware of how the source and target systems handle null fields.

Logging Status of your OnLine System

Logging status is one of the "gotchas" of moving data to and from OnLine. This usually gives you trouble when you are loading data into an OnLine system. Some of the utilities require that the logging modes of the sending and receiving database (OnLine to OnLine) be the same. No matter what tools you're using, it is usually better to load into a database that has logging turned off. Of course, this is not practical if you are loading into a production system using logging and you can't or don't want to turn the logging off. It's tempting to try to get around this problem by loading data into a nonlogging database and then either creating synonyms from a logging database into the new table or using INFORMIX-Star to load data from the new, nonlogging table into your production system. This does not work, as OnLine enforces rules that require similarity of logging status on each side of synonyms and INFORMIX-Star links.

Indexing Requirements

You should load into nonindexed tables and index the tables after the data is in place. If you are loading and indexing at the same time, you will have data pages interspersed with index pages in your tablespace. This causes the data to be fragmented and makes access to the data slower. This is especially noticeable with long, sequential, nonindexed reads of the data. If the data pages had all been contiguous, the reads would be quite efficient. The indexes would have also been more compact, as they would have been presorted. With data pages and index pages interspersed, the disk head has to jump around quite a lot to read the data. In addition, the entire process goes faster if the indexing is done later. Especially in versions later than 4.11, the engine supports parallel sorting via the PSORT environmental variables. If you have multiple processors, using this parallel sorting capability will make your sorts go much faster. There are three separate PSORT variables:

- PSORT_DBTEMP = list of filesystems for sorting and working storage
- PSORT_NPROCS = number of sort threads to use
- PSORT_MALLOC = amount of data to keep in memory before writing work files. This is an undocumented variable and performs best at 10240.

If you can, when you are unloading a table to a flat file for loading into another OnLine database, sort the output in the primary key order that is desired for the target table. That way, when the table is loaded, it is already clustered on the primary key. In addition, if a table is already in the proper sorted order, there is an environmental variable that you can set to tell the sort that the table is already sorted and that the engine does not need to perform a sort for this index. This variable is $NOSORTINDEX. Set it to 1 before creating the primary index for this table, and the sorting portion of your index build will go even faster.

Degree of Logical Consistency Between Tables

If you are dumping just one table or loading just one table, you usually don't have to worry too much about consistency, but it may bear some thought. If you are moving multiple tables that depend upon one another, you definitely need to consider whether you can unload them while database activity is occurring. First, you need to decide whether the data movement occurs when the database is online or when it is quiescent. Are others accessing or needing access to the tables? Does the table depend upon other tables for join information or lookup information? Can others access the table while the data movement is happening? Does the utility lock the table when unloading? All of these factors make a difference in deciding how you move data.

If you try to move two tables while the database is running, you could be facing some serious problems if changes were made to the first and second tables after the first had been unloaded and before the second had been unloaded. The tables could contain logically inconsistent data.

Time Frame

How much time do you have to do this job? Do you need to have a table locked for hours? Do you need the database quiescent for hours? Just how long will it take to move a few million rows?

UNIX Resources

If you're moving data to disk, do you have enough disk space? How much of load will the job place on your system?

OnLine Resources

This is an important factor. First and foremost, will loading the data create a long transaction problem? If you're loading into a logging database, this could definitely be a problem. Make sure that you have enough logfiles and that other activities that generate heavy logging are not happening at the same time. Make sure that your LTXHWM and LTEHWM logfile high water marks are set lower than the defaults, as the defaults are too high for most real-world applications. Use at most 60 percent and 70 percent for the respective numbers. Make sure that you have enough locks in the system to handle the locking load. If you're loading using SQL into an existing or newly created table, lock the target table before beginning the load. That way, you'll use only one table lock instead of thousands of row or page locks.

We'll now look briefly at the tools for moving data. For full details on the operations of each of the utilities, look to your manuals. This is just an overview of the capabilities and applicability of each tool. We'll explore the tools from fastest to slowest.

Tbtape -s   (archive and restore)

This is by far your tool of choice if you are moving an entire instance. It will move everything: all databases, all indexes, all extent data, even all wasted space. If you want to move just one database from one machine to another, you can always move everything and drop the ones you don't want. You may even be able to use your normal backup archives as a medium of transferring data to the new computer without doing any extra work on your source machine.

Obviously, this works only from one OnLine system to another. Depending upon the differences between versions, it may work from one OnLine version to another. If the versions are close enough and if the machines have similar page sizes and similar ways of representing data, it may even work from one brand of computer to another. If you're upgrading to a bigger computer using the same operating system, the same OnLine version, and the same architecture, this may be the way to go.

At least with OnLine versions prior to version 6.0, the host and target machines must have similar layouts. If you have a one gigabyte chunk on /dev/chunk1 on the source machine, you must have a similar (or larger) size device on the target machine. The general rule is that the target machine must have everything that the host machine has. If you're working on a disaster recovery plan, make sure that your backup machine at least equals your source in disk space allocated to OnLine.

Along with the archives that are necessary for recovery, be sure that you have copied to a safe place any other information that would be necessary to recreate your system's layout. Keep a copy of the tbconfig file and a copy of the tbstat -a output. Also keep a copy of the output of the tbcheck -pr command.

If you can use tbtape's archives and restores to move your data, you can expect to restart on the new system with it looking exactly like the old system with little or no effort.

Tbunload/Tbload

The tbload and tbunload utilities are a very fast means of moving tables and databases. They can work either on single tables or on entire databases. Like archive and restore, they work with binary pages of data and are very fast, similar in speed to the archive and restore utilities. Like archives and restores using tbtape they require compatible versions of On-Line, compatible page sizes and page format, and compatible integer representations. Unlike tbtape archives and restores, they do not require similar resources and identical chunk size and naming.

The tbunload and tbload programs also transfer index, extent, and other table information. One of the potential problems that can occur with the moving of indexes is the requirement that index names be unique over a database. You cannot have two indexes named index_1 within a database even if they are on separate tables. The names must be unique. The tbload utility provides for this by providing a -i parameter that will allow you to rename indexes during the move to preserve the uniqueness of index names.

The tbload and tbunload utilities are designed to move data to and from tape. If you want to use a disk file instead, you should first create the file and make sure that it has proper ownership and permissions and then treat the file just like a tape device. Of course, you should be certain that you will have enough space on the device to hold all the data.

If you succeed in moving a table or a database using tbunload/tbload, always run the tbcheck utility on the resulting table or database. I have seen situations where the tbload completed with no problems, the tables showed up on the new system, and the data seemed to be there. However, when the tbcheck utility was run, there were internal problems with the data. Check it out carefully before putting your trust in it.

Dbexport/Dbimport

This utility pair moves entire databases between OnLine and/or INFORMIX-SE systems in the form of ASCII files. They transfer entire databases and cannot be used to add tables to existing databases. They create database schema files and database export files. The schema files and the export files can be individually directed either to disk or to tape. The schema files used by these utilities are basic and do not include information about extent sizes, locking modes, dbspaces, or logging modes.

These schemas are generalized so that they can be used to transfer data to and from both OnLine and INFORMIX-SE systems. If you are planning to send the data files to disk, be sure that you have enough disk space to hold your entire database.

Schema files can be edited if they are sent to disk, or they can be replaced with complete schema files such as those generated by the newschema shell script that is included in the CD-ROM that accompanies this book.

During operation of dbexport, the source database is locked in exclusive mode, so it is not suitable for operation while the database is in use.

Dbload

The dbload utility does not have a reciprocal dbunload program. The dbload utility is used to insert ASCII formatted data into existing tables, with the loading parameters controlled by a command file. This utility is best suited for moving complex ASCII data into OnLine tables.

This utility is executed from the UNIX command line. It has many option flags that give you a lot of control over how the utility runs.

The load utility gives you detailed control over delimiters, frequency of commits to avoid long transaction problems, acceptable number of errors before abort, number of rows to skip at the beginning of a data file, and whether or not to lock the target table when loading.

The usage of the dbload utility is:

```
INFORMIX : 19> dbload
DBLOAD Load Utility          INFORMIX-SQL Version 5.00.UC2
Copyright (C) Informix Software, Inc., 1984-1991
Software Serial Number XYZ#C2999999

Usage:
dbload [-d dbname] [-c cfilname] [-l logfile] [-e errnum] [-n nnum]
[-i inum] [-s] [-p] [-r]

d       database name
c       command file name
l       bad row(s) log file
e       bad row(s) # before abort
s       syntax error check only
n       # of row(s) before commit
p       prompt to commit or not on abort
i       # or row(s) to ignore before starting
r       loading without locking table
```

The command files can handle two main types of data: data that is delimited by a defined delimiter character and tabular data that is character-position dependent. This flexibility of input formats makes dbload a very powerful tool for loading ASCII files from sources other than an OnLine database. The dbload utility can be combined with other UNIX utilities to create flexible systems that takes a datafile or report from another source, massages it with UNIX utilities into a format that dbload understands, and finally loads the data into OnLine through dbload.

One of the main features of the dbload command is the -n parameter. It is possible that if you try to load a very large table into a tablespace you will run into problems with running out of locks or creating a long transaction. The -n parameter allows you to get around either of these problems, as the value of n tells dbload to perform a COMMIT WORK every n rows. These periodic commits prevent dbload from using all of your locks and from trying to do the entire load in one transaction, causing a long transaction and possibly filling up all your logfiles.

Another very useful capability of dbload is the -e parameter. Unless you are using dbload, if you attempt to load duplicate rows into a table with unique indexes or unique constraints, you will bomb out with an error message that tells you that you have duplicate data. This can become a real pain if you are trying to eliminate these duplicates. You can use the -e parameter to tell dbload to ignore bad rows and to place them in an error file (the name of which is determined by the -l parameter). The value of e is the total number of bad rows you will accept before allowing dbload to fail.

If you have a case where you have partially loaded a table, or if you have two tables that have duplicates, and you want to consolidate them, you can use dbload to create one table. Unload the first table into a flat file using the SQL UNLOAD TO command. Then do a dbload with a very large value for the -e parameter, loading the second table from the flat file that contains the first table's contents. The dbload command will complain about the duplicate rows, but it will load all of the nonduplicate rows into the second table.

Writing and debugging the command files for dbload is as much an exercise in programming as is writing SQL statements or writing C programs. If you need to use dbload to move data, sit down with the manuals and the examples and see how it is done. You may want to look at the *.unl files in the $INFORMIXDIR/demo file tree for examples of the use of this program.

The command file for dbload contains the name of the file from which the dbload program gets the data to load into the table. This does not necessarily have to be the name of a file. If your flavor of UNIX supports *named pipes* created by the mkfifo UNIX command, the data source can be a named pipe. You can use this to move data from table to table or from database to database without worrying about long transactions or running out of locks. Create the named pipe and start a SQL UNLOAD TO "named_pipe" command from your source table. From another terminal, run dbload with "named_pipe" as the source of your data. The data will be unloaded from the source table and inserted into the target table.

Unload/Load To/From filename select_statement

This pair of SQL statements allows you to create delimited ASCII files from tables and to place the contents of delimited ASCII files into tables. They can be used either with isql or with dbaccess. The select_statement in the UNLOAD command can be any legal OnLine SELECT statement, so it is possible to create LOADS of partial tables or fragments of tables.

These commands are suitable for use on an operating production system provided you have covered the problems of ensuring adequate resources and have adequately addressed the issues of logging and concurrency of access. The UNLOAD SQL statement is very seldom a problem in any manner, unless you don't have adequate disk space, but using LOAD can create long transactions or can cause you to run out of locks. In cases like this, the dbload program may be better for your use.

Reports to a File

ASCII files can be generated using a report writer. If you use `isql`, you can use the ACE report writer that is included with `isql`. These report files, if used with the default report format, will create character-position dependent ASCII output files suitable for use with `dbload`. By modifying the SELECT statement in the report, the report writer could create a delimited report.

Output to filename WITHOUT HEADINGS

This SQL statement is similar to UNLOAD except that it does not place delimiters in the output file. This makes it suitable for creating output files that are character-position dependent. It can also be run with the WITHOUT HEADINGS constraint that causes OnLine to omit the names of the fields. The OUTPUT TO or the UNLOAD TO SQL statements can create files that can be read by the `dbload` program.

An interesting and useful feature of the OUTPUT TO statement in SQL is the ability to use the PIPE statement in place of an output file. This statement takes the output of the SQL command and pipes it into a UNIX pipeline. Use of this construct is one way that you can cause a UNIX command to execute from within your SQL statements.

For example:

```
OUTPUT TO PIPE " > /dev/null; ls -la" select * from dummy
```

Since SQL does not have the equivalent of a `system` command, this trick can simulate a `system` command. The contents of the pipe command needs to do something with the standard output of the SQL statement.

If you just want to execute a system command and don't care about the output of the SQL command, just redirect its output to `/dev/null` as in the example.

Of course, this command is also very handy for its intended purpose, which is to pipe the output of the SQL to a UNIX command. This allows for further processing of the output by UNIX. This pipeline can be as complicated or as detailed as UNIX will allow.

If you wish, your SQL output can provide the starting point for extensive post-processing outside of the database. In some instances, this can be quite useful, as there are a lot of tasks that can be efficiently completed in UNIX but are difficult, expensive, or impractical to do within SQL.

In fact, it is possible to pipe the output to a long series of UNIX commands, massage the output, pipe the output into files, and then use one of the IDS LOAD commands to retrieve the data back into the OnLine database. This gives you the capability of choosing your working tools based upon the job to be done instead of trying to attack everything using the OnLine tools.

Isql **and** Dbaccess

For many users, the isql or dbaccess program is all they know of the OnLine system. This menu-based program is ubiquitous and is often taken for granted. There is a lot of utility in Informix's implementation of isql, and much of this utility is often overlooked. This seems to be especially true with users who have moved over from another database system to an OnLine system. Dbaccess is a stripped-down version of isql that is included with the 5.0 series of products. Dbaccess does not include the menu-creation and report-writing capabilities of isql.

Different database management programs all use extensions to ANSI SQL to achieve more functionality. Users coming from database management systems that add many extensions to their SQL products sometimes feel restricted when in the SQL query portion of OnLine. Such things as extensive string functions are not present as they are in the SQL's of programs such as Oracle. Heavy users of ESQL/C seem to feel this loss the most. They may use only the embedded SQL capabilities of OnLine and may miss out on some of the other functions available through isql.

The I-SQL program contains five major areas of functionality. For the SQL developer, the one that gets the most attention is the Query Language section. This system allows the user to create, modify, save, run, and redirect the output of SQL statements. A user who spends most of her time in the Query Language module may believe that some of the more sophisticated features of other database management systems are not present in OnLine.

Of course, this is not true. The isql module is a suite of packages. The main features are a form-based query and user-interface program, a report generator, the Query Language module, a user menu generator and runner, and a database and table status module. As an example, much of the character manipulation and string management functions are found in the report writer application. You can do things here that you cannot do in the query management module such as concatenation of strings, control of output format, and the like.

The forms module provides a very handy "quick and dirty" method of dealing with the data in the tables. You can generate, compile, and run complex, multipage screen forms quickly and easily. This forms module is not as comprehensive as the INFORMIX-4GL product, but it is a handy tool for rapid development and management of database systems.

The user menu module is also very useful in developing a user interface for various purposes. Using the user menu options, you can easily integrate Informix programs, scripts, UNIX utilities, and other executables into a seamless whole. It doesn't give you all the bells and whistles that custom development in C or Microsoft Windows™ will give you, but it doesn't take you months to do it either.

In my opinion, these tools are underrated and underused. As a working DBA, you will need to provide many services and rapid response to your user community. You will find yourself needing to develop and use many programs, scripts, and data management schemes to do your job. You can make the choice to develop your tools with lots of options and user-interface gadgets or to develop them quickly and simply. If you decide to go for the utility over the flash, you probably have all the tools you need using isql and INFORMIX-4GL.

This book will not go into detail about `isql`, INFORMIX-4GL, and the SQL query language. We are assuming that the DBA either has experience with, or can read the manuals for these programs. However, we will include examples of user tools developed with INFORMIX-4GL, forms built in the forms generator, and menu programs running under the menu module. All of these examples are of tools that will be helpful or informative to the DBA. As you are studying the examples, remain open to other things that you can do using these tools. I'm taking a typical UNIX approach to this. Show you the tools, show you how they can work together, and then turn you loose to develop your own variants.

If you develop some particularly interesting or useful variants, get on the Internet and post them to the `comp.databases.informix` newsgroups. If they're handy for you, others can probably use them. Besides, it'll give you a moment or two of fame!

The Onstat Utility in IDS

*T*he onstat utility in Informix Dynamic Server should look very familiar to users who have used the earlier OnLine products. Onstat represents the evolution of the tbstat command in OnLine into the parallel processing world of Informix Dynamic Server. Many if not most of the commands from tbstat work exactly the same way in onstat. If you've seen a trick or idea from the last chapter, don't think that it applies only to OnLine engines. Try it with the later versions if there's any question of compatibility.

There have been a few minor evolutionary changes in the tbstat commands, with one revolutionary change that turns it into onstat. That revolutionary change is the onstat -g syntax, which adds the whole new world of parallel processing to the old tbstat command structure. When tbstat was transformed into onstat, tbstat had used up most of the alpha characters for its existing options. Rather than rework the option usage for IDS, onstat added a single option, "-g whatever" where "whatever" is a command restricted to use with IDS engines. Thus, with the "-g" option, onstat typically requires two parameters rather than the old one parameter.

ADDITIONAL CREDITS

Much of the information about the meanings of the fields in the onstat commands was copied directly from Informix's excellent *Administrator's Guide for Informix Dynamic Server, Version 7.3,* February 1998. It's hard to exercise a lot of poetic license with field descriptions, and I wanted to come clean with the admission that some of this was just cut-and-paste. The manuals have said this a lot better than I could ever say it.

Many of these manuals are now available online from the Informix Web site under the following URL:

```
http://www.informix.com/answers
```

The CD-ROM that accompanies this book contains two Adobe Acrobat (pdf) files. One is the full text of the Version 7.3 Administrator's Manual, and the other is the Performance Tuning manual. These were the latest and greatest versions at the time of publication of this book. If you want to see the latest version of the manuals at any time, go to the above Web page and download the latest versions. You will also need to download Adobe Acrobat from this URL:

```
http://www.adobe.com/acrobat
```

These digital versions of the manuals are absolutely wonderful. They are relatively complete and very clear, and Acrobat comes with a powerful digital search capability. The digital search capability is reason enough to get the digital version.

OPTIONS TO ONSTAT

Onstat -

This syntax simply shows the header to the command, giving version, status, uptime, and memory usage as in the same tbstat command. Be aware that beginning with IDS 7.3, the version is listed as "Informix Dynamic Server" instead of the "Informix-OnLine" that was listed in previous versions of both OnLine and IDS. If you have any scripts looking for

"OnLine" in this line, they need to be made smart enough to look for either "OnLine" or "Informix Dynamic Server."

```
$ onstat -
Informix Dynamic Server Version 7.30.UC3   -- On-Line -- Up 2 days 21:01:57 -18464 Kbytes
```

This header includes five important sections. The first section gives the version number of the OnLine engine. The second section shows the current operating mode. Possible values of the mode are:

- Off-line: Engine not running.
- Quiescent: No user can start a server process. User `informix` can use administrative options of `onmonitor`. Any user can use `onstat` or view options of `onmonitor`.
- Online: Fully usable by all users.
- Shutdown: System is in transition from online to quiescent or from quiescent to off-line. Cannot be canceled.
- Recovery: Moving from off-line to quiescent. Fast recovery is performed here.

There is an optional third field following the mode indicator that shows up only in cases in which data replication is present. If DR is active, a "P" will show up here if this is a primary server, and an "S" will show up for the secondary server.

The fourth section is the (checkpoint) indicator. If applicable, this section can contain:

- (CKPT REQ)   Some process has requested a checkpoint, and the engine is trying to initiate the checkpoint. This flag is often seen if the database is hung waiting for a checkpoint.
- (CHKT INP)   Checkpoint is in progress. Users have read-only access to the database. No changes to data are allowed until the checkpoint ends.

The fifth section shows the real time that the database has been running, that is, the time since the last database startup. The sixth and final section shows the amount of shared memory in use by OnLine in kilobytes. This is roughly the size of the output file generated by the `onstat -o` command.

A second header line will appear in the header if the engine is blocked for any reason. The following line will occur in these cases:

```
Blocked: reason()
```

The reason is one of the following:

- CKPT   Checkpoint
- LONGTX   Long transaction
- ARCHIVE   A dbspace is being backed up
- MEDIA_FAILURE   Media failure
- HANG_SYSTEM   An unspecified server failure
- DBS_DROP   Dropping a dbspace
- DDR   Discrete data replication
- LBU   Logs full: high water mark

This section on blocked systems and the third section on replication role are new with onstat and do not appear in the headers for the tbstat program.

Onstat - -

Invoking onstat with a double minus flag brings up a list of options for the onstat command. This is a standard form of invocation for Informix utility programs. The double dash option always brings up the options screen.

```
$ onstat --
usage: onstat [ -abcdfghklmpstuxzBCDFRX ] [ -i ] [ -r [<seconds>] ]
[ -o [<outfile>] ] [ <infile> ]
     a      Print all info
     b      Print buffers
     c      Print configuration file
     d      Print spaces and chunks
     f      Print dataskip status
     g      MT subcommand (default: all)
     i      Interactive mode
     h      Print buffer hash chain info
     k      Print locks
     l      Print logging
     m      Print message log
     p      Print profile
     s      Print latches
     t      Print TBLspaces
     u      Print user threads
     x      Print transactions
     z      Zero profile counts
     B      Print all buffers
     C      Print btree cleaner requests
     D      Print spaces and detailed chunk stats
     F      Print page flushers
     G      Print global transaction ids.
     P      Print partition buffer summary
     R      Print LRU queues
     X      Print entire list of sharers and waiters for buffers
     r      Repeat options every <seconds> seconds (default: 5)
```

```
       o     Put shared memory into specified file (default: onstat.out)
<infile> Read shared memory information from specified dump file

MT COMMANDS:
       all   Print all MT information
       ath   Print all threads
       wai   Print waiting threads
       act   Print active threads
       rea   Print ready threads
       sle   Print all sleeping threads
       spi   Print spin locks with long spins
       sch   Print VP scheduler statistics
       lmx   Print all locked mutexes
       wmx   Print all mutexes with waiters
       con   Print conditions with waiters
       stk   <tid> Dump the stack of a specified thread
       glo   Print MT global information
       mem   [<pool name>|<session id>] Print pool statistics.
       seg   Print memory segment statistics
       rbm   Print block map for resident segment
       nbm   Print block map for non-resident segments
       afr   <pool name|session id> Print allocated pool fragments
       ffr   <pool name|session id> Print free pool fragments
       ufr   <pool name|session id> Print pool usage breakdown
       iov   Print disk IO statistics by vp
       iof   Print disk IO statistics by chunk/file
       iog   Print AIO global information
       iob   Print big buffer usage by IO VP class
       ppf   [<partition number> | 0] Print partition profiles
       tpf   [<tid> | 0] Print thread profiles
       ntu   Print net user thread profile information
       ntt   Print net user thread access times
       ntm   Print net message information
       ntd   Print net dispatch information
       nss   [<session id>] Print net shared memory status
       nsc   [<client id>] Print net shared memory status
       nsd   Print net shared memory data
       sts   Print max and current stack sizes
       dic   Print dictionary cache information
       opn   [<tid>] Print open tables
       qst   Print queue statistics
       wst   Print thread wait statistics
       ses   [<session id>] Print session information
       sql   [<session id>] Print SQL information
       stq   [<session id>] Print stream queue information
       dri   Print data replication information
       pos   Print /INFORMIXDIR/etc/.infos.DBSERVERNAME file
       mgm   Print Memory Grant Manager information
       lap   Print light append information
       ddr   Print DDR log post processing information
       dmp   <address> <length> Dump <length> bytes of memory starting at <address>
       src   <pattern> <mask> Search memory for <pattern>, where <pattern>==(memory&<mask>)
```

Onstat (No Options)

Invoking `onstat` with no options is equivalent of using the "-pu" option. It gives the header, the `onstat` -p performance monitoring screen, and the `onstat` -u user information screen. We'll go over each of these individual options later in depth.

Onstat -a   Print all Info

Don't use this option unless you are willing to deal with a lot of data. The "-a" option is the same as `onstat -cuskbtdlp`.   This breaks out to the following `onstat` outputs:

- config file
- user information
- latches
- locks
- buffers
- tablespaces
- disk usage
- log usage
- performance profile

Onstat -b   Print Buffers

This `onstat` command prints information about Informix buffers that are actually in use at the time. To see the same information about all buffers, see the `onstat` -B command.

```
$ onstat -b
Informix Dynamic Server Version 7.30.UC3   -- On-Line -- Up 2 days 21:02:04 -- 18464 Kbytes
Buffers
address  userthread flgs pagenum  memaddr  nslots pgflgs xflgs owner    waitlist
```

The fields have the following meanings:

- Address: The address of the buffer header in the buffer table
- User Threads: Most recent user thread to access this address
- Flgs: May have the following values:
  - 0x01   Modified data
  - 0x02   Data
  - 0x04   LRU
  - 0x08   Error
- Pagenum: Physical page number on the disk
- memaddr   Buffer memory address
- nslots: Number of slot-table entries in the page (rows or parts of rows on the page)
- pgflgs: The following flag values, alone or in combination, show the type of page this entry is pointing to.

1	data page
2	tblspace page
4	free-list page
8	chunk free-list page
9	remainder data page
b	partition resident blobpage
c	blobspace resident blobpage
d	blob chunk free-list bit page
e	blob chunk blob map page
10	B-tree node page
20	B-tree root-node page
40	B-tree branch-node page
80	B-tree leaf-node page
100	logical-log page
200	last page of logical log
400	sync page of logical log

800   physical log

1000 reserved root page

2000 no physical log required

8000 B-tree leaf with default flags

- xflgs   Describes the locking mode of the buffer access
  - 0x10 share lock
  - 0x80 exclusive lock
- owner   Thread ID that set the above xflags
- waitlist   Address of the first user thread awaiting this buffer

At the bottom of both the onstat -b and onstat -B screen is the following header:

```
0 modified, 0 resident, 4096 total, 4096 hash buckets, 2048 buffer size
```

The "total" number is the number of total buffers as specified in the BUFFERS parameter in the ONCONFIG file.

Onstat -B   Print all Buffers

This is the same output as is provided with onstat -b, with the exception that *all* buffers, whether used or not, are included in the output. Beware: on a large system with many buffers this may be a very lengthy output, so don't use it unless you really want to see lots of data.

```
$ onstat -B
Informix Dynamic Server Version 7.30.UC3    -- On-Line -- Up 2 days 21:03:06 -- 18464 Kbytes
Buffers
address  userthread flgs pagenum  memaddr  nslots pgflgs xflgs owner     waitlist
c103cfe4 0           6   100001   c10bc800 97     1000   0     0         0
c103d038 0          806  800004   c10bd000 5      2      0     0         0
c103d08c 0          806  100008   c10bd800 0      1000   0     0         0
c103d0e0 0          806  10000e   c10be000 5      2      0     0         0
c103d134 0          806  100009   c10be800 0      1000   0     0         0
<snipped many lines>
0 modified, 0 resident, 4096 total, 4096 hash buckets, 2048 buffer size
```

Onstat -c   Print Configuration File

Onstat -c prints out the ONCONFIG file for the instance. IDS decides which config file to use by first looking at the value of the ONCONFIG environment variable in UNIX and in NT. If this variable holds a file name, this is the file that gets displayed. If the variable is null, onstat will display the onconfig file in $INFORMIDIR/etc for UNIX or %INFORMIXDIR%\etc in NT.

Onstat -d   Print Spaces and Chunks

The "-d" and "-D" options to onstat are similar in presentation. The onstat -d command displays information about the chunks in each dbspace. The onstat -D command shows the same information, with the exception that the chunk size and chunk free values have been replaced with chunk reads and chunk writes.

```
$ onstat -d
Informix Dynamic Server Version 7.30.UC3     -- On-Line -- Up 2 days 21:02:10 -- 18464 Kbytes
Dbspaces
address   number   flags    fchunk   nchunks  flags   owner      name
c18d8158  1        1        1        1        N       informix   rootdbs
c18d8a78  2        1        2        1        N       informix   config_data
c18d8b38  3        1        3        1        N       informix   eba_data
c18d8bf8  4        1        4        1        N       informix   demotest_data
c18d8cb8  5        1        5        1        N       informix   eba_data_r0
c18d8d78  6        1        6        1        N       informix   eba_data_r1
c18d8e38  7        1        7        1        N       informix   appldbs_data
c18d8ef8  8        1        8        1        N       informix   logspace_data
c18d8fb8  9        2001     9        1        N T     informix   tempspace_data
9 active, 2047 maximum
Chunks
address   chk/dbs  offset   size     free     bpages  flags pathname
c18d8218  1   1    0        10000    4671             PO-   /dbspace/inf/rock1/rootdbs
c18d8378  2   2    0        10000    8241             PO-   /dbspace/inf/rock1/config_data
c18d8458  3   3    0        20000    18423            PO-   /dbspace/inf/rock1/eba_data
c18d8538  4   4    0        20000    13483            PO-   /dbspace/inf/rock1/demotest_data
c18d8618  5   5    0        20000    19947            PO-   /dev/vg00/rraw0
c18d86f8  6   6    0        20000    19947            PO-   /dev/vg01/rraw1
c18d87d8  7   7    0        20000    17357            PO-   /dbspace/inf/rock1/appldbs_data
c18d88b8  8   8    0        10000    9947             PO-   /dbspace/inf/rock1/logspace_data
c18d8998  9   9    0        10000    9947             PO-   /dbspace/inf/rock1/tempspace_data
9 active, 2047 maximum
```

The first section, "Dbspaces," describes the dbspaces that make up the database.

- address   Address of the space in the shared-memory space table.
- number   Unique ID number of the space assigned at creation.
- flags   The following hexadecimal values:
                    0x0001 No mirror

                              0x0002 Mirror

                              0x0004 Down

                              0x0008 Newly mirrored

                              0x0010 Blobspace

- fchunk   ID number of the first chunk.
- nchunks   Number of chunks in the space.
- flags   Use the following letter codes:

                       Position 1:

                             M - Mirrored

                             N - Not Mirrored

                       Position 2:

                             X - Newly mirrored

                             P - Physically recovered, waiting for logical recovery

                             L - Being logically recovered

                             R- Being recovered

                       Position 3:

                             B - Blobspace

- owner   Owner of the space.
- name   Name of the space.

The second section is the Chunks section, and it gives information about the actual chunks that create the dbspaces. The fields mean:

- address   Address of the chunk.
- chk/dbs   Chunk number and the associated space number.
- offset   Offset into the device in pages.
- size   Size of the chunk in pages.
- free   Approximate number of free pages in the chunk.
- bpages   Size of the chunk in blobpages.
- flags   Chunk status information:

                       Position 1:

                       P - Primary

                       M - Mirror

                       Position 2:

                       O - On-line

D - Down

X - Newly mirrored

I - Inconsistent

Position 3:

B - Blobspace

- - Dbspace

T - Temporary dbspace

• pathname   Pathname of the physical device.

Onstat -D   Print Spaces and Chunk Statistics

This is just like onstat -d except that it shows reads and writes to the chunks rather than sizes and space free. This is more of a tuning tool to help you visualize how much activity a particular chunk or set of chunks will receive.

The meanings to the fields are the same as onstat -d, with the exception that the Chunks section has pages read and pages written in place of size and free as in onstat -d. Judicious use of this command can give the DBA a very good idea about the disk access patterns for the database. This is especially important because the speed and efficiency of disk access are the primary predictors of overall database performance.

One technique of maximizing performance is placing critical tables that see lots of activity into chunks that hold only that table and maybe its indexes. If they are in individual chunks, you can use onstat -D to monitor the reads and writes to the tables of interest. Using this technique can also allow you to choose some of the most common, time-intensive joins and place the major tables involved on separate disks to minimize disk thrashing during joins and queries. Doing this requires an intimate knowledge of the types of use that the database will see, but it is well worth the effort in terms of performance improvements.

```
$ onstat -D
Informix Dynamic Server Version 7.30.UC3    -- On-Line -- Up 2 days 21:03:23 -- 18464 Kbytes
Dbspaces
address   number   flags    fchunk   nchunks   flags   owner     name
c18d8158  1        1        1        1         N       informix  rootdbs
c18d8a78  2        1        2        1         N       informix  config_data
c18d8b38  3        1        3        1         N       informix  eba_data
c18d8bf8  4        1        4        1         N       informix  demotest_data
c18d8cb8  5        1        5        1         N       informix  eba_data_r0
c18d8d78  6        1        6        1         N       informix  eba_data_r1
c18d8e38  7        1        7        1         N       informix  appldbs_data
c18d8ef8  8        1        8        1         N       informix  logspace_data
c18d8fb8  9        2001     9        1         N T     informix  tempspace_data
9 active, 2047 maximum
Chunks
address   chk/dbs offset    page Rd   page Wr   pathname
c18d8218  1   1   0         0         0         /dbspace/inf/rock1/rootdbs
```

```
c18d8378 2    2    0         0         0         /dbspace/inf/rock1/config_data
c18d8458 3    3    0         0         0         /dbspace/inf/rock1/eba_data
c18d8538 4    4    0         0         0         /dbspace/inf/rock1/demotest_data
c18d8618 5    5    0         0         0         /dev/vg00/rraw0
c18d86f8 6    6    0         0         0         /dev/vg01/rraw1
c18d87d8 7    7    0         0         0         /dbspace/inf/rock1/app1dbs_data
c18d88b8 8    8    0         0         0         /dbspace/inf/rock1/logspace_data
c18d8998 9    9    0         0         0         /dbspace/inf/rock1/tempspace_data
9 active, 2047 maximum
```

Onstat -f   Print Dataskip Status

Sometimes a dbspace may be off-line for one of many reasons, including media problems, disk or table reorganization, or for some reason taken off-line on purpose. IDS provides the dataskip feature to instruct the engine as to how to respond when it finds a dbspace off-line. Earlier OnLine engines would simply generate an error and abort the query or even take the engine off-line in some cases. The value of dataskip can be one of the following:

- OFF for all dbspaces (behavior similar to OnLine)
- ON for all dbspaces   (Queries proceed even if some chunks are off-line)
- ON for some dbspaces

Dataskip can be set by one of several methods:

- Setting DATASKIP parameter in the ONCONFIG file
- Execution of the SET DATASKIP command in SQL
- Use the onspaces command to set dataskip

The onstat -f command shows the current dataskip status.

```
$ onstat -f
Informix Dynamic Server Version 7.30.UC3    -- On-Line -- Up 2 days 21:02:14 -- 18464 Kbytes

dataskip is OFF for all dbspaces
```

While setting dataskip can enhance availability of the system, the DBA must be aware of the status at all times to ensure that she knows that dbspaces are being ignored due to their off-line status.

Onstat -i   Interactive Mode

The onstat -i option allows onstat to run in an interactive mode, one command at a time. When in this mode, the prompt becomes "onstat>." When you go into this mode, you may see a sequence like the following:

```
$  onstat -i
onstat>  f

Informix Dynamic Server Version 7.30.UC3    -- On-Line -- Up 2 days 21:02:14 -- 18464 Kbytes

dataskip is OFF for all dbspaces
onstat>  r 5
onstat[5]>  whatever_command_option_you_want
^C (ends a repeating command)
^D (exits interactive mode)
```

One of the handy features of this mode is that there is an "rz" command that acts like the "r" command followed by a "z" command. This repeatedly executes a command, zeroing out the statistics profile after each execution. This is handy in providing an incremental picture of what's going on in the database.

Onstat -h   Print Buffer Hash Chain Information

This command gives you information about the hash buffers and the linked lists that comprise them.

```
$ onstat -h
Informix Dynamic Server Version 7.30.UC3    -- On-Line -- Up 2 days 21:02:32 -- 18464 Kbytes
buffer hash chain length histogram
   # of chains          of len
       2397             0
       1550             1
        105             2
         38             3
              4              4
              1              8
              1              9
       4096 total chains
       1699 hashed buffs
       4096       total buffs
```

- # of chains   Count of the # of hash chains for which the length is "len."
- of len   Length of the chains.
- total chains   Total number of hash chains (buckets) created.
- hashed buffs   Number of buffer headers hashed into the hash buckets.
- total buffs   The total number of buffers in the buffer pool.

Onstat -k   Print Locks

This invocation shows any locks that are placed within the database at any particular point
in time.

```
$ onstat -k
Informix Dynamic Server Version 7.30.UC3    -- On-Line -- Up 2 days 21:02:35 -- 18464 Kbytes
Locks
address   wtlist    owner    lklist    type     tblsnum   rowid    key#/bsiz
c0f1eb24  0         c18db79c 0         HDR+S    100002    20b      0
c0f1eb58  0         c18db2e8 0            S     100002    20b      0
2 active, 20000 total, 16384 hash buckets
```

The fields have the following meanings

- address: Address of the lock in the lock table.
- wtlist: Address of the first user thread waiting on this lock.
- owner: Shared memory address of the owner holding the lock.
- lklist: If owner holds more locks, this is the address of the next lock.
- type: Type of lock identified by the following flags:

HDR:	Header lock
B:	Byte lock
S:	Shared lock
X:	Exclusive lock
I:	Intent lock
U:	Update lock
IX:	Intent exclusive
IS:	Intent shared
SIX:	Shared, intent exclusive lock

- tblsnum: Tablespace number of the locked resource.
- rowid: Rowid that is being locked. Values mean:

= 0	Table lock
ends in 00	Page lock
< six digits and does not end in 0:	Probably a row lock
>six digits	Index key value lock

- key#/bsiz   Index key number or #bytes of varchar locked.

The analysis of locking problems is always an issue for the DBA. This `onstat` command is one of the primary tools that the DBA has available to assist in this endeavor. Identifying the job that is causing a locking problem invariably comes down to resolving user addresses and translating them into user names and jobs.

One thing that I have found useful in tracking down locking problems is to run an `onstat -a` and pipe it into a file:

```
$ onstat -a > myfile
$ grep whatever_address_youre_looking_for myfile
$ vi myfile
search for the address in question
```

You could just pipe the `onstat -a` output into `grep`, but all you would see is the actual lines that contained the subject address. This would not show the context information for the lines, and it is difficult to know whether you're looking at user information, thread information, or whatever, unless you are very familiar with the `onstat -a` output. If you first pipe the output to a file, you can then search for the address and see the context of the lines containing the address, making it much easier to understand the output.

Onstat -l   Print Logging Information

The `onstat -l` command provides information about the usage of physical and logical logfiles in IDS. This command works very much like the tbstat -l command, at least superficially. It differs in that it shows backed-up logfiles as 100 percent used rather than as 0 percent used as the `tbstat` command did. This may effect the usability of some scripts that are written for OnLine originally.

```
$ onstat -l
Informix Dynamic Server Version 7.30.UC3    -- On-Line -- Up 2 days 21:02:38 -- 18464 Kbytes
Physical Logging
Buffer bufused  bufsize  numpages numwrits pages/io
  P-2  0         16       1292     94       13.74
       phybegin physize  phypos   phyused  %used
       10003f   500      498      0        0.00

Logical Logging
Buffer bufused  bufsize  numrecs  numpages numwrits recs/pages pages/io
  L-1  0         16       39377    2313     180      17.0       12.8

          Subsystem    numrecs  Log Space used
          OLDRSAM      39377    4599840

address   number   flags    uniqid   begin      size    used    %used
c101c9a4  1        U-B----  421      100233     250     250     100.00
c101c9c0  2        U-B----  422      10032d     250     250     100.00
c101c9dc  3        U-B----  423      100427     250     250     100.00
c101c9f8  4        U-B----  424      100521     250     250     100.00
c101ca14  5        U-B----  425      10061b     250     250     100.00
```

```
c101ca30 6        U-B----  426      100715       250       250    100.00
c101ca4c 7        U-B----  427      10080f       250       250    100.00
c101ca68 8        U-B----  428      100909       250       250    100.00
c101ca84 9        U-B----  429      100a03       250       250    100.00
c101caa0 10       U---C-L  430      100afd       250       110     44.00
c101cabc 11       U-B----  416      100bf7       250       250    100.00
c101cad8 12       U-B----  417      100cf1       250       250    100.00
c101caf4 13       U-B----  418      100deb       250       250    100.00
c101cb10 14       U-B----  419      100ee5       250       250    100.00
c101cb2c 15       U-B----  420      100fdf       250       250    100.00
```

The first section is the physical log section.

- Buffer: Number of the physical log buffer currently in use.
- bufused: Number of pages of that buffer currently used.
- bufsize: Size in pages of the physical log buffer.
- numpages: Number of pages written to this current buffer.
- numwrites: Number of writes to the disk.
- pages/io: Numpages/numwrites = buffer efficiency.
- phybegin: Physical page number of first page in physical log.
- physize: Size of physical log in pages.
- phypos: Current page address in physical log.
- phyused: Number of log pages used.
- %used: Percentage of pages used.

Note that the first six data items refer to the physical log buffer, and the last group refers to the physical log itself, not the buffers. The second section concerns the logical logfiles.

- buffer: Logical log buffer number.
- bufused: Logical log buffer pages used.
- bufsize: Size in pages of the logical log buffer.
- numrecs: Number of records written.
- numpages: Number of pages written.
- numwrites: Number of writes.
- recs/pages: Numrecs/numpages. Determined by types of operations.
- pages/io: Numrecs/numwrites = efficiency of buffering.

The third section details specific information about the use and configuration of the logical logfiles. The major difference between IDS and OnLine in this area is that the sizing

of logical logfiles can vary in IDS and not in OnLine. In OnLine systems, changing the size
of logical logfiles was a major operation involving a reconfiguration of the system. In IDS
systems, logfile size is configurable for each logfile added.

- address: Physical address of the logical logfile.
- number: Logical log id number.
- flags: Status flags for the logfile in question. Values are:

    A   newly added logfile

    B   backed up

    C   logfile currently in use

    F   free and available to use

    L   contains the last checkpoint record

    U   used

- uniqid: Unique ID number of the log, not to be confused with number.
- begin: Beginning address of the logfile.
- size: Size in pages of the logfile.
- used: Number of pages used in the logfile.
- %used: Used/size = percentage full of logfile.

Onstat -m   Print Message Log

This invocation of onstat prints the last 20 entries in the message log. This file is specified in the MSGPATH parameter of the ONCONFIG file.

```
$ onstat -m
Informix Dynamic Server Version 7.30.UC3    -- On-Line -- Up 2 days 21:02:40 -- 18464 Kbytes
Message Log File: /informix/online.log
10:12:30  Checkpoint Completed:  duration was 1 seconds.
10:13:46  Logical Log 427 Complete.
10:17:33  Checkpoint Completed:  duration was 0 seconds.
10:22:37  Checkpoint Completed:  duration was 0 seconds.
10:27:37  Logical Log 428 Complete.
10:27:38  Logical Log 429 Complete.
10:27:40  Checkpoint Completed:  duration was 0 seconds.
10:32:42  Checkpoint Completed:  duration was 0 seconds.
11:03:01  Checkpoint Completed:  duration was 0 seconds.
13:24:24  Checkpoint Completed:  duration was 0 seconds.
13:29:27  Checkpoint Completed:  duration was 0 seconds.
13:34:30  Checkpoint Completed:  duration was 0 seconds.
13:39:33  Checkpoint Completed:  duration was 0 seconds.
13:44:36  Checkpoint Completed:  duration was 0 seconds.
13:49:39  Checkpoint Completed:  duration was 0 seconds.
```

```
13:54:42  Checkpoint Completed:  duration was 0 seconds.
13:59:45  Checkpoint Completed:  duration was 0 seconds.
```

Onstat -p   Print Profile

Onstat -p is a primary method of understanding the performance of an IDS database. If you learn one invocation of onstat well, this should be the one. This is the place to start looking to correct performance and configuration problems.

```
$ onstat -p
Informix Dynamic Server Version 7.30.UC3    -- On-Line -- Up 2 days 21:02:43 -- 18464 Kbytes
Profile
dskreads pagreads bufreads %cached dskwrits pagwrits bufwrits %cached
1700     1725     216848   99.22   2630     5961     40360    93.48

isamtot  open     start    read     write    rewrite  delete   commit   rollbk
206500   25385    37521    47516    11083    2480     1946     2405     4

gp_read  gp_write gp_rewrt gp_del   gp_alloc gp_free  gp_curs
0        0        0        0        0        0        0

ovlock   ovuserthread ovbuff   usercpu  syscpu   numckpts flushes
0        0            0        143.95   273.80   23       1644

bufwaits lokwaits lockreqs deadlks  dltouts  ckpwaits compress seqscans
160      0        209896   0        0        3        467      924

ixda-RA  idx-RA   da-RA    RA-pgsused lchwaits
31       0        17       47         12
```

Meanings of the fields follow:

First line of output:

- dskreads: Number of times the disk subsystem was read.
- pagreads   Number of pages read.
- bufreads   Number of times the buffers were read.
- %cached   Read cache percentage. Should be > 95 percent.
                     100 * (bufreads-dskreads)/bufreads.
- dskwrits   Number of times the disks were written to.
- pagwrits   Number of pages written.
- bufwrites   Number of writes to the shared memory buffers.
- %cached   Write cache percentage. Should be >85 percent.
                     100 * (bufwrites-dskwrites)/dskwrites.

The major item of interest on this first line is the first %cached number, which represents the cache read ratio. The higher this number, the better. Every page read from the buffers rather than directly from the disk represents a true savings of processing time, as the reads from disk are much more costly than are the reads from the disks.

Don't get too excited about tuning for cache write ratios. This number is somewhat misleading, in that *all* writes in IDS are cached, *all* the time. What the write cache percentage is telling you is the ratio of database updates to page flushes. Write caching is really controlled by two factors, checkpoint intervals and LRU configuration. To decrease write caching, decrease the checkpoint interval and increase the LRU_MAX_DIRTY parameters in the ONCONFIG file.

The only time when you need to consider tuning for the write cache percentage is when you are seeing foreground writes (fgwrites) in the onstat -F command, indicating that you do not have enough buffers in your buffer pool to handle the update load.

The data in the first line of output is specific for the database specified in the ONCONFIG file if you have multiple instances running at the same time on the machine.

The second line of output is concerned with lowest-level ISAM calls. The statistics in this line are global for the server. It includes all ISAM activity for all instances running on the server.

Field meanings are:

- isamtot   Total number of ISAM calls made.
- open   Number of times a tablespace is opened.
- start   Number of times an index position was changed.
- read   Number of times the read function was called.
- write   Number of times the write function was called.
- rewrite   Number of times the update function was called.
- delete   Number of times the delete function was called.
- commit   Number of times the iscommit() function was called.
- rollbk   Number of times transactions rolled back.

This second section is useful in determining an overall level of activity within both the server and in individual IDS instances within the server. By looking at the ratios between reads, writes, rewrites, and deletes, you can get a good feeling for the type of work that the server is doing at any one time. Since these are low-level function calls, they do not necessarily correspond with any SQL or other specific activities within the database, as they include overhead and other activities that have no real one-to-one relationship to the commands the database is receiving. Use it as a blunt tool and don't try to balance out the calls to the penny. That's an exercise in futility.

The third line is new for IDS 7.30 and it is not documented anywhere that I can find. It appears to be related to the clustering capability that was introduced in 7.3. This is a good time to mention that the Informix documentation folks are human. The will sometimes miss changes that come up with new versions. When you run across something that is not documented, first check the release notes for your engine. If it's not in the release notes, contact Informix Support and let them know that you've found something that they didn't document. They will be glad for the additional help and proofreading assistance!

The fourth line is related to use of system resources and a few other odds and ends:

- ovlock   Number of times the database ran out of locks.
- ovuserthread   Number of times number of threads was exceeded.
- ovbuff   Number times system couldn't find a free buffer.
- usercpu   Total user cpu times for all threads.
- syscpu   Total system times for all threads.
- numckpts   Number of checkpoints completed.
- flushes   Number of times buffers were flushed to disk.

The first and third items indicate overflow conditions for items that can be configured in the ONCONFIG file. An ovlock condition can be cured by increasing the LOCKS parameter in the ONCONFIG file. An ovbuff condition can be alleviated by increasing the BUFFERS parameter.

The usercpu and syscpu fields are measured in seconds and are updated every 15 seconds. You can use the total of usercpu and syscpu numbers over a designated time interval to measure how much time the database engine is receiving and how much of the computer the database engine is actually using. If the total of usercpu and syscpu times approaches the actual physical time elapsed, it indicates that your system is CPU-bound and could benefit from additional CPUs.

The next line of the output contains the following fields:

- bufwaits   Number of times user threads have to wait for a buffer.
- lokwaits   Number of times user threads wait to acquire a lock.
- lockreqs   Number of total requests for locks.
- deadlks   Number of times that deadlocks were detected and cured.
- dltouts   Number of times distributed deadlock timeouts occurred.
- chpwaits   Number of times a thread had to wait on a checkpoint.
- compress   Number of page compressions.
- seqscans   Number of sequential scans executed.

This line contains several interesting pieces of information. One of particular interest is the bufwaits field. If a thread is trying to access a buffer and after a given amount of time has not yet found an unlocked queue, that thread will begin spinning and/or sleeping waiting for the last queue it tried to obtain to become available. Each time this happens, the bufwaits field is incremented.

IDS systems have intermittent problems with very large numbers in the bufwaits field. Whether or not it is actually a problem with performance is an open question. Some users have identified what appears to be a bug in the algorithm that IDS uses to select the next LRU to try when an LRU is not ready for use. This bug appears to be related to the figures chosen for LRUS in the ONCONFIG file. Typically, these numbers are chosen as 32, 64, or 128. Empirical evidence indicates that LRUS values of 64 and 96 may be problematic. Changing them to 63 and 95 solved the problems for those users. If you are experiencing excessive bufwaits, try increasing or decreasing the LRUS parameter to an odd number and see if it cures the problem.

The final line of the `onstat -p` output is mainly concerned with the efficiency of the read-aheads configured in the database. Field meanings are:

- ixda-RA   Count of read-aheads going from index leaves to data pages.
- idx-RA   Count of read-aheads traversing index leaves.
- da-RA   Count of data-path-only scans.
- RA-pgsused   Number of pages used that the database server read ahead.
- lchwaits   Number of thread waits to gain access to a shared-memory resource.

To measure the effectiveness of your read-ahead parameters for sequential scans of data and index pages, use the following formula:

```
RA-pgsused / (idxda-RA  +  idx-RA  + da-RA )  >   .95
```

This formula uses an arbitrary percentage of 95 percent. If your percentage is significantly lower than this, your system may be reading pages ahead only to have to throw them away. Each time this happens, the page cleaners have to work harder and you have wasted some time manipulating the buffers. If this percentage is low, consider lowering the read-ahead pages parameters. If the number is consistently high and you are doing frequent sequential scans of index or data pages, consider raising the parameter in order to make better use of read-ahead in the sequential scans.

Onstat -s   Print Latches

This invocation option for `onstat` should probably be named to "print mutexes," as IDS now refers to latches as mutexes in most places. This is one of the few areas that has not had the name changed.

```
$ onstat -s
Informix Dynamic Server Version 7.30.UC3   -- On-Line -- Up 2 days 21:02:46 -- 18464 Kbytes
Latches with lock or userthread set
name       address  lock wait userthread
```

Meanings of the fields are:

- name

    Name of the resource being controlled by the mutex

archive	Dbspace backup
bf	Buffers
bh	Hash buffers
chunks	Chunk table
ckpt	Checkpoints
dbspace	Dbspace table
flushctl	Page-flusher control
flushr	Page cleaners
locks	Lock table
loglog	Logical log
LRU	LRU queues
physb1	First physical-log buffer
physb2	Second physical-log buffer
physlog	Physical log
pt tblspace	Tblspace
tblsps	Tblspace table
users	User table

- address   Address of the latch
- lock   Is the lock set? 0 or 1 (values are system-dependent)
- wait   Are any threads waiting on this latch/mutex?
- userthread   Shared memory address of the owner of the latch

The userthread value shows a different type of address than any of the other invocations of onstat. Since latches/mutexes can be held by both system and user threads, the value of this address is the thread-control block address rather than the RSAM task-control block address, which lists only user threads. The two addresses can be correlated through the onstat -g ath command, which lists both of the values for a thread.

Onstat -t   Print TBLspaces

Onstat -t lists information about active tablespaces, that is, tablespaces that are in use by a thread.

```
$ onstat -t
Informix Dynamic Server Version 7.30.UC3    -- On-Line -- Up 2 days 21:02:49 -- 1
8464 Kbytes
Tblspaces
 n address   flgs ucnt tblnum   physaddr npages nused  npdata nrows  nextns resident
 3 c18d92e8 0    1    100001   10000e   150    150    0      0      3      0
25 c18d9710 0    1    200001   200004   100    100    0      0      2      0
43 c18d9bf8 0    1    300001   300004   150    120    0      0      3      0
61 c18ffa30 0    1    400001   400004   50     35     0      0      1      0
63 c18ffd18 0    1    500001   500004   50     4      0      0      1      0
64 c190a910 0    1    600001   600004   50     4      0      0      1      0
65 c190ae50 0    1    700001   700004   200    180    0      0      4      0
95 c1d5ddc8 0    2    70001f   700022   8      6      3      39     1      0
    8 active, 245 total
```

Values of the fields are:

- **n**   Arbitrary counter incremented when a tablespace is opened
- **address**   Address of the table in the shared memory tablespace table
- **flgs**   Status of the tablespace:

0x01	Busy
0x02	Dirty (modified but not yet flushed to disk)

- **ucnt**   Number of userthreads accessing this table
- **tblnum**   Hex value of the tblspace number. Integer representation of partnum in the systables table
- **physaddr**   Physical address on the disk of the table
- **npages**   Number of pages in the table
- **nused**   Total number of pages used
- **npdata**   Number of data pages used
- **nrows**   Number of rows in the table
- **nextns**   Number of noncontiguous extents used
- **resident**   Indicates whether the table is memory resident 0=no 1=yes

The last field is new to IDS 7.30. This version allows the DBA to specify whether or not a table is made memory resident; that is, its pages are loaded into shared memory and never removed from shared memory.

Onstat -T   Print all Cached TBLspaces

There is an undocumented invocation of onstat that provides the same information as the onstat -t command, only it covers all of the cached tablespaces, not just the active ones. The meanings of the fields are the same as those of onstat -t.

Onstat -u   Print User Threads

After onstat -p, the onstat -u invocation is one of the most common and most useful versions of the onstat command. It gives information about current user threads in the instance.

```
$ onstat -u
Informix Dynamic Server Version 7.30.UC3    -- On-Line -- Up 2 days 21:02:52 -- 18464 Kbytes
Userthreads
address  flags    sessid  user    tty    wait      tout locks nreads   nwrites
c18da018 ---P--D 1        informix -      0         0    0     26       196
c18da4cc ---P--F 0        informix -      0         0    0     0        2322
c18da980 ---P--- 5        informix -      0         0    0     0        13
c18dae34 ---P--B 6        informix -      0         0    0     0        0
c18db2e8 Y--P--- 40       informix NTWS134 c1bf0d30 0    1     0        0
c18db79c Y--P--- 34       informix NTWS010 c1be8a08 0    1     109      0
c18dbc50 ---P--D 9        informix -      0         0    0     0        0
7 active, 128 total, 18 maximum concurrent
```

Meanings of the fields are:

- address   Address in the shared memory user table
- flags   Status of the session. Values are position dependent:

  Position 1:

B	Waiting on buffer
C	Waiting on checkpoint
G	Waiting on logical log buffer write
L	Waiting on a lock
S	Waiting on a latch/mutex
T	Waiting on a transaction
Y	Waiting on a condition. If this flag is set to "Y," it means that the process simply has no work to do. Most often, this means waiting for user input
X	Waiting on a rollback

Position 2:

o	Transaction active during I/O failure

Position 3:

A	Dbspace backup (archive) thread
B	Begin work
P	Informix-Star prepared for commit
X	Informix-TP/XA prepared for commit
C	Committing or committed
R	Rolling back or rolled back
H	Heuristically rolling back or rolled back

Position 4:

P	Primary thread for a session
	seen in PDQ queries using multiple threads

Position 5:

R	Reading
X	In a critical section

Position 7:

B	Btree cleaner thread
C	Terminated user thread awaiting cleanup
D	Daemon thread
F	Page cleaner thread
M	Onmonitor thread

• sessid	Session id. Unique id for session.
• user	Login name of the user
• tty	Tty port the user is using. machine name on NT.

- wait   Address of resource that this thread is waiting for
- tout   Amount of time left for the wait (above) .

                  0 = no wait, -1 = indefinite wait
- locks   Number of locks held by this thread
- nreads   Number of disk reads by this thread
- nwrites   Number of buffer cache writes by this thread

The very last line contains some footer information that may be of interest, especially the "maximum concurrent" item. This tells the maximum number of current users that the system has seen since either startup or since the last onstat -z. This is not a maximum allowed; it is a maximum observed.

Onstat -x   Print Transactions

Onstat -x is used only in X/Open environments and in some transactions managed by Informix-Star.

```
$ onstat -x
Informix Dynamic Server Version 7.30.UC3    -- On-Line -- Up 2 days 21:02:55 -- 18464 Kbytes
Transactions
address   flags userthread locks log begin isolation retrys coordinator
c1900018 A---- c18da018   0    0            COMMIT   0
c1900168 A---- c18da4cc   0    0            COMMIT   0
c19002b8 A---- c18da980   0    0            COMMIT   0
c1900408 A---- c18dae34   0    0            COMMIT   0
c1900558 A---- c18db2e8   1    0            COMMIT   0
c19006a8 A---- c18dbc50   0    0            COMMIT   0
c19007f8 A---- c18db79c   1    0            COMMIT   0
   7 active, 128 total, 9 maximum concurrent
```

Field meanings are:

- address   Shared memory address of the transaction
- flags   Position-sensitive status flags:

                  Position 1:

                        A   Thread attached to a transaction
                        S   TP/XA suspended transaction
                        C   TP/XA waiting for rollback

                  Position 3:

                        B   Begin work
                        P   Informix-Star prepared for commit

X	Informix-TP/XA prepared for commit
C	Committing or committed
R	Rolling back or rolled back
H	Heuristically rolling back or rolled back

Position 5:

G	Global transaction
C	Informix-STAR coordinator transaction
S	Informix-STAR subordinate
B	Both coordinator and subordinate

- userthread   User that owns the transaction
- locks   Number of locks held
- log begin   Log ID holding the BEGIN WORK
- isolation   Isolation level
- retrys   Number of times a recovery thread was started
- coordinator   Coordinator thread id if this is a subordinate thread

Onstat -z   Zero Profile Counts

This invocation zeroes out the statistics kept by `onstat`. After running an `onstat -z`, the statistics will look like the engine has just started. Don't confuse this with the statistics kept and managed by the UPDATE STATISTICS command. The statistics for `onstat` do not affect any queries or other database activities. They are the same statistics that show up in the system monitoring interface (SMI) tables.

Onstat -C   Print Btree Cleaner Requests

This command invocation is totally undocumented in current manuals. It will remain a mystery.

```
$ onstat -C
Informix Dynamic Server Version 7.30.UC3   -- On-Line -- Up 2 days 21:03:19 -- 18464 Kbytes
Btree Cleaner Info
```

```
btcleanr pool      flags pools npend  busypnum head      tail    free
c18dae34 c1c0e018 1     1     0      0        0         0       c1c0e040

nreqs    dups      success dfrmv    unnec    ditems   ditlks   cmprs palcs
0        0         0       0        0        0        0        0     0

outstanding requests
address  next      partnum  pagenum  keynum
0 pending, 1024 total, 1024 hash buckets, 1 pools
```

Onstat -F   Print Page Flushers

Onstat -F provides information about the activity of the tasks that flush the dirty buffers
from shared memory to disk. This is of special interest when you are trying to analyze
problems related to checkpoint duration and efficiency.

```
Informix Dynamic Server Version 7.30.TC3   -- On-Line -- Up 00:00:34 -- 9536 Kbytes

Fg Writes      LRU Writes    Chunk Writes
0              0             0

address  flusher  state   data
c18e4b8  0        I       0        = 0X0
states: Exit Idle Chunk Lru
```

Meanings of the fields are:

- Fg Writes   Number of foreground writes
- LRU Writes   Number of LRU writes
- Chunk Writes   Number of chunk (checkpoint) writes
- address   Address of this page cleaner thread
- flusher   Page cleaner number
- state   Flag which indicates current activity of the cleaner
  - C   Chunk write
  - E   Exit (timed out)
  - I   Idle
  - L   LRU queue
- data   More information from the state field

  if state == C data = chunk number being written

  if state == I data = LRU queue being written

  The data field is given both as an integer and as

  an = (hexnumber) following the integer

Onstat -G   Print Global Transaction IDs.

This is another `onstat` command that is totally undocumented. I assume that it relates to X/Open or TP/XA transactions as identified in the `onstat -x` commands. Figuring out the meanings of the headers is left as an exercise to the student. (Didn't you always want to be able to say that while you were in school?)

```
$ onstat -G
Informix Dynamic Server Version 7.30.UC3    -- On-Line -- Up 2 days 21:03:27 -- 18464 Kbytes
Global Transaction Identifiers
address  flags     fID  gtl  bql  data
0 active, 128 total
```

Onstat -P   Print Partition Buffer Summary

This is another Informix "mystery meat" command that is undocumented.

```
$ onstat -P
Informix Dynamic Server Version 7.30.UC3    -- On-Line -- Up 2 days 21:03:31 -- 18464 Kbytes
partnum  total   btree   data    other   resident dirty
0        2751    150     448     2153    0        0
1048578  2       1       1       0       0        0
1048579  17      7       10      0       0        0
1048580  15      8       7       0       0        0
...
7340207  2       2       0       0       0        0
7340208  1       1       0       0       0        0
7340209  3       2       0       1       0        0
7340210  1       1       0       0       0        0
7340211  1       1       0       0       0        0

Totals:  4096    703     1190    2203    0        0

Percentages:
Data  29.05
Btree 17.16
Other 53.78
```

Onstat -R   Print LRU Queues

The `onstat -R` command gives information about the contents of the LRU queues. The number of LRU queues is determined by the LRUS parameter in the ONCONFIG file. Each queue is actually composed of two queues, a free queue (FLRU) and a modified queue (MLRU). When IDS needs to find a free buffer page, it chooses a queue at random and takes the last entry in the FRLU and attempts to lock the buffer page. If it can get a lock, it uses that buffer page. If it cannot, it will pick another queue at random and attempt to lock its least recently used queue.

IDS 7.3 introduced the concept of priority levels within the queues. This is how IDS 7.3 allows for resident tables. When it becomes necessary to flush a queue and reuse the buffer page, the HIGH priority queues are the last ones to become eligible for reuse.

Since each queue is composed of two subqueues, there are actually LRUS * 2 queues.

```
$ onstat -R
Informix Dynamic Server Version 7.30.UC3    -- On-Line -- Up 2 days 21:03:35 -- 18464 Kbytes

8 buffer LRU queue pairs                         priority levels
# f/m  pair total   % of    length    LOW   MED_LOW   MED_HIGH    HIGH
 0 f       512     100.0%     512     275      231         6         0
 1 m                 0.0%       0       0        0         0         0
 2 f       512     100.0%     512     270      234         8         0
 3 m                 0.0%       0       0        0         0         0
 4 f       512     100.0%     512     271      234         7         0
 5 m                 0.0%       0       0        0         0         0
 6 F       512     100.0%     512     270      236         6         0
 7 m                 0.0%       0       0        0         0         0
 8 f       512     100.0%     512     277      230         5         0
 9 m                 0.0%       0       0        0         0         0
10 f       512     100.0%     512     274      232         6         0
11 m                 0.0%       0       0        0         0         0
12 f       512     100.0%     512     279      226         7         0
13 m                 0.0%       0       0        0         0         0
14 f       512     100.0%     512     279      227         6         0
15 m                 0.0%       0       0        0         0         0
0 dirty, 4096 queued, 4096 total, 4096 hash buckets, 2048 buffer size
start clean at 10% (of pair total) dirty, or 51 buffs dirty, stop at 5%
```

Meanings of the output fields are:

- #   Sequential number of the queue, beginning with 0
- f/m   Type of queue. Values are:

  - f   free, not modified (FLRU)
  - F   shortest free LRU
  - m   modified queue (MLRU)
  - M   modified queue being flushed to disk

- pair total   Total number of buffers in the FLRU and MLRU
- % of   Percentage of the queue in this subqueue
- length   Length in buffers of FLRU + MLRU
- LOW   Number of buffers with LOW priority
- MED_LOW   Number of buffers with MED_LOW priority
- MED_HIGH   Number of buffers with MEDIUM HIGH priority

- HIGH   Number of buffers with HIGH priority

The last two lines are summary information about the queue usage, showing total dirty (modified) along with the LRU_MAX_DIRTY and LRU_MIN_DIRTY parameters on the last line.

Onstat -X   Print List of Sharers/Waiters for Buffers

This invocation lists the details about sharers and waiters for any buffers that are either sharing a buffer or waiting to acquire a latch on a buffer. This is similar to the information found in the `onstat -b` and `onstat -B` commands.

```
$ onstat -X
Informix Dynamic Server Version 7.30.UC3   -- On-Line -- Up 2 days 21:03:40 -- 18464 Kbytes
Buffers (Access)
address  owner    flags pagenum  memaddr  nslots pgflgs scount   waiter
0 modified, 4096 total, 4096 hash buckets, 2048 buffer size
```

The fields have the following meanings:

- Address: Address of the buffer header in the buffer table
- owner   Thread ID that is using the buffer
- Flgs: May have the following values:

    - 0x01   Modified data
    - 0x02   Data
    - 0x04   LRU
    - 0x08   Error

- Pagenum: Physical page number on the disk
- memaddr   Buffer memory address
- nslots: Number of slot-table entries in the page (rows or parts of rows on the page)
- pgflgs: The following flag values, alone or in combination, show the type of page this entry is pointing to.

    1   Data page

    2   Tblspace page

    4   Free-list page

    8   Chunk free-list page

    9   Remainder data page

b	Partition resident blobpage
c	Blobspace resident blobpage
d	Blob chunk free-list bit page
e	Blob chunk blob map page
10	B-tree node page
20	B-tree root-node page
40	B-tree branch-node page
80	B-tree leaf-node page
100	Logical-log page
200	Last page of logical log
400	Sync page of logical log
800	Physical log
1000	Reserved root page
2000	No physical log required
8000	B-tree leaf with default flags

- scount   Number of threads sharing this buffer
- waiter   Address of any threads waiting on this buffer

Onstat -r opt sec Repeat opt Every <sec> Seconds

This invocation provides for endless repetition of the options given in "opt" every "r" seconds. This provides a methods of performing ongoing monitoring of a single or multiple series of onstat commands. For example:

```
$  onstat -ru 5
would repeat onstat -u every five seconds
$  onstat -rzu 5
would repeat onstat -u followed by onstat -z every five seconds
```

Onstat -o <outfile> Put Shared Memory into File

This invocation of onstat will place the entire contents of shared memory into a file named by the outfile parameter. If this parameter is omitted, it places the output in onstat.out. Be aware that this command will require enough disk space to hold the entire shared memory.

This option is especially useful in taking a snapshot of shared memory for later analysis. This is good if you have a problem you are attempting to chase down but you don't have the luxury of taking the time to do it right now. Run `onstat -o` and chase the problem down at your leisure. This is the Informix equivalent of a core dump file in UNIX.

Onstat <infile> <options>

This invocation runs the requested options against a shared memory file (created by `onstat -o`) instead of against the engine itself. This is similar to running UNIX utilities against a core dump file.

ONSTAT -G OPTIONS

The `onstat -g` command structure is completely new with IDS. There is no analogue in the OnLine system to these commands. Since Informix had used up most of the available alpha characters with OnLine, they decided to use `onstat -g` as a gateway into most of the additional features of IDS such as, parallelism, multithreading, parallel data query, and memory management. To do this, they added a third parameter to the `onstat` command. The generic term for the information presented with this command subfamily is "MT," for "multithreading."

To expedite reference to the `onstat -g` commands, here is a summary of the multithreading commands:

```
MT COMMANDS:
onstat -g
all    Print all MT information
ath    Print all threads
wai    Print waiting threads
act    Print active threads
rea    Print ready threads
sle    Print all sleeping threads
spi    Print spin locks with long spins
sch    Print VP scheduler statistics
lmx    Print all locked mutexes
wmx    Print all mutexes with waiters
con    Print conditions with waiters
stk <tid> Dump the stack of a specified thread
glo    Print MT global information
mem [<pool name>|<session id>] Print pool statistics.
seg    Print memory segment statistics
rbm    Print block map for resident segment
nbm    Print block map for non-resident segments
afr <pool name|session id> Print allocated pool fragments
ffr <pool name|session id> Print free pool fragments
ufr <pool name|session id> Print pool usage breakdown
iov    Print disk IO statistics by vp
iof    Print disk IO statistics by chunk/file
iog    Print AIO global information
iob    Print big buffer usage by IO VP class
```

```
ppf [<partition number> | 0]  Print partition profiles
tpf [<tid> | 0] Print thread profiles
ntu   Print net user thread profile information
ntt   Print net user thread access times
ntm   Print net message information
ntd   Print net dispatch information
nss [<session id>] Print net shared memory status
nsc [<client id>] Print net shared memory status
nsd   Print net shared memory data
sts   Print max and current stack sizes
dic   Print dictionary cache information
opn [<tid>] Print open tables
qst   Print queue statistics
wst   Print thread wait statistics
ses [<session id>] Print session information
sql [<session id>] Print SQL information
stq [<session id>] Print stream queue information
dri   Print data replication information
pos   Print /INFORMIXDIR/etc/.infos.DBSERVERNAME file
mgm   Print Memory Grant Manager information
lap   Print light append information
ddr   Print DDR log post processing information
dmp <address> <length> Dump <length> bytes of memory starting at <address>
src <pattern> <mask> Search memory for <pattern>, <pattern>==(memory&<mask>)
```

Not All Onstat –g Options are Documented

Informix has not documented many of the onstat -g subcommands. The official line is that onstat -g is for "support and debugging purposes" only. Although this section has drawn information from multiple sources, in many instances what you are seeing is the "unofficial" definitions of terms and fields used in the commands. Some of the commands are so oblique that I didn't even include them in this chapter, since I'm convinced that *nobody* knows what they do. In many cases, the options have changed or been dropped from one version of IDS to the next. In view of the unsupported nature of much of this material, use caution in interpreting what these commands tell you. Luckily, you cannot do any harm simply by running the commands, so experiment away.

One of the useful sources of information about some of the meanings of the flags and fields has come from the sysmaster.sql command script that is used by the engine when it initializes the sysmaster database. If you ever want to do a little interesting, not-so-light reading, take a look at this SQL file. The fields are fairly well documented and understandable, although it has its share of cryptic definitions. Also of use is the flags_text table in the sysmaster database. This is useful in decoding the meanings of some of the more esoteric flags.

As part of the research for this book, I requested that Informix provide detail about these onstat -g options. Even with the assistance of Informix Press and insiders within the company, I could not pry the information loose from Informix. This is a totally unacceptable attitude and I hope that someone at Informix will see fit to document these utilities and to share this important monitoring and tuning information with the customers who have spent so much time and money acquiring and learning their products. Such arrogance and refusal to share information are not what users expect from an open systems company.

Onstat -g all   Print All MT Information

The `onstat -g all` command presents all of the multithreading information with one command. This is usually more information than you will ever need to know at one time. It may be useful if you are writing scripts to gather and then process the information with `grep`, `sed`, `awk`, `perl`, or other utilities.

MONITORING THREADS

Onstat -g ath   Print all Threads

This option to `onstat` will print all information about all user threads in the instance.

```
$onstat -g ath
Informix Dynamic Server Version 7.30.UC3   -- On-Line -- Up 2 days 22:12:02 -- 18464 Kbytes
Threads:
 tid    tcb       rstcb      prty status              vp-class       name
 2      c19ab050  0          2    sleeping forever    3lio           vp 0
 3      c19ab2c0  0          2    sleeping forever    4pio           vp 0
 4      c19ab558  0          2    sleeping forever    5aio           vp 0
 5      c19ab7f0  0          2    sleeping forever    6msc           vp 0
 6      c19aba88  0          2    sleeping forever    7aio           vp 1
 7      c19abe40  c18da018   4    sleeping secs: 1    1cpu           main_loop()
 8      c19c3810  0          2    running             1cpu           soctcppoll
 9      c19c3e20  0          3    sleeping forever    1cpu           soctcplst
 10     c19c64c8  c18da4cc   2    sleeping forever    1cpu           flush_sub(0)
 11     c19c6c20  0          2    sleeping forever    8aio           vp 2
 12     c19c6eb8  0          2    sleeping forever    9aio           vp 3
 13     c19c7150  0          2    sleeping forever    10aio          vp 4
 14     c19c73e8  0          2    sleeping forever    11aio          vp 5
 15     c19c7680  0          2    sleeping forever    12aio          vp 6
 16     c19c7918  0          2    sleeping forever    13aio          vp 7
 17     c19c7bb0  0          2    sleeping forever    14aio          vp 8
 18     c19c7e48  0          2    sleeping forever    15aio          vp 9
 19     c19db128  0          2    sleeping forever    16aio          vp 10
 20     c19db390  0          2    sleeping forever    17aio          vp 11
 21     c19db628  0          2    sleeping forever    18aio          vp 12
 22     c19db8c0  0          2    sleeping forever    19aio          vp 13
 23     c19dbb58  0          2    sleeping forever    20aio          vp 14
 24     c19dbdf0  0          2    sleeping forever    21aio          vp 15
 25     c19de228  0          2    sleeping forever    22aio          vp 16
 26     c19de468  0          2    sleeping forever    23aio          vp 17
 27     c19deeb0  c18da980   3    sleeping forever    1cpu           aslogflush
 28     c19df268  c18dae34   2    sleeping secs: 43   1cpu           btclean
 44     c1a23560  c18dbc50   4    sleeping secs: 1    1cpu           onmode_mon
```

```
70        c1be8bd0 c18db79c 2    cond wait  netnorm       1cpu          sqlexec
76        c1bf0ef8 c18db2e8 2    cond wait  netnorm       1cpu          sqlexec
```

Meanings of the fields are:

- tid   Thread ID
- tcb   Address of the thread within the thread control block
- rstcb   Address within the RSAM task-control block
- prty   Priority of the thread
- status   Status of the thread

  Common status flags:

  cond wait: netnorm   Engine thread is waiting for

  client to give a command over tcp

  cond wait: smread   Engine thread is waiting for

  client to give a command over shared memory connection

- vp-class   VP class and VP number the thread last ran on
- name   Descriptive name of the thread

These field meanings are the same for these three onstat -g subcommands:

- onstat -g wai
- onstat -g ath
- onstat -g rea
- onstat -g act

Onstat -g wai   Print Waiting Threads

This invocation is a subset of the onstat -g ath command that shows only threads which are waiting for something. Field meanings are the same as onstat -g ath (above).

```
$ onstat -g wai
Informix Dynamic Server Version 7.30.UC3   -- On-Line -- Up 2 days 22:12:05 -- 18464 Kbytes
Waiting threads:
tid     tcb      rstcb    prty status               vp-class      name
2       c19ab050 0        2    sleeping forever      3lio          vp 0
3       c19ab2c0 0        2    sleeping forever      4pio          vp 0
4       c19ab558 0        2    sleeping forever      5aio          vp 0
```

```
5        c19ab7f0 0          2    sleeping forever       6msc      vp 0
6        c19aba88 0          2    sleeping forever       7aio      vp 1
7        c19abe40 c18da018   4    sleeping secs: 1       1cpu      main_loop()
9        c19c3e20 0          3    sleeping forever       1cpu      soctcplst
10       c19c64c8 c18da4cc   2    sleeping forever       1cpu      flush_sub(0)
11       c19c6c20 0          2    sleeping forever       8aio      vp 2
12       c19c6eb8 0          2    sleeping forever       9aio      vp 3
13       c19c7150 0          2    sleeping forever       10aio     vp 4
14       c19c73e8 0          2    sleeping forever       11aio     vp 5
15       c19c7680 0          2    sleeping forever       12aio     vp 6
16       c19c7918 0          2    sleeping forever       13aio     vp 7
17       c19c7bb0 0          2    sleeping forever       14aio     vp 8
18       c19c7e48 0          2    sleeping forever       15aio     vp 9
19       c19db128 0          2    sleeping forever       16aio     vp 10
20       c19db390 0          2    sleeping forever       17aio     vp 11
21       c19db628 0          2    sleeping forever       18aio     vp 12
22       c19db8c0 0          2    sleeping forever       19aio     vp 13
23       c19dbb58 0          2    sleeping forever       20aio     vp 14
24       c19dbdf0 0          2    sleeping forever       21aio     vp 15
25       c19de228 0          2    sleeping forever       22aio     vp 16
26       c19de468 0          2    sleeping forever       23aio     vp 17
27       c19deeb0 c18da980   3    sleeping forever       1cpu      aslogflush
28       c19df268 c18dae34   2    sleeping secs: 40      1cpu      btclean
44       c1a23560 c18dbc50   4    sleeping secs: 1       1cpu      onmode_mon
70       c1be8bd0 c18db79c   2    cond wait   netnorm    1cpu      sqlexec
76       c1bf0ef8 c18db2e8   2    cond wait   netnorm    1cpu      sqlexec
```

Onstat -g act   Print Active Threads

This is another subset of onstat -g ath, and the field definitions are the same as for the above two thread-listing invocations.

```
$ onstat -g act
Informix Dynamic Server Version 7.30.UC3    -- On-Line -- Up 2 days 22:12:10 -- 18464 Kbytes
Running threads:
 tid     tcb      rstcb    prty status             vp-class      name
 8       c19c3810 0        2    running                1cpu      soctcppoll
```

Onstat -g rea   Print Ready Threads

This is yet another onstat command using the same headings as onstat -g ath. It shows the ready queue, that is, threads that are ready to run and waiting to run. As long as your system is not hardware bound, if you continue to see many threads in a ready state, it may help to add additional virtual processors to service these threads. When adding virtual processors to the engine no longer reduces the ready queue, the system is hardware bound and the only solution is either to put up with decreased performance or to add additional physical CPUs to the system.

```
$ onstat -g rea
```

```
Informix Dynamic Server Version 7.30.UC3   -- On-Line -- Up 2 days 22:12:13 -- 18464 Kbytes
Ready threads:
 tid     tcb      rstcb    prty status            vp-class      name
```

Onstat -g sle   Print all Sleeping Threads

This command lists the threads that are sleeping, waiting for a timeout. Threads that are sleeping forever do not show up here.

```
$ onstat -g sle
Informix Dynamic Server Version 7.30.UC3   -- On-Line -- Up 2 days 22:12:16 -- 18464 Kbytes
Sleeping threads with timeouts: 3 threads
        tid   v_proc rstcb      name          time
        7      1     c18da018   main_loop()    1
        44     1     c18dbc50   onmode_mon     1
        28     1     c18dae34   btclean 29
```

Field meanings are:

- tid   Unique thread ID
- v_proc   Virtual processor number
- rstcb   RSAM task-control block address
- name   Type of thread
- time   Time left to sleep

Onstat -g spi   Print Spin Locks with Long Spins

This command lists spin locks that have been obtained after more than 10,000 spins for any virtual processor. When a virtual processor spins more than 10,000 times, this is called a *longspin*.

There are four things that you can do to reduce longspins:

- Reduce load on the system
- Reduce number of virtual processors
- Set no-age parameter
- Set processor affinity parameters

```
$ onstat -g spi
Informix Dynamic Server Version 7.30.UC3   -- On-Line -- Up 2 days 22:12:21 -- 18464 Kbytes
Spin locks with waits:
Num Waits   Num Loops   Avg Loop/Wait    Name
```

```
1          1          1.00               vproc vp_lock, id = 1
```

Onstat -g tpf   Print Thread Profiles

```
$ onstat -g tpf
Informix Dynamic Server Version 7.30.UC3   -- On-Line -- Up 2 days 22:14:57 -- 18464 Kbytes
Thread profiles
tid lkreqs lkw dl to lgrs isrd iswr isrw isdl isct isrb lx bfr bfw lsus lsmx seq
0   0      0   0  0  0    0    0    0    0    0    0    0  0   0   0    0    0
0   0      0   0  0  0    0    0    0    0    0    0    0  0   0   0    0    0
0   0      0   0  0  0    0    0    0    0    0    0    0  0   0   0    0    0
0   0      0   0  0  0    0    0    0    0    0    0    0  0   0   0    0    0
76  0      0   0  0  0    0    0    0    0    0    0    0  0   0   0    0    0
70  0      0   0  0  0    0    0    0    0    0    0    0  0   0   0    0    0
31  0      0   0  0  0    0    0    0    0    0    0    0  0   0   0    0    0
```

This output is completely undocumented, but I believe that the meanings are as follows:

- tid   Thread id
- lkreqs   Lock requests
- lkw   Lock waits
- dl   Deadlocks
- to   Lock Timeouts
- lgrs   Log records written
- isrd   ISAM reads (from disk)
- iswr   ISAM writes (to disk)
- isrw   ISAM rewrites (second write to a page)
- isdl   ISAM deletes
- isct   ISAM commits
- isrb   ISAM rollbacks
- lx   Long transactions
- bfr   Buffer reads
- bfw   Buffer writes
- lsus   Log space used
- lsmx   Max log space used
- seq   Sequential scans

MONITORING VIRTUAL PROCESSORS

Onstat -g sch   Print VP Scheduler Statistics

This command gives scheduling statistics about the individual virtual processors in the
Informix instance.

```
$ onstat -g sch
Informix Dynamic Server Version 7.30.UC3    -- On-Line -- Up 2 days 22:12:27 -- 18464 Kbytes
VP Scheduler Statistics:
 vp    pid    class    semops    busy waits  spins/wait
  1    825    cpu      0         0           0
  2    826    adm      0         0           0
  3    827    lio      0         0           0
  4    828    pio      0         0           0
  5    829    aio      0         0           0
  6    830    msc      0         0           0
  7    831    aio      0         0           0
  8    833    aio      0         0           0
  9    834    aio      0         0           0
 10    835    aio      0         0           0
 11    836    aio      0         0           0
 12    837    aio      0         0           0
 13    838    aio      0         0           0
 14    839    aio      0         0           0
 15    840    aio      0         0           0
 16    841    aio      0         0           0
 17    842    aio      0         0           0
 18    843    aio      0         0           0
 19    844    aio      0         0           0
 20    845    aio      0         0           0
 21    846    aio      0         0           0
 22    847    aio      0         0           0
 23    848    aio      0         0           0
```

When a CPU VP does not have a thread to run, the process performs a 'busywait'.
This is a loop of instructions designed to wait a short time. It does this rather than going into
a sleep state for two reasons. First, a thread may become eligible to run very soon, sooner
than any system call to wait could return, and second, there is no other more useful work to
perform at the time. "Spins" are the number of loops in a busy wait.

The busy wait count is the number of times the VP was looking for a thread and found
none. Spins is the number of iterations of the busy wait loop. If a thread becomes runnable
before the busy wait loop count expires, then the VP exits the loop and runs the chosen
thread.

If the busy wait loop is completed and there is still no work to do, the VP then waits using a semaphore operation. When a runnable thread becomes available, the VP be awakened to run it. In `onstat -g sch`, the semops column gives the number of times that the operation was completed and the thread was put to sleep awaiting awakening by a semaphore.

Onstat -g con   Print Conditions with Waiters

```
$ onstat -g con
Informix Dynamic Server Version 7.30.UC3    -- On-Line -- Up 2 days 22:12:47 -- 18464 Kbytes
Conditions with waiters:
cid      addr      name              waiter    waittime
679      c1be8a08 netnorm           70        6306
744      c1bf0d30 netnorm           76        7080
```

A condition is a mutex (latch). This command lists any conditions that have other threads waiting on those conditions. More detailed information can be found in the sysmaster table sysconlst.

Onstat -g glo   Print MT Global Information

This `onstat` command provides information about the CPU usage of virtual processors running in the instance. Typical systems will show the majority of the CPU usage in the CPU and AIO virtual processors.

The command gives various bits of information, including number of user sessions, number of threads, number of virtual processors, number of longspins, number of scheduler calls, thread switches, and yields. These last few pieces of information may be marginally interesting in viewing how the engine is handling thread switching, but there's not much you can do with the information. Thread switching and yielding is embedded deep into the engine and you have little or no control over it. It's interesting to watch, though.

The more interesting information is the summary and individual virtual processor information found at the end of the output.

```
$ onstat -g glo
Informix Dynamic Server Version 7.30.UC3    -- On-Line -- Up 2 days 22:57:03 -- 18464 Kbytes
MT global info:
sessions threads  vps      lngspins
1        29       23       0

          sched calls      thread switches yield 0   yield n   yield forever
total:    28403            21613           0         13655     1
per sec:  0                0               0         0         0
```

The above section deals with the activities of the threads and provides some interesting insights into how the IDS engine is accomplishing its multitasking features. When the engine is running virtual processors,each virtual processor can be assigned threads to run. Each thread is actually an area of shared memory that contains variables and stack space that is needed to run the thread. When one of the VPs reaches a point where it will be waiting for something, it politely gives up control of the processor by executing what is known as a "yield." There are three types of yields:

Yield 0

The thread relinquishes control and moves to the end of the ready queue. If no other thread is ready to execute, the yielding thread begins executing immediately.

Yield n

The thread puts itself to sleep and will wake up in n seconds.

Yield forever

The thread puts itself to sleep and will only wake up when another thread specifically activates it

```
Virtual processor summary:
    class       vps         usercpu     syscpu      total
    cpu         1           1.05        1.37        2.42
    aio         18          1.73        4.75        6.48
    lio         1           0.11        0.29        0.40
    pio         1           0.09        0.25        0.34
    adm         1           0.44        1.00        1.44
    msc         1           0.00        0.00        0.00
    total       23          3.42        7.66        11.08

Individual virtual processors:
    vp    pid       class       usercpu     syscpu      total
    1     825       cpu         1.05        1.37        2.42
    2     826       adm         0.44        1.00        1.44
    3     827       lio         0.11        0.29        0.40
    4     828       pio         0.09        0.25        0.34
    5     829       aio         0.10        0.25        0.35
    6     830       msc         0.00        0.00        0.00
    7     831       aio         0.10        0.25        0.35
    8     833       aio         0.10        0.27        0.37
    9     834       aio         0.10        0.26        0.36
    10    835       aio         0.09        0.26        0.35
    11    836       aio         0.10        0.27        0.37
    12    837       aio         0.11        0.27        0.38
    13    838       aio         0.10        0.27        0.37
    14    839       aio         0.09        0.28        0.37
    15    840       aio         0.09        0.27        0.36
```

```
16    841    aio    0.11    0.27    0.38
17    842    aio    0.09    0.26    0.35
18    843    aio    0.10    0.26    0.36
19    844    aio    0.09    0.26    0.35
20    845    aio    0.09    0.25    0.34
21    846    aio    0.09    0.30    0.39
22    847    aio    0.09    0.24    0.33
23    848    aio    0.09    0.26    0.35
             tot    3.42    7.66    11.08
```

This command allows the DBA to track VP usage. Run it during heavy load after an `onstat -z` (to clear the statistics in the internal tables), and time the amount of physical time elapsed during the run. Now look at the sum of the usercpu and syscpu columns for the first CPU-VP. If the accumulated time is near the elapsed time, the CPU-VP was running almost continuously and the CPU-VP count should be increased. CPU-VPs were the bottleneck.

This same principle can be used to evaluate the overall performance of the engine over a known time. Simply take the totals time for usercpu and syscpu and compare that time with the elapsed time. This can give you a feeling for the amount of the overall processor that is being utilized by the database engine.

MONITORING MEMORY USAGE

Onstat -g mgm   Print Memory Grant Manager Information

Queries that utilize the parallel features of the database may be expensive both in terms disk accesses and memory utilization. These decision support queries are identified by the fact that they are queries that run with a PDQ priority greater than zero. One of the things that the database administrator needs to be aware of is the status of the PDQPRIORITY for any queries that are running. If a query is run with a high PDQPRIORITY, it can hog the system resources to such an extent that the entire system slows to a crawl.

All memory and other resources used in DSS queries is controlled by the Memory Grant Manager in IDS. It controls:

- Number of concurrent queries (specified in DS_MAX_QUERIES in ONCON-FIG)
- Number of scan threads
- Number of PDQ threads
- Amount of memory and CPU resources used

What is a quantum?

No, we're not talking about particle physics or strange quarks here. This is complicated stuff, but it's not rocket science. When Informix allocates memory to decision support queries, it allocates the memory in chunks, the size of which is defined by the ONCONFIG setup of the engine. For each system, the minimal amount of memory allocated to a query is called a *quantum*.

A quantum is defined as

DS_TOTAL_MEMORY / DS_MAX_QUERIES

When a decision support query is submitted to the engine, the engine first registers the query with the Memory Grant Manager, which is the mechanism that allocates the memory and other resources for the query. MGM will reserve an amount of memory for the query equal to:

DS_TOTAL_MEMORY * (1 / 100 * PDQPRIORITY), rounded down to the nearest quantum

This shows the importance of managing the PDQPRIORITY correctly. If the PDQPRIORITY is set to 100 percent, the first decision support query will go out and reserve the entire contents of the decision support memory, thus blocking any further queries from running. We'll look at the output from `onstat -g mgm` in several sections, since the report is fairly long and each section is different:

```
$ onstat -g mgm
Informix Dynamic Server Version 7.30.UC3    -- On-Line -- Up 2 days 22:16:32 -- 18464 Kbytes
Memory Grant Manager (MGM)
------------------------

MAX_PDQPRIORITY:   100
DS_MAX_QUERIES:    2
DS_MAX_SCANS:      1048576
DS_TOTAL_MEMORY:   256 KB
```

This first section simply lists configuration data from the ONCONFIG file. The DS_MAX_SCANS parameter is usually defaulted to a very high number in the engine, in this case equal to (1024 * 1024). This parameter is the total number of scan threads that the engine may allocate.

When a DSS query on a fragmented table runs, the engine attempts to allocate a number of scan threads equal to:

reserved_threads = min (*nfrags*, (DS_MAX_SCANS * PDQPRIORITY / 100 *`MAX_PDQPRIORITY / 100`))

Usually, this will mean the number of threads reserved for a query will equal the number of fragments (nfrags) to be scanned. If for some reason the scan threads cannot be allocated, the query will be held in a ready state until the threads become free.

```
Queries:    Active      Ready    Maximum
                 0          0          2

Memory:     Total       Free     Quantum
(KB)          256        256        128

Scans:      Total       Free     Quantum
          1048576    1048576          1
```

The second section gives information about the number of active queries and number of ready queries, along with the DS_MAX_QUERIES parameter from the ONCONFIG file. If you see a positive number under "Ready," it means that something is blocking these queries from running and that you could possibly speed up performance by eliminating the blockage.

The next line gives total and free decision support memory, as well as the calculated figure for the smallest amount that can be allocated (the quantum). If you see a very small amount of free memory, you have another source of blockage.

The third line is the total and free number of scans, as well as the least number of scan threads that can be allocated at any one time.

```
Load Control:   (Memory)      (Scans)   (Priority)   (Max Queries)   (Reinit)
                 Gate 1       Gate 2      Gate 3         Gate 4       Gate 5
(Queue Length)        0            0           0              0            0
```

This next section gives a summary of the queries' status. When a query is registered with the MGM, one of the first things that MGM does is test for resources that may be required by the query. If any needed resources or conditions cannot be met, the query is held in a ready state and is added to a queue waiting for one of the following:

- Memory: Queries waiting for other queries to release memory. These other queries have already reserved all the available memory and no memory is now available.

- Scans: Your system has already reached the DS_MAX_SCANS parameter and this query has to wait until some scan threads free up. With the default 1048576 DS_MAX_SCANS, you should never see queries waiting here.

- Priority: The PDQPRIORITY does more than just allocate memory. Threads are run in order of PDQPRIORITY. If a query is run at a lower PDQPRIORITY, it cannot run until all queries with a higher priority have run.

- Max Queries: You've reached the DS_MAX_QUERIES parameter limit and this query cannot run until another query finishes.

- Reinit: If the user or DBA changes either of the Informix environmental variables DS_TOTAL_MEMORY or DS_MAX_PARAMETERS, the change does not become effective until all currently running queries are completed. Any new queries registered before this happens must wait in the reinit queue until all the other queries have completed and the parameters can be reinitialized.

```
Active Queries:
---------------

Session      Query  Priority      Thread        Memory       Scans    Gate
23                  c053f23 50                  c12345c1    1024/1024    3 / 4

Ready Queries:  None
```

This section gives more information about the queries that are active and queued up and waiting for resources. The session ID is the same as is found in `onstat -g ses`. The Thread column is the number of the primary thread that registered the query with MGM. The Memory field is not the amount of memory as might be expected, rather it is the number of internal calls to get memory.

Scans tells the number of scans used/allocated. The Gate field lists the queue that the query is waiting in (only for ready queries; an active query is not waiting for any resources).

```
Free Resource       Average #       Minimum #
-------------       ---------       ---------
Memory              0.0 +- 0.0          32
Scans               0.0 +- 0.0       1048576

Queries             Average #       Maximum #     Total #
-------------       ---------       ---------     -------
Active              0.0 +- 0.0          0            0
Ready               0.0 +- 0.0          0            0

Resource/Lock Cycle Prevention count:  0
```

This final section may be of more use than any of the others in tuning your PDQ usage. It gives the averages, minimums, and totals for various queries since either the engine was restarted or since any of the parameters were dynamically changed with an `onmode` command. The free resources section shows averages and minimums for memory and scans. The minimum number are minimum free numbers, not the minimums actually seen. In the queries section, you get averages, minimums, and totals for active and ready queues. The maximum field contains the maximum sizes of the queues during the period. Total field gives the total number of each queue. Here, you can get a count of exactly how many of your queries are running as DSS queries.

The Average fields in both sections have one interesting data item that you will not see in any other reports. Note that these numbers have a "+-" in them. The second number is actually a calculated standard deviation from the norms in the first numbers. If you are attempting to make some sense out of these numbers, make sure you understand the statistical concepts of standard deviation so that you don't try to make assumptions based on insufficient data. Basically, if the +- figure is large, it means that there was a lot of deviation from the averages. If you lay with your head in the oven and your feet in the icebox, you'll be comfortable in the mean, but the standard deviation will kill you.

Since MGM only reserves memory for queries and doesn't force its usage, you may find that it is overallocating memory resources for your DSS queries. If you suspect that's the case, check the output of the onstat -g mem command and see how much of the memory is actually being used by the query in question. If there's a lot of unused memory, you could benefit by running this query with a much lower PDQPRIORITY, thus freeing resources for other uses.

Onstat -g mem Print Pool Statistics

The amount of memory available to your DSS system is a primary factor in the system's overall performance. One task that the DBA has is to determine whether or not the system has enough memory for its intended use in the first place, and later to monitor the usage and allocation of this memory.

The memory being displayed is in the virtual portion of the shared memory segment. The DBA needs to continuously monitor memory utilization with the aim of either managing the utilization or detecting when the system needs more memory. Actual memory in use doesn't become an issue with IDS unless there is not enough of it, and then it becomes a big issue. When the system begins to start swapping or paging out in an attempt to deal with memory shortages, the system's performance goes down the drain. The virtual portion of shared memory is used by both OLTP and DSS queries, but requirements for OLTP are minimal. It's the DSS queries that use up the virtual portion of shared memory. DSS queries use the shared memory for various activities, including:

- Session pools
- Thread pools
- Sort pools
- Joins
- Sorts
- Group operations

The first issue is usually balancing the use of shared memory between DSS and OLTP queries. This is best done by manipulating the value of the DS_TOTAL_MEMORY parameter in ONCONFIG. Use this to restrict the amount of shared memory that is used by DSS. Then monitor the memory usage by OLTP queries and see how much memory the remaining queries utilize. If you find that the OLTP queries do not use all of the remaining portion of the virtual shared memory, increase the DS_TOTAL_MEMORY to take advantage of this unused memory.

For pure DSS systems, increase the DS_TOTAL_MEMORY to it's maximum, which is half the total shared memory configured in the IDS system. For such pure DSS systems, reduce the amount of BUFFERS in ONCONFIG and use as much of the memory as possible for DSS memory. If you do this, keep in mind that for sequential scans in DSS systems, the most efficient means of reading the tables are by light scans, and for a table to be eligible to use light scans, it must be larger than your total BUFFERS. All of this monitoring of memory usage is done by the onstat -g mem command. This command can be executed in one of three flavors:

- Onstat -g mem   Global memory information
- Onstat -g mem <pool name>   Memory usage for a named pool
- Onstat -g mem <session> Memory usage for a numbered session

Since the last two invocations are simply subsets of the first, we'll look at the global memory with onstat -g mem:

```
$  onstat -g mem
Informix Dynamic Server Version 7.30.TC3   -- On-Line -- Up 00:21:46 --9536 Kbytes
Pool Summary:
name         class addr      totalsize freesize #allocfrag #freefrag
resident     R     c002018   417792    12144    2          2
res-buff     R     c068018   835584    12144    2          2
global       V     c152018   540672    162672   612        55
mt           V     c154018   1417216   639760   888        45
rsam         V     c18c018   212992    760      87         1
aio          V     c1ce018   1720320   151632   198        47
gls          V     c1d2018   49152     2240     709        6
dictpool     V     c1d6018   49152     1936     34         5
procpool     V     c1d8018   8192      1992     9          1
XTF_mem      V     c20e018   409600    17464    4          3
main_loop()  V     c310018   40960     23680    115        4
2            V     c31c018   8192      3336     8          1
3            V     c33e018   8192      3336     8          1
4            V     c360018   16384     3048     207        1
lgflushpool  V     c4be018   8192      7912     3          1
aslogflush   V     c4c0018   16384     4632     108        1
btclean      V     c4d4018   16384     4632     108        1
onmode_mon   V     c4fe018   16384     4632     108        1
510          V     c502018   57344     27360    272        8
511          V     c4fc018   8192      3336     8          1

Blkpool Summary:
name         class addr      size      #blks
global       V     c15a1d8   0         0
```

The output is divided into two sections, the pool summary and the block pool summary. Both outputs share the following fields:

- Name   Pool name or session ID. The names that consist of numbers only are the session pools. In the example, we have session pools for session 3, session 4, session 510, and session 511.
- Class   R=resident, V=virtural
- Addr   Address in shared memory

The Pool Summary section has these fields that are specific to this section:

- Totalsize   Total size in bytes of the pool
- Freesize   Total unused bytes in the pool
- #allocatedfrag Number of allocated fragments
- #freefrag   Number of free fragments

The block pool summary uses these fields in addition to the first three that are common to both sections:

- size   Total size in bytes of the pool
- #blks   Number of 8K blocks

The major fields of interest are the pool names, classes, total and free sizes. By looking at these outputs, you can get a pretty good idea of how your memory is being used and what it is being used for.

Onstat -g ses   Print Session Information

In the onstat -g mem output above, we showed sessions 2, 3, and 4 as being active. We can use the onstat -g ses command to get more information about these sessions.

```
$ onstat -g ses 3

  Informix Dynamic Server Version 7.30.TC3    -- On-Line -- Up 00:43:59 -- 9536 Kbytes

session                                    #RSAM   total    used
id        user      tty      pid  hostname threads memory   memory
3         informix  -        0    -        0       8192     4856

Memory pools      count 1
name          class addr    totalsize freesize #allocfrag #freefrag
3             V     c33e018  8192      3336     8          1

name          free      used         name          free      used
overhead      0         120          scb           0         96
ostcb         0         40           sqscb         0         4552
fragman       0         48
```

We can also invoke the `onstat -g ses` command without giving it a session number. Depending upon how you get interested in a particular session, you may run `onstat -g ses` first and then drill down into a particular session of interest.

```
C:\INFORMIX\etc>onstat -g ses
Informix Dynamic Server Version 7.30.TC3    -- On-Line -- Up 00:46:49 -- 9536 Kbytes

session                               #RSAM     total      used
id       user     tty     pid    hostname threads memory    memory
1104     informix -       0      -        0      8192       4856
4        informix -       0      -        0      16384      13336
3        informix -       0      -        0      8192       4856
2        informix -       0      -        0      8192       4856
```

Onstat -g afr   Print Allocated Pool Fragments

The last two fields of the `onstat -g mem` command discussed allocated and free pool fragments. Use the next three `onstat -g` commands to further drill down and look at the actual composition of those fragments.

```
$ onstat -g afr 3
Informix Dynamic Server Version 7.30.TC3    -- On-Line -- Up 00:56:45 -- 9536 Kbytes
Allocations for pool name 3:
addr      size       memid
c33e000   120        overhead
c33e078   48         scb
c33e0a8   48         scb
c33e0d8   40         ostcb
c33e100   4456       sqscb
c33f268   48         fragman
c33f298   40         sqscb
c33f2c0   56         sqscb
```

Onstat -g ffr   Print Free Pool Fragments

Use this command to drill down into the information about memory pools to get information about free pool fragments.

```
$ onstat -g ffr 3
Informix Dynamic Server Version 7.30.TC3    -- On-Line -- Up 00:58:49 -- 9536 Kbytes
Free list for pool name 3:
addr      size
c33f2f8   3336
```

Onstat -g ufr   Print Pool Usage Breakdown

This command simply summarizes the individual pool fragment allocations from the
onstat -g afr command.

```
$ onstat -g ufr 3
Informix Dynamic Server Version 7.30.TC3    -- On-Line -- Up 01:00:50 -- 9536 Kbytes
Memory usage for pool name 3:
size      memid
120       overhead
96        scb
40        ostcb
4552      sqscb
48        fragman
```

Onstat -g seg   Print Memory Segment Statistics

This onstat -g command shows how much resident and virtual shared memory is allocated and used by the IDS engine.

```
$ onstat -g seg
Informix Dynamic Server Version 7.30.UC3    -- On-Line -- Up 2 days 22:13:20 -- 18464 Kbytes
Segment Summary:
id      key         addr       size      ovhd     class blkused  blkfree
4       1381451777  c0e96000   10706944  1204     R     1300     7
(shared) 1381451777 c18cc000   8200192   736      V     657      344
Total:   -          -          18907136  -        -     1957     351

(* segment locked in memory)
```

The id, key, and addr fields are implementation-specific means of identifying the
shared memory. They differ between NT and UNIX, which have different mechanisms for
handling shared memory. The major points of interest are in the size (total size in bytes),
class (Virtual or Resident), blkused (blocks used), and blkfree (blocks free) fields. The total
field should equal the final field in the header for onstat in Kbytes.

One highly implementation-specific caveat comes in systems running on the Hewlett
Packard HP/UX 10.XX operating system on PA-RISC processors. HP systems have some
problems with the algorithms for adding shared memory segments. These systems should be
monitored carefully with the onstat -g seg command, and they should never be allowed to grow beyond three shared memory segments. Once the fourth segment is added,
performance goes into the toilet. The trick here is to allocate enough shared memory at boot
time by adjusting the SHMVIRTSIZE parameter to the largest number that is likely to be
needed, and then adjust the SHMADD and SHMTOT parameters in the ONCONFIG file to
disallow any dynamic growth of the shared memory beyond the amount already configured
in the first three segments. This is a hardware limitation of the PA-RISC processor. This
processor has 4 special-purpose address registers that are the only way to access shared

memory. If you get more than 4 shared memory segments, the system is forced to thrash by swapping the shared memory base addresses into and out of these 4 registers.

Onstat -g rbm   Print Block Map for Resident Segment

The next two `onstat -g` commands show bitmaps for the resident and nonresident segments of shared memory. Each bit set represents an 8-kilobyte block in use. If the bit is not set, that block is not in use. This command lists the block usage for the communication message area of the resident section.

```
$ onstat -g rbm
Informix Dynamic Server Version 7.30.UC3   -- On-Line -- Up 2 days 22:13:26 -- 18464 Kbytes
Block bitmap for resident segment address c0e96000:
(bitmap address = c0e9625c, bitmap size = 292)
c0e9625c:ffffffff ffffffff ffffffff ffffffff ffffffff ffffffff ffffffff ffffffff
c0e9627c:ffffffff ffffffff ffffffff ffffffff ffffffff ffffffff ffffffff ffffffff
c0e9629c:ffffffff ffffffff ffffffff ffffffff ffffffff ffffffff ffffffff ffffffff
c0e962bc:ffffffff ffffffff ffffffff ffffffff ffffffff ffffffff ffffffff ffffffff
c0e962dc:ffffffff ffffffff ffffffff ffffffff ffffffff ffffffff ffffffff ffffffff
c0e962fc:fffff000 00000000 e0b60000 00000000 00000001 00000001 00000000 00000000
c0e9631c:00000000 00020000 c0e96000 52574801 52574801 00001000 00000001 00a36000
c0e9633c:007d2000 00000000 00000000 00000000 00000000 02000000 c0e96000 00000000
c0e9635c:00000000 00000000 c0e96000 c209e000 c0e9a800 00000000 00000000 00000000
c0e9637c:00000000
```

Onstat -g nbm   Print Block Map for Nonresident Segments

Prints block bit map for the nonresident segments, one bit per 8-kilobyte block. Bit set indicates block free. By converting the values to binary, you can determine how much of the nonresident (virtual) segment is actually in use at any one time. If you see "00000000" for many segments, this indicates that the virtual portion of shared memory is not being used to its fullest and you may be able to cut back on the nonresident portion, thus freeing up memory for other uses.

```
$ onstat -g nbm
Informix Dynamic Server Version 7.30.UC3   -- On-Line -- Up 2 days 22:13:31 -- 18464 Kbytes
Block bitmap for virtual segment address c18cc000:
(bitmap address = c18cc25c, bitmap size = 128)
c18cc25c:ffffffff ffffffff ffffffff ffffffff ffffffff ffffffff ffffffff ffffffff
c18cc27c:ffffffff ffffffff ffffffff ffffffff ffffffff ffffffff ffffffff ffffffff
c18cc29c:ffffffff ffffffff fffffffe ffffffff ffc22888 00000003 80000000 00000000
c18cc2bc:00000000 00000000 00000000 00000000 00000000 00000000 00000000 00000000
```

MONITORING DISK I/O

Onstat -g iof   Print Disk I/O Statistics by Chunk/File

Onstat -g iof is the onstat command that is most useful in monitoring reading and writing activity to and from the disk subsystem. Given the sensitivity of the database engine to disk access times, monitoring disk activity is of critical importance in extracting maximum performance from the IDS engine. The onstat -D command can give you similar information, but onstat -g iof is somewhat simpler and easier to understand.

This is true in OLTP systems and even more true in DSS systems. Decision support systems rely more on IDS's inherent parallelism and smart disk access to reduce the times needed for the many sequential scans that are typically seen in DSS systems. The major objective for disk tuning is to spread the activity as evenly as possibly across multiple fast disk drives. The general rule is "the more spindles, the better." Thus, if you have otherwise equally attractive opportunities to use either four 2-gig drives or one 8-gig drive, the four drive setup will give you better performance, assuming that other access factors are equal.

```
$ onstat -g iof


Informix Dynamic Server Version 7.30.UC3   -- On-Line -- Up 2 days 22:14:37 -- 18464 Kbytes
AIO global files:
gfd pathname          totalops  dskread dskwrite   io/s
  3 rootdbs                 0        0        0    0.0
  4 config_data             0        0        0    0.0
  5 eba_data                0        0        0    0.0
  6 demotest_data           0        0        0    0.0
  7 /dev/vg00/rraw0         0        0        0    0.0
  8 /dev/vg01/rraw1         0        0        0    0.0
  9 appldbs_data            0        0        0    0.0
 10 logspace_data           0        0        0    0.0
 11 tempspace_data          0        0        0    0.0
```

Chunk numbers are not listed in the onstat -g iof output, but the chunks are listed in the same order as in onstat -d. Field meanings are:

- gfd   Global file descriptor. Earlier numbers were created earlier
- pathname   Location of the chunk
- totalops   Total of all disk operations to the chunk
- dskread   Read operations from the disk
- dskwrite   Write operations from the disk
- I/O/s   I/O operations per second

The system from which this sample output was taken was inactive, but should you see one chunk with much more activities per second, you might want to run oncheck -pe to find which tables or fragments reside on the chunk and consider modifying either your table locations or your fragmentation strategy.

The ideal situation would be to have each chunk represent a different disk. What is really important for performance is not reads and writes by chunk but reads and writes per disk spindle. With a one-to-one chunk to spindle relationship, the disk activities become obvious. What this would mean, though, is that the maximum physical disk size that you could use would be 2 gigabytes, as that is the maximum chunk size that IDS can address. With the advent of larger disks and the need to go to larger disks, this is not always feasible. Another way to make it easier to analyze the data in that case would be to follow a stringent chunk naming convention. Thus, if you have four 2-gig chunks all residing on an 8-gig disk called diskA, name the chunks in such a way that you can identify the physical disk from the chunk name, something like this:

```
dAchunk1
dAchunk2
dAchunk3
dAchunk4
dBchunk5
dBchunk6, etc
```

While this will not alleviate any performance problems that arise from using larger disks, it will at least make the monitoring easier.

Onstat -g ioq   Print I/O Queue Information

This command seems to have disappeared from the "onstat - -" help screen, but as of IDS 7.30, it still existed in the utility. Whether this is a purposeful omission or not on Informix's part is open to discussion.

This command presents information about the IDS I/O queue lengths and operations. There is one line of output for every physical chunk in the system. These are identified by "gfd <number>" where gfd is the global file descriptor as in the onstat -g iof output. There is also one queue for each CPU-VP.

```
D:\INFORMIX\bin>onstat -g ioq
Informix Dynamic Server Version 7.30.TC3    -- On-Line -- Up 00:27:13 -- 9536 Kbytes
AIO I/O queues:
q name/id    len maxlen totalops  dskread dskwrite  dskcopy
   kio   0     0    0        0         0        0         0
   kio   1     0    3      121       113        8         0
   adt   0     0    0        0         0        0         0
   msc   0     0    1     1015         0        0         0
   aio   0     0    1       47        14        0         0
   pio   0     0    0        0         0        0         0
   lio   0     0    0        0         0        0         0
   gfd   3     0    0        0         0        0         0
   gfd   4     0    0        0         0        0         0
```

```
gfd   5      0       0        0        0        0        0
gfd   6      0       0        0        0        0        0
```

Meanings of the output fields are:

- q name   Type of I/O queue
- id   Either the gfd identifier or the VP number
- len   Current length of requests in the queue
- maxlen   Maximum number of requests in the queue
- totalops   Total operations
- dskread   Disk reads
- dskwrite   Disk writes
- dskcopy   Disk copies

If you notice an excessive number in the maxlen column for any of the aio queues, it may be possible to increase your disk performance by adding an additional AIO-VP thread.

To use this command to debug performance problems, look for abnormally high numbers in the len and totalops fields for a particular gfd, which will map to a particular chunk. If you see high numbers for particular gfds, your disk access is skewed and you should look at either moving some tables around or fragmenting large tables that are located on these devices.

Onstat -g iov   Print Disk I/O Statistics by VP

While `onstat -g ioq` gives you information about the queue lengths for the various disk chunks, the `-g iov` report gives you I/O per second, total I/O operations broken down into reads, writes, and copies. It also gives information about how many times these VPs were wakened from a sleeping state and how many I/O operations were performed on the average for each wakeup.

This is broken down by virtual processors, so you can get a feeling for how many virtual processors your system actually needs. In the sample below, there are 18 AIO-VPs and none of them is doing anything. If you were to see many VPs that had low numbers of I/O per wakeup during a relatively busy period, you would want to consider cutting back on the number of AIO-VPs and using their resources for other tasks.

In addition to the aio class of virtual processors, you will also see:

- msc   Handles miscellaneous writes, such as writes to the system log
- pio   Writes to the physical log
- lio   Writes to the logical log
- aio   "Normal" AIO-VPs which access data from the disk

```
$ onstat -g iov
Informix Dynamic Server Version 7.30.UC3    -- On-Line -- Up 2 days 22:14:34 -- 18464 Kbytes
AIO I/O vps:
class/vp s  io/s totalops  dskread dskwrite  dskcopy  wakeups  io/wup  errors
   msc  0 i   0.0       0        0        0        0        0    0.0       0
   aio  0 i   0.0       0        0        0        0        0    0.0       0
   aio  1 i   0.0       0        0        0        0        0    0.0       0
   aio  2 i   0.0       0        0        0        0        0    0.0       0
   aio  3 i   0.0       0        0        0        0        0    0.0       0
   aio  4 i   0.0       0        0        0        0        0    0.0       0
   aio  5 i   0.0       0        0        0        0        0    0.0       0
   aio  6 i   0.0       0        0        0        0        0    0.0       0
   aio  7 i   0.0       0        0        0        0        0    0.0       0
   aio  8 i   0.0       0        0        0        0        0    0.0       0
   aio  9 i   0.0       0        0        0        0        0    0.0       0
   aio 10 i   0.0       0        0        0        0        0    0.0       0
   aio 11 i   0.0       0        0        0        0        0    0.0       0
   aio 12 i   0.0       0        0        0        0        0    0.0       0
   aio 13 i   0.0       0        0        0        0        0    0.0       0
   aio 14 i   0.0       0        0        0        0        0    0.0       0
   aio 15 i   0.0       0        0        0        0        0    0.0       0
   aio 16 i   0.0       0        0        0        0        0    0.0       0
   aio 17 i   0.0       0        0        0        0        0    0.0       0
   pio  0 i   0.0       0        0        0        0        0    0.0       0
   lio  0 i   0.0       0        0        0        0        0    0.0       0
```

Onstat –g lsc   Print Light Scan Information

Under the appropriate circumstances, Dynamic Server can bypass the LRU queues when it performs a sequential scan. A sequential scan that avoids the LRU queues is termed a light scan. Light scans can be used only for sequential scans of large data tables and are the fastest means for performing these scans. System catalog tables and tables smaller than the size of the buffer pool do not use light scans. Light scans are allowed under Dirty Read (including nonlogging databases) and Repeatable Read isolation levels. Repeatable Read full-table scans obtain a shared lock on the table. A light scan is used only in Committed Read isolation if the table has a shared lock. Light scans are never allowed under Cursor Stability isolation.

```
C:\INFORMIX\bin>onstat -g lsc
Informix Dynamic Server Version 7.30.TC3 - On-Line  Up 00:14:54 -- 536 Kbytes
Light Scan Info
descriptor  address   next_lpage  next_ppage  ppage_left  bufcnt  ook_aside
```

There is an environmental variable, LIGHT_SCANS, that can be set to the value of FORCE in some IDS systems that may help you ensure that light scans are used. Try it in your engine to see if it helps.

Onstat -g iog   Print AIO Global Information

This command provides you with a summary of the types and numbers of AIO (async I/O) threads.

```
$ onstat -g iog
Informix Dynamic Server Version 7.30.UC3    -- On-Line -- Up 2 days 22:14:45 -- 18464 Kbytes
AIO global info:
6 aio classes
12 open files
64 max global files
```

Onstat -g iob   Print Big Buffer Usage by IO VP Class

Big buffers are used for long read and write operations. They are more efficient than normal buffers and reside in the virtual portion of shared memory. These big buffers are composed of several pages of shared memory. When the server needs to access multiple pages that are contiguous for either reads or writes, it will use big buffers. Examples are in sequential scan reads and some sorted writes. It also uses the big buffers during checkpoint writes. This is what makes the checkpoint writes more efficient than normal writes. Once a series of pages are read into a big buffer, they are then automatically copied into regular buffers.

The onstat -g iob command shows to what extent the various IO-VP classes are able to utilize these big buffers. It shows read and write activity as well as holes and holes per operation. The concept of holes is not defined anywhere in Informix documentation, so we are left to guess at the meanings.

This command doesn't really affect anything that happens in the database, but it will give you a feeling for just what is happening under the hood. There's not much you can do to act on this data, however.

```
$ onstat -g iob
Informix Dynamic Server Version 7.30.UC3    -- On-Line -- Up 2 days 22:14:49 -- 18464 Kbytes
AIO big buffer usage summary:
class                     reads                              writes
        pages   ops   pgs/op  holes  hl-ops hls/op     pages   ops   pgs/op
  kio     0      0     0.00     0       0    0.00         0      0    0.00
  adt     0      0     0.00     0       0    0.00         0      0    0.00
  msc     0      0     0.00     0       0    0.00         0      0    0.00
  aio     0      0     0.00     0       0    0.00         0      0    0.00
  pio     0      0     0.00     0       0    0.00         0      0    0.00
  lio     0      0     0.00     0       0    0.00         0      0    0.00
```

Onstat -g ppf   Print Partition Profiles

IDS can speed up DSS queries by using parallel threads to accomplish DSS queries. This is most useful when the tables in question are fragmented across multiple disk spindles. This onstat command allows the DBA to monitor many factors by partition. Among the most important data elements in this command are the isrd (ISAM read) and iswrt (ISAM write) fields. These do not correspond directly to disk reads and disk writes, but they are a good indicator of the amount of activity to those partitions.

```
$ onstat -g ppf
Informix Dynamic Server Version 7.30.UC3    -- On-Line -- Up 2 days 22:14:53 -- 18464 Kbytes
Partition profiles
partnum  lkrqs lkwts dlks  touts isrd  iswrt isrwt isdel bfrd  bfwrt seqsc
15       0     0     0     0     0     0     0     0     0     0     0
23       0     0     0     0     0     0     0     0     0     0     0
1048577  0     0     0     0     0     0     0     0     0     0     0
1048578  0     0     0     0     0     0     0     0     0     0     0
...
7340211  0     0     0     0     0     0     0     0     0     0     0
8388609  0     0     0     0     0     0     0     0     0     0     0
9437185  0     0     0     0     0     0     0     0     0     0     0
```

Field meanings are:

- partnum   Partition number
- lkreqs   Lock requests
- lkwts   Lock waits
- dlks   Deadlocks
- touts   Timeouts
- isrd   Read calls
- iswrt   Write calls
- isrwt   Rewrites (updates)
- isdel   Deletes
- bfrd   Buffer reads
- bfwrt   Buffer writes
- seqsc   Sequential scans

To relate the partnums to actual table names requires you to go to the system tables. The partnum field is found as partn in the sysfragments table. Also in sysfragments will be the tabid which is the table ID. Go to the systables table with the tabid and get the tabname. This will work only if there are actually fragmented tables in the database. If there are no fragmented tables, there will be no rows in the sysfragments table.

MONITORING NETWORK OPERATIONS

Onstat -g ntu   Print Net User Thread Profile Information
by VP

This command allows you to monitor network packet reads and writes in the IDS engine.

```
$ onstat -g ntu
Informix Dynamic Server Version 7.30.UC3    -- On-Line -- Up 2 days 22:15:01 -- 18464 Kbytes
global network information:
  #netscb connects    read      write    q-free  q-limits  q-exceed
    4/   6        0         0        0    1/   1  135/  10   0/   0

Individual thread network information (basic):
  netscb type    thread name    sid  fd poll    reads    writes q-nrm q-exp
c1c43b68 soctcp sqlexec          40   3   5        0         0  0/ 0  0/ 0
c1a6a018 soctcp sqlexec          34   2   5        0         0  0/ 0  0/ 0
c1a51628 soctcp soctcplst         3   1   5        0         0  0/ 0  0/ 0
c1a503f8 soctcp soctcppoll        2   0   5        0         0  0/ 0  0/ 0
```

In the example above, the first two threads are user (sqlexec) threads and the last two
are poll threads. Monitor the reads and writes by the user threads to find out how much load
individual user threads are placing on the network.

Onstat -g ntt   Print Net User Thread Access Times

This command provides user times for the various threads that are accessing network resources. This command is also totally undocumented, but it does show one piece of information that is difficult to find anywhere else. In the example printout, look at the
"soctcplst" entry. Off to the right is an address that includes a machine name, a socket/tcp-
port-number, and an Informix network protocol. This can be useful in investigating connections to your database that you cannot trace to SQL running in the engine.

The open and read times can also give you an idea how long a connection has been
active and when the last activity occurred. This can help you investigate long-running tasks
or connections.

```
$ onstat -g ntt
Informix Dynamic Server Version 7.30.UC3    -- On-Line -- Up 2 days 22:15:04 -- 18464 Kbytes
global network information:
  #netscb connects    read      write    q-free  q-limits  q-exceed
    4/   6        0         0        0    1/   1  135/  10   0/   0

Individual thread network information (times):
  netscb thread name    sid    open      read     write address
c1c43b68 sqlexec          40 13:35:22 13:39:32 13:39:32
c1a6a018 sqlexec          34 13:22:51 13:52:26 13:52:26
```

```
c1a51628 soctcplst        3 17:24:52 13:52:04          rock.shared.com|4001|soctcp
08/14/98

c1a503f8 soctcppoll       2 17:24:46
08/14/98
```

Onstat -g ntd   Print Net Dispatch Information

This command shows the number of accepted and rejected network packets arranged by
type of client. It can tell you a couple of things. First, the total number of packets read and
written can give you an estimate of the amount of work being done by various client types
and can help you investigate clients that may be placing an inappropriate load on the network. Look at the read and write columns for this data.

     You can also look for a large number of rejected entries that will help alert you to
network problems. These rejects can occur for several reasons:

*   Network timeout caused by network overload or other network problems
User table overflow. Check `onstat -p` and look for ovuserthreads greater than 0.

     If you are seeing excessive network timeouts, there are a couple of environmental
variables that you can set either in `setnet32` or in your user environment:

*   INFORMIXCONTIME   Wait time for a connection. Try increasing it.
*   INFORMIXCONRETRY   Number of times to retry a failed connection.

     For example, if you have INFORMIXCONTIME set to 1200 and
INFORMIXCONRETRY set to 20, the client will retry the connection every 1200/20 =
every 60 seconds for 20 times, for a grand total of 1200 seconds. If your network is very
busy or if you are connecting over a slow network such a RAS or PPP connection, you may
manipulate these connection parameters in an attempt to cut down on rejected connections.

```
$ onstat -g ntd
Informix Dynamic Server Version 7.30.UC3   -- On-Line -- Up 2 days 22:15:13 -- 18464 Kbytes
global network information:
    #netscb connects    read    write    q-free   q-limits  q-exceed
    4/   6        0        0       0      1/   1   135/  10    0/   0

Client Type    Calls    Accepted   Rejected       Read      Write
sqlexec        yes         42          0            0          0
srvinfx        yes          0          0            0          0
onspace        yes          0          0            0          0
onlog          yes          0          0            0          0
onparam        yes          0          0            0          0
oncheck        yes          0          0            0          0
```

```
onload        yes       0        0        0        0
onunload      yes       0        0        0        0
onmonitor     yes       0        0        0        0
dr_accept     yes       0        0        0        0
cdraccept     no        0        0        0        0
ontape        yes       0        0        0        0
srvstat       yes       0        0        0        0
asfecho       yes       0        0        0        0
listener      yes       0        0        0        0
crsamexec     yes       0        0        0        0
safe          yes       0        0        0        0
Totals                 42        0        0        0
```

Onstat -g dic   Print Dictionary Cache Information

IDS maintains a dictionary cache in the virtual portion of shared memory. Every time an SQL statement references one of the system tables, the information from the system table is cached in stored memory. Just about every SQL statement will require access to one of the system tables. This dictionary cache size cannot be modified with documented parameters, but there are two undocumented parameters that can affect the cache size. They are:

- DD_HASHSIZE   must be prime (default 31)
- DD_HASHMAX   Integer < 32767 (default 10)

Set these two parameters so that DD_HASHSIZE * DD_HASHMAX is greater than the estimated number of active tables in all databases (including remote databases) and you will cut down on thrashing in the dictionary cache.

The dictionary cache is ordered into a series of linked lists. When a table's dictionary data is cached, the engine chooses a list and adds the internal data structure to the list. The ordering is not sequential, so there is no easy way here to tell when the table's data was accessed, only that it was accessed and has not been deleted from the cache yet.

```
$ onstat -g dic
Informix Dynamic Server Version 7.30.UC3  -- On-Line -- Up 2 days 22:15:38 -- 18464 Kbytes

Dictionary Cache:  Number of lists: 31, Maximum list size: 10
list#  size  refcnt  dirty?  heapptr      table name
------------------------------------------------------------
  0     7      0       no    c1d15520     crm3@inf_rock1:informix.summ_mbr_ret_h_mg
              0       no    c1cef420     crm3@inf_rock1:informix.summ_mbr_ret_hdr
              0       no    c1d3c6e0     crm3@inf_rock1:informix.levels
              0       no    c1d39f20     crm3@inf_rock1:informix.mbr_points
              0       no    c1d08700     crm3@inf_rock1:informix.batch_history
              0       no    c1d28c20     crm3@inf_rock1:informix.batch_rpt_hdr
              0       no    c1d25020     crm3@inf_rock1:informix.sweepstakes_audit

  1     4      0       no    c1d3cee0     crm3@inf_rock1:informix.location_assoc
              0       no    c1d41020     crm3@inf_rock1:informix.mbr_id
              0       no    c1d62be0     crm3@inf_rock1:informix.summ_lp_level
```

```
            0      no      c1d39320    crm3@inf_rock1:informix.mbr_points_year

<many lines deleted for simplicity>
    29     4     0      no      c1d7b020    bsgsec@inf_rock1:informix.sysdefaults
                 0      no      c1d596c0    crm3@inf_rock1:informix.summ_lp_level_mg
                 0      no      c1d44020    crm3@inf_rock1:informix.item_group
                 0      no      c1c5fe80    crm3@inf_rock1:informix.sysdefaults

    30     5     0      no      c1d1c4c0    crm3@inf_rock1:informix.summ_lp_dg_mg_ig
                 0      no      c1cd9c20    crm3@inf_rock1:informix.summ_new_mbr_hdr
                 0      no      c1d63b40    crm3@inf_rock1:informix.summ_lp_level_pro
                 0      no      c1d0b1c0    crm3@inf_rock1:informix.sweepstakes_detail
                 0      no      c1cffc20    crm3@inf_rock1:informix.systableext

Total number of dictionary entries: 181
```

Meanings of the fields follow:

- list#   ID number of the hash list
- size   How many dictionary structures are in this list
- refcnt   How many current threads are referencing this data
- dirty   Has any of the dictionary data changed?
- heapptr   Pointer to the data structure in the heap
- table name   Fully qualified table name

This information in the dictionary cache is not changed by an `onstat -z`. It changes only when the capacity of the cache is reached and some data has to be dropped from the cache. It is also reinitialized whenever the engine is stopped and restarted.

Onstat -g opn   Print Open Tables

This command lists data about tables that are open at the time the command is run.

```
$ onstat -g opn
Informix Dynamic Server Version 7.30.UC3    -- On-Line -- Up 2 days 22:15:43 -- 18464 Kbytes
tid  rstcb      isfd  op_mode    op_flags    partnum     ucount ocount lockmode

76   0xc18db2e8 0     0x00000400 0x00000397 0x0070001f 2      2      0
76   0xc18db2e8 1     0x00000002 0x00000003 0x0070001f 2      2      0
76   0xc18db2e8 2     0x00000400 0x00000693 0x00700040 1      0      0

70   0xc18db79c 0     0x00000400 0x00000397 0x0070001f 2      2      0
70   0xc18db79c 1     0x00000002 0x00000117 0x0070001f 2      2      0
70   0xc18db79c 4     0x00000400 0x00000417 0x00700041 1      0      0
```

Field meanings are:

- tid   Thread ID of the thread that is using the table
- rstcb   Address of the thread in the RSAM thread-control block
- isfd   Unknown
- op_mode   Unknown
- op_flags   Unknown
- partnum   Partnum of the table
- ucount   Number of users accessing the table
- ocount   Number of opens
- lockmode   Flag indicating the lock mode of the query

    0   None

    3   Share mode

    7   Intent Exclusive (Update & deletes)

    9   Exclusive Lock=X

Onstat -g qst   Print Queue Statistics

In order to use this command, you first have to set up your engine to collect statistics on queue activity. This is done by setting the QSTATS parameter to 1 in the ONCONFIG file. This data collection will slow the engine down significantly and shoul be done only if the user is chasing down a particularly obstinate problem.

    This best done in conjunction with Informix Support, and we will not go into detail here.

```
D:\INFORMIX\etc>onstat -g qst
Informix Dynamic Server Version 7.30.TC3   -- On-Line -- Up 00:00:56 -- 9536 Kbytes
Mutex Queue Statistics
name      nwaits   avg_time max_time avgq maxq nservs   avg_time
```

    This command gives you information about the queues that control access to mutexes. It gives the name, number of wait events, average wait times, maximum wait times, average queue length and maximum queue length for the queues. The last two columns are so far undocumented.

Onstat -g wst   Print Thread Wait Statistics

Thread wait statistics is like queue statistics in that you first have to set the engine up to track thread waiting events. To enable the collection of wait statistics, set WSTATS to 1 in the ONCONFIG file. Beware that setting these data collections statistics can slow your server down significantly. Like queue statistics, this is best done in conjunction with Informix Support.

```
$onstat -g wai
Informix Dynamic Server Version 7.30.TC3    -- On-Line -- Up 00:00:47 -- 9536 Kbytes
Waiting threads:
 tid    tcb       rstcb    prty status                 vp-class     name
 2      c274200   0        2    sleeping forever        3lio         vp 0
 3      c274440   0        2    sleeping forever        4pio         vp 0
 4      c2746a8   0        2    sleeping forever        5aio         vp 0
 5      c274910   0        2    sleeping forever        6msc         vp 0
 6      c2c8230   c18e018  4    sleeping secs: 1        1cpu         main_loop()
 9      c2c9d28   0        3    sleeping forever        1cpu         soctcplst
 10     c2cc350   c18e4b8  2    sleeping forever        1cpu         flush_sub(0)

 11     c2cc590   0        4    sleeping forever        5aio         kaio
 12     c2ccb38   0        4    sleeping forever        1cpu         kaio
 13     c2cd170   c18e958  3    sleeping forever        1cpu         aslogflush
 14     c2cd4a0   c18edf8  2    sleeping secs: 19       1cpu         btclean
 30     c274fe0   c18fbd8  4    sleeping secs: 1        1cpu         onmode_mon
```

MONITORING SQL STATEMENTS

Onstat -g sql   Print SQL Information

This command is one of the most useful features found in onstat in IDS engines. OnLine systems provided no way for you to see exactly which SQL statements were being executed at any particular time. This left the DBA in the dark when trying to see exactly which SQL statements may be hogging system resources and bringing the system to its knees.

Users who are running ad hoc queries in OLTP systems are going to do bad SE-LECTS no matter how well you train them. A bad SELECT is defined as any SELECT statement that hogs a lot of the system resources. These can be such things as non-indexed reads against large tables resulting in sequential scans, disjoint queries that return a Cartesian product of the tuples, generating a million lines of output, or queries so constructed that they use bad optimizer paths. You'll even generate bad queries occasionally yourself. This is forgivable.

What is totally unforgivable in a system is to imbed system-hog queries into the code of a production system. During the development process, every SQL statement and every possible combination of dynamic SQL statements that may be created on the fly in response to user inputs should be tested and should have a SET EXPLAIN run against them. Dynamic SQL statements in particular are problematic, since by nature, the statements change in response to user inputs. Particular care should be given to front-end applications that generate dynamic SQL statements to make sure that they will not allow, or at least warn the user about, SQL statements that will hog up system resources.

Onstat -g sql gives you a tool to trace down these pathological queries and identify where the queries are coming from. I'd estimate that half of your production problems can be solved by eliminating these system hog queries.

What usually happens is that you'll receive reports or notice yourself that system performance suddenly goes into the toilet. This is the time to run an onstat -g sql.

Onstat -g sql can be run either globally or against a particular session. Here is a global run:

```
$ onstat -g sql
Informix Dynamic Server Version 7.30.TC3    -- On-Line -- Up 00:29:36 -- 9536 Kbytes

Sess  SQL          Current         Iso Lock      SQL ISAM F.E.
Id    Stmt type    Database        Lvl Mode      ERR ERR  Vers
583   SELECT       sysmaster       CR  Not Wait  0   0    7.30
```

This invocation gives you a simple list of the session ID, type of SQL statement (SELECT, UPDATE, INSERT, DELETE), the database used, isolation level, lock mode, SQL error code and/or ISAM error code, and front-end program version of all the sessions currently running. You can get some useful data from this. If you have a system that runs multiple types of clients, such as ESQL/C programs, dbaccess, Powerbuilder, and the like, the final field, F.E. Version, can often give you a hint as to what kind of job is running. You might have started your witch hunt by running onstat -u, looking for sessions that were doing a lot of reads, which often indicates a sequential scan. You could have used the SMI tables to discover sequential scans. Anyway, somehow you have gotten interested in finding out what a particular user thread is doing. In this case, we're interested in session ID #583:

```
$ onstat -g sql 583
Informix Dynamic Server Version 7.30.TC3    -- On-Line -- Up 00:30:56 -- 9536 Kbytes

Sess  SQL          Current         Iso Lock      SQL ISAM F.E.
Id    Stmt type    Database        Lvl Mode      ERR ERR  Vers
583   SELECT       sysmaster       CR  Not Wait  0   0    7.30

Current statement name : slctcur
Current SQL statement :
select * from systables
Last parsed SQL statement :
select * from systables
```

Running onstat -g sql with a session id after it gives you the same information about the thread that running without the session id did, plus it gives you the paydirt at the end of the report. This paydirt is the exact SQL code that is being run by the session, as well as the last SQL code that was parsed by the statement. Just seeing the SQL may tip you off that this is you resource hog. If you see someone running a query against a 100-million-row table with a where clause referencing an unindexed column, you know you've found the culprit.

Often though you won't be sure that this is the job that's causing the problem. The thing to do now is cut and paste the query text into your own query tool, slap a SET EX-PLAIN ON at the beginning of the statement, run it long enough to generate a query plan, and then interrupt the query. Of course, before running it, be sure that running the query won't lock a system table or something similar or otherwise screw up what's running in production. Then take a look at the query plan and see exactly what the query is doing. If this provides the smoking gun, it's time to break out the baseball bat and go visit either the user who's running the ad hoc query or the developer who let such a stupid piece of code get into a production system. This is much more fun than doing what you really should have done, which is use the baseball bat on yourself. After all, you *do* have a policy that all production SQL code has to be approved by the DBA, don't you?

A final point for the onstat -g sql <sessionid> command is the current statement name. This is the cursor or prepared statement name for the currently running SQL state-ment. If you are writing code that prepares and executes SQL statements, be sure that the names chosen for the cursors are meaningful. If they are, you can identify the running SQL more easily. For example, the cursor name should be coded to identify both the purpose of the cursor and the name of the program running it.

Onstat -g pos   Print DBSERVERNAME File

The DBSERVERNAME file is actually the $INFORMIXDIR/etc/.infos.servername file. This file is a temporary binary file that is created whenever you initialize shared memory for an instance and is deleted when you take the server off-line. The "servername" part of the filename is the DBSERVERNAME parameter from the ONCONFIG file. The IDS engine and its utilities refer to this file in order to address the server. The only way to get a human-readable view of this file is to use onstat -g pos. Do not delete this .infos file from the $INFORMIX/etc directory, as it is needed by the utilities. If you delete the file by acci-dent (it's hard because the filename begins with a period), you can re-create it by restarting the engine.

```
$ onstat -g pos
Informix Dynamic Server Version 7.30.UC3   -- On-Line -- Up 2 days 22:16:22 -- 18464 Kbytes
   1   7   0 infos ver/size 2 136
   2   1   0 snum     1 52574801 00000000 inf_rock1
   3   4   0 onconfig path /informix/etc/onconfig.rock1
   4   5   0 host rock
   5   6   0 oninit ver Informix Dynamic Server Version 7.30.UC3
   6   8   0 del
```

Onstat -g lap   Print Light Append Information

Light appends are append operations to a page which bypasses the normal buffer pool. They are used in the High Performance Loader (HPL) in certain instances in the express mode of operation. The onstat -g lap command is the primary means of looking at these light appends.

```
$ onstat -g lap
Informix Dynamic Server Version 7.30.UC3    -- On-Line -- Up 2 days 22:16:37 -- 18464 Kbytes
Light Append Info
session id  address   cur_ppage   la_npused   la_ndata   la_nrows    bufcnt
```

## CHAPTER 11

Exploring the Sysmaster Database

by Lester Knutsen

*T*his is the only chapter in the book that was not written by the author. A year or so ago, Lester Knutsen presented a paper on the subject of the SMI (System Monitoring Interface) tables to a standing-room-only crowd at the Informix World Users Group. Since then, his paper and the accompanying shell scripts for querying the SMI tables have become staples in the arsenals of hundreds or even thousands of DBAs across the world. I had originally resigned myself to digging through the documentation and writing a chapter on the SMI tables, and I wanted to be able to include Lester's scripts on the CD that comes with this book. When I e-mailed Lester, he graciously gave me permission to include the scripts, and included the paper as documentation for the scripts.

When I read the paper again, I remembered just how good it had been and realized that there was no way that I was going to do a better job on the subject than Lester had already done, so I e-mailed him back and obtained his permission to include the paper in the book. I'm getting tired of writing just about now, and I figured that you readers could use a break from my "breezy blue-collar writing style." Lester's paper was written before Informix changed the name from "OnLine" to "INFORMIX-Dynamic Server," so he refers to IDS as "OnLine". Be assured that he is talking about what we now know as IDS, that is, Versions 7 and above.

So, without further ado, I'll take a break and let Lester educate you about the finer points of the SMI tables.

Exploring the SMI Database

When you list all the databases on your INFORMIX server, you will see one called "sysmaster." This is a special database and is one of the new features that first appeared in INFORMIX-OnLine DSA 6.x and 7.x. This is a database that contains tables that can be used for monitoring your system. These are referred to as the System Monitoring Interface (SMI) tables. In this chapter we will explore some of the tables and views that are in this database.

The sysmaster database is described as a pseudo database. That means most of its tables are not normal tables on disk, but pointers to shared memory structures in the OnLine engine. The sysmaster database contains over 120 tables. Only 18 of these tables are documented in the INFORMIX-OnLine Dynamic Server Administrator's Guide, Volume 2, Chapter 38. The rest are undocumented and described by Informix as for internal use. The examples and references in this article are based on OnLine 7.23. I have also tested some of the examples with versions 7.10, 7.12, and 7.22. There are some minor changes between versions in the undocumented features and structures of these tables.

A warning: Some of the features discussed in this article are based on undocumented SMI tables and may change or not work in future versions of INFORMIX OnLine DSA.

This article will focus on users, server configuration, dbspaces, chunks, tables, and monitoring I/O using the sysmaster database. We will present how to create scripts to monitor the following:

- List who is using each database.
- Display information about your server configuration.
- Display how much free space is available in each dbspace in a format like the UNIX df command.
- List the status and characteristics of each chunk device.
- Display blocks of free space within a chunk. This allows you to plan where to put large tables without fragmenting them.
- Display I/O statistics by chunk devices.
- Display I/O usage of chunk devices as a percent of the total I/O, and show which chunks are getting used the most.

- Display tables and the number of extents, and number of pages used.
- Present a layout of dbspace, databases, tables, and extents similar to the command "tbcheck -pe."
- Show table usage statistics sorted by which tables have the most reads, writes, or locks.
- Show statistics of users sessions.
- Show locks and users who are waiting on locks.

A PRACTICAL EXAMPLE: WHO IS USING WHAT DATABASE

Let's begin with a very practical example of the sysmaster database's value. My interest in this database started a couple of years ago, while consulting on a project for a development group where I needed to know who had a database open and which workstation they were using to connect to the database. This was a development environment and there were continual changes to the database schemas. In order to make updates to the database schema, I would have to get the developers to disconnect from the database. The "onstat -u" utility would tell me which users were connected to the server, but not what database and what workstation they were using. Onstat -g ses told me the user and workstation, but not the database. Onstat -g sql told me the session ID and database, but not the user name and workstation. After some debugging, I found all the information I wanted in the sysmaster database. And, because it was a database, I could retrieve it with SQL queries. The following query shows the database, who has it open, the workstation they are connected from, and the session ID

Figure 1. Dbwho SQL script

```
------------------------------------------------------- dbwho.sql
select  sysdatabases.name database,          -- Database Name
        syssessions.username,                     -- User Name
        syssessions.hostname,             -- Workstation
        syslocks.owner sid                    -- Informix Session ID
from    syslocks, sysdatabases , outer syssessions
where
        syslocks.tabname = "sysdatabases"         -- Find locks on sysdatabases
and
        syslocks.rowidlk = sysdatabases.rowid     -- Join rowid to database
and
        syslocks.owner = syssessions.sid      -- Session ID to get user info order by 1;
```

Every user that opens a database opens a shared lock on the row in the sysdatabases table of the sysmaster database that points to that database. First we need to find all the locks in syslocks on the sysdatabases table. This gives us the rowid in sysdatabase which has the database name. Finally, we join with the table syssessions to get the username and hostname. I put all this together in a shell script that can be run from the UNIX prompt and called it dbwho. Figure 2 contains the shell script.

Figure 2. Dbwho shell script

```
#############################################################Program: dbwho
#       Author:   Lester Knutsen
#       Date:     10/28/1995
#       Description: List database, user and workstation of all db users
######################################################################
echo "Generating list of users by database ..."
dbaccess sysmaster - <<EOF
select
sysdatabases.name database,
syssessions.username,
syssessions.hostname,
syslocks.owner sid
from  syslocks, sysdatabases , outer syssessions
where syslocks.rowidlk = sysdatabases.rowid
and   syslocks.tabname = "sysdatabases"
and   syslocks.owner = syssessions.sid
order by 1;
EOF
```

One of the first things you will notice is that this script is slow. This led me to start digging into what was causing the slow performance. Running this query with set explain turned on (this shows the query optimizer plan) shows that there is a lot of work going on behind the scenes. Syslocks is a view, and it takes a sequential scan of six tables to produce the view. A temp table is created to hold the results of the syslocks view, and this is then joined with the other two tables. The tables sysdatabase and syssessions are also views. And the view syssessions uses a stored procedure, called bitval. Figure 3 contains the output from turning set explain on. In spite of these queries sometimes being a bit slow, these tables are a tremendous value and make it much easier to monitor your database server.

Figure 3. Output from "set explain on" for dbwho.sql

```
QUERY:
create view "informix".syslocks (dbsname,tabname,rowidlk,keynum,type,owner,waiter)
as      select x1.dbsname ,x1.tabname ,x0.rowidr ,x0.keynum ,
x4.txt [1,4] ,x3.sid ,x5.sid
            from   "informix".syslcktab x0 ,
       "informix".systabnames x1 , "informix".systxptab x2 , "informix".sysrstcb x3 ,
"informix".flags_text x4 , outer("informix".sysrstcb x5 )
where ((((((x0.partnum = x1.partnum ) AND (x0.owner = x2.address ) )
```

```
AND (x2.owner = x3.address ) ) AND (x0.wtlist = x5.address ) ) AND (x4.tabname =    'syslcktab' ) )
AND (x4.flags = x0.type ) ) ;

Estimated Cost: 713
Estimated # of Rows Returned: 51
1) informix.syslcktab: SEQUENTIAL SCAN
2) informix.flags_text: SEQUENTIAL SCAN
Filters: informix.flags_text.tabname = 'syslcktab'
DYNAMIC HASH JOIN
Dynamic Hash Filters: informix.syslcktab.type = informix.flags_text.flags

3) informix.systxptab: SEQUENTIAL SCAN
DYNAMIC HASH JOIN
Dynamic Hash Filters: informix.syslcktab.owner = informix.systxptab.address
4) informix.systabnames: SEQUENTIAL SCAN
Filters: informix.systabnames.tabname = 'sysdatabases'
DYNAMIC HASH JOIN
Dynamic Hash Filters: informix.syslcktab.partnum infor       mix.systabnames.partnum
5) informix.sysrstcb: SEQUENTIAL SCAN
DYNAMIC HASH JOIN (Build Outer)
Dynamic Hash Filters: informix.systxptab.owner = informix.sysrstcb.address
6) informix.sysrstcb: SEQUENTIAL SCAN
DYNAMIC HASH JOIN
Dynamic Hash Filters: informix.syslcktab.wtlist = informix.sysrstcb.address

QUERY:
select  sysdatabases.name database,
syssessions.username, syssessions.hostname,
syslocks.owner sid
from  syslocks, sysdatabases, outer syssessions
where syslocks.rowidlk = sysdatabases.rowid and   syslocks.tabname = "sysdatabases"
and    syslocks.owner = syssessions.sid order by 1

Estimated Cost: 114
Estimated # of Rows Returned: 11 Temporary Files Required For: Order By

1) (Temp Table For View): SEQUENTIAL SCAN
2) informix.sysdbspartn: INDEX PATH
(1) Index Keys: ROWID
Lower Index Filter: informix.sysdbspartn.ROWID = (Temp Table For View).rowidlk
3) informix.sysscblst: INDEX PATH
(1) Index Keys: sid (desc)
Lower Index Filter: informix.sysscblst.sid = (Temp Table For
View).owner

4) informix.sysrstcb: AUTOINDEX PATH
Filters: informix.bitval(informix.sysrstcb.flags ,'0x80000' )= 1
(1) Index Keys: scb
Lower Index Filter: informix.sysrstcb.scb = informix.sysscblst.address
```

HOW THE SYSMASTER DATABASE IS CREATED

The sysmaster database keeps track of information about the database server just like the system tables keep track of information in each database.

This database is automatically created when you initialize OnLine. It includes tables for tracking two types of information: the System Monitoring Interface (SMI) tables, and the On-Archive catalog tables. This chapter will focus on the SMI tables. There is a warning in the documentation not to change any information in these tables as it may corrupt your database server. Also there is a warning that OnLine does not lock these tables, and that all selects from this database will use an isolation level of dirty read. This means that the data can change dynamically as you are retrieving it. This also means that selecting data from the sysmaster tables does not lock any of your users from processing their data. As mentioned above, the SMI tables are described as pseudo-tables which point directly to the shared memory structures in OnLine where the data is stored. That means they are not actually on disk. However, because many of the SMI tables are really views, selecting from them does create temporary tables and generate disk activity.

A script located in your directory $INFORMIXDIR/etc. named sysmaster.sql contains the SQL statements to create the sysmaster database. The process of creating it is interesting and is outlined as follows:

- First the script creates real tables with the structures of the pseudo tables.
- Then the table structures of the real tables are copied to temp tables.
- The real tables are then dropped.
- The column in systables that contains partnum is updated to indicate they point to pseudo tables in shared memory.
- The flags_text table is created which has the interpretations for all the text descriptions and flags used in the SMI tables.
- The stored procedures are created that are used to create the views, two of which may be interesting:
    - bitval() is a stored procedure for getting the Boolean flag values
    - l2date() is a stored procedure for converting UNIX time() long values to dates
- Finally the script creates the SMI views.
- After the sysmaster script is run the system will execute another script to create the on-archive tables and views in the sysmaster database.

Warning: The sysmaster database is created the first time you go into online mode after you first initialize your system. Do NOT start creating any other database until this process is complete or you may corrupt your sysmaster database. You will need 2000 KB of logical log space to create the sysmaster database. If there are problems creating the sysmaster database, shut your OnLine server down and restart it. This will re-create the sysmaster database. Monitor your online.logfile until you see the messages showing the successful completion of building the sysmaster database in the online.log (Figure 4).

1.2   Figure 4. Online.log messages showing successful creation of sysmaster database

```
12:10:24  On-Line Mode
12:10:24  Building 'sysmaster' database ...
12:11:02  Logical Log 1 Complete.
12:11:03  Process exited with return code 1: /bin/sh /bin/sh -c
/u3/informix7/log_full.sh 2 23 "Logical Log 1 Complete." "Logical Log 1 Complete."
12:11:22  Logical Log 2 Complete.
12:11:23  Process exited with return code 1: /bin/sh /bin/sh -c
/u3/informix7/log_full.sh 2 23 "Logical Log 2 Complete." "Logical Log 2 Complete."
12:11:26  Checkpoint Completed:  duration was 3 seconds.
12:11:40  Logical Log 3 Complete.
12:11:41  Process exited with return code 1: /bin/sh /bin/sh -c
/u3/informix7/log_full.sh 2 23 "Logical Log 3 Complete." "Logical Log 3 Complete."
12:11:59  Logical Log 4 Complete.
12:12:00  Process exited with return code 1: /bin/sh /bin/sh -c
/u3/informix7/log_full.sh 2 23 "Logical Log 4 Complete." "Logical Log 4 Complete."
12:12:25  'sysmaster' database built successfully.
```

SUPPORTED SMI TABLES

There are 18 supported SMI tables in release 7.23 of INFORMIX-OnLine DSA. We will discuss the more important ones and a few unsupported ones in this chapter.

1.2   Figure 5. Supported SMI tables

Supported tables and views: (OnLine 7.23)

- sysadtinfo   Auditing configuration table
- sysaudit   Auditing event masks table
- syschkio   Chunk I/O statistics view
- syschunks   Chunk information view
- sysconfig   Configuration information view
- sysdatabases   Database information view
- sysdbslocale   Locale information view
- sysdbspaces   Dbspace information view
- sysdri   Data replication view
- sysextents   Table extent allocation view
- syslocks   Current lock information view
- syslogs   Logical Log status view

- sysprofile   Current system profile view
- sysptptof   Current table profile view
- syssessions   Current user sessions view
- sysseswts   Session wait times view
- systabnames   Table information table
- sysvpprof   Current VP profile view

DIFFERENCES FROM OTHER DATABASES

There are several key differences between the sysmaster database and other databases you might create. Reminder that this is a database that points to the server's shared memory structures and not to tables that are stored on disk. Some of the differences are:

- You cannot update the sysmaster database. Its purpose is to allow you to read information about the server. Trying to update its tables should generate an error message but may corrupt the server.

- You cannot run dbschema on these table to get their structure. This will generate an error message. (**Joe Lumbley's note:** But you can massage the sysmaster.sql script to simply create the tables and views in another database, removing the statements to drop the tables and recreate them as pseudotables. This will allow you do a few neat things with the SMI database. I'll explain at the end of Lester's paper.)

- You cannot drop the sysmaster database or any tables within it. Again, this should generate an error message.

- The data is dynamic and may change while you are retrieving it. The sysmaster database has an effective isolation level of dirty read even though it looks like a database with unbuffered logging. This prevents your queries from locking users and slowing down their processing.

- However, because the sysmaster database uses unbuffered logging, its temp tables are logged.

- You can create triggers and stored procedures on the sysmaster database, but the triggers will never be executed. Again, this is because this is not a real database but pointers to shared memory.

The sysmaster database reads the same shared memory structures read by the command line utility "onstat." The statistical data is reset to zero when OnLine is shut down and restarted. It is also reset to zero when the "onstat -z" command to reset statistics is used. Individual user statistical data is lost when a user disconnects from the server.

Now, let's examine some of the more interesting tables in the sysmaster database and what else can be done with them.

SERVER INFORMATION

This first section will look at how you determine the state and configuration of your INFORMIX-OnLine server from the sysmaster database. We will look at four tables and how to use them.

Server configuration and statistics tables

- sysconfig   ONCONFIG File
- sysprofile   Server Statistics
- syslogs   Logical Logs
- sysvpprof   Virtual Processors

Server configuration parameters: sysconfig

The view sysconfig contains configuration information from the OnLine server. This information was read from the ONCONFIG file when the server was started. Have you ever needed to know from within a program how your server was setup? Or, what TAPEDEV is set to?

View sysconfig

Column	Data Type	Description
cf_id	integer	unique numeric identifier
cf_name	char(18)	config parameter name
cf_flags	integer	flags, 0 = in view sysconfig
cf_original	char(256)	value in ONCONFIG at boottime
cf_effective	char(256)	value effectively in use
cf_default	char(256)	value by default

Example queries:
To find out what the current tape device is:
```
select cf_effective from sysconfig where cf_name = "TAPEDEV";
```

To find the server name:
```
select cf_effective from sysconfig where cf_name ="DBSERVERNAME";
```

To find out if data replication is turned on:
```
select cf_effective from sysconfig where cf_name = "DRAUTO";
```

Server profile information: sysprofile

The sysprofile table is a view based on values in a table called syshmhdr. Syshmhdr points to the same shared memory area as the `onstat` utility with the -p option. When you zero out the statistics with "`onstat -z`," all values in the syshmhdr table are reset to zero.

View sysprofile

Column	Data Type	Description
name	char(16)	profile element name
value	integer	current value

One of the best uses of this data is for developing alarms when certain values fall below acceptable levels. The Informix documentation says that tables in the sysmaster database do not run triggers. This is because the updates to these tables take place within OnLine shared memory and not through SQL which activates triggers. However, you can create a program to poll this table at specified intervals to select data and see if it falls below your expectations.

Logical logs information: syslogs

Syslogs is a view based on the table syslogfil. This is an example where the SMI views are a great tool in presenting the data in a more understandable format. Syslogfil has a field called flags which contains status information encoded in Boolean smallint. The view syslogs decodes that data into six fields: is_used, is_current, is_backed_up, is_new, is_archived, and is_temp, with a 1 if true or a 0 if false.

View syslogs

Column	Data Type	Description
number	smallint	logfile number

uniqid	integer	logfile uniqid
size	integer	pages in logfile
used	integer	pages used in logfile
is_used	integer	1 for used, 0 for free
is_current	integer	1 for current
is_backed_up	integer	1 for backed up
is_new	integer	1 for new
is_archived	integer	1 for archived
is_temp	integer	1 for temp
flags	smallint	logfile flags

Virtual processor information and statistics: sysvpprof

Sysvpprof is another view that is more readable than the underlying table sysvplst. As with the view syslogs in the above paragraph, this view has data that is converted to make it more understandable. This time the flags are converted to text descriptions from the flags_text table.

View sysvpprof

Column	Data Type	Description
vpid	integer	VP id
txt	char(50)	VP class name
usecs_user	float	number of secs of user time
usecs_sys	float	number of secs of system time

The following query on the base table sysvplst achieves the same results as the view.

```
--vpstat.sql
select   vpid,
txt[1,5] class,
pid,
usecs_user,
usecs_sys,
num_ready
from        sysvplst a, flags_text b
where       a.flags != 6
and         a.class = b.flags
and b.tabname = 'sysvplst';
```

SQL Output

Vpid	class	pid	usecs_user	usecs_sys	num_ready
1	cpu	335	93.61	30.46	0
2	adm	336	2.0	0.11	0
3	lio	337	1.15	5.98	0
4	pio	338	0.19	1.13	0

```
5      aio    339    0.94        4.27        0
6      msc    340    0.15        0.14        0
7      aio    341    0.81        5.72        0
8      tli    342    1.79        3.02        0
9      aio    343    0.52        2.50        0
10     aio    344    0.28        1.16        0
11     aio    345    0.09        0.86        0
12     aio    346    0.16        0.48        0
```

DBSPACE AND CHUNK INFORMATION

Now let's look at the SMI tables that contain information about your disk space, chunks, and dbspace. There are four tables that contain this data.

- Sysdbspaces   DB Spaces
- syschunks   Chunks
- syschkio   I/O by Chunk
- syschfree*   Free Space by Chunk

Note: Syschfree is not a supported table.

Dbspace configuration: sysdbspaces

The sysmaster database has three key tables containing dbspace and chunk information. The first one is sysdbspaces. This is a view that interprets the underlying table sysdbstab. Sysdbspaces serves two purposes: it translates a bit field containing flags into separate columns where 1 equals yes and 0 equals no, and, it allows the underlying table to change between releases without having to change code. The view is defined as follows:

View sysdbspaces

```
Column         Data         TypeDescription
dbsnum         smallint     dbspace number,
name           char(18)     dbspace name,
owner          char(8)      dbspace owner,
fchunk         smallint     first chunk in dbspace,
nchunks        smallint     number of chunks in dbspace,
is_mirrored    bitval       is dbspace mirrored, 1=Yes, 0=No
is_blobspace   bitval       is dbspace a blob space, 1=Yes, 2=No
is_temp        bitval       is dbspace temp, 1=Yes, 2=No
flags          smallint     dbspace flags
```

The columns of type bitval are the flags that are extracted from the flags column by a stored procedure called bitval when the view is generated.

Chunk configuration: syschunks

The syschunks table is also a view based on two actual tables, one for primary chunk information, syschktab, and one for mirror chunk information, sysmchktab. The following is the layout of syschunks:

View syschunks

Column	Data Type	Description
chknum	smallint	chunk number
dbsnum	smallint	dbspace number
nxchknum	smallint	number of next chunk in dbspace
chksize	integer	pages in chunk
offset	integer	pages offset into device
nfree	integer	free pages in chunk
is_offline	bitval	is chunk offline, 1=Yes, 0=No
is_recovering	bitval	is chunk recovering, 1=Yes, 0=No
is_blobchunk	bitval	is chunk blobchunk, 1=Yes, 0=No
is_inconsistent	bitval	is chunk inconsistent, 1=Yes, 0=No
flags	smallint	chunk flags converted by bitval
fname	char(128)	device pathname
mfname	char(128)	mirror device pathname
moffset	integer	pages offset into mirror device
mis_offline	bitval	is mirror offline, 1=Yes, 0=No
mis_recovering	bitval	is mirror recovering, 1=Yes, 0=No
mflags	smallint	mirror chunk flags

Displaying free dbspace

Now, we will take a look at several ways to use this dbspace and chunk information. One capability I have always wanted is a way to show the amount of dbspace used and free in the same format as the UNIX "df -k" command. The sysmaster database contains information about the dbspaces and chunks, so this can be generated with an SQL script. The following is an SQL script to generate the amount of free space in a dbspace. It uses the sysdbspaces and syschunks tables to collect its information.

```
---dbsfree.sql - display free dbspace like UNIX "df -k " command
database sysmaster;
select  name[1,8] dbspace,            -- name truncated to fit on one line
```

```
            sum(chksize) Pages_size,        -- sum of all chunks size pages sum(chksize) - sum(nfree)
            Pages_used,
            sum(nfree) Pages_free,          -- sum of all chunks free pages round ((sum(nfree)) /
            (sum(chksize)) * 100, 2) percent_free
from        sysdbspaces d, syschunks c
where       d.dbsnum = c.dbsnum
group by 1
order by 1;
```

Sample output

```
dbspace         pages_size       pages_used        pages_free       percent_free
rootdbs              50000            13521             36479              72.96
dbspace1            100000            87532             12468              12.47
dbspace2            100000            62876             37124              37.12
dbspace3            100000              201             99799              99.80
```

Displaying chunk status

The next script lists the status and characteristics of each chunk device

```
--chkstatus.sql - display information about a chunk
database sysmaster;  `
select
            name dbspace,               -- dbspace name
            is_mirrored,                -- dbspace is mirrored 1=Yes 0=No
            is_blobspace,               -- dbspace is blobspace 1=Yes 0=No
            is_temp,                    -- dbspace is temp 1=Yes 0=No
            chknum chunknum,            -- chunk number
            fname  device,              -- dev path
            offset dev_offset,          -- dev offset
            is_offline,                 -- Offline 1=Yes 0=No
            is_recovering,              -- Recovering 1=Yes 0=No
            is_blobchunk,               -- Blobspace 1=Yes 0=No
            is_inconsistent,            -- Inconsistent 1=Yes 0=No
            chksize Pages_size,         -- chunk size in pages
            (chksize - nfree) Pages_used, -- chunk pages used
            nfree Pages_free,           -- chunk free pages
        round ((nfree / chksize) * 100, 2) percent_free, -- free
        mfname mirror_device,           -- mirror dev path
            moffset mirror_offset,      -- mirror dev offset
            mis_offline ,               -- mirror offline 1=Yes 0=No
            mis_recovering              -- mirror recovering  1=Yes 0=No
from     sysdbspaces d, syschunks c
where d.dbsnum = c.dbsnum
order by dbspace, chunknum
```

Displaying blocks of free space in a chunk: syscchfree

In planning expansions, new databases, or when adding new tables to an existing server, I like to know what blocks of contiguous free space are available. This allows placing new tables in dbspaces where they will not be broken up by extents. One of the sysmaster tables tracks the chunk free list, which is the available space in a chunk.

Table syschfree

```
Column  Data Type      Description
chknum  integer        chunk number
extnum  integer        extent number in chunk
start   integer        physical addr of start
leng    integer        length of extent
```

The next script uses this table to create a list of free space and the size of each space that is available.

```
--chkflist.sql - display list of free space within a chunk
database sysmaster;
select
            name dbspace,  -- dbspace name truncated to fit
            f.chknum,           -- chunk number
            f.extnum,           -- extent number of free space
            f.start,            -- starting address of free space
            f.leng free_pages   -- length of free space
from    sysdbspaces d, syschunks c, syschfree f
where d.dbsnum = c.dbsnum
and     c.chknum = f.chknum
order by dbspace, chknum
```

Sample Output

dbspace	chknum	extnum	start	free_pages
rootdbs	1	0	11905	1608
rootdbs	1	1	15129	34871

I/O statistics by chunk devices: syschkio

Informix uses a view, syschkio, to collect information about the number of disk reads and writes per chunk. This view is based on the tables syschktab and symchktab.

View syschkio

```
Column         Data Type    Description
chunknum       smallint     chunk number
reads          integer      number of read ops
pagesread      integer      number of pages read
writes         integer      number of write ops
pageswritten   integer      number of pages written
mreads         integer      number of mirror read ops
mpagesread     integer      number of mirror pages read
mwrites        integer      number of mirror write ops
mpageswritten  integer      number of mirror pages written
```

The following script displays I/O usage of chunk devices. It uses the base tables so the mirror chunks can be displayed on separate rows. It also joins with the base table that contains the dbspace name.

```
--chkio.sql - displays chunk IO status
database sysmaster;
select
name[1,10] dbspace,        -- truncated to fit 80 char screen line chknum,
"Primary" chktype,
reads,
writes,
pagesread,
pageswritten
from    syschktab c, sysdbstab d
where   c.dbsnum = d.dbsnum
union all
select
             name[1,10]        dbspace,
             chknum,
             "Mirror"       chktype,
             reads,
             writes,
             pagesread,
             pageswritten
from    sysmchktab c, sysdbstab d
where   c.dbsnum = d.dbsnum
order by 1,2,3;
```

Sample Output

dbspace	chknum	chktype	reads	writes	pagesread	pageswritten
rootdbs	1	Primary	74209	165064	209177	308004
rootdbs	1	Mirror	69401	159832	209018	307985

A better view of your I/O is to see the percent of the total I/O that takes place per chunk. This next query collects I/O stats into a temp table, and then uses that to calculate total I/O stats for all chunks. Then each chunk's I/O is compared with the total to determine the percent of I/O by chunk. The following script uses the one above as a basis to show I/O by chunk as a percent of the total I/O.

```
--chkiosum.sql - calculates percent of IO by chunk
database sysmaster;
--Collect chunk IO stats into temp table A
select
name dbspace,
chknum,
"Primary" chktype,
reads,
writes,
pagesread,
pageswritten
from    syschktab c, sysdbstab d
where   c.dbsnum = d.dbsnum
union all
select
             name[1,10] dbspace,
             chknum,
```

```
                 "Mirror"     chktype,
                 reads,
                 writes,
                 pagesread,
                 pageswritten
from     sysmchktab c, sysdbstab d
where    c.dbsnum = d.dbsnum
into temp A;

--Collect total IO stats into temp table B
select
sum(reads) total_reads,
sum(writes) total_writes,
sum(pagesread) total_pgreads,
sum(pageswritten) total_pgwrites
from A
into temp B;

--Report showing each chunks percent of total IO
select
dbspace,
chknum,
chktype,
reads,
writes,
pagesread,
pageswritten,
             round((reads/total_reads) *100, 2) percent_reads, round((writes/total_writes)
             *100, 2) percent_writes, round((pagesread/total_pgreads) *100, 2) per-
             cent_pg_reads, round((pageswritten/total_pgwrites) *100, 2) percent_pg_writes
from     A, B
order by 11;-- order by percent page writes
```

Sample output for 1 chunk
```
dbspace                 datadbs
chknum                  9
chktype                 Primary
reads                   12001
writes                  9804
pagesread                         23894
pageswritten            14584
percent_reads           0.33
percent_writes          0.75
percent_pg_reads                  37.59
percent_pg_writes                 1.86
```

DATABASE AND TABLE INFORMATION

The next five tables we will look at store information on your tables and extents. They are:

- sysdatabases   Databases
- systabnames   Tables

- sysextents   Tables extents
- sysptprof   Tables I/O

Information on all databases on a server: sysdatabases

This view has data on all databases on a server. Have you ever needed to create a pop-up list of databases within a program? This table now allows programs to give users a list of databases to select from without resorting to ESQL/C. The following is the definition of this view:

View sysdatabases

```
Column          Data Type       Description
name            char(18)        database name
partnum         integer         table id for systables
owner           char(8)         user name of creator
created         integer         date created
is_logging      bitval          unbuffered logging, 1=Yes, 0= No
is_buff_log     bitval          buffered logging, 1=Yes, 0= No
is_ansi         bitval          ANSI mode database, 1=Yes, 0= No
is_nls          bitval          NLS support, 1=Yes, 0= No
flags           smallint        flags indicating logging
```

The following is a script to list all databases, owners, dbspaces, and logging status. Notice the function dbinfo is used. This is a new function in 7.X with several uses, one of which is to convert the partnum of a database into its corresponding dbspace. This function will be used in several examples that follow.

```
--dblist.sql - List all databases, owner and logging status
database sysmaster;
select
dbinfo("DBSPACE",partnum) dbspace,
name database,
owner,
is_logging,
is_buff_log
from sysdatabases
order by dbspace, name;
```

Sample Output

dbspace	database	owner	is_logging	is_buff_log
rootdbs	central	lester	0	0
rootdbs	datatools	lester	0	0
rootdbs	dba	lester	0	0
rootdbs	roster	lester	0	0
rootdbs	stores7	lester	0	0
rootdbs	sunset	linda	0	0
rootdbs	sysmaster	informix	1	0
rootdbs	zip	lester	1	1

Information about tables: systabnames, sysextents, and sysptprof

Three tables contain all the data you need from the sysmaster database about tables in your database. The first of these is a real table defined as follows:

Table systabnames. All tables on the server

Column	Data Type	Description
partnum	integer	table id for table
dbsname	char(18)	database name
owner	char(8)	table owner
tabname	char(18)	table name
collate	char(32)	collation assoc with NLS DB

View sysextents. Tables and each extent on the server

Column	Data Type	Description
Dbsname	char(18)	database name
tabname	char(18)	table name
start	integer	physical addr for this extent
size	integer	size of this extent

The view sysextents is based on a table, sysptnext, defined as follows:

Table sysptnext

Column	Data Type	Description
pe_partnum	integer	partnum for this partition
pe_extnum	smallint	extent number
pe_phys	integer	physical addr for this extent
pe_size	integer	size of this extent
pe_log	integer	logical page for start

View sysptprof. Tables I/O profile

Column	Data Type	Description
Dbsname	char(18)	database name
tabname	char(18)	table name
partnum	integer	partnum for this table
lockreqs	integer	lock requests
lockwts	integer	lock waits
deadlks	integer	deadlocks
lktouts	integer	lock timeouts
isreads	integer	reads
iswrites	integer	writes
isrewrites	integer	rewrites
isdeletes	integer	deletes
bufreads	integer	buffer reads
bufwrites	integer	buffer writes
seqscans	integer	sequential scans
pagreads	integer	disk reads

```
        pagwrites        integer              disk writes
```

These tables allow us to develop scripts to display tables, the number of extents, and pages used. We can also present a layout of dbspace, databases, tables, and extents similar to the command "tbcheck -pe." And finally, we can show table usage statistics sorted by which tables have the most hits based on reads, writes, or locks. These scripts will enable a DBA to monitor and tune the database server.

Extents are created when a table's initial space has been filled up and it needs more space. OnLine will allocate additional space for a table. However, the table will no longer be contiguous, and performance will start to degrade. Informix will display warning messages when a table reaches more than 8 extents. Depending on a number of factors, at approximately 180 to 230 extents a table will not be able to expand and no additional rows can be inserted. The following script lists all tables sorted by the number of extents. The tables that show up with many extents may need to be unloaded and rebuilt.

```
--tabextent.sql - List tables, number of extents and size of table.
database sysmaster;
select  dbsname,
tabname,
count(*) num_of_extents,
sum( pe_size ) total_size
from systabnames, sysptnext
where partnum = pe_partnum
group by 1, 2
order by 3 desc, 4 desc;
```

Sample Output

dbsname	tabname	num_of_extents	total_size
rootdbs	TBLSpace	8	400
sysmaster	syscolumns	6	56
sunset	inventory	3	376
sunset	sales_items	3	96
sunset	sales_header	3	48
sunset	parts	3	48
sunset	customer	3	40
sunset	syscolumnext	3	32
sunset	employee	3	32

Sometimes it is helpful to see how the tables are interspersed on disk. The following script lists by dbspace each table and the location of each extent. This is similar to the output from "oncheck -pe."

```
--tablayout.sql - Show layout of tables and extents
database sysmaster;
select dbinfo( "DBSPACE" , pe_partnum ) dbspace,
dbsname[1,10],
tabname,
pe_phys start,
pe_size size
from    sysptnext, outer systabnames
where   pe_partnum = partnum
order by dbspace, start;
```

Sample output

dbspace	dbsname	tabname	start	size
rootdbs	rootdbs	TBLSpace	1048589	50
rootdbs	sysmaster	sysdatabases	1050639	4
rootdbs	sysmaster	systables	1050643	8
rootdbs	sysmaster	syscolumns	1050651	16
rootdbs	sysmaster	sysindexes	1050667	8
rootdbs	sysmaster	systabauth	1050675	8
rootdbs	sysmaster	syscolauth	1050683	8
rootdbs	sysmaster	sysviews	1050691	8
rootdbs	sysmaster	sysusers	1050699	8
rootdbs	sysmaster	sysdepend	1050707	8
rootdbs	sysmaster	syssynonyms	1050715	8

I/O performance of tables

Have you ever wanted to know which tables have the most reads, writes, or locks? The last script in this article shows the performance profile of tables. By changing the columns displayed and the sort order of the script, you can display the tables with the most reads, writes, or locks first.

```
--tabprof.sql
database sysmaster;
select
dbsname,
tabname,
isreads,
bufreads,
pagreads
--uncomment the following to show writes
--iswrites,
--bufwrites,
--pagwrites
--uncomment the following to show locks
--lockreqs,
--lockwts,
--deadlks
from sysptprof
order by isreads desc; -- change this sort to whatever you need to monitor.
```

Sample Output

dbsname	tabname	isreads	bufreads	pagreads
zip	zip	334175	35876509	1111
sysmaster	sysviews	259712	634102	1119
sysmaster	systables	60999	240018	1878
zip	systables	3491	8228	543
sysmaster	sysusers	2406	8936	87
sysmaster	sysprocauth	1276	5104	12
sunset	systables	705	2251	26
sysmaster	sysprocedures	640	2562	21
sysmaster	syscolumns	637	1512	49
stores7	systables	565	136	16

```
sysmaster      sysdatabases   534          2073         902
```

USER SESSION INFORMATION

This last set of SMI tables deals with users and information about their sessions. These tables were used in our example script "dbwho" at the beginning of this chapter.

- Syssessions   Session data
- Syssesprof   User statistics
- Syslocks   User locks
- Syseswts   Wait times

User session and connection information: syssessions

This view contains information from two shared memory structures, the user control and thread control table. This tells you who is logged in to your server and some basic data about their session.

View syssessions

```
Column       Data Type      Description
Sid          integer        Session id number
Username     char(8)        User name
uid          smallint       User UNIX or NT id
pid          integer        User process id
hostname     char(16)       Hostname
tty          char(16)       TTY port
connected    integer        Time user connected
feprogram    char(16)       Program name
pooladdr     integer        Pointer to private session pool
is_wlatch    integer        Flag 1=Yes, 0=No, wait on latch
is_wlock     integer        Flag 1=Yes, 0=No, wait on lock
is_wbuff     integer        Flag 1=Yes, 0=No, wait on buffer
is_wckpt     integer        Flag 1=Yes, 0=No, wait on checkpoint
is_wlogbuf   integer        Flag 1=Yes, 0=No, wait on log buffer
is_wtrans    integer        Flag 1=Yes, 0=No, wait on transaction
is_monitor   integer        Flag 1=Yes, 0=No, monitoring process
is_incrit    integer        Flag 1=Yes, 0=No, in critical section
state        integer        Flags
```

The following is a quick query to tell who is using your server.

```
--sessions.sql
select  sid,
username,
```

```
pid,
hostname,
l2date(connected) startdate -- convert UNIX time to date
from    syssessions
```

Sample Output

```
        Sid     username    pid     hostname    startdate
        47      lester      11564   merlin      07/14/1997
```

This next query lists all users and their session status. The objective is to show who is blocked waiting on another user, lock, or some other OnLine process. The five fields are yes/no flags where 1 = yes and 0 = no. If all the fields are 0, then none of the sessions are blocked. In the following example, one session is blocked waiting on a locked record.

```
--seswait.sql
select  username,
            is_wlatch,      -- blocked waiting on a latch
            is_wlock,       -- blocked waiting on a locked record or table
            is_wbuff,       -- blocked waiting on a buffer
            is_wckpt,       -- blocked waiting on a checkpoint
            is_incrit       -- session is in a critical section of transaction
                            -- (e.g. writting to disk)
from    syssessions
order by username;
```

Sample Output

username	is_wlatch	is_wlock	is_wbuff	is_wckpt	is_incrit
lester	0	1	0	0	0
lester	0	0	0	0	0
lester	0	0	0	0	0

User session performance statistics: syssesprof

This view syssesprof provides a way to find out at a given point in time how much of your server resources each user is using. The view contains the following information.

View syssesprof

Column	Data Type	Description
sid	integer,	Session Id
lockreqs	decimal(16,0)	Locks requested
locksheld	decimal(16,0)	Locks held
lockwts	decimal(16,0)	Locks waits
deadlks	decimal(16,0)	Deadlocks detected
lktouts	decimal(16,0)	Deadlock timeouts
logrecs	decimal(16,0)	Logical Log records written
isreads	decimal(16,0)	Reads
iswrites	decimal(16,0)	Writes
isrewrites	decimal(16,0)	Rewrites
isdeletes	decimal(16,0)	Deletes
iscommits	decimal(16,0)	Commits

```
isrollbacks              decimal(16,0)   Rollbacks
longtxs                  decimal(16,0)   Long transactions
bufreads                 decimal(16,0)   Buffer reads
bufwrites                decimal(16,0)   Buffer writes
seqscans                 decimal(16,0)   Sequential scans
pagreads                 decimal(16,0)   Page reads
pagwrites                decimal(16,0)   Page writes
total_sorts              decimal(16,0)   Total sorts
dsksorts                 decimal(16,0)   Sorts to disk
max_sortdiskspace        decimal(16,0)   Max space used by a sort
logspused                decimal(16,0)   Current log bytes used
maxlogsp                 decimal(16,0)   Max bytes of logical logs used
```

This table contains data since the user logged on. Each time a user disconnects, his data is lost so you cannot use this data for charging the user for server usage. Also, when a DBA resets the server statistics with the command "tbstat -z," all profile data is reset to zero. I like to monitor the number of locks used by each user and their buffer usage. The following is an example query.

```
--sesprof.sql
select  username,
syssesprof.sid,
lockreqs,
bufreads,
bufwrites
from    syssesprof, syssessions
where   syssesprof.sid = syssessions.sid
order by bufreads desc
```

Active locks on the server: syslocks

This view contains information about all active locks on your server. It can be very large; if you have a lot of users and your server is configured to handle a large number of locks, you could end up with hundreds of thousands or more records in this view. This view is composed of six tables, and queries on this view will create a temp table which is logged to your logical log. The performance may be a bit slow because of the sheer volume of data produced by this view. However, the data this view contains can be very helpful to understanding how your system is performing.

View syslocks

```
Column       Data Type      Description
dbsname      char(18)       Database name
tabname      char(18)       Table name
rowidlk      integer        Rowid for index key lock
keynum       smallint       Key number of index key lock
owner        integer        Session ID of lock owner
waiter       integer        Session ID of first waiter
type         char(4)        Type of Lock

             Types of Locks
```

```
B        - byte lock
IS       - intent shared lock
S        - shared lock
XS       - repeatable read shared key
U        - update lock
IX       - intent exclusive lock
SIX      - shared intent exclusive
X        - exclusive lock
XR       - repeatable read exclusive
```

Basically there are three types of locks: a shared lock (S), an exclusive lock (X), and an update lock(U). A shared lock allows other users to also read the data but none may change it. An exclusive lock does not allow anyone else to lock that data even in shared mode. An update lock prevents other users from changing data while you are changing it.

There are five objects that can be locked in OnLine.

- Database   Every user that opens a database places a shared lock on

  the database to prevent someone else from dropping the database while it is in use. This shows up as a lock on the sysmaster database and the sysdatabase tables, and the rowid will point to the record containing database name.

- Table   A table lock shows up as a lock on a table with a rowid of 0

  and a keynum of 0.

- Page   Page level lock = rowid ending in 00. All rows on the page are locked.

- Row   A row level lock will show with an actual rowid (not ending in 00).

- Key   A key lock will show with a keynum.

If a row has indexes that need to be updated a key lock will place locks on the indexes for that row.

One of the key data elements missing from this view is the username and session id (sid) of the user who has a lock. The following query adds the user's name and session id and uses the underlying tables to improve performance. It also puts the data into a temp table from which you can select subsets of data much more quickly than if you were to repeat the query.

```
--locks.sql
select   dbsname,
b.tabname,
rowidr,
keynum,
e.txt          type,
d.sid          owner,
g.username     ownername,
f.sid          waiter,
h.username     waitname

from           syslcktab a,
```

```
                    systabnames b,
                    systxptab c,
                    sysrstcb d,
                    sysscblst g,
                    flags_text e,
                    outer ( sysrstcb f , sysscblst h  )
where    a.partnum = b.partnum
and               a.owner = c.address
and               c.owner = d.address
and               a.wtlist = f.address
and               d.sid = g.sid
and               e.tabname = 'syslcktab'
and               e.flags = a.type
and               f.sid = h.sid
into temp A;

select            dbsname,
tabname,
rowidr,
keynum,
type[1,4],
owner,
ownername ,
waiter,
waitname
from A;
```

Example SQL Output

```
dbsname           sysmaster
tabname           a
rowidr            0
keynum            0
type              X
owner             47
ownername         lester
waiter
waitname
```

The above example SQL output shows the row from syslocks that displays the exclusive lock I created on the temp table "A" while running the query. A more important use of this query is to find out when one user is waiting on the lock owned by another user. When a user has a database object locked, the first user waiting on the object can be displayed. (This will only occur when a user has set lock mode to WAIT.) The following script displays only the users that have locks where someone else is waiting on their process. There is one key difference between this script and the one above. The tables sysrstcb and sysscblst in this script do not use an outer join, so only rows that have waiters will be returned. In this example "linda" has an update lock on a row and "lester" is waiting for that update to complete.

```
--lockwaits.sql
database sysmaster;
select  dbsname,
b.tabname,
rowidr,
```

```
keynum,
e.txt    type,
d.sid    owner,
g.username ownername,
f.sid    waiter,
h.username waitname

from     syslcktab a,
            systabnames b,
            systxptab c,
            sysrstcb d,
            sysscblst g,
            flags_text e,
            sysrstcb f ,
            sysscblst h

where    a.partnum = b.partnum
and      a.owner = c.address
and      c.owner = d.address
and      a.wtlist = f.address
and      d.sid = g.sid
and      e.tabname = 'syslcktab'
and      e.flags = a.type
and      f.sid = h.sid
into temp A;

select   dbsname,
tabname,
type[1,4],
owner,
ownername ,
waitname
from A;
```

SQL Output

```
Dbsname    tabname       type   owner   ownername    waitname
stores7    items         U       29     linda        lester
```

Wait status and times on objects: sysseswts

This is a supported view that shows all sessions that are blocked and waiting on a database object. It shows the amount of time a user has been waiting. On a well tuned system this table should be empty. However, when the table is not empty, it provides useful information on what is causing your performance to slow down.

View sysseswts

Column	Data Type	Description
Sid	integer	Session ID
reason	char(50)	Description of reason for wait
numwaits	integer	Number of waits for this reason
cumtime	float	Cumulative wait time for this reason
maxtime	integer	Max wait time for this reason

SOME UNSUPPORTED EXTRAS

Several of the SMI tables are not documented and not officially supported. These could change in future releases. Two additional unsupported tables I have found helpful are systrans and syssqexplain.

User transactions: systrans

Three of the fields in systrans are very helpful to determine what logical log number a transaction began in, and the current logical log number in use by a transaction.
Key systrans fields:

```
Column          Data Type        Description
tx_id           integer          pointer to transaction table
tx_logbeg       integer          transaction starting logical log
tx_loguniq      integer          transaction current logical log number
```

This can be used to create a script to determine what logical logfiles have active transactions. The output of this will tell you what logical logs are free and available for reuse. This first script lists all user transactions and what logs they are using.

```
--txlogpos.sql
select
t.username,
t.sid,
tx_logbeg,
tx_loguniq,
tx_logpos
from    systrans x, sysrstcb t
where   tx_owner = t.address
```

SQL Output

```
Username             sid    tx_logbeg tx_loguniq   tx_logpos
informix             1      0              16       892952
informix             7      0              0        0
informix             8      0              0        0
lester               53     0              0        0
informix      12     0                     0        0
lester        51     14                    16       0
-------------------------------------------------------------------------
```

This shows that my logical logs numbered 14 to 16 are in use by transactions. Another helpful use of this view is to summarize the transactions by logical logs. This next script show my transaction status by logical log.

```
--logstat.sql

database sysmaster;
```

```
--select transaction data into a temp table

select  tx_logbeg,    tx_loguniq
from    systrans
into temp b;

--count how may transactions begin in each log
select tx_logbeg, count(*) cnt
from B
where tx_logbeg > 0
group by tx_logbeg
into temp C;

--count how many transactions currently are in each log
select tx_loguniq, count(*) cnt
from B
where tx_loguniq > 0
group by tx_loguniq
into temp D;

--join data from counts with syslogs
select
uniqid,
size,
            is_backed_up,    -- 0 = no, 1 = yes log is backed up
            is_archived,     -- 0 = no, 1 = yes log is on last archive
            c.cnt    tx_beg_cnt,
            d.cnt    tx_curr_cnt
from    syslogs, outer c, outer D
where   uniqid = c.tx_logbeg
and     uniqid = d.tx_loguniq
order by uniqid
```

SQL Output

uniqid	size	is_backed_up	is_archived	tx_beg_cnt	tx_curr_cnt
10	500	1	1		
11	500	1	1		
12	500	1	1		
13	500	1	1		
14	500	1	1		
15	500	1	1		
16	500	0	1	1	2

This shows that all logs are backed up except the current one, and it has two active transactions.

User queries: syssqexplain

Have you ever wanted to run a query to see what your users were doing? The view syssqexplain contains some of the data from a user's session, including the SQL that they are currently executing. Try this query on your system sometime to see your user's SQL.

```
--syssql.sql
select  username,
sqx_sessionid,
sqx_conbno,
sqx_sqlstatement
from syssqexplain, sysscblst
where  sqx_sessionid = sid
```

SQL Output

```
username            lester
sqx_sessionid  55
sqx_conbno      2
sqx_sqlstatement select username,sqx_sessionid, sqx_conbno, sqx_sqlstatement
                  from syssqexplain, sysscblst where sqx_sessionid = sid

username            lester
sqx_sessionid  51
sqx_conbno      0
sqx_sqlstatement update items set total_price = 300 where item_num = 1
    ----------------------------------------------------------------------
```

CONCLUSION

The sysmaster database is a great tool for a DBA to monitor the Informix server. If you have any questions or suggestions please send me E-mail at lester@advancedatatools.com. Also, if you have any creative scripts for monitoring your server with the sysmaster database, please send them in and I   may include them in the future publications.

Contact Information for Lester Knutsen

Lester Knutsen
Advanced DataTools Corporation
4216 Evergreen Lane, Suite 136,
Annandale, VA 22003
(703) 256-0267 or (800) 807-6732
lester@advancedatatools.com
www.advancedatatools.com

Notes

Lester does wonderful work. I thank him for his contribution to this book and suggest that if anyone in the vicinity of Washington, D.C. needs consulting or training services that they contact Lester. He is also very active in the Washington Area Informix Users' Group and has made many significant contributions to the body of Informix knowledge.

Thanks to his generosity, I have been able to include all of these scripts with the CD-ROM that comes with this book. I've left them totally unchanged, but I have one suggestion for those who may wish to use them in conjunction with the SQL-Editor front-ends from Informix. This front-end has an annoying habit in that every time you want to do a "database sysmaster" or choose the sysmaster database from the GUI, it will give you a pop-up screen warning you that you are working with the sysmaster database. To get around this behavior, take out all of the "database sysmaster;" commands and address include the "sysmaster" name in each table in the FROM statements, like this;

Change from:

```
DATABASE sysmaster;
SELECT * from sysprofile;
```

Change to:
```
SELECT * from sysmaster:sysprofile;
```

This will also allow you to choose a user database from the GUI and keep using it while making these queries to the sysmaster database as needed. Informix probably wouldn't approve of this, but I keep Lester's scripts (and my own) in the $INFORMIXDIR/bin subdirectory on my Windows machines. This is the default place that the GUI looks for scripts, and it makes it very easy to use these and other scripts.

THE HTML VERSION OF THE SYSMASTER DOCUMEN-
TATION

Earlier, I make a parenthetical comment in Lester's article about a method that allows the user to make a "fake" copy of the sysmaster database. You may have wondered why I did that. Since the dbschema program will not report on pseudotables, in order to get a schema generated for the sysmaster database, you have to massage the sysmaster.sql script that is used by Informix to generate the sysmaster database in the first place. Be sure and work on a copy.

If you haven't looked at this sysmaster.sql script, you might find it interesting anyway. It has documentation for most of the fields that are found in the sysmaster tables. Anyway, to create the "fakesmi.sql" script, change the "create database sysmaster with log" command in the first section of the script to something like "create database fakesmi with log." Then go down to the statement that says "select tabid from systables". It's on line 1278 in the NT 7.30.UC1 sysmaster.sql script file. Beginning here is where they start doing something tricky that turns normal tables into pseudotables. Delete everything from here down until where it drops all of the temp tables it created and before it creates the flags_text table (Line 1448 on NT 7.30). Before you run the script, do a text search to make sure that the word "systables" is not used in any SQL statement. Wouldn't want to destroy your sysmaster database, would you? If you run the new script, you'll have a real database with real tables that looks just like sysmaster. I'll include the "doctored" script on the CD in case you feel a need for it.

So why would you want to butcher up a creative, well documented script to create a database that you don't need and that might actually damage a database that you really need?

A year or so ago a company called Technology Investments came out with a group of ingenious PERL scripts that did all sorts of trick things with Informix databases. The tools were called "ztools," and many of the denizens of comp.databases.informix served as beta testers for them. The ztools product line was subsequently either sold or licensed to BMC Software, the makers of the Patrol line of monitoring tools, and BMC now sells the ztools under another name. Many of the ztools based their work on a program called "zschema" that ran a dbschema against an Informix database and massaged it in various ways.

One of the ztools was a program called "zweb," which generated marvelous data dictionaries from an existing Informix database and converted them into HTML which could be viewed and managed from any frames-capable Web browser. Zweb needed to be able to actually see the database and run "zschema," which ran dbschema against the database. Thus, since dbschema could not run a schema against the sysmaster database, none of the ztools would work with sysmaster.

The output from zweb allows you to search the schema of the sysmaster database in many ways, including cross-reference searches like "which tables have a partnum column." I've included the Web based data dictionary generated by zweb in the CD in the HTML subdirectory. Enjoy.

I have to include a *"Kids, don't try this at home"* disclaimer on this creation of a fake SMI database. Due to the risk of destroying your sysmaster database, I recommend that you do not try this on a production machine and that you try it only if you are very sure of what you are doing. Besides, I've included the HTML output and there is really no reason for you to try this yourself.

How Do I? Tips and Tricks for OnLine Engines

This chapter consists mostly of scripts, programs, and techniques for accomplishing specific tasks that often cause problems for DBAs for Versions 5 and older OnLine engines. This chapter has not been changed significantly from the first edition of the book.

CAN I USE THESE SCRIPTS WITH IDS?

Many of the scripts and techniques will work as well for IDS as they do with OnLine. In fact, many of the scripts were modified by Carlton Doe for his initial book on the IDS engine, *INFORMIX-OnLine Dynamic Server Handbook*, also from Informix Press. I'm including Carlton's modified scripts in the CD-ROM that accompanies this book, although I'm not discussing the IDS versions.

What strikes me as I go through this chapter for the second edition of this book is exactly how far we've come from OnLine to INFORMIX-Dynamic Server. While many of the scripts will actually function properly in the IDS world, they are no longer needed because IDS has provided us with more sophisticated tools, better monitoring, and better control of the database than we had just three years ago. Many of the things done in this chapter with scripts can be done with SMI queries in IDS. Using SMI can be a much more useful technique simply because you do not have to be resident on the particular machine in order to get the information. Using SMI, you can monitor a remote machine much more easily than ever before. Using the graphical user tools currently provided on Windows NT gives you levels of monitoring and control that were never possible with OnLine engines.

Much of the initial usefulness of this chapter was that it allowed the DBA to work around limitations in the engine. Many of those limitations and restrictions are now gone, but the techniques and rationale behind the method of scripting has remained the same.

Personally, much of my current scripting is done with PERL rather than the UNIX or MKS shells. Almost anything you could do with the earlier shells can be done much easier and more elegantly with the PERL language. A perfect example is the excellent set of tools that were written by Technology Investments and called ztools. These tools are now sold by BMC software. The scripts were written in PERL and did not even require the Informix extensions to the language. They would run an Informix utility from within PERL and parse the output to provide the data they needed.

While the individual scripts and programs should be useful in the day-to-day operations of your database, it is likely that you will have to massage and modify the programs for your own use. What you as a DBA should take from this chapter are concepts and approaches for how to use various tools to do your bidding. The goal here is to give you a place to start and to point you in the direction of creating your own database tools.

ONLINE-SPECIFIC SCRIPTS

Just about every program will use the UNIX utilities to massage data. If you do not have a good background in UNIX, you need to get a few good books on UNIX and work at writing scripts. UNIX scriptwriters tend to develop intimate relations with several of the utilities at the expense of others. I am no exception. I use a lot of awk, grep, sed, and csh concepts. If you have other preferences, feel free to exercise your scriptwriting in the way you feel most comfortable.

With UNIX, there are usually several ways to accomplish a given task, from the most awkward to the most elegant approach. I make no claim as to the elegance of these DBA scripts. If you can modify them and make them prettier, faster, and more elegant, go to it.

All of these scripts and programs were developed "under the gun" as part of real business systems. Often, it is necessary to take shortcuts and to use brute force to accomplish jobs within a given time frame. These scripts are ample proof.

There, I think I've apologized enough for the inelegance.

RUN SQL FROM THE COMMAND LINE

Although isql is a menu-driven program, it follows the standard UNIX I/O conventions. This allows input and output to and from I-SQL to be redirected and to come from or go to UNIX devices such as terminals and files. It is also possible to pass parameters to isql from the command line or from files or scripts.

Note that in all of the included scripts, we are assuming that you are using isql and not dbaccess. If you use dbaccess instead of isql, just replace all instances of isql with dbaccess and the programs should work the same.

As example, take the sample script dbcat:

```
#!/bin/csh
echo "select * from $2;" | $INFORMIXDIR/bin/isql $1
```

The syntax is dbcat database_name table_name. The database_name is passed as parameter $1 and the table_name is passed as parameter $2. This concept can be extended in the C-Shell by using aliases to provide complete SQL services directly from the command line. To do this, place the following aliases in a file called aliases.rc.

```
alias alter  "echo 'alter \!:*;'  | $INFORMIXDIR/bin/isql $DB"
alias create "echo 'create \!:*;' | $INFORMIXDIR/bin/isql $DB"
alias delete "echo 'delete \!:*;' | $INFORMIXDIR/bin/isql $DB"
alias drop   "echo 'drop \!:*;'   | $INFORMIXDIR/bin/isql $DB"
alias grant  "echo 'grant \!:*;'  | $INFORMIXDIR/bin/isql $DB"
alias insert "echo 'insert \!:*;' | $INFORMIXDIR/bin/isql $DB"
alias rename "echo 'rename \!:*;' | $INFORMIXDIR/bin/isql $DB"
alias revoke "echo 'revoke \!:*;' | $INFORMIXDIR/bin/isql $DB"
alias select "echo 'select \!:*;' | $INFORMIXDIR/bin/isql $DB"
alias update "echo 'update \!:*;' | $INFORMIXDIR/bin/isql $DB"
alias info   "echo 'info \!:*;'   | $INFORMIXDIR/bin/isql $DB"
```

These aliases receive the name of the requested database through the $DB environmental variable. The aliases are defined when you run the command source aliases.rc. Each time this file is sourced, the aliases are redefined. To make these aliases point to another database, reset the $DB environmental variable and then run source aliases.rc. If you need to access only one database, or if you work predominantly with one database, you may want to set the $DB environmental variable in your .cshrc file and add the contents of aliases.rc to the end of your .cshrc file.

The thing that makes these aliases work is the \!:* in the first half of the aliases. It takes the first word of the command, either alter, create, delete, etc., and turns it into an alias. Whenever you type the first word, that is interpreted as an alias. The rest of the command line is indicated by the \!:* structure. It is passed to the echo statement that is sent to isql by the magic \!:* clause. This construct works only in the C-Shell.

Another way to pass parameters to a script running `isql` is to use a UNIX *here document*. This type of script instructs the shell to take the command and the input from the same source. For example, look at the sample script, `get_accounting_data`:

```
#!/bin/csh
$INFORMIXDIR/bin/isql $1 << EOF
SELECT  * from accounts_payable
WHERE   date = "$2" and
code = "$3";
EOF
```

Running this script would allow you to pass a database name as `$1` and `date` and `code` as `$2` and `$3`. In the here document, the key is the `<<` construct. This means that the shell is to use the code immediately following the `<<` as a marker delimiting input to the script. Using "EOF" as a marker, the first "EOF" indicates the beginning of the input.

The entire select statement, up to the semicolon that immediately precedes the last "EOF" is then taken as input to the `isql` command. The handy part is that the shell first interprets any shell parameters before it evaluates the input. This is what allows you to pass the parameters.

FIND OUT HOW MUCH SPACE IS BEING USED BY TABLES

`Tbstat -d` gives you an output that shows the raw information necessary to calculate the free space in your database, but it is not organized in a way that is easy to comprehend.

This script, a C-Shell script called `dbdf`, does a much cleaner job:

```
#!/bin/csh
#dbdf
$INFORMIXDIR/bin/tbstat -d | grep / | grep -v bpages | sort +2 -3 -n |awk
'{printf("%s\t%s\t%s\t%s\n", $3,$5,$6,$8)}' > /tmp/c$$
$INFORMIXDIR/bin/tbstat -d | grep informix | awk '{print $2, $8}' > /tmp/s$$
join  /tmp/s$$ /tmp/c$$ > /tmp/j$$
awk '\
BEGIN {name=""} \
{total[$2]+=$3; free[$2]+=$4} \
END { for (space in total) printf("%-12s is %.2f percent full and has %6d free pages \n", space,
(1-free[space]/total[space])*100,free[space])}' /tmp/j$$ | grep -v log
rm /tmp/c$$ /tmp/s$$ /tmp/j$$
```

This script uses `tbstat -d` and massages the output with `grep` and `awk`. It creates three temporary files in the `/tmp` directory that are erased at completion of the script. These files will be cXXXXX, sXXXXX, and jXXXXX where the XXXXX is the script's process id number (PID). This PID number is created by the `$$` construct as used in `rm /tmp/c$$ /tmp/m$$ /tmp/j$$`. The second `tbstat` command makes one assumption. It assumes that the owner of all of the Informix chunks is user `informix`. If for some reason you have a custom installation that does not follow this convention, you will need to modify the grep informix. The last statement before the UNIX command rm /tmp/c$$ contains another section of code that you may want to modify. It uses a grep -v log to exclude any lines that contain the word log. All of my logs are in separate dbspaces that are called logSOMETHING. Since the space utilization of these logspaces does not vary (the logs are allocated and take up space whether they're full or not), I'm not interested in monitoring changes in the space utilization of these dbspaces. If you use similar conventions in naming your chunks and dbspaces, you may want to use a similar exclude statement.

Place the script in your $INFORMIXDIR/local_bin directory and chmod it to be executable by whomever you wish to give the right to run dbdf. This program does not understand multiple OnLine instances. If you want to make it do so, you'll have to pass it a parameter for the name of the $TBCONFIG file and have it set the $TBCONFIG environment variable to the passed value and then run the script.

FIND DUPLICATE VALUES IN A TABLE

There are several reasons that you may want to find duplicate values in a table. The main reason is when you are attempting to build a unique index on a field and the index build crashes with a SQL duplicate value error. This error message does not go far enough in that it tells you it has a problem, but it does not tell you where the duplicate value occurs. All that you know is that you have a duplicate value somewhere.

There are several approaches to solving this problem, and one good method for avoiding it. If you initially build the table with a unique index on the field in question, you will avoid the duplicates in the first place. This requires planning ahead. You have to know in advance that you want field x to be unique.

Even if you know in advance that you need a unique field, it is often not possible to prebuild the index. This often happens when you are loading a table from outside sources. When doing this type of a load, you may wish to do it without indexes for performance reasons. When you try to build the index, you get the duplicate key error.

Assuming that you are loading from an outside data source, you have the option of using UNIX commands on the raw data files prior to trying the LOAD. You can use the UNIX sort -u command to presort the data.

If the data is already in a table, you can use SQL to identify the duplicate entries. Given the following table;

```
CREATE TABLE person (ssn  char(11), name char(20));
```

assume that you are getting a duplicate key error on ssn. To identify the duplicate ssn entries, use the following SQL statement:

```
SELECT ssn FROM person
GROUP BY ssn
HAVING count(*) > 1;
```

The GROUP BY/HAVING combination allows you to pick out the duplicate values in the ssn field. A slightly more complex query will give you all of the data instead of just the ssn:

```
SELECT * FROM person
WHERE ssn in
( SELECT ssn FROM person
GROUP BY ssn
HAVING count(*) > 1)
      )
```

CLEAN OUT TABLES

There are two distinct parts to the problem of cleaning out tables. The first part is knowing that the tables need to be purged. The second part is the mechanical question of how to do it.

We'll cover the mechanical aspects here. Look to the sections on database monitoring and table proliferation for methods of discovering which tables need to be cleaned.

Assuming that you know that table x needs to be purged, how do you go about it? If you have determined that the table needs to be completely emptied, you may be tempted to use this SQL statement;

```
DELETE FROM x;
```

to remove all of the rows. This is OK for a small table, but it can take a significant amount of time on larger tables. To completely empty a large table, it is easier to drop the table and re-create it. Use the dbschema utility to create SQL statements that will re-create the table:

```
dbschema -d dbname -t tabname mk_tabname.sql
```

Then go into isql and drop the table;

```
DROP TABLE tabname;
```

Finally, re-create the table from the script you just created with dbschema;

```
isql dbname < mk_tabname.sql
```

Note, however, that the dbschema utility does not preserve dbspace, extent, and locking information. If you use dbschema, be sure to modify the mk_tabname.sql script to include the proper dbspace, extent, and locking information.

A better solution to the problem of preserving this information is to use the newschema script included in the next section. The newschema script creates a more complete schema.

RE-CREATE A TABLE WITH THE SAME PARAMETERS AS THE ORIGINAL

As mentioned above, the Informix dbschema program has some noted limitations. While it will create all of the SQL statements necessary to rebuild the table in its most basic form, some very valuable information is lost. This is the information regarding the extent sizes and the locking mode of the table.

As the DBA continues to tune the database, it becomes very important to keep the tables within the minimum number of extents. It is often necessary to adjust the extent sizes of a table to make sure that it uses its space most effectively and to make sure that its access speed is maximized. When rebuilding the table, much accumulated tuning work would be lost if the latest EXTENT SIZE and NEXT SIZE parameters were lost. The newschema script is designed to capture this otherwise lost information and to create a schema program that is truly useful.

Newschema is composed of two parts. The first is a report in the isql report-writer, ACE. The second part is a script that merges this information with the output of the OnLine dbschema program to provide the information needed.

The ACE report is called storage.ace. If you do not have the isql package containing ACE, the same report could be written in SQL.

```
database
admin <--(*NOTE* Put your own database name here)
end
define
param [1] which_table char(50)
variable mode char(4)
end
output
top margin 0
bottom margin 0
left margin 0
end
select
tabname,
owner,
locklevel,
fextsize,
nextsize
from systables where tabname = $which_table
end
format
on every row
```

```
if locklevel = "P" then
begin
let mode = "PAGE"
end
if locklevel = "R" then
begin
let mode = "ROW"
end
print "EXTENT SIZE ", fextsize using "######",1 space,"NEXT SIZE ",nextsize using "######",1
space,"LOCK MODE ", mode clipped
end
```

The above ACE program is compiled by using the isql Forms Compile option or by using the appropriate command line options to compile the program. The output program will be called storage.arc.

The following C-Shell script needs to be placed in the DBA's path. I suggest creating a $INFORMIXDIR/local_bin directory and placing all of the included DBA scripts and programs in it. Set the $INFORMIXLOCALBIN = XXXXXXXX environmental variable to point to the location of this local directory. If you place all of your site-specific scripts in a local bin directory, this directory will be preserved with subsequent Informix installs and upgrades. If you have put your scripts in the $INFORMIXDIR/bin directory, you will someday need to decide which are your "local" scripts and which are the "real" Informix distribution programs. You might as well do it right the first time.

The actual script that makes use of the storage.arc report is newschema.

```
#!/bin/csh
#newschema
set INFORMIXLOCALBIN = $INFORMIXDIR/local_bin
$INFORMIXDIR/bin/dbschema -d $1 -t $2 /tmp/tempschema$$
set storage_option = `$INFORMIXDIR/bin/sacego -s -d $1 $INFORMIXLOCALBIN/storage $2`
cat /tmp/tempschema$$ | sed "s/ );/ ) $storage_option ;/" > /tmp/tempschema2$$
cat /tmp/tempschema2$$ >> $3
rm /tmp/tempschema$$ /tmp/tempschema2$$
```

The newschema program is similar in concept to the Informix dbschema program with the exception that it works for one table at a time. Invocation is as follows:

```
newschema   database_name   table_name   destination_file_name
```

This script will append its schema to the destination_file_name, which makes it usable in creating schemas for multiple tables. This is done by using one of my most-often-used UNIX tricks, taking input from a file. Suppose you wanted to do a newschema for all tables in database admin. The first job would be to create a UNIX file of the tables in the subject database. The SQL commands for this would be:

```
DATABASE admin;
SELECT tabname FROM systables WHERE tabid > 99;
```

These SQL statements take advantage of the fact that all of the internal tables that OnLine creates for a database will have a `tabid` in the `systables` system table of less than 99. Anything greater than 99 must be a user table. Place the output of this script into a file called `targets` (or whatever else you want to name it). This can be by using the `isql` query language and using the Query-Language menu option followed by the Output option to place the output in a new file, `target`. If you are using the SELECT alias under C-Shell, it would be nice if you could simply type from the UNIX prompt:

```
SELECT tabname FROM systables WHERE tabid > 99 > target
```

Unfortunately, the shell will not understand this construct in conjunction with an alias. If you are using C-Shell with the history mechanism, you can get around it by using the following series of commands:

```
SELECT tabname FROM systables WHERE tabid > 99
```

You then get an output to your screen. Then you type

```
!! > target
```

The `!!` (bang bang) command repeats the last command and puts the output in `target`. The next step is to clean out everything but the tablenames from the file `target`. This is easily done using a word processor. If you're after a system that can be run without human intervention or if you simply want to make the script more elegant, you could populate the `target` file by using an ACE report instead of `isql`. The report writer gives you a lot more flexibility in formatting and layout than `isql`. For this case, `isql` works fine, because we're just doing this to show you the techniques.

Okay, you now have a file called `target` that contains only the names of the tables you want to include in your schema. Now comes time for the UNIX wizardry that makes the job work. You want to tell UNIX to run `newschema` on every table in `target` and put the output in the file called `mk_admin.sql`. Write a C-Shell script called `newschema_alldb` that looks like this:

```
#!/bin/csh
foreach table (`cat target`)
$INFORMIXLOCALBIN/newschema  admin  $table  mk_admin.sql
end
```

When you run this script, it does a `newschema` on each table in the `target` file and appends it to `mk_admin.sql`. You can then re-create the database by running the SQL script from within `isql`. This method of massaging an output file and then running multiple jobs against it is a most handy tool, especially for all of those "quick and dirty" jobs that you want to do. The same type of approach can be taken with either the Bourne or Korn shells. However, I'm a C-Shell bigot, so I'll leave it to you to translate the scripts if you care to use any of the lesser shells.

CLEAN SELECTED DATA OUT OF A TABLE

The above methods are workable if you want to delete all rows from a table. What about when you need to delete only some of the rows? Or you need to move some of the rows out of the table and archive them in another table. This is a common task in database management, and it is one that seems to be forgotten many times in the design of applications.

Programmers seem to spend a lot of time figuring out how to put data into tables, but they often do not spend quite as much time devising methods to remove obsolete data. In many ways, the database is a black hole to developers. They tend to think that they can continue to add data to it forever. But the DBA knows different. We have to clean these things up!

As a DBA, you should be a strong advocate for an entire life-cycle approach to designing your applications. Every time a developer approaches you with a request for a new table, you should inquire about how the data gets into the table and how it goes away. Get the developers to thinking about means of keeping the data current and getting rid of the trash. Data does not have to be kept online forever.

There are also significant technical problems with deleting specific rows from a table, especially a large, frequently used table. The SQL delete statement will place locks on the table being deleted from. The level of locking will be the lock level as established for the table unless an explicit table lock is placed on the table. If the locking granularity is either row or page, it is possible that a long delete will overflow your lock table. Such a delete is also considered a transaction and could possibly throw you into a long transaction situation with regard to your logfiles. The same problems apply to updates to tables and to saving rows to history tables. The history table problem can be broken down into two parts, inserting the row into a history table and deleting the row from the old table.

The major problem here is that the deletes, updates, or movements of data are done in one big transaction. Solving the problem requires that the tasks be broken into smaller manageable units.

The following 4GL program is called `sample.4gl` and it utilizes a concept I have called *flutter locks*. Flutter locks are locks that are placed and released on small units of data. As such, they are much less intrusive in day-to-day operations. When using programs similar to `sample.4gl`, you can have archiving and table cleanup programs that will peacefully coexist with an active user community.

Programs using flutter locks should pay careful attention to the concept of a *transaction*. A transaction is a group of statements that should be completed as a unit. If any of the parts are not completed, none of the statements is executed. For most deleting and archiving situations, these transaction units can be made at the row level. Either a row needs to be deleted or it doesn't. In an archive situation, the transaction should consist of two parts. First, copy the row to the new table. Second, delete the row from the old table. Most of the time you really don't need the very broad transaction units utilized by the DELETE or UPDATE SQL statements. These statements interpret the transaction as, "DELETE all of the rows covered by the WHERE clause or ROLLBACK all of the rows." If your application requirements really require such an all-or-nothing level of transactions, using a flutter lock program will not solve the problem. Such instances are rare, however.

In the case of an archive program in which you are moving rows based upon certain criteria, the world will not fall in if you miss a row or two. They'll get archived next time the program runs. One very important implication of using a flutter lock program for deleting or row archiving is that the jobs can be easily interrupted. Try interrupting a long SQL DELETE statement after it's worked for an hour, and you'll see about an hour of rollback. Even worse, imagine what happens if you've had a DELETE or UPDATE SQL statement going on for several hours and your system crashes. Your fast recovery on restart will be anything but fast. Your system will probably be down for hours recovering.

Using flutter locks allows you to perform this "transaction chopping" and to completely avoid most of these problems. I have chosen to demonstrate this in I-4GL rather than in ESQL/C. The same programming concepts are available in both tools.

The general concept of the program is to first open a cursor in which you select the rows on which you wish to operate. You may then wish to DELETE the data, archive the data to another table, or perform other SQL operations on the data. The key thing to note is that this outer cursor is opened using the parameter WITH HOLD. This causes the program to maintain its position within the list of rows that need to be acted upon.

For each row in the outer cursor, the program goes into the table, does its BEGIN WORK, locking the rows, does its DELETE or UPDATE statement, and does its COMMIT WORK. Then it goes out to the outer cursor again and picks its next row, etc. Without the hold cursor, each time it went out to the outer cursor, the SQL statement would have to be reevaluated and a new SELECT done.

When you get your rows from the cursor, you can do any amount of work you wish in the inner sections. An archive requires an INSERT into another table and a DELETE from the old table, but you can perform much more complicated tasks within the inner loop.

Just remember to think about keeping the actual work within the transaction to an absolute minimum. Also, it is necessary for you to closely monitor the success or failure of the jobs done within the transaction. If the status indicates that the work failed, you need to be sure to roll back the entire transaction explicitly.

A couple of things to note about the sample.4gl program. First, don't worry about trying to work through the outer_count and quitflag variables. They are in there so that you can group the transactions into bigger transactions, maybe committing after every 100 or 200 executions. There are cases in which the overhead cost of doing a BEGIN WORK/COMMIT WORK for every single row in the outer cursor would be prohibitive.

Rather than COMMITTING after every single, *atomic transaction*, this code allows you to group several hundred such atomic transactions together. Either they all succeed or they all fail. If you need the capability, it is available. I've found that committing after every atomic transaction does not create a problem with resources in most cases. Also, note that the 4GL program follows the PASCAL conventions of including comments within pairs of curly braces:

```
{ this is a comment }
```

```
joe 58>  cat sample.4gl
DATABASE admin
GLOBALS
DEFINE s_order RECORD like order.*
DEFINE s_order_tran RECORD like order_tran.*
DEFINE counter INTEGER
DEFINE outer_count INTEGER
DEFINE quitflag INTEGER
DEFINE total INTEGER
END GLOBALS

MAIN
CALL startlog("d_order.errors")
ALTER TABLE order LOCK MODE (row)
IF status < 0 THEN
WHILE status < 0
SLEEP 2
ALTER TABLE order LOCK MODE (row)
END WHILE
END IF
{ comment:  all of this status checking is to be sure that the lock }
{           mode really gets changed. The row locking makes the program }
{           even less intrusive to users.   }
{ NOTE:  this will cause short lockouts during operations.  Make sure that }
{           this short lockout will not crash other users }
ALTER TABLE order_tran LOCK MODE (row)
IF status < 0 THEN
WHILE status < 0
SLEEP 2
ALTER TABLE order_tran LOCK MODE (row)
END WHILE
END IF
DECLARE drop_order CURSOR WITH HOLD FOR
select * from  order where
due_date < current - 3 units month
AND
start_date < current - 3 units month
FOR UPDATE

{ comment:  this is the outer cursor.  The "with hold" is critical }
{           the "for update" is what allows you to do a delete inside }
{           the loop with a "current of cursor" clause  }

DECLARE copy_order CURSOR WITH HOLD FOR
INSERT INTO order_hist VALUES (s_order.*)
{ doesn't always need to have "with hold" }
LET outer_count = 0
LET quitflag = 0
OPEN drop_order
OPEN copy_order
WHILE TRUE
```

```
LET counter = 0

WHILE counter < 1
{comment:  if you wanted to change your number of transactions per }
{          commit, change the 1 to however many rows you want to work }
{          between transactions.  }

BEGIN WORK
{    this is the beginning of the transaction.  Keep the transactions short }
FETCH drop_order into s_order.*
IF status = NOTFOUND
THEN COMMIT WORK
LET quitflag = 1
EXIT WHILE
END IF
{ always check to see that the statement completes properly }
PUT copy_order
{ first, insert into the history table }

IF status < 0 THEN
ROLLBACK WORK
CALL errorlog("ERROR........SKIPPING")
EXIT WHILE
END IF
INSERT INTO order_tran_hist SELECT *
FROM order_tran
WHERE order_number = s_order.order_number
AND   order_type   = s_order.order_type
{ do a little more work with another table while we're in the loop }
IF status < 0 THEN
ROLLBACK WORK
CALL errorlog("ERROR........SKIPPING")
EXIT WHILE
END IF
DELETE from order_tran
WHERE order_number = s_order.order_number
AND   order_type   = s_order.order_type

{delete from the other table}
DELETE from order
WHERE current of drop_order
{delete the current row in the outer cursor table }
LET counter = counter + 1
COMMIT WORK
LET total = outer_count + counter
DISPLAY total

{ provide a heartbeat to the standard out to let us know the program' }
{ still alive and where it's working.  You can direct the standard out }
{ of the compiled program by invoking the program as : }
{      sample.4ge >! sample_log &     }

END WHILE
IF quitflag = 1
THEN EXIT WHILE
END IF
LET outer_count=outer_count + 1
END WHILE

ALTER TABLE order LOCK MODE (page)
```

```
IF status < 0 THEN
WHILE status < 0
SLEEP 2
ALTER TABLE order LOCK MODE (page)
END WHILE
END IF
{ put the tables back in their old lock mode }
ALTER TABLE order_tran LOCK MODE (page)
IF status < 0 THEN
WHILE status < 0
SLEEP 2
ALTER TABLE order_tran LOCK MODE (page)
END WHILE
END IF
END MAIN
```

The `sample.4gl` program is compiled within the INFORMIX-4GL program or directly with a command-line interface. It can be run from a command-line interface, or it can be put into your `cron` file to run automatically.

KNOW IF ONLINE IS RUNNING

Occasionally, the DBA needs to be reassured that the database has not aborted and is still running. This need for reassurance often occurs after the DBA mistakenly kills a `sqlturbo` backend or does something else stupid.

The DBA wants a quick check to see if he needs to start making excuses about why he crashed the database.

This information is also useful in writing scripts and programs that execute across the network on multiple machines. There are many reasons that a script would benefit by being aware whether or not OnLine was running on machine B.

I find the `ok` script handy in cases like this:

```
INFORMIX 23>  cat ok
#!/bin/csh
if ( `$INFORMIXDIR/bin/tbstat - |grep RSAM |awk '{print $5}'` == On-Line ) then
echo "  ....'saaaaaaawwwwwright......"
else
echo "Mucked Again"
endif
```

Feel free to change the `echo` statements to give you any cute and/or nasty comments that you wish to display. Run the script with no parameters.

CONVERT TABLE NUMBERS TO TABLE NAMES

All of the `tbstat` outputs refer to tables by `tblnum`, which is a hex number. In true, user-friendly fashion, OnLine uses an integer number to identify the tables in the `systables` system table. To convert between the two, you need to use the following SQL conversion:

```
SELECT tabname, hex(partnum) FROM systables;
```

This will give you a list of table names and `tblnums` (as used in `tbstat`) for all of your tables. The OnLine manual recommends that you keep a hard copy of this list available to use for debugging.

A somewhat better approach is to create the following script, `table` in your `$INFORMIXLOCALBIN` directory:

```
joe 67> cat table
#!/bin/csh
set search = $2
set SEARCH = `echo $2 | tr "[a-f]" "[A-F]" `
$INFORMIXDIR/bin/isql $1 << EOF
OUTPUT TO PIPE cat WITHOUT HEADINGS SELECT "$1" as database,tabname , hex(partnum) as tablenumber
from systables WHERE hex(partnum) MATCHES "*$SEARCH*" or tabname MATCHES "*$search*";
EOF
```

The `table` program is invoked as :

```
table database_name tblnum_fragment
table database_name table_name_fragment
table database_name
```

The `tblnum` as used in the `tbstat` outputs is a seven-digit hex number, and it's sometimes possible to make an error in entering it. That's why the `table` script does a MATCH and not an equals. If you see a `tblnum` of `300021e`, you can just enter the fragment `21e` and you'll get a listing of all matching tables. You can also enter either the complete table name or a fragment of the name and receive all matching table names and their `tblnum` equivalent IDs.

FIND DATABASE NAMES FROM A SCRIPT

The DBA sometimes needs to be able to run scripts or programs that will take an action on every database in an OnLine instance. An example would be if the DBA wanted to do some reports of space utilization by database. Another example would be running an UPDATE STATISTICS command in SQL for all databases. OnLine does not make it easy to do this. The information is readily available, since `isql` asks you to choose a database before you do any work from the menu, but there is no simple and straightforward way I know to do this from a script.

In this case, we need to take the brute force approach. This information is available in the tbcheck -pe output as part of the fully qualified table names. The following script, named find_db_names, will output the names of your databases:

```
$INFORMIXDIR/bin/tbcheck -pe |grep systables |grep -v WARNING | tr ":" " " | awk '{print $1}' |
sort -u
```

This script is pretty slow, and it's certainly an awkward approach, but it works. Since it uses tbcheck -pe, it does not lock up any tables and can be run with no danger to an operating Informix system.

FIND DATABASE NAMES FROM AN ESQL/C PROGRAM

If you have access to ESQL/C, there is a somewhat more elegant approach to determining the names of databases. The following program utilizes an undocumented function in ESQL/C. As such, the function is subject to change at any time by Informix. As a general rule, Informix does not recommend that users use undocumented functions and they take no responsibility for any problems that you may have in the use of undocumented functions.

Just remember that Informix may change this at any time. Until then, this program is much faster than the find_db_names shell script.

This program is called find_db_names.ec:

```
main()
{
#define MAXSPACES 256#define MAXSTRINGS (15 * MAXSPACES)
char *name[MAXSPACES];
char space[MAXSTRINGS];
int basecount=0;
int answer=sqgetdbs(&basecount, name, MAXSPACES,
space, MAXSTRINGS);

if (answer==0 && basecount >0)
        {
int i;
for (i = 0; i < basecount; ++i)
printf("%s\n", name[i]);

        }
}
```

`o compile this program, compile it with ESQL/C using the following command line:

```
:sql -o find_db_names find_db_names.ec
```

When this successfully compiles, you will have an executable program called find_db_names. If you use this compiled version of find_db_names, you can either overwrite or rename the script version presented above. Either one can be used with the other scripts in this book. If you do not have ESQL/C, it may be worth your while to try to find someone else who is running your version of UNIX who does have ESQL/C. If you can get a compiled version of this program you will find that it is definitely an improvement over the script version.

Maintain a Current UPDATE STATISTICS

The operations of the OnLine optimizer depend upon the data that is collected from runs of the SQL UPDATE STATISTICS command. This command looks at the distribution of data in the tables and indexes and stores it internally. Based upon this information, the optimizer decides the best way to execute your SQL statements. If the statistics information is stale or nonexistent, you could get SQL statements that perform poorly.

Get your users and developers into the habit of running an UPDATE STATISTICS FOR TABLE tablename every time they create a new table, create a new index, or significantly modify the distribution of data within a table. If you already have your users trained in the use of the SET EXPLAIN ON command in SQL and they are optimizing their own queries, be sure that they run the UPDATE STATISTICS before they do the SET EXPLAIN ON.

It is also a good procedure to have UPDATE STATISTICS in your UNIX cron file to be run occasionally. Once a night is not too much. Since UPDATE STATISTICS when invoked without a FOR TABLE clause works on a database level, you first need to feed the program the information about the names of your existing databases. This script is named update_statistics:

```
#!/bin/csh
echo "Please wait.........."
foreach db (`$INFORMIXLOCALBIN/find_db_names`)
echo "TIME: `date`   UPDATING STATISTICS FOR DATABASE:   $db"
$INFORMIXDIR/bin/isql $db << EOF
update statistics
EOF
end
```

This script includes an echo statement that can be removed if you want it to operate silently. I usually prefer to run the script with a redirection of the output to a logfile so that I can verify when the last updates were done. This information is not easily available unless you keep track of it yourself.

GET TABLE INFORMATION

It is advantageous for the DBA to be able to make ad hoc inquiries about database elements such as tables, columns, indexes, and rows. Users always seem to be asking about table structure, existing indexes, and the like. It is very handy to have a command-line program that will allow these types of questions to be answered from the UNIX command line.

The section above on running isql from the command line contains a C-Shell alias called info that pipes information to isql. The same could be done with a standard shell script if you are not a csh user. The csh alias is:

```
alias info    "echo 'info \!:*;'    | $INFORMIXDIR/bin/isql your_database"
```

This alias is invoked in several ways, depending upon the information that the DBA wants to locate. This alias uses one of the more obscure SQL commands called INFO. The command does not seem to be used very often by SQL users. They are missing a very useful tool. It just goes to show that you should go through the reference manuals occasionally just to see if there is something there that you don't usually use. Several possible ways to call this alias are:

```
INFORMIX 3>info tables

Table name

"dba".a31save        "dba".a_ab091993     "dba".a_ap091993
"dba".a_di091993     "dba".a_ia081993     "dba".a_ia091993
"dba".a_io091993     "dba".a_it091993     "dba".a_model_type
"dba".access_6       "dba".access_60      "dba".access_61
"dba".access_64      "dba".access_65      "dba".access_67
"dba".is_system      "dba".isboxes        "dba".ka_calendar
"dba".key_acct       "dba".key_acct_mem   "dba".key_acct_code

INFORMIX 4>info columns for sample_table
Column name          Type                           Nulls
system_num           smallint                       no
sys_code             char(5)                        yes
name                 char(30)                       yes
phy_city_loc         char(3)                        yes
system_type          smallint                       no
access_meth          smallint                       no
start_date           datetime year to second        no
end_date             datetime year to second        no
change_num           integer                        no

INFORMIX 5>info status for sample_table
Table Name           system
Owner                dba
Row Size             64
Number of Rows       216
Number of Columns    9
Date Created         06/24/1992
```

```
INFORMIX 6>info indexes for sample_table
Index name          Owner   Type    Cluster  Columns
sample_ci           dba     dupls   Yes      system_num

INFORMIX 10>info access for sample_table
User      Select        Update        Insert  Delete  Index  Alter
bull      All           All           Yes     Yes     No     No
chris     All           All           Yes     Yes     No     No
danny     All           All           Yes     Yes     No     No
```

MAKE A FAST RECOVERY GO FASTER

This is a trick question. It can't be done in OnLine. If your system comes down ungracefully, either because of a crash or because you initiated an immediate shutdown, you will be forced to go into recovery mode when you restart the database system. The length of time for fast recovery depends upon how much work has been done since the last checkpoint. If you absolutely have to bring the system down ungracefully, try to do a checkpoint before the shutdown. It will help speed up the recovery process. This is one thing to consider when establishing the frequency of your checkpoints. Spacing your checkpoints further apart may make the interruptions that they cause to processing less intrusive, but you'll take the risk of longer recovery times. You need to decide upon a balance between performance and speed of recovery.

IDS systems have an ONCONFIG parameter called RECOVERY_THREADS that allows the DBA to specify how many threads are started to handle fast recovery. Increasing this parameter will affect the recovery speed, but only in IDS systems.

As part of the recovery, the OnLine system will roll back any transactions that were working at the time of the shutdown and that were not yet committed. If you have a very long transaction working at the time of shutdown, your recovery time will be much longer. You can get a feel for how long it will take to recover by looking at how much logfile data you have. Recovery, especially in cases caused by long transactions, can take hours. Remember this when you're designing applications. This is another reason to keep your transactions short. You can alleviate these types of problems to a large extent by using programs with flutter locks that keep transactions as short as possible.

You will sometimes need to decide whether or not to bring the database down ungracefully. At least you have a choice here. In a crash, you have no choices at all. When making this decision, you must think about what is going on in your system and how long it will take for the recovery to take place. You may save some time by bringing the database down to stop a rogue process, but doing so may increase your recovery time. It's sort of a case of "pay me now or pay me later." Either way, it will take some time. You need to watch these things, especially if you are running a production database and your users need to have it working all the time.

You will eventually be faced with a fast recovery time that seems to go on forever. Maybe someone crashed the system while a long job was going on. Maybe someone brought the database down without checking for active transactions. Anyway, your database, which usually takes about 15 seconds for fast recovery on a restart, has already been cranking away for 15 minutes and the users are beginning to call, wondering when the database will be back up. You need to know how long it will take to recover.

First, run `tbstat -1` to check the status of your logfiles. If you've followed my suggestions, you've monitored your recovery times and have a rule of thumb for how long it takes to recover per logfile. This number is a very rough estimate. Sometimes it can be off by several factors of ten. During recovery, you cannot access the database. This means that the system tables are not available to you. However, the `tbstat` utility will run during recovery. Usually, what takes a lot of time during fast recovery is the rollback of transactions that were not committed when the system went down. You can do a `tbstat -u` and see which daemons are running during the recovery. This will be a very simplified output. All that will show up are the daemons for fast recovery and rollforward. Nobody else can be in the system.

A common cause of long recovery times is bringing the database down in the middle of long inserts into a table or deletes from a table. If you know, for example, that a table was being built from scratch, that is, it had no rows in it (or if you knew how many rows it initially had), you can get a very good estimate of your rollback time. Do a `tbstat -t` command and look at the number of rows in any table whose `tblnum` does not end in `00001`. This will be the table that is being rolled back. Then run several `tbstat -t` commands and note whether this number of rows is increasing or decreasing. If it is a scratch-built table, your recovery will go on until the number of rows equals zero. You can run several `tbstat -t` commands and calculate the rate at which the rows are being deleted. Extrapolate that number and you'll have an estimate of the rollback time. If it's a delete, and if you know how many rows were originally in the table, the number of rows will be increasing. You can perform the same extrapolation in the opposite direction to get an approximate rollback time.

None of this will make the recovery go any faster, but it'll help you make decisions about what to tell your users. If nothing else, having an accurate estimate and an explanation of why the rollback is occurring will make you look somewhat more in control of the situation.

KNOW WHAT A CERTAIN USER IS DOING

Database administrators spend a lot of time monitoring the database, looking for things that could cause problems. After a while, it is usually possible to identify several of your peers who need to be looked in upon occasionally. After about a thousand repetitions of "DBA, I've got a job I want to kill, would you do it?" I developed the following scripts:

The first is called `seeuser` and it tells you what a certain user is doing in the database. Since I get tired of deciphering the `flag` codes in the `tbstat` output, I also put a legend at the bottom of the output telling me what each code means:

```
JOE 71> cat seeuser
#!/bin/csh
if ( $#argv == 0 ) then
echo -n "Enter the USER NAME you want to check on ( . for all) :  "
set target = $<
else
set target = $1
endif

echo Looking at INFORMIX jobs for $target
echo "\
Users \
address   flags   pid     user     tty      wait      tout locks nreads nwrites"
echo " "
$INFORMIXDIR/bin/tbstat -u | grep $target | grep -v grep
echo "\
          ^ ^ ^ ^  \
          | | | |  \
POSITION  1 2 3 4  \
\
1 WAITING ON: B(uffer) C(heckpoint) L(ock) S(latch) X(rollback) G(log)\
2 TRANSACTIONS: B(egin work)  T(in a transaction)  R(ollback)  A(rchive)\
3 STATUS:     R(eading)     X(inside a write, checkpoints frozen)\
4 PROCESS:    M(Monitor)   D(aemon)  C(Dead, awaiting cleanup) F(PageFlusher)"
```

You can invoke `seeuser` with or without parameters. If you use no parameters, the script will prompt you to enter the name of a user to check on, or to enter a period to check on all users. You can also invoke the program with a user name as a parameter. In either case, user could be anything that shows up in a `tbstat -u` output. For example, you could type a `seeuser L` and it would show you any users who were waiting for a lock to release (It has an L in the first field of the flag field). Of course, it would also show you anything that user Lincoln or firewaLL was doing, too, but you wouldn't use capital letters in a user name, would you?

There's another variant of the `seeuser` script called `checkon`. This gives you all that `seeuser` does but also includes any UNIX processes owned by the user. Here is the `checkon` script:

```
INFORMIX 83> cat checkon
#!/bin/csh
echo LISTING ALL jobs for $1
echo " "
ps -fu $1
echo " "
echo Looking at INFORMIX jobs for $1
echo " "
echo "\
address   flags   pid     user     tty      wait      tout locks nreads nwrites"
```

```
$INFORMIXDIR/bin/tbstat -u | grep $1 | grep -v grep
echo "\
           ^ ^ ^ ^  \
           | | | |  \
POSITION   1 2 3 4  \
1 WAITING ON: B(uffer) C(heckpoint) L(ock) S(latch) X(rollback) G(log)\
2 TRANSACTIONS: B(egin work)  T(in a transaction)  R(ollback)  A(rchive)\
3 STATUS:    R(eading)    X(inside a write, checkpoints frozen)\
4 PROCESS:   M(Monitor)   D(aemon)    C(Dead,awaiting cleanup) F(PageFlusher)"
```

This script is a little more particular with input than the seeuser script is. This is because of the UNIX ps command in the third line. Depending on your UNIX flavor, you may need to modify this line anyway because different versions of UNIX have some differences in the ps command. Here, ps is looking for a complete user name. If your user name does not match, the script will fail on the ps command but will give you the tbstat output anyway. You could change the command to a simple ps command piped into grep something like this.

```
ps -aux | grep $1
```

instead of the ps -fu $1. This would allow you to use a partial username.

TRANSLATE A UNIX USER ID TO A REAL NAME

This short script is helpful when you're looking at the OnLine logfile trying to find out why something strange has happened. In the logfile, OnLine will tell you that a certain PID (process identifier) owned by a certain user has caused a problem. For example, the following two lines appeared in a logfile just before the database aborted and crashed:

```
11:42:24  Process Aborted Abnormally: pid=26630 user=129 us=e0002bf0 flags=1
11:42:24  Process Aborted Abnormally (latch): pid=26630 user=129 flags=1
```

Here, a backend, process ID #26630, was killed by user #129 at 11:42 while holding a latch, causing the system to abort. To find the name of user 129, run the following script, called username:

```
INFORMIX  73> cat username
grep $1 /usr/passwd | awk -F: '{printf("The culprit is %s, aka: %s\n",$1,$5))}'
```

Feel free to change the "culprit....etc." to your favorite pejorative comments. The script is invoked as username user_number, for example, username 129.

RUN AN ARCHIVE IN THE BACKGROUND AND MONITOR IT

The OnLine archiving programs assume that there will be a user sitting at a terminal monitoring the archiving process. Many times this is not a realistic option due to staffing problems. If you have large-capacity tapes, you can place the archiving and automatic backup of logfiles in the background and monitor them through log files. These techniques will work only if you are *absolutely sure* that you will not need to change tapes in the middle of an archive. Another reason to buy big DAT tape drives!

Refer to the chapter on "Understanding the Concepts" for a more detailed discussion on archives and the limitations of the OnLine archiving system. In that chapter we presented the following script, called do_level_1_archive:

```
INFORMIX 73> cat do_level_1_archive
#!/bin/csh
date
$INFORMIXDIR/bin/tbtape -s << EOF
{note, this line is a control-m, or carriage return.   don't type note}
1
EOF
```

Running the do_level_1_archive script will send the output of the tbtape command to the standard output, your current screen. For running in the background, this is not what we want. I use a script to drive the do_level_1_archive script and redirect the output. This script is called run_level_1_archives.

```
INFORMIX 74: cat run_level_1_archives
#!/bin/csh
$INFORMIXDIR/local_bin/do_level_1_archive >& $INFORMIXDIR/archive.log &
```

This script provides us with several useful features. First, it lets the archive run in the background, and second, it gives us a logfile to check to see how far along the archive has progressed. The tbtape program uses the UNIX curses screen I/O functions and is designed to provide screen output, not file output. As such, the output looks like one long character string to UNIX. The tbtape command does provide a running count of the percentage complete on the archive. To return a percentage complete string out of the archive.log file, use the peek_arc script.

```
tail -30c $INFORMIXDIR/archive.log
```

You'll see peek_arc used in the status script later that pulls many of these one-liner and other scripts together into a dashboard to look at the performance of the OnLine engine.

LOCATE AREAS OF HIGH DISK ACTIVITY

As you do such activities as archiving, you often want to get a feel not only for what percentage of the job is done, but also for exactly where in the database the program is now working. This is helpful in being able to predict how long something is going to take to complete as well as for getting a feeling for the performance of your system. As disk I/O is the slowest thing that your computer system does, you need to know where your disk input and output are occurring. We've shown a simple script called `hotspot` in the `tbtape -D` utility explanation earlier. Let's gussy it up a little and make it a little more useful. The new script is called `watch_hot`.

```
INFORMIX 75> cat watch_hot
#!/bin/csh
while ( 1 == 1)

$INFORMIXDIR/bin/tbstat -z
sleep 5
$INFORMIXDIR/bin/tbstat -D | grep /
end
```

There are not many changes from `hotspot`, but this script continues until you press BREAK or CONTROL-C, zeroes the statistics between each run, and shows you only the relevant chunk information. You can change the sleep period to whatever you like if you want to use `watch_hot` for a while and monitor your disk activity. As in the `hotspot` script, remember that the `tbstat -z command` will zero out the performance statistics each time it is run (every five seconds in this case).

If you have some programs that are monitoring the statistics, this will no doubt interfere with them. Don't confuse the statistics maintained to monitor performance with the statistics maintained in the UPDATE STATISTICS command in SQL. They are two entirely separate sets of statistics.

TELL IF CONTINUOUS BACKUP OF LOGFILES IS RUNNING

For many applications, it is wise to have the added security of continuous backup of logfiles to tape. If you're running a database with logging, it is very important to stay on top of freeing up logfiles. The best way to do this is to have `tbtape -s` running as much as possible. Even if you are using mirrored devices to hold your chunks, you need to think in terms of avoiding a single point of exposure to failure. This means running archives to tape regularly and it means backing up your logfiles to tape regularly. It also means physically separating the tapes from the computer. All of the redundancy and fault tolerance in the world won't save you if your computer room catches fire and everything in it burns.

If you have two tape devices available, it is possible to have continuous backup of logfiles running at all times. Note that I said possible, not recommended. Even with large tape backup devices, it is risky to backup your logfiles until the device fills. If you have a catastrophic tape error, it is possible that you could destroy hundreds of logs if you have a very large tape drive and had been running the logfile backup for a while. Why take the chance? Tape is cheap.

If you have only one tape drive available, you're forced to be conservative. You have to shut down continuous backup of logfiles to run your database archives. When you complete your archives, you have to put a log tape in the tape drive and restart the logging. This more or less forces you to swap log tapes at least once a day as a part of the archive/log cycle. Even if you have two tape drives, this is a good habit to get into. Plan on swapping out your log tapes at least daily, maybe more often if you have a very busy database. This also cuts down your exposure to massive data loss due to a bad tape. Once logfile data has been backed up to tape, it's lost to you. You can't undo it without restoring the database and re-applying logfiles. If you have backed up some logfiles to tape and find that the backup is questionable, do an archive immediately. It's the only way that you can ensure recovery.

If you are starting and stopping logfile backup or alternating archiving and logfile backup, you have the danger of human error. Someone may forget to start the logfile backup. Another point of exposure is errors on your tape device. If your tape device goes offline while continuous backup of logfiles is running, you will not always get notification in your online logfile. Here's where a script comes in handy to check to see if logging is still on. This script is called `logging`.

```
INFORMIX 94> cat logging

#/bin/csh
ps -efa  | grep "tbtape -c" | grep -v grep > /dev/null
if ($status == 0) then
set CONTINUOUS = "ON"
else
set CONTINUOUS = "OFF"
endif
echo $CONTINUOUS
```

The logging script is run with no parameters and returns either ON or OFF. You'll see it in the status dashboard script later. Closely kin to this is the archiving script that tells you whether or not an archive is running.

```
INFORMIX 95> cat archiving
#!/bin/csh
ps -efa  | grep "tbtape -s" | grep -v grep > /dev/null
if ($status == 0) then
set ARCHIVING == "ON"
else
set ARCHIVING == "OFF"
endif
echo $ARCHIVING
```

You'll find this script called in the status program also, in conjunction with the peek_arc script.

KILL A BACKEND

Informix OnLine versions earlier than 6.0 maintain a two-process architecture. Whenever a tool such as I-SQL or ESQL/C or I-4GL makes a request of the database, the tool is considered a client process. This client process spawns a server process that does the actual access to the database. This server process is called a "backend" process.

OnLine takes great pains to ensure the consistency of the data in the database. Whenever something occurs that could potentially destroy this consistency, OnLine will immediately abort. When the database is restarted, the fast recovery process will roll back any processes that are not completed and would therefore cause the inconsistency.

One of the major actions that can cause the database to become inconsistent is the premature death of a backend process. If a backend is killed before it has the chance to ensure the consistency of the database, it can abort the entire database and cause a database crash. There are two specific instances in which a prematurely killed backend can cause an abort:

- The backend dies while in a critical section (writing to the database)
- The backend dies while holding a latch.

You can't depend on being able to look at a tbstat output to see whether or not these circumstances apply. By the time you try to kill the process, the circumstances may have changed.

This means that you should *never, never, never use a kill -9 on a backend*! Did I make my point? Sometimes you can get away with it. There may even be occasions where you go ahead and break this rule, hoping that you'll dodge a bullet and be able to kill the backend without aborting the database. If you do ignore it, be prepared for crashing the system. Use the kill -9 command only as a last resort.

Why would you want to kill a backend? Many times, a user has started a query and then realizes that she is joining every table in your database with every other one and the query should generate a few billion rows. Maybe someone has started an update that was wrong and will destroy your biggest database table. Maybe someone's killed a client process and the server process is still running. There are many reasons why you may be tempted to kill a query. Sometimes it's best just to let the query continue to run if it will not destroy a table or eat up a lot of system resources. If the query is running from within isql, it is usually possible to press the BREAK or CONTROL-C key and gracefully stop the query. That's usually the user's first option.

Assuming that you've determined that a query should be terminated, how do you kill a backend properly? The recommended method is with the following command:

```
tbmode -z PID_OF_THE_BACKEND_PROCESS
```

The tbmode -z command usually succeeds in killing the process. After running the tbmode -z command , run tbstat -u. The entry for the process should be gone or should have an R in the second position of the flags field. This indicates that the process is being rolled back. If this is not the case, try the tbmode command several times. If the query is still cranking away, it's time for a few more desperate measures. Try

```
kill -15 PID_OF_THE_BACKEND_PROCESS
kill -13 PID_OF_THE_BACKEND_PROCESS
```

These UNIX kills are caught properly by the engine and are safe, posing no danger to your database. Like the tbmode command, try them several times if needed. You may need to change user to root to get the appropriate permissions to kill the backends. Again, check the tbstat -u output to see if the processes are dead or in rollback.

There are some processes that seem to be unkillable. Anything that is creating an index will be unkillable. UPDATE STATISTICS commands seem to be unkillable. Many of these unkillable processes are so deep into their programming loops that they are not checking their global `killflags` that the signal sets in the backend. Be patient in trying to kill with a `kill -15` or a `kill -13`. The processes may not go away immediately.

There's one final method of killing a `sqlturbo` process. This is definitely a last-ditch effort. When you do it, be ready to crash the system because it is definitely dangerous. Informix Technical Support doesn't even acknowledge the existence of the technique. They certainly don't recommend it. I don't even recommend it. But if you're faced with having to bring down a production database to kill a job and you've tried everything else short of a `kill -9`, what do you have to lose?

This method depends upon your flavor of UNIX having some kind of process control. Do a `man` on `kill` and look for some sort of kill that will halt a process in the same way that the CONTROL-Z key halts it for process control. If you can't find it in the `man` page, try running a `kill -l` to list the options. Also, look for the reciprocal command that re-starts the stopped job. On my Pyramid, the stop command is `kill - STOP PID` and the restart command is `kill -CONT PID`, where `PID` is the UNIX process ID of the process you want to kill.

The problem with trying to use `tbstat` information to decide whether or not you can safely kill a process is that `tbstat` is instantaneous and that your process may either ac-quire a latch or enter a critical phase in the time it takes you to read the `tbstat` output and execute your `kill` statement. To do this safely, you have to stop the process completely, check it with `tbstat` while it is stopped, and then either do your `kill` or restart the proc-ess and stop it again, checking each time to see if the stopped process is safe to kill.

Run the `kill - STOP` command and continue running `ps` until the process is get-ting no more processor time. Then do a `tbstat -u`. Look to see if the third position of the flag field is anything but an X, which indicates that the job is not in a critical section, writing to the database. Note the value of the first column, which is the address of the user process. Now look at the last column of the `tbstat -s` output, which tells you the owner of any latches. Does your offending process own a latch? If it doesn't, and if it's not in a critical section in the `tbstat -u` output, and if the process really is stopped, kill the process with a `kill -9`. If it is in a critical section or if it's holding a latch, run the `kill -CONT` or whatever command restarts the process, let it run a while, and repeat the process. If you can stop the process when it's in a safe status, you have a decent chance of killing it without harm.

Remember, this is a last-ditch measure. Although I have used it for several years without harm to the database, I've seen stranger things happen to databases. I would use this only if I were prepared to restart the database from a crash and to recover from an archive. About the only thing that would justify it is if a process is destroying a table that, if the table were gone, I would have to recover from tape anyway.

IDENTIFY TEMPORARY TABLES

Temporary tables are created in the OnLine system either explicitly or implicitly. Explicit temporary tables are created with the CREATE TEMP TABLE or the SELECT ... INTO TEMP ... command variants in SQL. Implicit temporary tables are created by the engine in the process of executing certain queries. None of these temporary tables ever receives an entry in any of the system tables, and thus it is difficult to see exactly what is going on with temporary tables.

These temporary tables are stored in the `rootdbs` dbspace unless they have been explicitly created in another dbspace. The `rootdbs` is always the first dbspace in an OnLine system, and its dbspace number is 1. Since the high-order bit of the `tblnum` output in `tbstat -t` represents the number of the dbspace, all default temporary tables will have a `tblnum` beginning with 1.

For versions of OnLine greater than 3.3, sorting is no longer done in the `rootdbs`. In these later versions, sorting is done in the directory identified by the $DBTEMP variable, in `/tmp` if $DBTEMP is not set, or in the directories specified in $PSORT_DBTEMP if you are using the parallel sorting option, PSORT. The only table that should normally reside in the `rootdbs` is the `tablespace tablespace`, which is identified with a final 1 in the `tblnum`. Thus 1000001 identifies the only non-temp table in the `rootdbs` in the default installation. Any other tables beginning with 1 should be temporary tables.

This is assuming that you are not placing ordinary databases and tables in the `rootdbs`. For maximum flexibility you should not be placing data in the `rootdbs`. The `rootdbs` is the only dbspace that cannot be dropped. If you have your databases located other than in `rootdbs`, you can always rebuild the dbspace on a larger device should your needs change. If you have tables in `rootdbs`, you lose this flexibility. As long as you have your initial three logfiles in `rootdbs` and as long as your physical logfile is in `rootdbs`, you probably don't want to add to the I/O load there anyway.

IDS allows you to designate the location for your temporary files. In many cases, it will make sense to place your temporary files in a separate dbspace custom designed to hold the temporary tables. Again, for flexibility, having them in anywhere but `rootdbs` will give you more options. If you are not yet on 6.0, you may want to go ahead and set up a dbspace for temporary files and build your explicit temporary files with the IN DBSPACE option to place them in the correct dbspace. This will allow you to have a somewhat easier transition to 6.0.

Temporary tables are deleted when the SQL statement that has created them is finished or when the database initializes. When a system crash occurs, the SQL statements do not complete and temporary tables can remain. It is possible to initialize OnLine with a `tbinit -r` command that tells the engine not to bother removing temporary tables. This may make the database initialization somewhat faster, but it runs the risk of leaving temporary tables lying around when they are not in use. I know of no way to actually use the data that's in these zombie tables.

KNOW WHEN SYSTEM IS IN A CHECKPOINT

Checkpoints can be disruptive to your users in that some user processing is halted during a checkpoint. Depending upon how long the checkpoint takes, users may experience a temporary "freeze" in their activities. Often, these users will call the DBA with a complaint that "the database is down" as soon as one of their queries gets delayed. It's handy for the DBA to have a quick script that lets her know the checkpoint status. This script is called checkpoint.

```
INFORMIX 37>  cat checkpoint
#!/bin/csh
$INFORMIXDIR/bin/tbstat -
echo Current time is: `date`
grep Checkpoint `grep MSGPATH ${INFORMIXDIR}/etc/${TBCONFIG} |
awk '{print $2}' ` | tail -5
```

This script is also useful in monitoring the frequency of your checkpoints. If you find that your checkpoints are coming too close together, you should consider retuning the database to provide longer times between checkpoints.

Actually, any of the tbstat invocations will include the header that gives the checkpoint status, but the simple minus option gives only the header. The grep statement in line 3 is a little more complicated than usual because we are picking up the value of $TBCONFIG and getting the message file name from the $TBCONFIG file rather than hard coding it into the script. This makes it possible to report on various OnLine instances just by making sure that the $TBCONFIG is set for the proper instance. This technique of getting data from the $TBCONFIG file rather than hard-coding it into the script is a useful programming technique if you are running multiple instances of OnLine.

MONITOR AND REPORT ON TABLE SIZES

Tables in an OnLine database seem to take on a life of their own, especially in a heavily used system with many developers. It is a twofold problem. First, there's the problem of proliferation of tables. This will be addressed later in a table warehouse program.

The second part of the space problem concerns the growth of existing tables. In other sections, we have seen various programs for performing data archiving and table cleaning, but to do any of these, the DBA needs to know where the problem lies. We need a way to track the size and space utilization of tables.

At first glance, this seems to be an easy task. Just write a report that looks at the system catalogs. There are a couple of problems to this, the main one being that the data in `systables` is not always accurate. The system catalogue `systables` has a field called `npdata` that nominally contains the number of pages used by the table. However, this table is updated only when the SQL statement UPDATE STATISTICS is run. On top of that, even when update statistics is run, the number in `npdata` is not always accurate. It seems to be an approximation.

There are only two reliable ways to get the accurate data that actually represents the real utilization of the disk. This involves using the OnLine utilities `tbstat` or `tbcheck`.

The `tbstat -t` output contains a column called `npages`. This is an accurate number and represents the actual number of pages on the disk that are currently allocated to the table and to all of its indexes. Some of these pages may be empty, but it doesn't matter. The table still has these pages allocated. The data about a table only shows up in `tbstat -t` if the table is in use when the utility is run. One way to do this is to do an `isql` retrieve from the menu on one terminal while running a `tbstat` on another. This is fine for one time checks but is not practical for compiling reports.

Another source of accurate data is `tbcheck -pt`. The output from this utility has a row called `Number of pages allocated` that gives an accurate page count. However, this utility has two drawbacks. The first is that it places a lock on the target table and prevents users from updating the table. This is even more disruptive because the report for a table of significant size can take a while to complete, keeping it locked for a longer period of time. This can be overcome, but not without manual intervention. The information that you want appears quickly after the utility is started. As soon as you see the data you want, you can break out of the utility by pressing CONTROL-C. You will not keep the table locked for long. The main problem, however, is the same as with the `tbstat` command. It doesn't lend itself well to creating reports.

The solution for running reports lies in the `tbcheck -pe` utility. This utility does not lock tables, so it can be run at any time without disrupting access to the database. It does have a few drawbacks, but they can be handled. The first drawback is that the output from `tbcheck -pe` uses a significant amount of space. The second drawback is that the data is arranged in the form of an extent-by-extent report and does not provide summary data for tables. If you've read this far, you can probably expect that the next thing we see will be a script that massages the data.

Actually, we'll be doing something a little more complicated here. Since the extent data can be useful, we'll create our own system table and keep the extent data there. First, create a database called `dba` (or whatever you want to call it, or even keep it in `rootdbs` if you insist). Place the following table `extent_sizes`, in the database:

```
create table extent_sizes
{database char(8),
owner char(8),
tabname char(20) not null,
extents decimal(7,1),
```

```
dbspace char(12) );
revoke all on extent_sizes from "public";
create index ext_tabname on extent_sizes (tabname);
```

The program that runs the tbcheck, massages the data, and then loads it back into the extent_sizes table is called last_table_sizes.

```
INFORMIX 92> cat last_table_sizes
$INFORMIXDIR/bin/tbcheck -pe >! $INFORMIXDIR/last_tbcheckpe
cat $INFORMIXDIR/last_tbcheckpe | /bin/grep : | /bin/grep -v Chunk: | /bin/grep -v WARNING |
/bin/grep -v SAM | /bin/awk '\
BEGIN      {FS = " "} \
/DBSpace/ {dbspace = $4;next} \
{printf("%s  %s\n",$0,dbspace)} ' \
| awk '{print $1,$3,$4}' | /usr/bin/tr ":" "|" | /usr/bin/tr "." "|" | tr -s " " " " | tr " "
"|" > $INFORMIXDIR/tempsizes
$INFORMIXDIR/bin/isql dba << EOF
DELETE FROM dba:extent_sizes;
LOAD FROM "tempsizes" INSERT INTO dba:extent_sizes;
SELECT database,owner[1,3],tabname,dbspace, count(*) as extents, sum(extents) as pages FROM
extent_sizes GROUP BY database,owner[1,3],tabname,dbspace ORDER BY pages desc;
EOF
/bin/rm $INFORMIXDIR/tempsizes
```

A few notes about the last_table_sizes script are in order. The second section beginning with cat $INFORMIXDIR/last_tbcheckpe is one long pipeline. Where it hits an end-of-line, use the backslash (\ ) to continue the line. None of the punctuation here is a backtick (`). This script uses just single and double quotes.

The final section is an isql command that first cleans out all of the rows of extent_sizes and then repopulates the table using a load from the destination of the long pipeline above. The report goes to standard output. If you wish, you can put the script in your cron file to run every night. If so, use a command like this.

```
$INFORMIXLOCALBIN/last_table_sizes > $INFORMIXDIR/last_table_sizes &
```

The resulting report looks like this.

```
database owner tabname        dbspace        extents        pages
admin    dba   loader_data    slowdbspace       17        210795.0
admin    dba   vmx_config     dbspace1          12        135349.0
admin    dba   person_addr    dbspace1          28        127767.0
admin    dba   mem_grp_code   dbspace1          14         82542.0
admin    dba   ticket_desc    dbspace1          41         71839.0
admin    dba   access_pre     dbspace1           6         67556.0
```

If you wish, you can then delete the last_tbcheckpe file, but if you can afford the space, leave it around. This file, if updated daily, can provide much valuable information about the general layout of your system. You can get valuable space utilization data as well as table fragmentation information by looking at the file.

Another good thing to do in your `cron` file is to move the `last_table_sizes` file into an archive directory before creating the new one. You can then do a UNIX `zip` or a `compress` on the old file if you wish. Keeping the `last_table_sizes` data around for a while can let you track and report on table and extent growth over a period of time. This sort of data is most helpful when you are trying to forecast future database needs. I keep the data around for a year and have written INFORMIX-WingZ programs to extract the data and draw impressive charts and graphs of table size growth. This is great when you're going to management requesting more hardware!

While the `last_table_sizes` report gives you useful information in terms of absolute number of extents and number of pages, it is often good to get this information in percentages. This lets you answer questions such as "What percentage of my database does table XXX occupy?" Since we have now gone to the trouble of building and populating a table with extent sizes in it, and updating it nightly, why not get a little more mileage out of the data?

The `last_percentage` script is very similar to `last_table_sizes`, with the exception that this scripts that the `extent_sizes` table is already populated.

```
INFORMIX 99> cat last_percentage
$INFORMIXDIR/bin/isql dba << EOF
SELECT database, owner, tabname,dbspace[1,8], count(*) as extents , sum(extents)/26165  as
percent
FROM dba:extent_sizes
GROUP BY database, owner, tabname,dbspace[1,8]
ORDER BY percent desc
EOF
```

This script gives you the following report:

database	owner	tabname	dbspace	extents	percent
admin	dba	loader_data	slowdbsp	17	8.06
admin	dba	vmx_config	dbspace1	12	5.17
admin	dba	person_addr	dbspace1	28	4.88
admin	dba	mem_grp_code	dbspace1	14	3.15
admin	dba	ticket_desc	dbspace1	41	2.75

You will need to make one change in the script to customize it to your environment, or change the script to handle this automatically. The SELECT statement divides the `sum(extents)` by 26,165 in my sample. Your number will be different. Do a `tbstat -d` and look at the chunk data. Add up all of the `size` columns for chunks that you want to consider as the total available. Divide this number by 100 and use the result instead of 26,165. You may want to exclude your `rootdbs` and logfile chunks as not being available for use. You may also want to play a little with the figures to give you some "fluff factor." Users are going to scarf up any amount of space you have. You might want to keep a little bit hidden.

Sometimes, you want information similar to that from the `table` script, only with information about the actual space utilization. The following `tabuse` script simply runs the UNIX `grep` command against the `last_tbcheckpe` file:

```
INFORMIX 43>  cat tabuse
#
#tabuse
echo " "
echo "ACTUAL DISK USAGE REPORT FOR TABLES IN ALL DATABASES"
echo This data is as of:  `ls -la $INFORMIXDIR/last_table_sizes | cut -c 32-44`  based on the
$INFORMIXDIR/last_table_size file
echo " \
database owner tabname            dbspace        extents          2K pages"
echo "name                                       used             used"
echo \ "======================================================================="
echo " "
grep $1 $INFORMIXDIR/last_table_sizes
```

The spacing of the echo statements may need to be adjusted if you are typing the program into your system. Just put in or take out some spaces to make it line up correctly on your terminal. Depending on your UNIX version, you may also need to alter the cut statement. Adjust the columns until the cut returns only the date.

This script does not provide real-time data. If you have your `last_table_sizes` script running in `cron`, tell your users to look at the top line of the `tabuse` output to see when the `last_tbcheckpe` file was generated.

Since we're using a `grep` statement, you can invoke the script by typing the command `tabuse any_fragment` where `any_fragment` is any text that can be found on a line in the `last_tbcheckpe` file. Thus, you could query by table name, table name fragment, database, owner, or dbspace.

This can be a useful utility. It's an example of a general method of doing things that would otherwise be very difficult or take a lot of time. In cases where real-time data is not absolutely critical, generate a work file for the data during a slow period and query the work file during heavy use periods.

FIGHT TABLE PROLIFERATION

If your users and developers have resource privileges on the database, you will find that you are constantly having to play "table janitor." It's funny how tables named `temp_XXX` are never really temporary and how tables that were going to hang around for "just a coupla' days" become institutionalized as part of your database.

What we need is a tool that will allow the DBA to monitor the tables in a database, know what should be there and what shouldn't be there, and notify the DBA when certain tables should be removed.

This is a situation that is quite common to UNIX system administrators. Any time that you have a community of users who are utilizing common resources, you have to deal with resource hogs. While many users are quite diligent about taking out their trash, there are many others who are pack rats. "I never saw a table I didn't like," seems to be their motto. Whether or not you are able to enforce some level of control over this situation depends on how much actual leeway you have in removing other people's tables.

You can send e-mail harassing and whining to the users about removing old tables, and you'll probably get fairly decent results. Nobody's out there just to fill up your database. The only problem is that you will be forced to be the police, and frankly, you have better things to do.

The UNIX system administrators solve this problem by having "file eater" daemons that automatically delete old files. The users know that these file eaters are there and they know how to protect their important files, but they have to take affirmative action to do it. The responsibility is on the users, not on the administrator. Here is a method of doing the same thing with OnLine tables.

The basis of this "table warehouse" is a database table that establishes ownership and longevity for all tables in your database. This table is called `auth_tables` and is in your dba database. It is designed to join with the various `systables` in each of your user databases, with the join being on two fields, `tabname` and `owner`. These fields should be unique within each database and will uniquely identify tables. Create the `auth_tables` table using this SQL script:

```
INFORMIX 1>cat mk_auth.sql
create table auth_tables
   (
tabname char(18),
owner char(8),
database char(8),
good_til datetime year to day,
user char(10),
application char(10)
   );
revoke all on auth_tables from "public";
create index auth_tables_x1 on auth_tables(tabname,owner);
```

The `tabname` and `owner` fields are identical to their counterparts in `systables`. This is where the tables join. The `good_til` column is a "drop-dead date" for a particular table. When a user creates a table that should remain in the database, the user must register the table information with you. The user field should be the person who takes responsibility for the table, not necessarily the owner in `systables`. The application should be the name of the application or module that uses the table. If the table is temporary, the user should give you a good_til date at which time the table can be removed. Tables that are permanent should have a date far out in the future, like 3000-12-31. Users should be taught that any table that is not registered in the auth_tables table is subject to immediate deletion after one publication of its table name in a warning e-mail message to everyone.

You may wish to be a little more lenient with unregistered tables. If you can identify the owner of an unregistered table, you may wish to modify the scripts to send them an e-mail message. If a table is not registered, you will not have a good_til, a user, or an application field, since you don't have an entry in the auth_tables database. If the table is not registered, you will have to make do with the owner name in systables. If your system does not enforce individual table ownership, the only way that you can notify an anonymous owner or user of a table is by an e-mail posting to all users.

There are several ways that you can initially populate your auth_tables database. If you are just beginning with OnLine, you can develop a system in which all tables that go into the database must be manually registered with you. If you have an existing application, put together a group and do a thorough cleaning of your database, getting rid of all the junk. Then go into the individual systables tables in each database and insert the tabname, owner, and database name into auth_tables. You may have to make several tries at it, but try to get all of the "legal" core tables identified as fully as possible with user, application, and good_til entries as appropriate. The following ACE form oktables should be helpful. Note that this is just a default form on auth_tables with headings added.

```
INFORMIX 3>cat oktables.per
database dba
screen size 24 by 80
{

Authorized Tables in the Database
tabname         [f000                  ]
owner           [f001     ]
database        [f002     ]
good_til        [f003       ]
user            [f004       ]
application     [f005       ]

}
end
tables
auth_tables
attributes
f000 = auth_tables.tabname;
f001 = auth_tables.owner;
f002 = auth_tables.database;
f003 = auth_tables.good_til;
f004 = auth_tables.user;
f005 = auth_tables.application;
end
```

Compile this form and use it to get all of your legitimate forms registered in your `auth_tables` table. Now the task is to create reports that show you which tables are candidates for execution. Since we are going to kill these tables, I've chosen a good Texas term for them, "outlaws." That's the name of the report script.

```
INFORMIX 4>cat outlaws
#
if ( $#argv == 0 ) then
set database = "admin"    <------You need to change this to your default
endif
if ( $#argv == 1 ) then
set database = ${1}
endif
$INFORMIXDIR/bin/isql $database << EOF
SELECT
systables.tabname,
systables.owner,
systables.created,
systables.nrows,
systables.npused * 2048 as bytes

FROM      systables, OUTER dba:auth_tables

WHERE     systables.tabname = dba:auth_tables.tabname AND
          systables.owner   = dba:auth_tables.owner   AND
                              systables.tabid > 99     AND
systables.tabtype = "T" AND
systables.tabname not in (select tabname from
dba:auth_tables where good_til > current)
and systables.tabname not matches "rev_*"
and systables.tabname not matches "access*"
and systables.tabname not matches "usage*"
and systables.tabname not matches "a_*"
and systables.tabname not matches "tmp_*"
and systables.tabname not matches "crev*"
ORDER by bytes desc
EOF
```

This script has a few things that are specifically designed for my database applications that you will need to change to fit your needs. First, you can invoke the script with or without a database name. If it is invoked without a database name, it defaults to my main database, `admin`. Of course, you'll need to change this. Based upon some of our earlier scripts, you may remember that the `npages` field in `systables` is not necessarily an accurate count of real size, but it is close enough. I just want to be able to tell the users in a general way how much space this table takes up. I have this number multiplied by 2048 for a 2K page size. If your system uses 4K, change the script. All of the SQL statements that are connected by AND are required. At the end, you see several statements that are connected by "and." These are optional and are local to my system. In my system, we have many tables that are legitimate but can be identified by the first characters in the name. The rest of the name is dependent upon the process ID that created the tables. These last SQL clauses cause these "wild card" table names to be accepted as legitimate tables. If you want to get fancy, you could put these names in a table and do the exceptions from fragments of names from the table. It's easier the way I did it. The `outlaws` script gives you a report similar to this:

```
INFORMIX 50>outlaws
tabname           owner    created        nrows         bytes

ry_invoice_def    rodney   10/06/1993     24600        3149824
zip_xref          dba      03/28/1993     43635        2078720
djcmv3            support  01/08/1994      2474         362496
conn11024         chris    01/17/1994      2024         188416
```

One of the drawbacks (or features, depending on whether you wrote it or I wrote it) to `outlaws` is that it must be run for each database. If you wanted to run it once for all of your databases, you could use our old friend `find_db_names`. Write a short script called `find_all_outlaws`, and run it with no parameters. The reports will be placed in files called `XXXXX.outlaws`, where XXXXX is the name of each of your databases.

```
INFORMIX> cat find_all_outlaws

foreach database (`$INFORMIXLOCALBIN/find_db_names`)
echo "`date`:  OUTLAWS REPORT for database: $database" >! ${database}.outlaws
$INFORMIXDIRLOCALBIN/outlaws $database >> ${database}.outlaws
endScript
```

THE STATUS SCRIPT

In this chapter, we've seen a lot of individual scripts and programs that enable the DBA to deal with different parts of the database. Now, it's time to pull them together and create a "dashboard" for the OnLine system.

Of all the tools that come with OnLine, there is nothing that provides a quick, one-page peek into the engine. Various invocations of `tbstat` will allow you to look at individual items, but nothing gives you a quick status report. If the OnLine system is a database engine, certainly there should be a dashboard. Like a dashboard, the `status` script gives you or your users one place to look for indications of current problems or problems to come.

This script depends upon having other scripts located in your `$INFORMIXDIR/local_bin` directory. It requires the following scripts:

- logging
- archiving
- thislog
- dbdf

Here is the code for the `status` script:

```
INFORMIX 103>  cat status
#!/bin/csh
clear
set INFORMIXLOCALBIN = "$INFORMIXDIR/local_bin"
echo "Please wait....."
set list = ( `$INFORMIXDIR/bin/tbstat -p | fgrep -v e` )
set dskreads = $list[1]
set pagreads = $list[2]
set bufreads = $list[3]
set readcache = $list[4]
set dskwrits = $list[5]
set pagwrits = $list[6]
set bufwrits = $list[7]
set writecache = $list[8]
set isamtot = $list[9]
set open = $list[10]
set start = $list[11]
set read = $list[12]
set write = $list[13]
set rewrite = $list[14]
set delete = $list[15]
set commit = $list[16]
set rollbk = $list[17]
set ovtbls = $list[18]
set ovlock = $list[19]
set ovuser = $list[20]
set ovbuff = $list[21]
set usercpu = $list[22]
set syscpu = $list[23]
set numckpts = $list[24]
set flushes = $list[25]
set bufwaits = $list[26]
set lokwaits = $list[27]
set lokreqs = $list[28]
set deadlks = $list[29]
set dltouts = $list[30]
set lchwaits = $list[31]
set ckpwaits = $list[32]
set compress = $list[33]

if ( $lokwaits > 0 ) then
@ lokhold  =  ( $lokwaits * 100  ) / $lokreqs
@ lokfigure = 100 - $lokhold
else
@ lokfigure = 100
endif
if ( $lchwaits > 0 ) then
@ lchhold =  ( $lchwaits * 100 ) / $isamtot
@ lchfigure = 100 - $lchhold
else
@ lchfigure = 100
endif
fgrep Checkpoint $INFORMIXDIR/online.log | tail -6 >! ~/temp_stat
#ps - efa > ~/tempjobs
ps -a > ~/tempjobs
@ NUMBERFULL = `$INFORMIXDIR/bin/tbstat -l | grep -v RSAM | grep U | wc -l`
endif
@ cpunum = `echo $syscpu | awk -F. '{print $1}'`
@ usernum = `echo $usercpu | awk -F. '{print $1}'`
```

```
if ( $cpunum == 0 ) then
@ cpunum = 1
endif
@ ratio = $usernum / $cpunum
echo "\
INFORMIX STATUS:COMPUTER NAME:    TIME: `date` \
`$INFORMIXDIR/bin/tbstat -` \
CPU UTILIZATION: \
`uptime` \
\
RATIOS: READ CACHE   WRITE CACHE   LOCK HIT%   LATCH HIT%   USER/SYSTEM\
        $readcache            $writecache          $lokfigure           $lchfigure
        ${ratio}-1 \
WAITS: CHECKPOINTS    BUFFERS          DEADLOCKS     \
          $ckpwaits            $bufwaits                $deadlks "
echo "\
LOGS:  There are now ${NUMBERFULL} log(s) in use.  This includes the current log:\
`$INFORMIXLOCALBIN/thislog`"
echo "\
\
CHECKPOINTS:  The last six checkpoints occurred as follows:\
`cat ~/temp_stat | sed 's/Checkpoint Completed/  /g'`"
echo \
=======================================================================
echo -n "  CONTINUOUS BACKUP OF LOG FILES: `$INFORMIXLOCALBIN/logging`   ARCHIVE:
`$INFORMIXLOCALBIN/archiving` "
echo  " "
sh $INFORMIXLOCALBIN/dbdf

$INFORMIXDIR/bin/tbstat -d  >! ~/temphold99
fgrep PD ~/temphold99 > /dev/null

if ($status == 0) then
echo "CAUTION:  A CHUNK IS DOWN"
endif
rm ~/temp_stat* ~/temphold* ~/tempjobs*
echo " "
```

This script is designed to be relatively portable across systems. I've avoided hard coding anything into the system, with the exception of some of the code in the dbdf script that excludes page usage in my logspaces. Since the logfiles are preallocated, the space usage does not vary. You may or may not want to see the data.

The screen output looks like this:

```
Please wait.....
INFORMIX STATUS:COMPUTER NAME: batman  TIME: Fri Jan 21 15:40:11 CST 1994
RSAM Version 4.10.UD4   -- On-Line -- Up 3 days 17:41:18 -- 18704 Kbytes
CPU UTILIZATION:
3:40pm  up 3 days, 17:46,  79 users,  load average: 12.94, 13.50, 13.27
RATIOS: READ CACHE   WRITE CACHE   LOCK HIT%   LATCH HIT%   USER/SYSTEM
             98.39          97.10        100          100        9-1
WAITS: CHECKPOINTS       BUFFERS               DEADLOCKS
           125            9941                     5

LOGS:  There are now 2 log(s) in use.  This includes the current log:
e06d26f0 11      U---C-L  3214      70f4f4      30000     13435    44.78
```

```
CHECKPOINTS:  The last six checkpoints occurred as follows:
12:59:42     13:31:53     14:04:41     14:22:41     14:56:41     15:33:37
=========================================================================
  CONTINUOUS BACKUP OF LOG FILES: OFF     ARCHIVE: OFF
rootdbs      is 37.34 percent full and has 167305 free pages
dbspace2     is 23.56 percent full and has 206379 free pages
dbspace1     is 89.84 percent full and has 166120 free pages
slowdbspace  is 92.90 percent full and has  61061 free pages
(Chunk down warning appears here if applicable)
```

The screen does tend to get a bit crowded. In fact, if you have more than four or five dbspaces in your system that are reported by the dbdf script, your report may scroll off the page. If this is the case, you could either reformat the screen output, taking out some of the blank lines that I put in for readability, or you could pipe the result through the UNIX more utility, which would allow the user to page through the output.

Understanding the Status Screen

The first four lines of the screen give you basic status and identifying information about the system. It includes the computer name (from the UNIX hostname utility, some UNIX versions may not have this utility) and the status date on the first line. The second line is the header from tbstat and tells you the RSAM version of OnLine, its status (online, offline, checkpoints), its uptime, and the size of its shared memory segment. The fourth line gives you the output from your UNIX uptime utility so that you can get a feel for the load on your system.

The RATIOS section gives you the read cache and write cache figures from tbstat -p. A well-tuned system will have 95+ percent for read and 85+ percent for write cache hit rates. The next two numbers are derived from tbstat -p output. The LOCK HIT % entry gives you the percentage of time that requests for locks were successful. It is calculated by this formula:

```
lock hit %  =   100  -  ( lock waits  x  100) /(lock requests)
```

This number should be close to 100 percent at all times. If this number begins to drop, it means that jobs are having to wait for locks to be released. Look for applications that are holding locks for too long or for problems with long transactions.

The LATCH HIT % statistic is similar to the LOCK HIT % statistic and shows you the number of times that latch requests were successful. There is no statistic available for the number of latch requests issued by the engine, so we used the statistics for the total number of ISAM calls. This gives a count of the number of database primitives that were executed. The formula for this calculation is

```
latch hit % =  100  -  ( latch waits x 100)/ (number of isam calls)
```

This number should also remain at 100 percent. If it starts to go down, look at contention for resources such as buffers, logfiles, etc.

The WAITS line tells you the actual number of times that processes had to wait for checkpoints to complete and for buffers to get free. Use this in conjunction with the LATCH HIT and LOCK HIT percentages if you begin to see slowdowns. The DEADLOCKS number gives the number of times that the engine has taken action to avoid a deadlock situation. This is not the number of times the engine has been deadlocked. Theoretically, a deadlock cannot happen. If your DEADLOCKS count is large, look to your applications. Jobs are failing and are being rolled back because of these potential deadlocks. You have a design error somewhere.

The LOGS lines give you a count of the number of logs that are not yet freed by being backed up to tape. This count also counts the number of logs that have been backed up but have not been released, because they hold information regarding uncommitted transactions. Watch the number of logs carefully. If it gets close to your total number of logfiles, you could be looking at a long transaction rollback. Check this screen to be sure that you have continuous backup of logfiles running. If it is running and if you have many logs in use, run a tbstat -u and look for transactions that have a lot of reads or writes. They are probably the long ones. The second LOGS line shows you the information about the CURRENT logfile. It is in the same format as the tbstat -l output.

The CHECKPOINTS lines show you the times of the last six checkpoints. If these checkpoints are closer together than you usually see, look for some jobs running that are causing a lot of logging. Long inserts and long deletes are a common culprit here. Unless you begin to get into logfile problems, there's not a lot that you can do. If you find that the checkpoints occur too frequently, you may need to tune the database.

The line immediately after the double lines gives you a quick status of your logging and archiving processes. If you are doing archives using the scripts in this section, you will be piping the output to the archive.log file. If so, when you are doing an archive, the percentage complete will appear after ARCHIVE. If not, it will just read ON or OFF. Continuous backup of logs will be a simple ON/OFF display.

The final section gives you dbspace by dbspace figures of percentage used and free pages. The final section will give you a warning about chunks that are offline if you have any. Note that this script does not consider mirroring chunks. If you are using Informix mirroring, you may wish to modify the script to show the mirror chunk data.

Common DBA Tasks

*T*here are many tasks that the DBA needs to be able to do on a regular basis, and that is what this chapter will cover.

INSTALLING AND SETTING UP ONLINE

At some point, you will need to be able to install and set up an Informix OnLine or IDS system. This will occur during an initial installation, during an installation on or upgrade to a new computer system, or during an upgrade to your existing system. As installations go, the Informix install process is usually relatively painless, but of course there are exceptions.

There seems to be a rule that software companies spend 20 quadrillion man years developing their products and about 10 minutes writing the install programs. Be very wary of all install programs, not only for Informix, but for all computer software. The rule seems to be uniform. If you have a chance, look at scripts before you run them, just to be sure that they don't do something stupid. Do this especially for upgrades. Install programs are often unclear about the extents they go to to preserve your existing data and environments. The better ones will warn you and ask your permission before making any modifications to anything critical. The worst ones will merrily blow away your data, configuration files, user files, and the like and not even bother to let you know what they've done.

Informix has gotten much better with the install programs for its Windows-based products. These install programs are very well thought out and for the most part will almost allow you to do a hands-off install. These install programs understand the relationships between the various Informix modules and will usually identify potential conflicts and give you guidance as to how to handle any unusual situations.

Luckily, Informix has a fairly robust set of install routines. In most cases, an upgrade will try to preserve existing data and environments. If the documentation does not make it clear, call Informix Technical Support. They may not, and probably will not, immediately know the answer, but they will research it for you.

In all cases, make a complete backup of your system before trying any type of installation procedure or upgrade. Back up your UNIX file system, making sure that you get all of your critical files. Do a complete, level 0 archive of your database, and back up all logfiles to tape. Don't scrimp or try to save time by not doing the backups. There's no such thing as a "safe" upgrade.

Maintaining a Logbook

A basic need common to all computer administration is the need to document and track the system configuration. Installation of software, changes to tuning parameters, changes or upgrades of the operating system, system crashes, and calls to support all need to be written down somewhere for future reference. Too often, the DBA gets so involved in solving the immediate problems that the job of documenting the problem gets a very low priority. A common train of thought is "Of course I'll remember what changes I'm making."

For the same reason that software must be rigorously documented, all of the primary and side issues of administering the database should be documented. Software that you install today may need to be reinstalled next year. You'll need the serial numbers, installation manuals, and software protection codes later. When you've discovered that something unusual has happened to your data two months ago and you're just now finding out about it, you'll want to know what types of tuning or database changes you made then. Some day you'll want to take a couple of weeks of vacation and let your assistant handle the database while you're gone. This person won't remember all of the things that you did. For all these reasons, you need to keep a logbook.

Computer people seem to want to try to do everything on the computer. That's why software developers can sell thousands of copies of home budget, recipe tracking, and videotape tracking programs that get used once or twice at the most. It's tempting to want to keep track of your database management activities using (surprise, surprise) the database.

Avoid this. Take the simple, low-tech approach. Use a physical logbook that you write in with a pen. (Try it, I'm sure it'll come back to you. It's the way you did it in elementary school.)

Make a big thing out of the logbook. Get a nicely bound book. Make it look good. You want something that gives you an incentive to use it and to keep it up. If you use some plain, ordinary notebook, you'll find yourself tearing pages out of it when you need to write down the plumber's phone number. The logbook is something you want to keep. Besides, if you make a production out of it, it'll be more convincing if you need to pull it out to convince a manager or a vendor that you know what you're talking about. True, it's a little thing, but little things count.

What should you keep in the logbook? At the very minimum, you need to have:

Telephone numbers	hardware and software vendors, service vendors, important staff members, facilities people (A/C, electrical, etc.), modem numbers for your incoming lines
Serial numbers	hardware, software (with key codes, too), O/S versions and revision levels version numbers of all installed software
Configuration data	disk layout documentation, mirroring and striping information, sample .profile or .cshrc files, scripts that set environment variables
Written procedures	startup and shutdown procedures, archive plan, logging procedures, emergency procedures, shutdown and startup procedures for applications, support policies, documentation for local utilities, location of full Informix manual set

Site-specific data	contents of your `tb/onconfig` file, `tb/onstat -a` output, `tb/oncheck -pe` output, `dbschema` output

For the most part, most of the items listed above are one-shot items. Sure, there's a lot of information to put together, but after it's done you'll only have to change it occasionally.

Other items need a running log that is more or less a system diary. These sections need to be added to as events happen. They need to be logged with a date and time.

Tuning changes	What parameters did you change? What were you trying to do? What was the result of the change? Is this a permanent change?
User complaints	What was the problem? Was it fixed? How? Is it a training issue?
System crashes	When did the system go down? Was there any data lost? What was the problem? How was it fixed?
Downtime	Was this scheduled or unscheduled downtime? Who was affected? How long was the system down? Who started it back up? Was there preventative maintenance done?
Support calls	Date and time of call to Informix Technical Support. Whom did you talk to? What was the case number they gave you? What did they recommend? Did it work? Is this a continuing problem? What was their response time?

Software changes   Full information about any new software
                        installed. Information on any upgrades
                        made.

This list is just the beginning of an outline, but you should get the general idea. This may be a pain to do right now, but when you find yourself with Informix licenses for 20 computers trying to figure out which versions are where and how to upgrade everyone to the same version, you'll be glad you took the time.

The Installation Procedure

Before you attempt an install or an upgrade, look through the documentation included with the software. Informix usually includes a booklet that details install procedures for the entire release set. These booklets are done by overall version of the product. Thus, if you have a 5.01 install, you may be installing a 5.01 engine and earlier, possibly 4.11 tools. There should be separate install booklets for the 5.01 and the 4.11 software. They'll probably say the same thing, but read through them to see if anything's different. You'll also get lots of registration forms and license forms. Put them aside and handle the paperwork later. You will, however, receive an envelope with the software serial number and installation key codes with each set of disks or tapes that make up one product. Be sure to keep track of which codes go with which products. I always try to write the serial number and key codes on the installation media. If you do this, be sure to maintain tight physical control over the media.

The booklets and distribution media will contain commands for loading the media. Take these with a grain of salt. The actual commands are probably right, as are the flags to the commands, but you'll probably have to do some interpretation of the device names. Just know the device names for your tape drives and/or floppy devices, and you'll get through it with no trouble.

UNIX Installs

It is very important that you have created the `informix` user and group properly. Check the installation booklet carefully to see if there are any restrictions on proper user or group numbers for `informix`. The instructions will tell you to place certain environmental variables such as `$INFORMIXDIR` into your environment. It's best to create the `informix` login first, then re-login as `informix`. You can check that you have the proper variables in place by using the UNIX `echo` command, as in `echo $INFORMIXDIR`. If the outputs are correct, you have the variables set correctly for your login. The actual installs are done as user `root`.

The actual installations usually follow a similar sequence of events.

1. Load the software as `root` in the `$INFORMIXDIR` directory.
2. Run the install script named `./installXXXX` (XXXX is the product name).

Running the install script usually consists of entering the software serial number and key code and then watching the install script move things into the proper places. Part of the process is *branding* the code, which is Informix's means of protecting its software from pirates. If for some reason the install doesn't go properly, it is usually better to reinstall from the installation medium. If something got branded improperly or didn't get done at all, you'll have problems in the future.

The order of installation is important in installing Informix products. Usually, the order is:

1. Install tools first (earliest versions first)
2. Install the engine
3. Install communications products like INFORMIX-Connect and INFORMIX-CLI.

A good mnemonic for remembering the order is TEN, for Tools, Engine, and Network. If you have any questions about the proper installation order, contact Informix Support for the latest information. With varying product families and varying versions, the TEN order does not always hold true, but it is a good place to start.

Be sure to completely install one product before you copy the media from the next product. The process should be copy media, run `install`, copy media, run `install`, etc.

After all of the products are on the disk and have been installed properly, you need to initialize the database. Initializing the database needs be done only once. If you are upgrading from a prior version, do not initialize the database. It will destroy all of your data if you do. Refer to the installation booklets for the initialization process, but I'll give you a few suggestions covering items that may not be clear in the documentation.

First, plan your install. Know which devices you are going to use for disk chunks. The best procedure for handling disk chunks is to create symbolic links to them. Don't ever use the full UNIX name for the devices. If you do, you will not be able to swap out those devices when they break. If you use links, you can simply replace a broken device with an equivalent one no matter what it is called. You then link the new device to the old device name and continue merrily on your way.

Make sure that all of these devices are owned by the `informix` user and that they have the proper access permissions. Informix is very picky about permissions, and the error messages are not always clear that they're complaining about permissions. In fact, if anything doesn't work correctly in the installation process, look at your permissions. If one of the install scripts did not complete properly, it may not have changed the permissions of the software correctly. If you already have a running engine, run a directory of all of the Informix code for future reference. There may be a time that you'll want to come back and compare your permissions with a known good system.

Also, be prepared to relink your kernel several times to get Informix to run properly. One common problem is with shared memory and semaphore limits. Have your UNIX system administrator (or the system administration manual) handy. It is a good idea to check the release notes after all of the software is installed but before you try to initialize the engine. These release notes are in the `$INFORMIXDIR/release` directory. In later IDS systems supporting Global Language Support (GLS), these release notes will be found further down in this directory tree divided into subdirectories based upon locales and GLS options. If your machine's release requires any special kernel parameters, they will be found in a file called `*ONLINE*`. Go through everything in the release notes directory. It'll save you a lot of time down the line

Windows NT Installs

As mentioned earlier, Informix has gotten much more sophisticated with the install programs for the Windows-based products. Most of these programs now come on CD-ROM, and the install often consists mainly of sticking the CD-ROM into the drive and letting Windows run it automatically. If Windows does not automatically run the CD-ROM, change over to it and look for either an "install.exe" or a "setup.exe" program. Run that program, answer a few questions, enter your serial number and key code, and you're off and running.

Pay particular attention to the requirements for Windows service packs. These are occasional operating system patches released by Microsoft. If the engine requires a particular service pack, be sure that it is installed on your system.

If this is an upgrade, the install program will usually recognize that you have existing Informix products and will ask you whether you want to just reinstall the product, reinstall and reconfigure it, or reinstall and reinitialize it. Be sure that you are certain what you are doing. It's always pretty scary when you are doing an upgrade and you don't know whether the install program will blow away all of your existing data. The install is actually pretty forgiving of this, but be careful.

If you want to take a "belt and suspenders" approach to doing a reinstall on an existing IDS system on NT, copy the rootdbs file over to a file with another name. Even safer is to rename the subdirectory in which the rootdbs resides. That way, even if the install program mistakenly chooses to reinitialize the database, you can recover from it. To be totally safe, take a copy of your ONCONFIG file before starting the upgrade also.

Versions of IDS on NT prior to 7.30 do not give you the option of setting up your chunks on raw disks. I've actually seen very little cost in performance to using the NTFS filesystem for your dbspaces. One thing that using the NTFS disk files gives you is some very tricky disaster recovery options. All of the information about chunk names, disk locations, chunk sizes, and dbspace locations is kept in the rootdbs. The only thing that refers to the location of the rootdbs is the ONCONFIG file. This means that as long as your ONCONFIG file is intact and as long as the rootdbs and other database disk files are in the same locations on the same drives as before, you can recover from many kinds of disaster.

As an example, I was doing an upgrade from 7.23 IDS to 7.30 IDS on NT and ran into problems because of some services that would not disappear (ISM storage manager services, and I still haven't figured it out). Due to some ill-advised monkeying with the registry and the attempt to manually delete some program files, I was trapped in a Catch-22 situation. I couldn't use the commands to uninstall properly, because I had deleted needed files. I couldn't install properly, because the services wouldn't go away. But I did have a 7.23 engine running on another system on the network. I didn't want to try to reinstall the old version for fear of destroying my existing data.

I copied the ONCONFIG file into the $INFORMIXDIR\bin directory on the new server and created a parallel directory structure for the rootdbs alongside the directory holding the rootdbs of the working server, only in a subdirectory with the same name that the broken rootdbs came from. I then used NT drive mapping to map the drives on the old machine to the same drive names on the new machine. When I was finished, the working machine had the ONCONFIG file from the broken machine (the good ONCONFIG was appropriately saved) as well as the identical drive structure and file locations as the broken machine had had. The files were actually the same files as before on the broken machine, only mapped over to the new machine. When I restarted IDS on the nonbroken machine, everything came up properly and I was able to do a dbexport of the broken database. (I know, I should have done it before trying the upgrade, but I was getting complacent.) I was then able to completely rebuild the broken server and reimport the data. I had done something similar to this once before after changing the computer name of an NT machine running an IDS server. Don't ever rename the computer that holds an IDS server. If you do, you will have to reinstall all the software and reconfigure the system. The computer name is imbedded deep inside the Informix system, and changing the name is a major operation. Also, keep the name of the NT machine short and simple (fewer than 8 characters), and don't use a dash anywhere in the name. IDS has problems with this.

Since Informix uses the NT and Windows 95 registry extensively, don't attempt to deinstall Informix products on these platforms without running the uninstall programs that are included with the products. These uninstall programs will clear out the proper registry entries as well as remove icons and menu items from the Windows environment.

DESIGNING THE DATABASE

Once your system is correctly installed and running properly, the job becomes one of deciding how to structure and organize the data. Decisions made at this time can have lasting impact upon the performance and usability of the database.

Depending upon the scope of the duties assigned to you as DBA, you may or may not have responsibilities in the actual design of the database. Even if you do not actually design the database, you need to be aware of the factors relating to the design decisions. You need to be able to provide Informix-specific information relating to performance and design.

This task requires an understanding of the database structure, an understanding of the needs of your users, and an understanding of the resources and capabilities available to your system.

Understanding your Database Structure

It is important to differentiate between knowledge of the structure of the database and knowledge of the contents. It is possible for the DBA to administer a large, complex database with little or no knowledge of what the actual data looks like. In a smaller, simpler system, the DBA may wear DBA, developer, and even user hats. As a system grows larger and more complex, the users, developers, and DBAs develop more stratified views of the system. Each views the database from his or her own level of abstraction. The users don't care about the structure but understand the data. The developers understand part of the structure and part of the data. Finally, the DBA understands how pieces fit together but doesn't necessarily understand what the pieces are.

This stratification of knowledge can be a help or a hindrance. In any case, the DBA must deal with the highest levels of abstraction, for it is only here that the overall operations of the system can be maximized. If you can work with and understand the lower levels of abstraction, by all means do so, but start from the top.

Normalization of the Database

If you are inheriting an existing database system, you will probably be more or less stuck with the database design. It becomes more and more difficult to make wholesale changes in the structure of a database with time. As more applications are developed that access the database, you tend to get more and more locked into the structure dictated by the original designers. Remember this if you are in the enviable position of starting at the beginning. Either you or your successors will have to live with your design decisions for a long time.

We're not going to get into a long discussion on normalization. There are books devoted to the subject, and there is an entire calculus devoted to the theory of database design. Besides, it's probably academic if you are dealing with a legacy database. There's not much you can do to change it anyway. Instead, we will look at the extremes of not normalized versus fully normalized databases.

Most databases have had at least some attempt at normalization. With relational databases such as Informix, some degree of normalization is expected, if only from the fact that it is a buzzword that lots of people know and few people understand. A totally non-normalized database would essentially be a flat file. All data items would be in one table. This environment would be extremely wasteful of space and would be a poor performer, but it would have some advantages. It would be easy to understand. Users could do ad hoc queries without having a detailed knowledge of the structure of the database.

The fully normalized database will have the data elements spread out in many tables that can be joined to extract needed data. A database in the fourth normal form is usually more efficient in the use of disk storage and computer resources. It can also be more difficult to understand both for the end users and for the DBA. Often, a highly normalized database can suffer a performance penalty because of the amount of joining that is needed to access data. In these instances, some denormalization of the database can help improve performance. For example, your application may access information in two tables very often using a particular join. In this case it might be advisable to denormalize and put the data together in a single table to eliminate the constant joining. Even though the normalized version may actually be more efficient in use of overall resources, the perceived speed of access to your users may be more important than milking the absolute maximum efficiency from the database.

Even in databases that begin as a normalized database, we often see a "creeping denormalization." Sometimes this denormalization is intentional, but more often it is the result of expediency. Developers may add redundant tables "just this once" or for a "temporary project." The lesson here is that normalization of the database is a constant process. If you have a normalized database, you have to enforce normalization throughout the development process, not just in the initial design phase.

Don't be enslaved by the theoretical arguments for or against various normal forms. While it may be interesting to decide how many angels will fit on the head of a pin, the answer will probably change tomorrow. Look at the overall balance between database efficiency and usability. Don't be afraid to denormalize when there are good reasons.

TABLE MANAGEMENT

The tables are the reason for the existence for the database system. Using the "black box" theory of databases, users tend to believe that once they have created a table, everything is automatically taken care of and handled by the omnipotent and omniscient database management system. For the user, it is often enough to allow his understanding to stop at this point. Ask a user where his data resides, and you'll probably get "in a table" as an answer.

One of the most important DBA functions is the arrangement and management of the tables and indexes in the database system. Unless the basic requirements of efficient table and index layout are achieved, the entire system starts off at a disadvantage and optimum performance becomes an illusive dream. Once the system is set up properly, the DBA must continuously monitor these aspects of the database system. It will always be evolving, and the DBA needs to be able to at least stay abreast of the changes. To effectively set up and maintain a database system, the DBA needs to have a deeper understanding of the physical layout of tables and indexes. This understanding must start with the sizing and physical storage of tables within databases.

Sizing and Physical Storage

Database tables are stored either in normal UNIX or NT files or on raw devices. Raw device storage is more efficient and much more common than UNIX file system storage. Since tables are not stored in individual files that are visible to UNIX, the DBA has to use Informix utilities to view table data.

Much useful information is contained in the table `systables`. Every database managed by Informix will have a separate set of system tables. These tables can be inspected either by the `isql` utility, by the `dbaccess` utility, by INFORMIX-4GL or other client programs, by GUI-based Informix clients, or by embedded ESQL code.

Data about physical storage locations on disk is available through use of the `tb/oncheck` utility. This utility is very useful and is one of the few ways that the DBA can see how the physical data is actually stored and arranged. IDS systems can also duplicate much of the data from `oncheck` by running queries against the sysmaster tables. See Chapter 11 for examples.

When a table is first created, a typical SQL statement to create the table might be:

```
CREATE TABLE test_table
    (
field1  SMALLINT,
field2  SMALLINT
)IN dbspacename EXTENT SIZE XXX NEXT SIZE YYY
```

IDS systems also have the option to use a FRAGMENT BY clause to allow the data to be intelligently located across multiple disk devices.

From a physical storage standpoint there are three interesting areas of this SQL statement. They are discussed in the next three sections.

in <Dbspacename>

Here, DBSPACENAME would be replaced with the name of one of your system's dbspaces. At table creation time, this is one way that you can specify where to put the table. Physical table location is most important when trying to place active tables in preferred locations on the disk. If you have some tables that are very active, you may wish to create dbspaces that are made up of chunks from your fastest disk devices. You may also wish to create dbspaces composed of chunks on different devices or controlled by different disk controllers to separate two tables that often get accessed together. Such a scheme would allow simultaneous access of both tables without the disk thrashing that would be caused if both tables were on the same disk and accessed by the same read head.

In the absence of the IN <dbspacename> clause, the table will be placed in the default dbspace for the current database. When the database is first created, it can be created in a particular dbspace by the following SQL:

```
CREATE database databasename IN dbspacename;
```

If the IN <dbspacename> clause is omitted, the database will be placed in the rootdbs, which is usually a very bad idea.

Extent Size

This is the size in kilobytes of the first extent of the table. Whether the table has one row or hundreds, it will still occupy this amount of space in the database. This space is reserved at table creation time and is released only if the table is recreated. Due to the internal layout of Informix OnLine engines, it is better if an entire table will fit within a total of eight extents. If the number of extents goes above eight, the engine has to access another page from disk each time the table is accessed. It is best to try to build your tables so that the first extent will contain all the data and indexes. Putting the majority of data into the first extent ensures that most of the data will be located in a contiguous area of disk, with resulting performance gains in long sequential reads. This is less critical in IDS systems, which keeps the free extent list in SMI tables rather than in memory caches.

Next Size

When the first extent is filled, the Informix engine automatically allocates an additional extent of NEXT size in kilobytes. As these extents are filled, more are allocated. Once an extent is allocated, it is not released unless the table is rebuilt. This means that when left alone, tables will grow in size or remain the same in size. They never decrease in size without manual intervention.

There are some cases in which the engine modifies the NEXT SIZE. There is an internal limit to the number of extents that Informix engines can physically assign to a tablespace. This limit varies with the Informix version. For example, in Version 4.XX the limit is approximately 200 extents. If a table is created using the default EXTENT SIZE and NEXT SIZE, it is possible for the table to grow to its maximum number of extents, preventing it from growing any further.

To partially alleviate this limitation, the engine does several things to minimize the number of extents used. In the first case, when Informix is allocating a NEXT extent, it will try to allocate it contiguous to the previous extent. If it is possible to do this, it considers the added extent space to simply be an enlargement of the last extent and does not call it a separate extent. This can sometimes cause confusion to the DBA when she is looking at `tb/oncheck -pe` outputs. Although the CREATE TABLE statement for the table may specify a NEXT SIZE the real extents may vary in size from that specified.

Another approach the engine takes to reduce extent usage is called *extent doubling*. Whenever the number of extents in a table reaches a multiple of 32, the NEXT SIZE parameter is automatically doubled. For example, in a table created using the default eight pages of EXTENT and NEXT sizes (16K on 2K page machines), the 32nd extent will be 16K in size. The 33rd extent will be 32K in size.

At any time during the life and growth of a table, you can alter the NEXT SIZE parameter by using the ALTER TABLE SQL statement. This will not affect existing extents in use, but the next extent to be allocated will be given the new size. This allows a certain amount of tuning to be done to table allocation schemas after the table is created.

Finally, if a dbspace begins to get full, the NEXT SIZE parameter will be limited to the actual available space in the dbspace. For example, suppose your NEXT size is 64K and when it comes time to allocate another extent to the tablespace, there is only 40K of contiguous space left in the tablespace. The final extent will be 40K, not 64K. This will allow all of the space in the dbspace to be used. If there are other noncontiguous spaces left in the tablespace, they will be used for further table needs in order of decreasing size.

Correct use of EXTENT SIZE and NEXT SIZE can allow creation of extremely large tables without choking the engine. There is one case, however, that can cause a problem. It involves the creation of implicit temporary tables. You will remember that these implicit temporary tables are created by the engine for various internal uses. These tables are created with default extents and they are not under user control. It is possible for these implicit temporary tables to reach their maximum number of extents at about 8 megabytes due to the limitations on the number of extents.

Reclaiming Space

One way to recover the extents allocated to a table is by dropping and re-creating the table. This can be done explicitly with commands to drop and re-create the table or implicitly as part of a command that re-creates the table as a side effect of doing something else.

Dropping and Re-creating the Table

This is the most flexible method of recovering space that is no longer needed by a table. The DBA simply creates a dummy table in the correct dbspace, copies the data from the original table into the new table, drops the original table, and then renames the new table the same as the old. Since the DBA is recreating the table totally, the new table can be in whichever dbspace is needed, with whatever FIRST SIZE and NEXT SIZE are desired. Sometimes, especially in systems with very large tables, this is not possible due to a shortage in disk space. In certain cases, attempting to recreate the table becomes a time-consuming and risky proposition that entails unloading the table to tape, re-creating it with the proper sizing, and finally reloading from tape. Due to my inherent distrust of tape devices, this is not something I will do lightly.

Implicitly Re-creating the Table

There are several SQL commands that re-create a table as a side effect of doing another job. In general, any *Data Definition Language* (DDL) statement can cause a table to be rebuilt. For example, the following command causes the table sample to be rebuilt.

```
ALTER TABLE sample  ADD newfield integer
```

The table must be rebuilt because of the addition of the new column, `newfield`. Any such DDL command can cause the table to be rebuilt. Statements that create cluster indexes also force a physical rebuild of the table.

```
ALTER INDEX xxxxxxx TO CLUSTER;
CREATE CLUSTER INDEX  yyyyyy ON tabname (colname);
```

Both these SQL statements make use of the main property of clustered indexes, that is, a clustered index rearranges the physical layout of the table. It essentially creates a new table with the rows rearranged in the order of the cluster index. This has the by-product of freeing up unused NEXT extents. It does not allow placing the table in another dbspace or altering the FIRST EXTENT or NEXT EXTENT numbers. It simply releases any extents that are not used.

When a new cluster index is created, or when an existing index is altered to cluster, the engine creates a temporary copy of the table that is dropped when the index is completed. If the table is very large, this could result in space problems during this process. Be sure that you have enough space available in your system to create the large temporary table needed. This table will be the same size as the existing table.

IDS systems have additional tools for reorganizing the tables, the most efficient of which is

```
ALTER FRAGMENT ON TABLE tablename INIT IN spacename
```

IDS systems beginning with version 7.30 also have the capability of doing an in-place table reorganization that does not require that there be enough space in the database to hold a temporary copy of the table. Note that an in-place reorganization of the table will not reorganize extents or reclaim used pages.

Altering a Table

Later versions of IDS (I'm not sure when this began. Check your own version.) have a feature that is quite useful for those cases when you need to add a column to a table. In earlier versions, any table alter required that the engine go through the entire table adding an additional column. In later versions, if you *add a field to the end of the table*, the alter table is almost instantaneous as the engine does not have to traverse the entire table. If you try to alter the same table by inserting a field between two existing fields, the traversal still occurs. This speedup of the alter table is quite helpful, especially in data warehouse systems that may have hundreds of millions of rows in a table.

AVOIDING AND CURING UNPLANNED TABLE FRAGMENTATION

There are several practices that you can follow to eliminate and cure unplanned table fragmentation. It is important to realize the difference between planned and unplanned fragmentation. Planned fragmentation occurs when the DBA makes a purposeful decision to locate various chunks of the table on different disk devices to improve disk access performance. This type of fragmentation is a feature of the IDS engine that was enacted to enhance the DBA's ability to intelligently locate disk chunks and indexes for top performance.

Unplanned fragmentation can happen with either OnLine or IDS engines. This happens when the engine is forced to allocate extents for a table in such a way that they are not contiguous with the other data in the table. This forces the disk heads to thrash about and slows disk I/O speed significantly. To avoid this unplanned fragmentation, estimate the anticipated size of your tables and create them with proper FIRST and NEXT SIZE parameters. Doing this means that the engine will create larger, contiguous extents for the data and indexes to occupy. If you have created tables with a large enough FIRST extent parameter, you can be sure that the data will be compact and relatively easy for the engine to get to without forcing it to jump all over the disk.

It is also possible to reduce table fragmentation by intelligent use of the bulk loading utilities. As a general rule, it is preferable to do your loading into tables that have no indexes, creating them after the load. This has the advantage of being faster, especially in versions of OnLine newer than 5.0 that have improved indexing algorithms. The second advantage is that your data pages and index pages become contiguous. All of the data pages are together and all of your index pages are together. When you do your bulk loads with the indexes already built, your extents will have a few data pages followed by a few index pages, followed by more data pages, etc. When you do your bulk loads with no indexes in place and create the indexes later, the data pages are grouped together, followed by the index pages. If you create your indexes one at a time after the data is loaded, the index pages will become even more effectively located, with pages for one index being together followed by pages from the next index, etc. Having these pages located contiguously makes it easier for the engine to access them without thrashing all over the disk. This also allows the use of *big buffer reads*, which use more efficient reading mechanisms if the data is located contiguously.

You can cure fragmented tables in the same way that you drop unused extents from tables by re-creating the tables or by altering indexes to cluster. Actually, any DDL command that alters the table, such as adding a column or changing the structure of the table will cause a rebuild of the table, but altering to cluster is the most innocuous approach.

The benefits of defragmenting tables begin to go away as the table is used and modified. If you begin to notice a slow degradation of access time and performance, look at table fragmentation. It often occurs so slowly that you don't notice it. It should be noted that there is one surefire way to avoid unplanned fragmentation of tables. If you place each of your active tables in its own dbspace and continuously monitor the space for adequate free space, you will not experience any unwanted fragmentation. This strategy can also help in several other areas, such as in archiving just one table.

INDEX MANAGEMENT

The indexes in your database are absolutely the single most important determinant in the performance of the OLTP database. An awful database design that has a good index structure will almost always out-perform a wonderful design that is indexed poorly. The importance of indexes becomes more important as the table sizes get larger.

Indexes seem to be even more of a "black box" than tables. DBAs often do not understand the actual layout of the indexes. Books have been written about different methods of indexing, so the area can be somewhat intimidating. For our purposes, a simple explanation of the indexing mechanism should suffice.

B+tree Indexes

Informix indexes use the b+tree method of indexing. Basically, this is a method that stores the key values and pointers to the `rowids` of the rows containing that key value. These key/pointer pairs can be searched to retrieve the `rowids` of matching rows. Using the indexes means that a search has to inspect far fewer pages to find the needed rows than would be necessary if a sequential scan of the entire table were to be needed.

The key/pointer information is stored in fixed-size data structures called nodes. The first node is called the *root node*. When the table is small, an index could possibly be no larger than this root node. Accompanying the key value will be a pointer that points directly to the `rowid` of the row. As the table grows larger and more and more key values need to be indexed, the root node may fill up. At this time, additional nodes may be added. This is known as adding a level to the tree. When a level is added to the tree, the root level no longer contains pointers to the actual `rowids`. Each entry in the root node now points to a new node in the tree.

At the lowest level of the tree, the pointer will point to an actual `rowid`. The nodes that actually point to the `rowids` are known as *leaf nodes*. They are the end point of the search. As additional levels and additional nodes are added to the tree, the index becomes larger and more complex.

Since an index must accommodate change in the table's data, it is possible that some of the nodes will fill up and some will become too empty. The engine attempts to balance and prune the b+tree to maximize the usability of the index. To do so, it occasionally merges adjacent nodes into one, splits full nodes into two, or shuffles key/pointer pairs from one index to another. For the most part, these activities are completely invisible, even to the

DBA. However, their tracks can be seen by inspecting the logfiles using the `tb/onlog` utility. (Be careful with `tb/onlog`. It will freeze your database while you're looking at logs in use. If you must inspect logs, look at logs on tape, where they're harmless.)

How Indexes are Stored

Pages containing index data are stored within the dbspace that contains the tablespace in OnLine systems. IDS systems allow the options of detaching and fragmenting the indexes and building them in dbspaces chosen by the DBA. Index pages contain nothing but index data and miscellaneous overhead items relating to the index. Each page of index data is a b+tree node.

These pages are not allocated in any particular order. Thus, a dbspace may be composed of random index and data pages. To further complicate matters, the dbspace may contain data from multiple tables and multiple indexes, all thrown into one big pot.

If the data and index pages for a particular table become strewn across the disk, table fragmentation can occur. This fragmentation means that the engine has to work a lot harder to get to the data it wants. As a general rule, avoid this type of fragmentation.

MEETING USERS' NEEDS

No two database systems are the same. Some may be composed of data that is accessed only through canned programs that are fully optimized. Others may be decision support applications that see a lot of nonstructured, ad hoc query activity. Others may have data that remains in the system for years. Still others may move data through the system in a day and then throw it away. These different modes of use and purpose must be understood by the DBA if he is to manage the entire system.

The purpose of the database is to make the information contained in the database tables accessible in some form to the users. The most controlled access is a system of structured access in which all data flows through well-defined programs. This is the typical form of access in most current database applications designed for end users. Essentially an extension of the "big iron" philosophy, it stresses centralized control over the data resources.

At the other end of the spectrum is a more free form type of access in which users execute many ad hoc queries. As users become more empowered by the client/server paradigm, DBAs can expect to field more requests for this type of access, with the opportunities and pitfalls that accompany it.

Additionally, different types of users may view a database management system in completely different ways. The DBA has to understand all of their uses and needs.

Understanding the Needs of your Users

Different levels of database users can expect to view the database in different ways: users at different levels need different information about what is going on inside the system. Of course, the lines between different types of users are fuzzy at best. It's fun to generalize, but it's also impossible. You are dealing with people, and they will tend to distribute themselves all over the spectrum. I'm certain you will recognize most of your users somewhere in this list.

End Users

The database is usually invisible to the end user. They simply do not see the database: they see the applications. In most cases, the end users do not even know that the application is based upon a database. For them, the whole system, from hardware to application programs, is known simply as "the computer." They do not make the differentiation between hardware, software, and applications.

The end user mostly runs "canned" programs. These programs were either bought from others or developed by other users, the programmers. End users want results, answers, numbers. Give results to the end users and they'll be happy.

End users also want fast response times. The system is not only important to them, often it is the major tool that they use to do their job. If a query that has been coming back in three seconds starts to take six seconds, expect to hear from the users. They are your first line of alert to problems.

Advanced Users

Advanced users are at a point somewhere between end users and programmers. They still get their information from the existing applications, but they have discovered that much more information exists. They will try to get to it either by having programmers write them hundreds of reports or by pushing for client/server tools that let them use the database's data from within their comfortable, PC-based tools. In the absence of client/server orientation, these advanced users may be intercepting print spool files from the print queue or requesting that their reports be formulated to fit their spreadsheets. These advanced users still probably have little or no knowledge of the underlying database.

Advanced users in client/server environments usually learn SQL because their spreadsheets or other client programs accept SQL commands. These users learn a subset of the database's structure and often use tools such as advanced 4GLs and data import/export tools to integrate their PCs with the database. These advanced users often use third-party tools as well.

Programmers

Programmers can run the gamut from inexperienced to very sophisticated. Either type can make incredible demands upon the DBA. Given exposure to the database, the novice programmers usually learn the system quickly. Using programmatic interfaces like ESQL/C, programmers soon begin to view the database as just another function call. As long as they can get the results they are seeking, they do not care much about the inner workings of the database. They tend to view the database as yet another "black box."

The sophisticated programmers often know as much about what's going on "under the hood" as the DBA does. At least, they can seem to know as much. If their knowledge transfers to the overall workings of the database system, these gurus can become quite a resource. Often, however, their in-depth knowledge is restricted in breadth. Many times, they will be generalizing from other databases or from generic experience and will engage you for hours in esoteric discussion of paging algorithms. They can easily suffer from a typical DBA problem, that is, focusing too narrowly in one area. It is possible to write tight, high-performance code that pushes the database to its absolute limits of performance. It's also possible that this same code can bring the system to its knees if the developer has neglected to see how the code interacts with other programs.

Executives

Executives have their own set of needs in understanding the database. Dealing with executives requires the best technical expertise that the DBA can bring to bear, but it also requires at least an awareness of the politics of the situation.

Depending upon the background of the executive, their needs can be met from anything from a confidently delivered "I've got it handled" to a detailed technical explanation. Know which to use and when.

Remember that executives have the same goals you have. They want to accomplish a task efficiently and with the least effort and expenditure. If you can communicate your needs and requests to them in such a way that they can relate it to the overall needs of the organization, you will receive more satisfactory responses.

The quality movement is currently very big in corporate environments. It's been my experience that once companies get on the total quality bandwagon, you can use the jargon and techniques of your particular quality dialect to your advantage. If you phrase your requests and suggestions using the approved quality dialect you'll find that most executives will be more receptive. If you're asking for additional disk space to make your administration job easier, you may or may not be listened to. If you need the same disk space to improve the process of retaining information and making it available to your internal customers on a more timely basis, you'll have a lot better chance of getting your disks. You've requested the same disks in both cases, but the second request is phrased in such a way that only opponents of quality could refuse.

A more recent bandwagon that just everybody is jumping onto is the Y2K problem, caused by legacy code that does not handle the proper conversion from dates in the 1900's to dates in the 2000's. A lesser-understood part of the Y2K problem is the inability of much software to decide whether or not the year 2000 is a leap year (it is). Recently, it seems that everyone has something to say about the Y2K problem, and DBAs are finding that they can couch many of their upgrade requests in terms of "Y2K remediation" and get more support than if they phrased it in other terms.

Even the TV preachers are getting into the Y2K game. I've heard claims that the year 2000 will be the date of Armageddon because of all of the computer failures that will occur. These prophets of doom seem to appear at every century mark, predicting the end of the world. They are now urging people to hoarde food and weapons in preparation for the Y2K bug. It turns out that what all of us software people thought was only sloppy programming was actually the work of the devil. So, if you're involved in Y2K remediation efforts, you can feel secure in knowing that you're doing God's work. Hey, I don't mind. Just don't let them convince you to take vows of chastity or poverty.

DBAs

The DBA needs to be able to understand the mechanics at the lowest level of database operations. DBAs also need to have an overall picture of the operation of the system as a synergistic whole. Knowledge of the low-level operations are critical when debugging the system, as problems often seem to revolve around just one item that refuses to work properly. This in-depth knowledge of the architecture also helps the DBA deal with his own system gurus and with the Informix helpline personnel.

If nothing else, the DBA needs to maintain professional control over database operations. The ability to explain, argue fine points, and to solve unusual problems can do nothing but enhance the DBA's professional stature.

Being able to see the overall picture is at least as important. In many organizations, database design, applications programming, and providing ad hoc data to advanced users are spread across several departments and across many individuals. The DBA has to be able to integrate the different pieces and make them work together in an efficient whole.

Often, there is nobody else with a sufficiently broad job description to handle this most important task.

DESIGN CONSIDERATIONS IN DATABASE SYSTEMS

This section will be applicable to you only if you have the luxury of building your database system from scratch. If you are starting with a blank sheet of paper, an empty computer room, and a bottomless bank account you can build a nearly ideal system.

Of course, an ideal system designed to spec today, delivered by the vendors in three months, and operable in 9 to 12 months will never be ideal when it goes into production. At current rates of hardware and software development, something new and better seems to come along every 3 to 4 months. So, the ideal system is just that, an ideal. System vendors themselves never have ideal systems, so why should you expect it for yourself?

In real life, you are probably inheriting an existing system. You have time and budget constraints, you have to maintain production (whatever that means in your environment), and you have a backlog. Welcome to the real world.

Still, the design issues that you would face in building a state-of-the-art system from scratch are applicable to you even if you have an existing system. As your system grows and matures, you will probably have opportunities to upgrade your system, add peripherals, upgrade the software, and modify your applications. Who knows, your company may land a big contract and the CEO might come into your office some day with a blank check.

So what is a state-of-the-art system? The answer, of course, is highly time-dependent. What is hot and new as I am writing this chapter will be old news in a year. You'll find the latest and greatest in current magazines. Maybe you'll see it from your hardware vendors, but in my experience if you don't ask for it, you'll never find out from vendors. An amazing attitude from people who make a living selling you things!

Your hardware decisions will mainly concern choice of equipment manufacturers, processor layout, and peripheral layout. We'll stay away from questions of who makes the best hardware, because there is no correct answer. Your best manufacturer is the one who makes something you feel comfortable with and from whom you can get the best service. I've always found that the service component is much more important than the hardware end. If you have a company that gives you A+ hardware and B- service, you'll probably be much less pleased than with a company giving you B+ hardware and A+ service. Hardware is something that you agonize over while making the original choices and then find ways to live with for the rest of the life cycle. As long as it works and performs adequately, you'll probably be happy. Service is something that you have to live with daily. When you need support or service, odds are you're in a bind and you need it NOW. You probably have users screaming at you and you cannot put up with lackadaisical support or service. Go for the service! With luck, you can get both good hardware and good support, but don't hold your breath.

Hardware

Computer systems continually evolve. A decade ago, proprietary systems were the way to go. You would get all of your hardware and software from one source and that one source would hold your hand forever and handle all of your needs. The end result of this commitment to proprietary systems was that the user became locked into one vendor. Purchasers of systems began to realize that this limited their flexibility and their bargaining power with their system vendor.

Systems are now evolving toward the concept of open systems. Rather than being locked into one "big iron" vendor, you pick the best pieces from best vendors and somehow make them all work together. The glue that ties it all together is the UNIX operating system and the evolving standards that are being adopted by vendors. These standards include UNIX for the operating system, TCP/IP for networking, X-Window for graphical displays, C and C++ as programming languages, and SQL for the database language. Informix is a major player in the open systems movement, with database engines that run on everything from PCs to mainframes. Personal computers, even those not running UNIX or UNIX-derivatives, also play in the open systems arena. Microsoft Windows™, Microsoft Windows NT™, and OS/2 systems are increasingly finding themselves used in connection with UNIX servers. These personal computers often serve multiple purposes, ranging from acting as terminals talking to UNIX boxes over the network to serving as X-Window displays using the PC's intelligence to emulate an X-Window terminal. Personal computers are also serving as full-fledged clients in distributed applications, with the PCs handling the input/output and the graphics and the UNIX servers handling the database management.

In recent years, NT has moved more and more into the mainstream of database environments. When Informix introduced server products on NT, everybody thought they were crazy. This tune will change as more people see NT systems performing on a par with, or better than, their UNIX brethren. This is happening now, and will continue into the future because of the rapid pace of hardware advancement.

It is a fact of life that with the size of the Intel-compatible Windows NT/Windows 95 market, as soon as someone comes out with faster chips or faster busses or faster peripherals, the next day they will be running on NT. Most UNIX systems are more proprietary and will lag behind the rapid pace of development of the PC-based hardware. I can buy an Intel-based PC today that is twice the speed and half the cost of the one I bought a year ago, and it will run Informix 7.30 on NT out of the box. Any inefficiencies in O/S design will be more than made up for in hardware speed. Fast hardware can cure a lot of ills.

There are other options for running Informix on this latest and greatest hardware. Operating systems such as UNIXWare will run on commodity hardware and give you the robustness of UNIX along with the ability to keep pace with hardware developments.

A somewhat surprising advance in database functionality is now happening with the Linux operating system. Linux is a UNIX variant that is essentially free. You can buy a CD with Linux on it for $50 or less. Many UNIX fans are adopting Linux as the software of choice because of its low price and robustness. Linux fans swear that Linux is more reliable and less liable to crash than NT, and it runs on commodity Intel processors. Many organizations are reluctant to bet the farm on an operating system that nobody owns and that nobody supports. That's the line, anyway. What really happens is while there is no central owner who supports Linux, the actual support is done by all of the users and sellers of the product. Since the source code of Linux is freely available, if someone else can't fix your problem you have the option of breaking out your C compiler and fixing it yourself. Try that with NT!

Informix has recently made available the Informix-SE engine on Linux and has made it available free for download over the Web. Plans call for porting other products to Linux and for developing a means of supporting the products on Linux.

A big advantage of the open systems concept is scalability. By choosing to remain compliant to standards, a system can grow and evolve as your needs change. Applications running on an SCO UNIXWare server on a personal computer can easily be ported to larger minicomputers or even mainframes as long as the basic database and language tools are available. This flexibility also extends to your choice of vendors. You are no longer married for life to a hardware or software manufacturer. If you find that you've made a bad choice or two, or if the vendor is no longer providing you with what you need, you no longer have to scrap everything and begin anew. The vendors realize this and are beginning to behave in a more competitive manner. They now see that users and purchasers have choices. This will give users much more leverage with vendors.

Processor Decisions

In today's market, the rising stars in the hardware arena are the multiprocessor or parallel processing systems. We are discovering that several less powerful processors that can cooperate inside one box can often outperform one super-fast processor. By breaking tasks up into pieces that can be farmed out to multiple processors, the central processing unit can often get much more work done and provide a higher level of throughput.

In some systems, the multiprocessing or parallel processing paradigm can also allow for more tolerance for failure, as the processors can fill in for each other should one fail. This is by no means universal. In fact, in some multiprocessing arrangements, failure of any one processor will bring the system down, giving you a higher probability of failure.

The OnLine product provides for various levels of support for multiple and parallel processors. This is version-dependent. Beginning with OnLine 4.1, Informix provided the `psort` capability that will farm out sorts to multiple processors if your system has them. This was enhanced in Version 5.0. INFORMIX-Dynamic Server provides more utilization for multiple processors in the areas of sorting, indexing, archiving, and database access. Version 7.X provides support for fully parallel architectures and provides outstanding performance for both OLTP and DSS needs.

Clustered Systems

Beginning with the 8.X series of servers, Informix has provided support for clusters of either UNIX or NT systems. Using what Informix calls a "shared-nothing" design, these systems allow multiple IDS engines to cooperate and share data and queries, providing almost linear performance increases as additional systems are added to the cluster. In traditional SMP and MPP environments which share busses and other resources, increases in the number of processors give rise to a diminishing return in processing performance as the shared resources begin to become saturated.

The shared-nothing systems scale much better, since they each handle their own resources and give the DBA much better granularity of control over what happens in each system. In addition to the 8.X (XPS) family, NT versions of IDS beginning with 7.30 have the capability of operating in such clusters.

The first commercially available NT clusters were produced by Tandem. In 1995, Stratus introduced the Radio line of NT cluster systems that won "Best New Product" at several major computer shows. Radio depended upon a 100-megabit network backbone that connected dual-processor off-the-shelf Intel systems into a virtual machine that was designed for fault-tolerance. The fault-tolerance was provided by software running on each node of the cluster.

Microsoft is now working on its "Wolfpack" clustering scheme, which should bring clustered systems into the mainstream. As more such developments occur, the penetration of NT into the "big iron" world should continue to increase.

Disk Storage Systems

Much of the work that a database system does revolves around taking information that is stored on a hard disk drive and making it available for user processes. On most computer systems, the slowest thing that happens is transferring data to and from a hard disk. It's obvious that if a product depends so heavily on something that is relatively slow, management of the slow resource takes on a critical role.

This is the case with Informix. Many of the setup and tuning strategies the DBA employs to extract the best performance from the system have to do with reducing the amount of time the system spends accessing the disks. Thus, we have a large emphasis on caching data items in the shared memory where access is many times faster than from disk. A lot of time can be spent in trying to physically place tables in areas of optimum ease of access on the disk. The aim is to cache the data in shared memory if you can, but if you have to go to the disk, go there with as little relative motion of the disk drive heads as possible. When you have to move data from the disk to shared memory, the data movement should be as fast as possible and involve the least possible movement of the disk heads.

From these requirements, it is obvious that you should have the fastest disk storage system that you can obtain if you are looking for peak performance. Since the disk system is such a common bottleneck to high performance, improvements in this area can often pay impressive performance dividends.

In the area of disk layout, there are four main areas that you need to consider, actual disk configuration, disk striping, mirroring, and *RAIDs* (Redundant Arrays of Inexpensive Disks).

Physical Disk Configuration

No matter what your disk system type, you need to carefully consider how you use it to get the best performance. The choices that you make regarding placement of the rootdbs, placement of your logfiles, placement of your physical logs, and placement of your most active tables can make a big difference in performance.

If you have multiple disks, it is usually better to place the database components on different physical drives from the UNIX or NT filesystems used by your applications. This way, movement of the disk heads caused by UNIX or NT jobs does not interfere with those belonging to Informix. If you can place these areas on separate controllers, so much the better.

I'm assuming that you are using raw devices for your data areas. They will show a uniform improvement over UNIX filesystems for the simple reason that the work that UNIX would do to maintain a filesystem is redundant for a chunk. Informix is running its own routines to manage its chunks, and there's no need to duplicate them. The situation of raw vs. cooked filesystems becomes murkier with the NT port. Versions prior to 7.30 did not have the option of using raw filesystems. They had to use NT's NTFS filesystem. Nonetheless, performance was very good. The jury is still out on the use of raw devices in IDS 7.30+ on NT.

If you have multiple raw disks available for your database, you have to decide how to divide up the space. Often, an inexperienced DBA will simply create one large rootdbs and place everything there. This is not usually a good idea for several reasons. The rootdbs can never be dropped. To get rid of it, you have to reinitialize your database and restore the data from tape or other sources. As such, space that you devote to rootdbs in Informix is space that you can never get back. If you need to make changes or allocate resources, you have to rebuild.

On the other hand, if you have a reasonably sized rootdbs with separate dbspaces for various tables or databases, you maintain some flexibility in dealing with change. You can move databases or tables from dbspace to dbspace a lot easier than by re-creating everything from scratch. These convenience and flexibility items are in addition to the performance issues that can be addressed by having separate dbspaces for different database components.

You may have some disks that perform better than others. If so, this is where you want your most active tables. You can put them there by creating dbspaces on the fast devices and using the IN DBSPACE clause of your table creation statements. You'll find that some tables and some portions of the database system will get a lot more writing activity than others. Put these on the faster devices. Good candidates for placement on faster devices are your physical and logical logfiles.

Disk Striping

Disk striping is a method of creating logical disks that are actually composed of several physical disk devices. Disk striping is also known as RAID 0. Striping is supported on many UNIX and NT machines and is often beneficial to database performance. With striping, a logical disk is composed of data tracks that are interleaved across several devices. Thus, you can give a command calling for accesses to the disk and have the heads of several devices move at once to retrieve the data. In some cases, this can improve performance. It makes actual physical placement of tables and dbspaces on disk less critical, as the striped volume is distributing the read load across many spindles. It also cuts down on the possibility of contention, or forcing a disk head to make large jumps from disk request to disk request.

Striping is an operating system function. Informix does not know or care about how the volume is laid out. As long as the engine can execute calls to the logical volume and receive data, it does not matter whether the underlying device is a physical device or a logical device.

Striping is a powerful tool in your search for performance. If you have it available to you, it is almost always better to use it than not to. If you have an efficient, reliable striping method, you do not really have to worry about the physical location of tablespaces and dbspaces in your system. This can drastically cut down on your possibility of error and on the amount of time you spend fiddling with disk layout. With striping, you can do it once and let UNIX take care of it in the future.

Disk Mirroring

Both striping and mirroring are actually subsets of the RAID concept, each being a different RAID level. Mirroring is also known as RAID 1. There are two choices for mirroring with Informix engines. You can either let the operating system or hardware handle the mirroring, or you can let Informix handle it.

If you enable operating system mirroring, the O/S handles it much like a striped device. When one side of the mirror device has a data change, the drivers automatically make the change on the other side. Mirroring is not really a positive performance issue. It is more of a redundancy issue. Using mirrored devices allows you to survive a failure of a physical drive and to continue running on the other device. Mirroring actually slows performance down somewhat, but the added fault-tolerance makes it often worth the cost.

The other approach to mirroring is to let Informix handle the mirroring. Whenever you create a chunk, you can tell the engine that you want to mirror it. To do so, you must have twice the space normally required on your drives. Thus, to mirror a 1-gigabyte chunk, you would need to have two 1-gigabyte chunks available, a primary chunk and a mirror chunk. The database engine will automatically apply changes from the primary chunk to the mirror chunk. Informix mirroring is somewhat slower than operating system or hardware mirroring, especially if your mirroring is built into your hardware.

The natural question is "Which one is better?" I generally tend toward taking the O/S mirroring over the Informix mirroring in systems that need to minimize maintenance and upkeep. Mirroring that is integrated into either your hardware or your operating system can be more highly optimized for your specific environment. Informix mirroring is a fairly generic product. It works the same for all environments, while the native mirroring is often more highly tuned. From an operations standpoint, they both seem to provide the same level of security.

For situations where the DBA is proactive and sophisticated, Informix mirroring is often a better idea. This mirroring gives the DBA some additional options for moving and relocating disk devices that can prove very helpful if the DBA is savvy enough to take advantage of them. In modern RAID designs, the write speed penalty for RAID 1 is not usually significant. These systems make extensive use of intelligent drivers and caching controllers. The read performance of RAID 1 is often better than with a JBOD, because the RAID offers parallel read capabilities, reading from either the primary or the mirror.

RAID

Both mirroring and striping are considered to be low level RAID implementations. RAIDs utilize several physical disks that are addressed as one logical disk. Various levels of RAID systems lay out the disks in ways that can provide performance gains as well as increase reliability.

A good RAID implementation can provide several advantages to a state-of-the-art system. First, the individual disks that comprise a RAID system are usually less expensive than traditional disks used with larger minicomputer systems. These disk drives are often 4 to 9 gigabyte drives designed to be used with personal computers. These disks are priced more for the PC market than for the minicomputer market and are relatively inexpensive compared to those sold strictly for the high-end markets.

Second, RAIDs provide a level of redundancy and can survive the failure of one or more of the individual disks. Some of the better implementations also allow a *hot swap* capability in which a bad disk can be replaced without taking the system offline. After the bad disk is replaced, the RAID will begin the process of resynchronizing the disks so that the redundancy is restored.

Not only can you get better performance due to the striping capability of RAIDS, you can also get a level of tunable performance. Some systems can allow different levels of RAID redundancy in different parts of the file system.

As an example, some areas such as physical and logical logs in Informix will see a lot of write activity and little or no reads. If these areas can be put in an area that is tuned for writing, not for random reading, the overall performance will improve.

RAID 5 is a common choice for database systems. It provides improvements in reading speed with a fair degree of fault-tolerance, at the cost of sometimes significant degradation of write speeds. If your system is write-intensive, RAID 5 is probably not the way to go.

AVOIDING MISTAKES IN THE DEVELOPMENT PROCESS

The concept of distributed databases is a most attractive one to the modern corporation. Coupled with the flashy, icon-driven front ends that are becoming more and more available in the marketplace, this concept is almost too attractive to resist. What could possibly be wrong with downsizing applications from mainframes to minicomputers and even desktop PCs? What could possibly be the problem with allowing data to be owned where it originates? What could be the drawbacks of allowing end users to step up from dull, dumb terminals to the modern-looking interfaces as typified by the Microsoft Windows environment.

The answer is, there's nothing intrinsically wrong with the concept. True, the technology is still in its infancy and there are bugs that need to be worked out. Modern-day PCs capable of running Windows are as powerful as the minicomputers of several years ago. Desktop PCs can now have more than 128 megabytes of memory and can have many gigabytes of hard disk storage. Modern network operating systems are approaching the flexibility and performance of mainframe and minicomputer operating systems such as UNIX. Even more powerful desktop machines are on the way. Even better operating systems and application software packages are being released on an almost daily basis. Costs seem to be going down, making downsizing look better and better every day.

So where's the drawback? Is there a drawback? Are we really living in computer heaven? Can you really get something for next to nothing? An example taken from the real world may shed some light on some of the things that can go wrong.

The OSCAR Syndrome

Several years ago a medium-sized corporation had a legacy software package that had been running for years on a mainframe. The application was a database that managed several gigabytes of data. This was the main application for the firm, mission critical in the truest sense of the word. The firm could not live without it.

The problem with the old legacy system was that the ongoing costs, which included rental of time on another firm's mainframe, came to about $500,000 a year. The director of Information Services saw that downsizing the application to a network of UNIX machines could save the company millions. Without the approval or knowledge of the CEO, he began a secret project to begin to port the legacy application to UNIX. He hired a programmer out of his regular budget and put that programmer to work with an Oracle database. This went on for several months until the programmer completed a demo application.

The director of Information Services then presented the demo to the officers of the company. The demo was a smash hit. The old green-screen CRTs of the legacy system were replaced with color PCs with pop-up windows. Whenever a data item crossed a threshold of criticality, the data was shown in blinking red. Users who saw the demo were thrilled with it. Management saw visions of cost savings. The PR people saw a showcase application that would certainly impress new customers. This company was going to become a technology leader! After much wrangling and ego bashing, the new program was called OSCAR and funds were allocated.

Now the project began to pick up steam. Five outside consultants were hired to develop the entire system. The team was given carte blanche. They were given their own offices, away from the rest of the developers so that they could concentrate on OSCAR alone. They began an exhaustive series of Joint Application Development (JAD) meetings with users, soliciting their input and trying to design a user interface that the users would love.

Everything was done to empower the end users, knowing that their approval and participation in the project would ensure its success.

Eventually, plans were made for the actual implementation of OSCAR, Phase I. Remote locations were wired for the UNIX terminals. PCs were bought to serve as terminals. Several mid-range UNIX machines were purchased. Beta testing went off without a hitch. Life was wonderful. A few weeks before the scheduled implementation there was only one little hitch.

Phase I was not going to totally replace the legacy system. It was going to offload a few of the processing modules and remove some of the load from the mainframe. The mainframe database was to feed data to the UNIX machines, the UNIX boxes would do some processing, and eventually give the data back to the mainframe. Finally, someone asked the critical question. How were they going to keep the databases in sync? What happened if data on the mainframe was changed while the UNIX box was working on the same data? Nobody had given serious thought to the problems of data concurrency.

The interface was wonderful. Users were excited. But OSCAR would never work. The department was eventually outsourced after blowing $6 or $7 million.

What's the lesson learned from OSCAR? Everyone involved fell into a trap that is very easy to fall into. Data concurrency was only the executioner's blade. If it had not been concurrency, it would have been something else. The project was doomed to failure from the start.

The emphasis was on the front end. The interface. The GUI. This was the sexy part of the project. It was flashy, attractive, a wonderful tool for selling the project to the users. It was also the last thing that should have been done. The prototype turned into the project. As an afterthought, the team turned to the underlying architecture. By then, they had committed themselves too deeply. The architecture would never work.

Readers may say this was an incredibly stupid mistake. It was. They may say that nobody is that stupid anymore. They're wrong.

In their rush to please their internal customers, data processing shops are giving users unprecedented input into the projects being written for them. Users see a flashy demo running on a minimal database and think that this is the real application. They think that the job is finished when it has not even started.

There are several lessons to be learned from the OSCAR experience. First, a prototype should never take more than a few weeks to develop. If you need to muster the political and executive support, go ahead and build a flashy interface with circles and arrows and a paragraph on the back of each one. Don't spend a lot of time worrying about which tools to use. Don't spend endless months benchmarking different products, at least not yet. Once you've gotten approval for the project, go right to work on the underlying architecture. Move data around. Update it. Insert it. Get the data flows and the data accessibility right. Once you are sure you can move the data into the right places, concentrate on the flashy screens. Choose your tools. Bring the users in and let them become your partners in building the interface. Just don't do it until the underlying structure is tested and proven.

GUIs and flashy screens are downright seductive. The excitement of seeing your applications almost magically change from a green and white terminal to a brilliant color monitor is almost too much for anyone to resist. Sure, get excited about the interface. Just don't confuse it with the real application.

MONITORING AND TROUBLESHOOTING

The Most Common Cause of Database Crashes for OnLine Systems

In an environment with many programmers who are familiar with UNIX, your most common problem will occur when somebody kills an engine process. Informix does not take lightly to the untimely death of a sqlturbo engine or an oninit process. This often causes the database to abort, necessitating a restart and recovery that can take anywhere from minutes to hours. In general, if a sqlturbo process is killed with a kill -9 command while it is in a critical section of code or when it is holding a latch, the engine will abort.

This problem can best be solved by enforcing a prohibition that no one but the DBA can kill -9 a sqlturbo process. It's safe for anyone to kill -15 a process. The problem here is that if a UNIX user gives a kill -15 command, the process will not necessarily die immediately. If the sqlturbo process goes into a rollback status because it received the command in the middle of a transaction, the process will remain around until the rollback completes. An impatient user may try a few kill -15 commands and finally try for a sure kill with kill -9. If the system is in rollback, OnLine will probably crash. If the process was holding any locks or if it was in a critical write process, the OnLine system will crash. The Informix command tbmode -z command works in the same way. The job doesn't immediately disappear.

Both kill -15 and tbmode -z are safe to use any time, as long as the user is prepared to be patient. It's usually best to have the users check with the DBA if the jobs don't die within about 15 minutes.

Processes that take longer than about 15 minutes can pose a quandary even to the DBA. It's possible that the query is a disjoint query and that the system is trying to process millions of rows. You could be in a long transaction on the verge of either going into forced rollback or filling up all your logs, causing a crash. If the DBA can't identify exactly what's happening, it is usually best to let the process finish its job, unless this will cause other problems in the database such as filling up the logs. If the runaway job begins to affect performance or response time, the DBA usually needs to kill it.

By the time the DBA sees the typical rogue sqlturbo process, the user has probably already tried to kill it with kill -15 or tbmode -z. It's probably in rollback. Rollback can be identified by the flags --R--X-- in the tbstat -u output. Using the UNIX ps command will tell the DBA whether the sqlturbo process is getting any time. If so, your rollback is in process. No matter what you do, the rollback has to complete. It'll either complete with the system online, or it will complete during the recovery stage of database startup. Online is usually best.

The worst case for the DBA is the process that was written in ESQL/C or one that has other reasons why the process only recognizes a kill -9. Here, if you absolutely have to stop the process, a kill -9 command is your last resort. If your UNIX operating system has process control (do you have a bg command to put a job in the background?), read the next paragraph before doing a kill -9. Otherwise, do it and cross your fingers.

Some UNIX operating systems that support placing jobs in the foreground or background have another option to the kill command that could possibly give you an out in the above situation. These versions of UNIX often have options to the kill command that allow you to stop execution of a process and restart it. On a Pyramid these options are kill -STOP and kill -CONT. These options are not universal, and they are not uniform between versions of UNIX. Check your manpage with man kill to see if you have these options. If you can stop the process by process control or by using your version of the kill -STOP command, you may see that the UNIX ps command shows that the process is eventually getting no time and is in a sleeping state. You can then use tbstat -u and check the flags for the sqlturbo you want to kill. If the flags don't show an X indicating that the process is not in a *critical state*, you have a chance. If it is in a critical state, use your equivalent of the kill -CONT command to restart the process. Keep stopping and starting it until it gets no time according to ps and doesn't have an X flag in the tbstat -u output, meaning that it is not in a critical section of code. Note the address column of the tbstat -u output for the sqlturbo process that you are trying to kill. Run a tbstat -s command and look for that address in the address column of the output. If the address is there, your process is holding a latch and doing the kill -9 will abort the engine. If the process is not holding a latch, you are safe in doing a kill -9. If it doesn't work and you really needed to kill the process, you haven't lost anything. You would have had to run the kill -9 command anyway.

No matter what you do, no matter how careful you are, you will crash like this sometimes. If the consequences are bad enough, the users usually learn to make the DBA kill the tough jobs.

Most of these problems have gone away with the introduction of the multithreaded architecture of the IDS engines. The only jobs that a user could kill would be the various oninit processes that comprise the executables of the engine. Killing one of these has nothing but bad effects, with the best being an immediate crash of the system and the worst being the need to restore from an archive. There's no point in even considering killing an oninit process unless it's the last thing you try prior to rebooting your system.

Thawing out a Frozen System

One of the true tests of the DBA's understanding of the system occurs when everything just suddenly freezes up. Nothing is getting done. Users find their screens just sitting there, Jobs either fail or disappear into the ether. The calls start coming in and the DBA has to go to work.

After learning that there is a problem, the first thing to do is to isolate it. Is the operating system up? If you are getting no screen response to your keystrokes, the problem is probably somewhere upstream of Informix. Either the OS is down or there is some sort of communication problem between the terminals and the system. How about the network? Call the system administrator and/or the network guru.

Assuming that you can actually communicate with the computer, run the Informix tb/onstat -u command. If it comes back with a shared memory error, your engine is down. Go into your online.log (or whatever you are naming it in your $TB/ONCONFIG file) and look at the bottom of the file. Look for lines with the word *abort* in them.

If you can identify the job that caused the abort, you will probably need to chase down the culprit and string him up by his thumbs. The username script is useful here.

Other than as a postmortem investigation, there's nothing else you can do. If the system has crashed, use tb/onmonitor or tb/onmode or one of the NT GUIs to bring it back up and hope that you aren't facing a long recovery period.

If you do not get a shared memory error when running tb/onstat -u, take a look at the flags column of the output. If you haven't committed all the flags to memory, run the seeuser script to look at the output with the added "training wheels" of informative column headings. The first character of the flag field will usually indicate the problem. If many or most of the processes show a "C," an "S," a "G," or an "L" in the first field, these jobs are waiting for something to happen. Usually, you can correlate this information with the information in the tb/onstat header and figure out why the engine is waiting.

If you are still in the dark about the situation, go back to the online.log. Look toward the end, or at the approximate time of the initial problem report. Look for any kind of error message that you aren't used to seeing. This implies that you have to know what is normal and what is odd. That's why you should always be monitoring your online.log. Any time you shut the system down or start it up, take a peek at the online.log file and verify that all is OK. Look for anything out of the ordinary.

If you don't find anything by looking at the online.log, run a few tb/onstat commands. Run a tb/onstat -p and see if anything is out of place. You may find high numbers in the deadlocks section or you may find high numbers in the ovlock, ovuser or other resource limitations sections. Run the status program. It will help you spot anything that looks out of place.

If you're still frozen up, run a tb/onstat -l command. Are your logfiles full? Shame on you. You probably haven't backed up your logs, or you've failed to turn on continuous backup of logfiles. Go in and do a manual backup of your logfiles and you'll be moving again.

Still lost? Try running a few iterations of watch_hot and see if your system is getting any disk activity. If it is, something's going on. Do you know what it is? Maybe it's a backend run amok or a disjoint query. Run your ps UNIX command. Do you see any processes with lots of time on them? They may be the culprits. If these are onit processes, don't be alarmed at high user times. It's normal. What's not normal is if these onit processes are sucking up all of your CPU time. This usually means that some massive query is running or that the engine has shunted itself out into the bushes and needs to be rebooted.

If you see some backends that are running wild, trace them down using ps. If all of your jobs are run as individual users, the job will be easier. Who owns the sqlturbo? What else is she doing? One frequent cause of sqlturbos running amok often occurs when you are running INFORMIX-4GL. This product sometimes leaves the sqlturbos running if the 4GL process is either killed or orphaned. There is no known cure for this other than a DBA (or a script) that watches for processes that are running with no frontends attached.

In IDS systems, you won't see sqlturbo processes. Instead look at onstat -g sql and see what is running. Beware that on very busy SMP systems, onstat -g sql may never return. The system tables that this command accesses may be changing so fast that onstat can't keep up with them. Do a few onstat -D commands and see where the disk reads and writes are occurring. If nothing's happening but the CPU is still hogged up, suspect an engine run amok. On IDS systems, check for any jobs that are running with a very high PDQPRIORITY. These jobs may be hogging up all of the decision support memory. Run an onstat -g mgm and look for jobs that are held up at one of the gates.

If all of your jobs are run as a particular user, it may be more difficult to track down the particular job causing a problem. Look at the PID (process ID) and PPID (parent process ID) of the offending backends. Trace the ownership of the offender. The offender's PPID will be the PID of the job that started it. You may have to trace it back through several levels, but eventually you'll come up with some job that started the problem.

Or maybe you won't. Oftentimes a job that starts a series of processes will either be killed when the user realized that it was doing the wrong thing or will simply die of its own accord or when it begins to consume so many operating system resources that the kernel kills the job. These "orphan" or "zombie" processes often cause problems with Informix, as the child processes can continue to run even if the parent is no longer viable. In these cases, you often have to take a chance on killing the process or just letting it run until the operating system finally gets around to killing it.

Jobs that Just Fail

Sometimes you will need to troubleshoot problems that are less drastic than the wholesale freezing up of your system. Maybe a program is not behaving as planned, or maybe a job being run by one of your users fails for no apparent reason.

The approach is essentially the same as listed above except that you are often under less pressure to solve it because everyone else is still running normally. Avoid the temptation to put the troubleshooting job off until later. Usually when something like this comes up, it is a warning about other potential problems that are just lurking around and waiting for a chance to grab you.

In solving problems with specific jobs, it is most important that you get a full report of the symptoms and error messages from the user. Have them write down any error messages they get, or better yet, tell them not to touch the terminal until you have a chance to come see it. Don't ever assume that just because a user tells you something that it is either correct, complete, or relevant. Users often think they are doing one thing while they are really doing something completely different.

You still follow the logical progression of identifying and isolating the symptoms, checking the logs and utilities, forming a theory about the problem, and acting on the theory. Make lots of use of your logfiles. If the user's job has methods of logging errors or tracing execution, use them.

Many, if not most, of your jobs that fail are caused by inconsiderate or uninformed user activity. This is defined as a user who is not following the general rules of courtesy and sanity in a multiuser database environment.

Some of the rules that are often broken are:

- Careless use of transactions
- Failure to promptly commit or roll back a transaction
- Creation of long transactions
- Trying to update or delete from a large, heavily-used table while the system is busy
- Careless query formulation
- Creation of disjoint queries that return billions of rows
- Failure to lock a table in exclusive mode while doing mass inserts into it or deletes from it. This causes the system to exceed the allowed number of locks.

If you find that the job that is failing is a long one or one that acts upon many rows, suspect either locking problems or long transaction problems. Either one should show up in the `online.log` as well as in specific error messages returned by the failing job.

If all else fails, consider whether your problem is really in the engine at all. Could you be reaching some sort of resource limits in the operating system? Could it be a terminal problem or a glitch on the line?

Above all, try not to be too dogmatic in your approach to troubleshooting. Try to be skeptical and flexible. Some of the worst troubleshooting problems are caused by red herrings. All the evidence seems to be pointing to one particular area. You've recently been having problems in just that area, and now, here it is again! Don't be too quick to make that assumption. It often seems that system problems come in clumps with complex failures of multiple systems at once. Unless you keep an open mind and look at each problem as an individual entity, you'll find yourself, like Alice, "chasing rabbits."

## CHAPTER 14

The Database Tuneup

*I*n the foreword to the second edition I rhapsodized about the straightforwardness and other virtues of the common automobile repair manual. In this chapter, I'll attempt to emulate that style of writing and outline a basic procedure that will allow you to tune an Informix database.

So why am I pushing this auto repair analogy so far? I want all of the DBAs reading this to take off their white lab coats and put on their overalls because proper database tuning will require them to poke around in places they usually don't poke. I want to demystify the tuning process. It's not rocket science, but a lot of users and DBAs are intimidated by database tuning and would rather do almost anything else but tune the database. If the database tuning process is approached with a methodical attitude and the guidelines found in this chapter are followed, the reader should be able to tune for most types of applications.

An author always has the question of how to address his readers. I think it makes the most sense in this context to address you as "consultants," for that is usually the role that you will be filling. That means that anyone that owns or uses the database you are tuning will be "clients." Actually, I think that just about all knowledge workers should view themselves as consultants. A consultant is hired and kept around only as long as she is needed. It's not really any different if you work for a large corporation Such terms as "job security" are practically oxymorons now anyway. If you think of yourself as a consultant no matter where you work, you'll better appreciate the need to deliver value. In most organizations, you're only as good as your last assignment.

PRODUCTION VERSUS DEVELOPMENT SYSTEMS

Tuning is an iterative and often time-consuming process. It's also a major inconvenience to users of a production system. Many of the tuning changes you will be making will require a database shutdown and restart. Some may require reconfiguration of the operating system or a kernel relink on UNIX systems. Some of the changes may make the situation worse than before.

Your tuning strategy must first consider the environment in which you'll be working. I'm making an assumption that you've never seen the system before, that you're just walking in the front door for the first time. You can either tune on a development or a production system. There are tradeoffs for each one. If you're tuning on a development system, you should be able to demand full control of the system. This means that there won't be someone else changing up the operating system or trying to reconfigure the database. You'll probably be able to start and stop the system with minimum hassle and inconvenience. You probably will have to contend with other developers on the system at the same time. Try to understand what they're doing and whether there will be someone on the production system doing the same thing. Developers and coders habitually put different types of loads on a system than users do. If your production users are running a fairly "canned" application, with little or no ad hoc querying and all querying done through your "canned" application, the loads will be consistent and will have consistent problems. On a development system, there's a lot more ad hoc querying going on as well as a lot of bad SQL that is in the process of being discarded. A major challenge is providing a production-level user load on a development system. A lot of times this is complicated by the fact that the development system is seldom an exact hardware duplicate of the production system. The development system often a less powerful sibling of the production system. Sometimes it is last year's production system,

Tuning on a production system is another matter entirely. Depending on the exposure of the system within the organization, one production database can affect many people within an organization. Random database restarts or operating system reboots will not endear you to the users. If you're lucky, you'll have a window after normal working hours that will allow you to tune. If you're in a 24 x 7 environment, tuning can be difficult or even impossible. You'll have a lot less leeway in tuning a production system, and your technique will be much more restrained and conservative. Aggressive experiments you may be able to try on a development system are often best forgotten in the production system.

Doing it Right the First Time

This chapter assumes the most common type of tuning environment, in which you're called in to tune up an existing system. You'll have some sorts of constraints placed upon your tuning activities depending upon your environment. If, by some freak of chance, you are tuning a production database before it actually goes production, you are in the rare position of being able to do it correctly the first time

If you can interject tuning issues early into the development process, you'll avoid many of the difficulties of tuning an active production system. The key to doing the development properly is to test at very high volumes and to resolve the tuning issues before the system goes into production. This is a lot more work and requires a lot more time than less rigorous testing does. It often requires a larger development system, one at least as large as a typical production system. Of course, your eventual production system can be the development system before it goes production. This is in many ways an ideal situation. Early development is done on the development machine. Volume testing should be done on the production machine prior to placing it in production.

Generating enough client load for testing a typical large database system is always a challenge. It often makes sense to combine your volume testing with some training or client acceptance procedure. While you're testing volume on the database, the trainees or client-side testers are generating volume for your testing. This "real" volume is quite valuable for testing purposes, since real users develop ways to crash systems that developers would never find by themselves. This real volume can be combined with workload generated by automated testing programs and with batch-processing, should the production system do batch processing. The idea is to simulate real volume as much as possible and for as long as possible.

This is an ideal way to move a new system into production. In many cases a system is rushed into production for revenue or other competitive reasons before being adequately tuned.

Informix Versions

This chapter is written from a Version 7.X perspective, but many of the same approaches are equally applicable to Version 5.X. Where possible, I'll note differences between versions. Otherwise, assume the information is specific to Version 7.

GETTING YOUR MARCHING ORDERS

When you are evaluating a new tuning assignment, you need to get examples of specific problems that you are to solve. Many times you'll just hear a very unspecific "the system's slow," but often you'll be presented with a detailed laundry list of problems with the system. Typical things that you'll see are:

- Performance slowing down
- System hangs or freeze up
- System crashes
- Specific queries take too long
- Random errors
- Jobs failing "for no reason"
- Contention errors
- Extent sizing problems

Unfortunately, these errors do not always come with neat little labels on them that tell you where they come from. For example, poor UNIX kernel configuration can result in seemingly random errors that seem to make no sense. Usually, a system's owners and users have the best instincts for the system's problems. Listen to them. They're a great resource. Get them to prioritize the problems, so that you can work on the most important issues.

It's important to establish an understanding about ground rules on the system. If you're on a production system, you need to know the rules about anything that will impact production work. Negotiate on this. In order to tune a production system properly, you will have to impact production to some extent. Make sure that whoever is signing your check knows this and is prepared for it. In any tuning exercise, it's possible that you'll stumble onto a bug or underlying problem that nobody expects. There's a possibility that you'll take the whole system down to such an extent that you'll have to recover from backups or even have to reinstall the operating system from scratch. This is a worst-case scenario, but you need to prepare for it. Make sure that you have access to all of the people and/or passwords that you need for the duration of the tuning effort. On a UNIX system, you will at least need the Informix user password. If you can get the root password, so much the better. Many of the utilities you'll use to inspect kernel parameters require root access. If you can't get root access, get access to the system administrator. If you're working on the system after hours, know how to get hold of anyone you need.

The underlying idea behind this stage is to set your and your client's expectations properly for the coming tuning task. You need to know what's needed by the client, and your client needs to know what's possible and what to expect.

BEFORE YOU START

Make sure that you have a current backup of the entire system, not just the database. Make sure that all of the operating system is backed up, with any flatfiles or temporary files that your application may use. Make sure that your backups contain enough configuration information to restore the system from scratch. On NT systems, do a database backup; then shut down the database and do a full NT system backup. Make sure you have current boot or repair disks in case the worst happens.

Compare this process to the way that the production database is currently being backed up. If there are any glaring differences, point them out. Part of a tuneup should be checking out the safety features anyway. Does the current backup procedure have any holes or area that is missed?

READ THE ONLINE.LOG

The online.log is the first place you'll visit. Be sure that you know how (if any) old logfile backups are stored. You'd like to be able to go back to the initial install in your logfiles if possible. Often, a client doesn't see the utility of keeping old logs. If this is the case, suggest they be saved and compressed or saved and archived on tape. Old logfile information can be very useful in tracing problems in the system.

There are several things that you look for in your first inspection of the online.log file. First of all, it's not always called online.log. This log is named in the $ONCONFIG file. For our purposes, though, it'll be online.log. A second thing you're looking for is "smoking guns" that indicate serious errors that have been encountered. These errors will be tagged with a "WARNING" label in the online.log. Any time you find a smoking gun, you need to know exactly what happened. You'll be more interested in recent errors in the logs. I prefer to read the logfile backward, starting at the end and working toward the beginning.

Get your users into the habit of logging errors and problems that they encounter, making sure that they log the exact date and time, along with any error messages they receive. If you have the dates and times, you can then check the online.log for error messages that appeared at that time.

Reading the logfile is only the first step of the tuneup process. Even if you find an obvious smoking gun, don't jump to the conclusion that this is either the only or even the primary problem. Once you have isolated and analyzed any warning messages in the logfile, don't just declare the tuneup project a success. Go through the entire process and at least hit on all the major areas, even if you think you've solved the problem early in the exercise.

THE OPERATING SYSTEM

The addition of Microsoft NT to the list of Informix-supported operating systems means that we can no longer just assume that an Informix application is running on UNIX. Currently, most large Informix databases are running on UNIX, but the NT systems are making inroads into what used to be strictly UNIX territory.

Most operating system tuning will be on UNIX systems, mainly due to the fact that NT is not easily tunable. On NT, the database will either run or it will not. There's not a lot of area in between.

UNIX is totally different. UNIX is the only major operating system that allows you to completely recompile the OS kernel in order to change operating system parameters. In fact, the process of creating a new kernel is actually recompiling and relinking the operating system.

If your target system is UNIX, you'll need to verify that the kernel was relinked with the proper parameters. Kernel tuning is done differently in different flavors of UNIX. If the system has a system administrator, consult with him and get him to relink the kernel for you. If not, go to your manuals and be sure that you understand the process.

If you are relinking the kernel, be sure that you save a copy of the current (working) version of your kernel. Also, be sure that you know how to boot up under the old kernel as well as under the new one.

Read the Release Notes

The release notes for your version of Informix will be found in the $INFORMIXDIR/release directory tree. With the implementation of global language support, there may be subdirectories under the release   For example, for a system running U.S. English, the release notes may be found in /usr/informix/release/en_us/0333. Whenever you are familiarizing yourself with a new Informix installation, always go through all of the files in the release notes.

The release notes will contain the most recent information about your particular port of Informix. The files containing kernel parameters will be named something like "ONLIN*." The correct file will usually contain semaphore parameters, shared memory parameters, process parameter, and information about whether various parameters are supported under your current release. You'll also often find information about such features as forced residency, kernel async I/O (KAIO), processor affinity, processor aging, and supported interface/protocol combinations. You may also find information about operating system patches that should be present on your system. If these patches are not in place, make sure that you manage to have them installed.

Note that these recommended kernel parameters come from the development group that actually did the port. Their parameters are parameters that have worked on their development machine. There is no guarantee that these parameters are the most efficient or the most optimal parameters. The only guarantee is that someone, somewhere got an Informix server to work using them. They are a place to start, not commandments chiseled into stone.

Inspect the Kernel

Once you know the required kernel parameters, check your current kernel's parameters. This usually requires root access to the system. If you have a system administrator, have her do the inspection and/or relinking.

Consider Other Applications

Unless the Informix server is the only application on the hardware, you must consider all of the other applications that are running on the server. If they have special shared memory or semaphore requirements, you will need to consider their kernel requirements in addition to Informix's kernel configuration requirements.

There are no hard and fast rules here. I generally try to err on the side of too many kernel resources rather than too few. Sometimes this liberal approach may lead to a bloated kernel. If the kernel grows unnecessarily large, its performance may be less than optimal. Always compare the size of your "before" and "after" kernels. If your "after" kernel is significantly larger than the "before" version, you may find that you've slowed the system down rather than sped it up. Kernel tuning is somewhat of a black art. It may take a bit of trial and error to get it right. You'll probably never be 100 percent sure that the kernel is right. For many of us, just having it right enough so that the database doesn't crash will be good enough. Look at kernel tuning as a go/no-go situation. It either works reliably or it doesn't. If it works reliably and without glaring evidence that there are problems, it is probably good enough to run in production. If you need to spend your time tweaking something, you'll find that you get more "bang for the buck" by concentrating on other areas such as indexing and analysis of your SQL code.

SYSTEM CONFIGURATION

Once you are comfortable that you have a properly configured kernel, you can begin to analyze other aspects of the system. Informix databases are complex systems, and all of the parts need to be working together correctly in order to achieve maximum performance. It's possible, though, to boil the complexity down to a few general areas that need to be considered in all instances:

- Memory
- CPU usage

- Disks
- Connectivity

Any of these elements can create a processing bottleneck that will slow the entire system down. Your task as a tuner is to uncover and eliminate these bottlenecks.

Database tuning is a continuous process because most databases change significantly over time. Tables grow. Disks fill up. New queries are run. What you get is sort of an onion effect. As you eliminate the biggest bottlenecks, other bottlenecks become visible. You never see the lower-level bottlenecks until the top-level ones are corrected. At some point, you either declare a victory and state that the system is tuned as well as it will ever be or you decide that the costs of further tuning do not outweigh the benefits gained from eliminating the remaining bottlenecks.

Although the title of this chapter is "The Database Tuneup," it could also be titled "The Database and Application Tuneup." It's futile to spend too much time tuning at the database internals level. Most systems will benefit most from tuning at the table, index, and application levels. Unless there are glaring problems with the Informix setup, your time will be best spent by optimizing your indexes, your SQL statements, and your table placement across the disks. If pressed to give a highly unscientific estimate, I'd guess that 10 percent of performance problems are at the Informix setup and configuration level and that the other 90 percent are at the application and table layout level.

This doesn't mean to ignore the Informix setup. Indeed, this is the first thing to inspect because you will not be able to successfully tune the 90 percent of problems that are application related until the 10 percent of problems that are setup related are addressed. The setup and configuration issues will affect just about everything that goes on in the database. Problems in this area will make it more difficult to identify application problems. This is a case of "a rising tide raises all boats." Fix the configuration problems and everything will run better. You can then concentrate on individual items that are not performing well.

Memory

The amount of shared memory available to Informix is a very important factor of the tuning equation. A server uses shared memory for many functions, the most critical being:

- Page buffers contain copies of pages read from disk. Since accessing data in RAM is much faster than accessing it from disk, you gain a tremendous performance advantage from getting the page from shared memory as opposed to having to read it from disk.
- Logical log buffer.
- Physical log buffer.
- Big buffers, which are used to enhance performance during sequential scans.
- Stored procedure and data dictionary caches.

- In-memory sorting.

There are two things you need to know in order to start tuning memory utilization. You need to know how much total memory you have available from the operating system, and you need to know how much memory you are currently using.

Total available memory does not necessarily mean the total amount of RAM on the system. It means the maximum amount of shared memory that you have available for use by the Informix database engine. Part of this maximum number is the amount of shared memory and the number of shared memory segments that you have configured into the kernel.

You need to consider the memory needs of any other applications running on the machine and the memory needs of the operating system. The optimum situation is to have nothing running on your Informix server machine other than the server itself. On the other end of the scale, one of the worst situations you can be in from a tuning standpoint is having multiple databases from different vendors all running on the same computer and competing for resources. This becomes even more complicated if the databases are administered and controlled by different people. It often becomes a tug of war between multiple DBAs and system administrators, all of whom want their particular systems to run optimally. Avoid this situation like the plague.

Unfortunately, it can be difficult to assign exact memory needs for the OS and for other programs. The major component that governs shared memory utilization is the BUFFERS parameter in the $ONCONFIG file. Tuning the BUFFERS entails changing the parameter and stopping and restarting the server. Informix recommends that you establish your buffer needs as follows:

- Start with an arbitrary number of buffers.
- Let the system run under load.
- Check the read and write cache hit rates.
- Increase the number of buffers and repeat the second two steps.
- If the cache hit rate increases, increase the number of buffers and try again.
- Keep doing this until you either run out of shared memory, the OS starts swapping, or until you fail to get an improvement in the hit rates. Then lower the BUFFERS until none of these things happens.

It's most important that you do not increase the memory usage to the point that the system starts swapping. Swapping is the kiss of death for UNIX performance. When your system swaps, entire processes are removed from memory and are saved off to your swap partition. When the processes need to run, they are copied from the swap partition back into memory, at a great cost in performance. You can spot swapping by sudden slowdowns of everything running on the system. The behavior is just like the freeze-up that occurs during an Informix checkpoint, except that it involves all processes, not just the Informix-related ones.

Your best tool on a UNIX machine for detecting swapping is the `sar` command. Check with your system administrator and see if he runs sar in data collection mode. When run like this, sar runs all the time and stores its data in a file that can later be analyzed by running sar against the output file. This is really the only way to spot swapping with sar. If you use sar in its interactive mode, you'll only see the results for the time that you're running it, and it will be very difficult to catch your system "in the act" of swapping. Be aware of the fact that running sar in the data collection mode may be detrimental to performance, as it consumes CPU cycles. If your system doesn't have sar, it may have other performance-monitoring utilities such as vmstat or iostat that can serve the same purpose. If you're not sure, check with your system administrator. There are different viewpoints on this, but I get concerned if I see any indication that the system *ever* swaps. Memory is cheap enough nowadays that adding physical memory to a system to avoid swapping makes a lot of sense. When you compare the cost of adding memory to the personnel and opportunity costs of spending time trying to shoehorn applications into limited memory, most often throwing hardware at a problem ends up being the cheapest solution.

The simplest way of seeing how much memory your Informix instance is using is to look at the first line of any of the `onstat` outputs. Memory use in kilobytes is the last number in the first line of the output. A more detailed analysis of memory allocation for the instance can be found by running `onstat -g mem`.

```
$ onstat -g mem
INFORMIX-OnLine Version 7.22.UC1   -- On-Line -- Up 22:50:42 -- 31240 Kbytes
Pool Summary:
name          class addr      totalsize freesize #allocfrag #freefrag
resident      R     c1d00018  15351808  12136    2          2
res-buff      R     c2ba4018  8404992   14184    2          2
global        V     c33b2018  147456    36088    376        19
mt            V     c33b6018  1646592   597520   645        42
rsam          V     c33b8018  212992    4472     218        1
aio           V     c33f0018  835584    114008   221        40
gls           V     c33f4018  24576     2480     348        2
dictpool      V     c33f8018  90112     5184     83         7
procpool      V     c33fc018  8192      7104     4          1
XTF_mem       V     c341a018  24576     15152    4          2
main_loop()   V     c34a4018  16384     856      114        1
2             V     c34b0018  8192      3368     7          1
3             V     c34be018  16384     3120     206        1
btclean       V     c35e2018  16384     6592     108        1
onmode_mon    V     c35fe018  16384     6592     108        1
13            V     c3602018  8192      3368     7          1

Blkpool Summary:
name          class addr      size      #blks
global        V     c33b2098  0         0
```

CPU Usage

This is one area where Version 5 differs significantly from Version 7. One of the major advantages of the later versions of Informix is that it is optimized for symmetric multiprocessing systems.

OLTP VERSUS DSS SYSTEMS

On-line transaction processing systems and decision support systems have radically different tuning needs. A typical OLTP system depends heavily upon indexes to achieve fast response from the database. In these systems the goal is to cache as much data in the buffers as possible, to reduce the number and frequency of disk accesses, and to do most or all of the data accesses through the use of indexes. There will often be multiple indexes on tables to support the major queries against them. The general approach in OLTP systems is one of finesse, in which the architect attempts to understand and prepare the system in advance for specific queries that will be run against the system.

Decision support systems usually handle very large quantities of data and the specific queries that are executed against the system are not usually known in advance. These systems depend more upon brute force than finesse. Where sequential scans are the kiss of death in OLTP systems, they are the norm in DSS systems. The DSS system is typically tuned to run sequential scans as efficiently as possible with little or no dependence on indexes.

Given the differences in requirements between the two types of systems, tuning a hybrid system that does both can be a major challenge for the DBA. Some of the tuning parameter and considerations to consider in tuning these different types of system are listed and explained in the following section.

Logging versus Nonlogging Databases

OLTP systems are most often concerned with managing transactions and are interested in being able to rollback any transactions that fail. These systems typically use either buffered or nonbuffered logging to accomplish this. In addition, they are concerned with being able to restore the database back to its condition an instant before a crash, so they need the logging to be able to restore from an archive and then roll forward the logs to the last transaction committed before a crash.

Decision support systems usually have less reliance on transactions than do OLTP systems. A majority of the work in most DSS systems consists of long queries with few if any inserts or updates. They often dispense with logging altogether and run as nonlogged databases. They are concerned with frequent requirements to load large quantities of data and often have daily, and sometimes even hourly, loads from other sources. Logging just slows these systems down. Due to the lack of user- or transaction-based inserts and updates, DSS systems are not always concerned with recovery of a database by using log rollforward. In such systems, it is often more expeditious to restore the last archive and then re-run any subsequent database loads than it is to maintain the logfiles needed for rollforward and to suffer the performance degradations inherent in using a logging mechanism.

This becomes more complicated in a hybrid system that has a mix of OLTP and DSS characteristics. One of the areas of complication is that a logging database cannot access the data from a nonlogged database directly. This is also a complication in which you have separate OLTP and DSS systems, with the OLTP system providing data to the DSS system for decision support analysis. Even though you are able to tune the two systems differently to meet their respective needs, if the DSS system takes the information directly (through SQL statements rather than by unloading to a flatfile and then loading into the DSS system) from the OLTP system the two systems need to share a logging mechanism.

BUFFERS

OLTP systems depend upon IDS's caching mechanisms to ensure rapid data access. These types of systems typically need to have large numbers of buffers configured to help in this task. Since total memory in most systems is usually restricted by economics or system limitations, typical OLTP systems usually benefit from allocating their total memory more to the resident portion, which holds the buffers, and less to the virtual portion, which holds the decision support memory.

DSS systems usually benefit from allocating as much memory as possible to the virtual portion with less allocated to the buffers. In systems that do large sequential scans of large tables, the entire table will probably not fit into your available buffers anyway. Keeping the number of buffers low in such cases has an additional benefit in DSS systems. The fastest way to access data in long sequential scans is by using the light scans that avoid buffering of the data. Light scans are used only if the total table size is larger than the amount of buffer space. In such cases, attempting to use a large number of buffers may actually cause you to avoid using light scans.

Again, it's a matter of balance when you have hybrid systems. Tune the system to make the most use of the buffers, and then allocate enough memory for the decision support queries also.

OPTCOMPIND

The OPTCOMPIND configuration variable is often misunderstood. The engine comes out of the box with OPTCOMPIND defaulted to 2. This means that the engine makes its query optimization "solely on costs." With OPTCOMPIND set to 0, the optimizer gives preference to nested-loop joins over sortmerge joins or hash joins. One would think that you get best performance when the joins are decided upon solely upon costs, but that's not always the situation. For most applications that use indexes to get to the data rows, a nested loop join will always be faster than either a sortmerge join or a hash join. Sortmerge and hash joins come into their own when doing large joins of the unindexed tables typically found in DSS systems. A general rule of thumb for tuning is to start with OPTCOMPIND at 0 for OLTP systems and at 2 for DSS systems. If you find that specific queries are being wrongly optimized, try to change the query path either by rewriting the SQL, running UPDATE STATISTICS with different options, using optimizer directives in 7.3 and above, or finally, changing the OPTCOMPIND.

I'd say that at least 20 percent of all Informix performance problems regarding slow queries that I have seen in the comp.databases.informix newsgroup are solved by setting OPTCOMPIND to zero.

PDQ settings

The parallel data query settings will differ between OLTP and DSS systems. Although it is not a hard and fast rule, DSS systems will depend heavily upon the parallelism built into the IDS server to handle many of its long sequential scans. This will be most effective if the tables are fragmented across many disk spindles. OLTP systems, on the other hand, will try to have indexes created that will minimize the use of sequential scans. Often, OLTP systems will have the PDQPRIORITY set to zero to completely avoid interpreting any queries as DSS rather than OLTP queries.

This may be a bit of overkill and it is probably because users and/or DBAs who are used to OLTP systems have been burned several times by parallel queries and have chosen to totally eliminate the possibility that the engine will try to interpret their carefully orchestrated and designed queries as DSS queries by accident.

RA_PAGES

A lot of the time spent by the engine in reading from the disk system is spent in positioning the disk heads to the point where reads should start. Many of the tasks involved in tuning for disk performance will be attempting to reduce the disk head positioning time. Also time-consuming is the time spent processing a page once the read has begun. Once your disk system has begun a read, the cost of reading further contiguous pages is relatively low. IDS can take advantage of this by setting two Informix ONCONFIG parameters, RA_PAGES and RA_THRESHOLD. When a sequential scan of either index pages or data pages is begun, the engine will bring in RA_PAGES worth of data and will begin. When the number of unprocessed pages in memory falls to RA_THRESHOLD, another read command will be issued, again bringing in RA_PAGES worth of data. During sequential scans, the idea is to keep the disk reading at top speed while avoiding pulling in too many pages and causing the page cleaners to have to clean a buffer page to make room for the next set of pages.

OLTP systems will try to avoid any sequential scans and will not typically alter the default read-ahead parameters. In these systems, the DBA will typically not be concerned with read-aheads. If they detect a long sequential scan that would benefit from using read-aheads the DBAs of OLTP systems will typically create an index to eliminate the scan rather than trying to make the scan more efficient.

DBAs with DSS systems will be more concerned with read-aheads and will try to keep increasing the efficiency of the read-aheads in order to speed up their scans. See the section on `onstat -p` for instructions on how to monitor the effectiveness of your read-ahead parameters.

Hardware Differences in DSS versus OLTP Systems

The type of system that you are running will influence the type and quantity of hardware that you will need. While everyone wants more memory, more and faster processors, faster and more reliable disks, and faster bus speeds, there are a few items that differ between OLTP and DSS systems.

RAID versus JBOD

Decision support systems typically store much more data online than do OLTP systems. Many of the larger and even medium-sized data warehouses can grow into the terabyte range. These systems will usually have some sort of a disk farm with tens or hundreds of physical disk drives. OLTP systems are usually somewhat smaller, although they can get to be a respectable size themselves. For DSS systems, the large data storage requirements usually mean that it is better to use the largest disks possible. One large disk is usually much more cost-effective than several smaller ones. A disk farm using large drives is more compact and easier to manage than a farm made of smaller drives. OLTP systems often like to use a larger number of smaller disks in order to spread the disk access out over more disk spindles and heads, thus increasing overall disk access performance.

One of the main decision points when you get to managing large disk farms is whether to run them as RAIDs or JBODs (just a bunch of disks). There is always a great bit of discussion about whether RAID systems make any sense in a database environment. The four most common RAID implementations are:

- RAID 0: Striped disks. These are hardware-controlled striping schemes that distribute the data across multiple drives and usually show improved read performance over JBOD, with no redundancy or failsafe features.

- RAID 1: Mirrored disks. These are hardware-mirrored disks and they provide redundancy and reasonable protection from data loss. The hardware handles all the mirroring. They incur little or no performance penalties over JBOD. The mirroring doubles the non-mirrored system's disk costs.

- RAID 0+1: Mirrored and striped. Hardware-controlled combination of RAID 0 and RAID 1. Provides good read performance, reasonable write performance, and hardware redundancy. By paying attention to the sizes of the stripes and the physical layout of the system, very good performance can be had in addition to hardware redundancy. Again, the mirroring doubles the cost of disks. RAID0+1 is the mirroring of two striped sets. RAID1+0 is similar, but it is the striping of N mirrored pairs of disks. RAID10 improves upon RAID01 in recovery time, as RAID01 has to recover an entire stripe set, while RAID10 must only recover the damaged drive, not the entire stripe set.

- RAID3: Striped, with one dedicated parity drive and synchronized spindles. Newer systems perform the parity comparison in hardware. RAID3 corrects data loss immediately through the use of parity.

- RAID5: Striped with distributed parity across all drives. This provides good protection from failures, as long as two drives don't fail at the same time. RAID5 usually exacts a penalty in write performance, but can often be viable solution that balances performance with protection and costs. RAID5's write performance can be greatly increased by adding large hardware memory caches to the system. RAID5 can also be a factor in causing overconfidence in the ability of the hardware to avoid failure. There are instances in which partial data losses can occur in RAID5, since RAID5 only uses parity to recover when a drive physically and catastrophically fails.

All of the hardware RAID solutions take some control of disk placement and disk usage away from the operating system and away from Informix and place it in hardware. In many cases, this will completely negate the built-in intelligence that IDS has with regard to fragmentation and parallel operations. When you go into a striped environment, the controller automatically fragments the data for you. While this may be easier, it robs you as DBA of the ability to fine-tune your disk access patterns.

Another question that often comes up is whether to use Informix's mirroring or to use hardware mirroring. Informix's mirroring is highly efficient and can approach the performance of hardware mirroring from a raw disk access speed perspective. Using Informix's mirroring will allow the DBA to do such tricky things as moving disk chunks from drive to drive by dropping and re-creating mirrors on the other drive. Informix's mirroring also allows intelligent reading from either the primary or the mirror drive based on load and access speed.

In general, DSS systems will tend to want to use the disk farm as a JBOD in order to take maximum advantage of Informix's fragmentation and parallelism. Since massive loads are the norm for DSS systems, the write penalties inherent in RAID5 are also a factor that will cause problems. OLTP systems are often real-time systems that cannot afford any slowdown or downtime due to disk problems, and often some form of RAID, usually RAID 0+1, will make more sense from a fault tolerance and performance standpoint.

System Memory

Both OLTP and DSS systems can benefit from as much memory as they can handle. The major difference between the two will be in how that memory is allocated.

Resident vs. Virtual Memory

OLTP systems will usually benefit from having as many buffers as possible, while DSS systems will benefit from using that memory for DSS queries instead (see BUFFERS, above).

Data loading

A common function in DSS systems is a nightly data load from another source. Often, the system will need to be tuned to maximize this loading speed. Things to look at here are:

- LRU_MAX_DIRTY: In another chapter, I suggested that both LRU_MAX_DIRTY and LRU_MIN_DIRTY be reduced to force the system to perform writes in between checkpoints and to minimize the delays in access time due to long checkpoints. This is less important when you are loading data, and you want to use the most efficient means of loading data with no concern for interruptions for checkpoints.
- CKPTINTVL: The same logic as above. Data loading will cause more frequent checkpoints anyway.
- PHYSFILE & PHYSBUFF: A larger physical buffer will cause more work to be done between checkpoints.

Indexes

OLTP systems are much more tolerant of many indexes than are DSS systems. Excessive indexes in DSS systems may be detrimental for several reasons. First, data loads will become slower with each additional index you load. Second, the existence of many indexes may cause the optimizer to try to treat your DSS queries as OLTP queries and actually slow down your system.

TABLE FRAGMENTATION

IDS engines support the intelligent placement of tables across multiple disks or across multiple files on a disk. This is known as table fragmentation, and contrary to the terminology commonly used in computer systems, fragmentation in this case is a good thing. Fragmentation occurs at table create or table alter level. In the table creation statement the DBA can specify a scheme for placing the table data into different dbspaces based on certain conditions exhibited by the data.

There are two methods of table fragmentation:

- Round-robin: This type of fragmentation attempts to evenly distribute all of the data across all of the listed dbspaces for the table. In a non-fragmented table that consists of multiple dbspaces, the dbspaces are filled in order of creation. Until the first space gets full or very close to full the second dbspace receives no data.

- By expression: In fragmentation by expression, the DBA establishes logical or mathematical expressions that determine which dbspace a particular row will go into. For example, a table of part numbers may be fragmented such that parts #1 through #10000 will be placed in the first dbspace, #10001 through #20000 in the next dbspace, and so on.

How Your Data is Distributed

It is important for you to understand how your data is distributed before you embark upon a fragmentation strategy. In a case where you have an existing table or have a table that you believe will be distributed in the same way as the new table, the best way to explore your data distribution is a two-step process. First, run an UPDATE STATISTICS HIGH or UPDATE STATISTICS MEDIUM. This generates the distributions. Note that a plain old UPDATE STATISTICS is the same as UPDATE STATISTICS LOW and does not generate distributions.

To see the distributions, run this command:

```
$ dbschema -d your_database_name -hd your_table_name
```

This will generate a distributions report that looks something like this:

```
DBSCHEMA Schema Utility        INFORMIX-SQL Version 7.30.T
Copyright (C) Informix Software, Inc., 1984-1998
Software Serial Number XXXXXXXXX
{

Distribution for informix.systables.tabname
Constructed on 10/02/1998
Medium Mode, 2.500000 Resolution, 0.950000 Confidence

--- DISTRIBUTION ---
     (              GL_COLLATE         )
  1: (   1,    1,   GL_COLLATE         )
  2: (   1,    1,   GL_CTYPE           )
  3: (   1,    1,   VERSION            )
```

```
 4: (    1,     1, sysblobs           )
 5: (    1,     1, syschecks          )
 6: (    1,     1, syscolauth         )
 7: (    1,     1, syscoldepend       )
 8: (    1,     1, syscolumns         )
 9: (    1,     1, sysconstraints     )
10: (    1,     1, sysdefaults        )
11: (    1,     1, sysdepend          )
12: (    1,     1, sysdistrib         )
13: (    1,     1, sysfragauth        )
14: (    1,     1, sysfragments       )
15: (    1,     1, sysindexes         )
16: (    1,     1, sysobjstate        )
17: (    1,     1, sysopclstr         )
18: (    1,     1, sysprocauth        )
19: (    1,     1, sysprocbody        )
20: (    1,     1, sysprocedures      )
21: (    1,     1, sysprocplan        )
22: (    1,     1, sysreferences      )
23: (    1,     1, sysroleauth        )
24: (    1,     1, syssynonyms        )
25: (    1,     1, syssyntable        )
26: (    1,     1, systabauth         )
27: (    1,     1, systables          )
28: (    1,     1, systrigbody        )
29: (    1,     1, systriggers        )
30: (    1,     1, sysusers           )sertype
31: (    1,     1, sysviews           )sertype
32: (    1,     1, sysviolations      )
Constructed on 10/02/1998
Medium Mode, 2.500000 Resolution, 0.950000 Confidence
```

The first number (followed by a colon) is simply a sequential bucket number. The second number is the total rows in that bucket. The third number is the number of unique rows. The final value is the high value for that bucket. In the sample case, we're looking at the system table "tabname," and all of the rows are unique, so the distribution is even across all the rows.

By analyzing the output of this dbschema command, you can get an idea of how the data is distributed across key values. Based upon this, you can better decide upon a fragmentation scheme.

Round-Robin Fragmentation

This type of fragmentation is the simplest fragmentation scheme to implement, as there is no effort to place the rows in specific dbspaces. Instead, the emphasis is on evenly distributing the data across all of the dbspaces in the fragmentation scheme. This type of fragmentation is best if you are sure that most of the queries against the table will be sequential scans that access all rows in the table and that WHERE clauses will not be very selective. In such cases where all the rows will be accessed a round-robin fragmentation scheme will distribute the reads fairly evenly across all available dbspaces. The dbspaces should be placed on different disks, preferably on different controllers if possible.

This scheme is also good for data loading, as it eliminates "hot spots" caused by trying to load all rows into one or two dbspaces. Optimally, you should have enough AIO-VPs available to allow one for each fragment. This is consistent with the general rule of one per physical disk since you should have one fragment per disk in an ideal situation.

Another benefit of round-robin fragmentation also ties into the data loading efficiency. If one of the dbspaces in a round-robin fragmented table is down, an INSERT statement will simply ignore it and place it in the first available dbspace. If the same thing occurs in a table fragmented by expression and the desired dbspace is offline, the INSERT statement will fail. A round-robin scheme is good in cases in which you don't know the distribution of values in the table, as it will spread the load out as evenly as possible.

Fragment by Expression

This type of fragmentation is good for cases in which you know the distribution of data and do not expect to have to do full table scans to access the data. This type of fragmentation can almost be viewed as a very high-level form of indexing for DSS tables that do not have indexes.

One of the benefits of fragmentation by expression is the possibility of fragment elimination. This occurs when the fragmentation scheme is such that some or most of the fragments can be eliminated from consideration for table scans. This occurs when the WHERE clause is selective enough to allow the engine to decide which fragments could possibly hold all candidate rows.

The ideal way of creating a fragmentation expression is to create non-overlapping fragments on a single column in the table. Such a fragmentation scheme would be something like:

```
FRAGMENT BY EXPRESSION
member_id > 1 and member_id <= 10000  in dbspace1,
member_id > 10000 and member_id  <= 20000 in dbspace2,
member_id > 20000 and member_id  <= 30000 in dbspace3;
```

- WHERE clause: Range statement using a relational operator ($<$, $>$, $<=$, or $>=$)
- WHERE clause: Equality statement using an equality operator ($=$, IN)

In this case, one or two fragments may be eliminated depending upon the exact formulation of the WHERE clause. A WHERE clause such as either of the following would not allow any fragments to be eliminated:

- WHERE member_id > 5000 and member_id < 25000;
- WHERE member_id IN (5000, 15000, 25000);

If one or more fragments can be eliminated from scanning in a DSS query, the query will perform faster than if all fragments had to be scanned. Note that this can be of benefit even if all of your fragments are on one large RAID drive. Even though you do not gain any of the benefits of being able to selectively place rows on different disk drives, you still can eliminate the number of rows that have to be scanned. In the example above, assume that the member_ids are sequential from 1 to 30,000. Without fragmentation a sequential scan would have to scan 30,000 rows no matter what. With fragmentation, the query could possibly scan as few as 10,000 rows.

The fragmentation formula can be as simple or as complicated as you like, and it can be based upon more than one column in the table. While such formulas may have some applications, in general it is better to stick with a simple, nonoverlapping formula. One reason for this is that when rows are inserted or updated in the table, the formulas have to be evaluated until one of them is true in order for the row to be placed in the proper dbspace. If more than one are true, the first true one determines placement. If you use complicated formulas, your loading and updating activities can be slowed significantly. Don't use formulas that require any type of data conversion in these fragmentation expressions. This will also slow your activities significantly. Don't use dates or datetimes in the fragmentation clause since they are internally converted to integers.

There are two other ways of fragmenting by expression that can be used if you absolutely have to, but they each allow fragment elimination only for equality WHERE clauses and not for range WHERE clauses:

- Overlapping or noncontiguous fragments on a single column
- Non-overlapping fragments on multiple columns

Both of these schemes may have some use in limited applications, but you should strive for a simple nonoverlapping fragmentation scheme on a single column.

Another way to increase performance with a fragmentation scheme is to pay attention to the order of statements in the fragmentation clause. The earlier example should really be written like this for maximum performance:

```
FRAGMENT BY EXPRESSION
member_id <= 10000 and member_id > 1 in dbspace1,
member_id <= 20000 and member_id  > 10000 in dbspace2,
member_id <= 30000 and member_id  > 20000 in dbspace3;
```

The only difference is in the order in which the inequalities are evaluated. In the first case, all of the member_ids are greater than 1, so that clause is always evaluated. A logical AND statement only evaluates the second portion of the statement if the first part is TRUE. When you place the most restrictive part of the clause first, you are giving the engine the option of determining that the entire AND statement is FALSE after evaluating the more restrictive first part and without having to evaluate the second part.

In the first example, to insert a member_id of 27000, here is the series of calculations that would be done:

```
member_id > 1              TRUE so evaluate
member_id <= 10000         FALSE so evaluate
member_id > 10000          TRUE so evaluate
member_id <= 20000         FALSE so evaluate
member_id > 20000          TRUE so evaluate
member_id <= 30000         TRUE so it goes in dbspace3
```

With the orders reversed in the fragmentation clauses the logic flow would look like this:

```
member_id <= 10000         FALSE, so ignore the second half of the formula
member_id <= 20000         still FALSE, ignore second half of 2nd formula
member_id <= 30000         TRUE, so evaluate the second part
member_id > 20000          TRUE, so it goes in dbspace3
```

By arranging the fragmentation statements so that the most restrictive part is first, we performed the insert with four compare operations in the second instance versus six compare operations in the first. This can make a significant difference when you are inserting millions of rows.

If you know that your data distribution is skewed, you can also gain performance by arranging the FRAGMENT BY clause so that the most common data elements are evaluated first, thus avoiding subsequent comparisons. If you use a FRAGMENT BY/REMAINDER IN clause, the REMAINDER dbspace is always scanned, so avoid using REMAINDER if you can.

In this example, the fragmentation is non-overlapping and based upon a single column. There is only one possible fragment for any row with a given value. In this case, any WHERE clause based upon member_id may allow fragment elimination:

Fragmentation by Hash Expression

This method is one type of FRAGMENT BY EXPRESSION that can also help you divide your data evenly across multiple dbspaces while giving you the advantages of fragment elimination. Suppose you want to fragment by the value of an integer, member_id and you want to fragment across three dbspaces. Do it like this:

```
FRAGMENT BY EXPRESSION
mod(member_id, 3) = 0 in dbspace1,
mod(member_id, 3) = 1 in dbspace2,
mod(member_id, 3) = 2 in dbspace3;
```

As long as the distribution of member_ids is random, the data will be distributed evenly across the the three dbspaces. On the other hand, if all of your member_ids were multiples of 3, dbspace1 would be full and the other two would be empty..

Other Benefits of Fragmentation

A good table fragmentation scheme can benefit both OLTP and DSS systems. Table fragmentation becomes more important as the tables get larger. In addition to the well-known benefits of fragmented tables with regard to intelligent access to the disk system, there are several additional features that can come into play in deciding if and how to fragment your tables.

One often overlooked benefit from fragmenting a large table by expression is that the fragmentation can be done with the aim of making it easier to manage moving data out of the main table into a history table. For example, suppose you have a financial table that is fragmented such that January transactions go onto disk A, February transactions go onto disk B, etc. When it comes time to delete January transactions from the table or to move them into a history table, this is easily done with an "ALTER FRAGMENT/DETACH" statement. This type of action would be more important in an OLTP than in a DSS system, since OLTP systems typically need to keep the table sizes smaller than DSS systems.

Fragmenting and Locating Indexes

IDS systems have alleviated some of the problems that earlier OnLine systems had with interleaving index pages with data pages by giving the DBA more flexibility in locating and fragmenting indexes. The CREATE INDEX clause with no special parameters behaves like OnLine systems and places the index in the same dbspace as the table. There are two new options:

```
CREATE INDEX blah_blah on tablename(column) in dbspace1;
CREATE INDEX blah_blah on tablename(column)
FRAGMENT BY EXPRESSION
     column  < 20000    in indexspace1,
     column >= 20000    in indexspace2;
```

These two options allow you much more flexibility in managing your index layouts than OnLine did. As a rule, if you fragment your indexes it is better for the indexes to use the same fragmentation scheme as the table. The only allowable fragmentation method for indexes is FRAGMENT BY EXPRESSION. You cannot use round-robin index fragmentation. If your table is fragmented round-robin and you do not specify an IN DBSPACE clause for the index, the index will be fragmented in the same round-robin manner, bringing your indexed reads down to a crawl. Always specify an IN DBSPACE clause for a round-robin fragmented table.

Extent Sizes for Fragmented Tables and Indexes

With a non-fragmented table, whenever you specify a EXTENT SIZE clause the first extent is given that size and subsequent extents get the NEXT SIZE. This changes when you fragment your tables. In a fragmented table, the EXTENT SIZE refers to the initial extent size for *each fragment*, not for the whole table. If you don't realize this, you may be creating your fragments much larger than you actually need.

You cannot specify EXTENT SIZE for fragmented indexes. Their extents are calculated as a fixed percentage of the extent sizes of the fragments..

Understand your Database Setup

When you are tuning a database, especially one that may be new to you, it is important to get right down to the hardware and operating system levels if you want to really obtain the best performance. Only by knowing exactly what is happening under the covers can you extract the maximum amount of performance out of a system, no matter what it is used for. Simply doing `onstat` or `oncheck` commands will not tell you about the underlying nature of the system you are tuning.

Disk Layout

Since much of the work of database tuning involves minimizing delays spent in accessing the disk system, it is incumbent upon the tuner to understand exactly how the disks are connected to the system. You need to know such things as:

- How many physical disks are there?
- How many disk controllers?
- Which disks are on which controllers?
- How fast are the disks?
- Are some faster than others?
- What other applications are hitting what disks?
- What disk is the operating system on?
- Where is the swap space located?

These questions are all useful in determining how to place your tables on the disk. Also important is some knowledge of the applications running. If you know that you have two large tables, Table A and Table B, that are frequently joined, it would be a good idea to place them on different disks and on different controllers. This allows you to bring as many spindles into play as possible and to reduce access times when these tables are joined.

Raw or Cooked Files

On most systems, raw disk access is faster than access through the operating system. To achieve maximum performance you need to be sure that all of your chunks are on raw partitions. This is not immediately obvious from `onstat` or oncheck outputs. You need to be sure that the underlying devices are raw devices.

Proper File Types

In UNIX systems, storage devices can be two different types of devices, block-special devices or character-special devices. Informix runs best on character special devices. These devices can be identified either by their names or by their permission flags. For example, here is a listing of some UNIXWare devices:

```
crw-rw-rw-   1 root     sys      89,34747 Sep 23  1995 vfs3b
crw-rw-rw-   1 root     sys      89,34748 Sep 23  1995 vfs3c
crw-rw-rw-   1 root     sys      89,34749 Sep 23  1995 vfs3d
crw-rw-rw-   1 root     sys      89,34750 Sep 23  1995 vfs3e
```

These devices are all found in the /dev/rdsk subdirectory. The "rdsk" indicates that they are character-special devices, and the "crw-rw-rw-" flags verify it. The "r" in "rdsk" actually stands for "raw". The following devices on an HP/UX 11.0 system in the /dev/dsk subdirectory are block special devices:

```
brw-r-----   1 bin      sys      31 0x005000 Apr  4 20:30 c0t5d0
brw-r-----   1 bin      sys      31 0x012000 Apr  4 20:30 c1t2d0
brw-r-----   1 bin      sys      31 0x013000 Aug 31 16:10 c1t3d0
brw-r-----   1 bin      sys      31 0x014000 Aug 12 16:51 c1t4d0
```

The only way to be sure that you are using the correct types of devices is to trace down every link to the proper device in the /dev directory structure and verify that they are the correct type.

The block and character devices are actually the same disk devices, and they represent the same physical space. The only difference between them is the way that they are read. In cases where you may be using a block-special device and really want to use a character-special device, you can just change the links to the the appropriate device in the "rdsk" subdirectory. The data doesn't need to be moved.

Using the wrong type of raw file can be a very subtle performance problem. The system will never complain about using the wrong file type. It will just never perform as well as it should. There are no other symptoms.

No Overlapping Tracks

While you are at the operating system level inspecting the devices that the chunks are made of is a good time to check for chunks that overlap or have gaps in them. This one is both subtle and easy. It's easy because you will have no difficulty in determining when you have a problem. If you have overlapping tracks, something very bad will happen and you will be hard-pressed to ignore it. The problem is that it will not happen until you happen to try to use the portion of the disks that overlap. Until then, you'll just hum along as though nothing were wrong. When you are tracking down the block or character status of the disk devices, check the major and minor device numbers to verify that you or an earlier DBA have not mistakenly used the same device or parts of the device in multiple chunks. Informix will just check the names of the chunks. If you have linked two different names to the same device, Informix will merrily accept the fact and allow you to overwrite one chunk or part of a chunk with another. The only way to check this is to understand the mechanism that your UNIX uses to divide up the devices.

A common occurrence in UNIX is for there to be one name for the device that includes all of the disk, another name for the first 250 or so megs, a different name for the first 500 megs, etc. When you're checking this out, check with the UNIX system administrator to be sure that your system is not using the same portion of the disks for different chunks.

Trust me, it will eventually come back to bite you if you ignore this. I speak from painful experience.

UNDERSTAND THE APPLICATION

Before you can successfully tune a system, you have to understand the types of applications that run on it. We've gone into fairly extensive detail about the tuning differences between OLTP and DSS systems, and that should give you some general rules for tuning, but they are just general guidelines. Every system is different, and they all have different requirements. Don't just take for granted that you know how the system is being used. Check it out firsthand.

Understand not only what types of applications run, but also when they run and how long it takes. Be sure that you are aware of any processing windows, especially any hard windows that cannot be violated.

A good example was a major credit card processing application that I was contracted to tune. The company processed millions of dollars a day and had a hard deadline at 5:00 in the afternoon. If they had not completed their daily bank deposit by that time, the bank began assessing monetary penalties for every five minutes that it was late. When the end-of-day process ran slowly, it became the most important process in the entire shop. Forget that I had reduced OLTP response time for the operators by 20 percent. Forget that they were able to process 30 percent more work in a day. The only thing that mattered was that they make that five o'clock window.

Tuning is not only making the system run faster. It is also making the right parts of the application run faster. From a purely political standpoint, when an operator had to wait 30 seconds for a logon to complete, it was no big deal. When the CEO had to wait the same 30 seconds, it was time to call in the cavalry.

Application Tuning Hints

A complete tuneup of a database system should also include an analysis of the actual code of any programs that are running on the system. This assumes that you can get access to the source code. Without source code access, you are restricted to using `onstat -g` to see what SQL is executed and making inferences from there. The best way to do this is through a process of code review during development.

Code Reviews

Most database code is written by developers who do not have an in-depth under-standing of the database. They may be writing code at a lowest-common-denominator level with the goal of having the code run against multiple databases. They probably do not un-derstand the optimizer. In many cases, they may be duplicating the functions of an earlier program that was written in COBOL to run against ISAM files. They consider themselves successful if the screens look the same as the specifications and if the rows in reports match the ideal results that they have been given to verify against.

The best way to conduct code reviews is during the development of the software. As a minimum, all developers should be required to run SET EXPLAIN against all queries that they code for the application. Make it a rule with no exceptions. No SET EXPLAIN, no quality assurance clearance. A better method is to have the DBA personally approve any SQL that goes into the application. By doing this, the DBA will get to know the application very well and will be able to determine indexing and fragmentation schemes that will best suit the application.

Even if the coders are very good, they may still not know the intricacies and pitfalls of a particular database system. Someone who is a wizard with Sybase may assume that the same techniques work in Informix. Sometimes this can be an expensive assumption.

PREPARED Statements

A good example of this is in the area of prepared SQL statements. Informix is some-what unique in that it is very sensitive to optimizing and communications times. What this means is that every time a SQL statement is generated by an application, whether it be an ESQL/C program or `dbaccess`, several steps have to take place. The program has to parse the statement, manipulate variables, and submit the query to the engine. When it gets to the engine, the engine has to parse and recognize the statement, obtain information from the system tables, optimize the query plan, accept any variables, execute the query, and finally send the results back to the client. In all, there are about 10 time-consuming steps that the engine has to complete before returning data to the client.

If this is a singleton statement that is only executed one time, this is no big deal. The engine just takes the steps and goes on to do the next job. It is different, though, if the same statement is repeated thousands or even millions of times in a program. Redoing these 10 steps a million times can seriously impact the performance of a program. This usually happens when the query is imbedded deep within a loop. Look at these two sections of pseudocode:

```
FOR x = 1  to  1000
FOR y = 1 to 1000
EXEC SQL SELECT * from mytable
WHERE blah_blah = x and
Foo_bar    = y;
DONE
DONE
```

This select statement has to go through all 10 steps a million times. Now look at the next section of code:

```
PREPARE mystatement from "SELECT * from mytable
WHERE blah_blah = :x and
Foo_bar    = :y";
FOR x = 1  to  1000
FOR y = 1 to 1000
EXECUTE mystatement using :x, :y;
DONE
DONE
```

The PREPARE/EXECUTE combination parses and optimizes the statement one time, when the statement is prepared. All that is required for each execution is for the client to pass the required :x and :y variables to the engine. The engine doesn't have to parse or optimize the statement again. It just runs the query and returns the results.

The performance gains are impressive. I have seen performance improvements in specific programs in the range of 5000 percent. That's a fifty-fold speed increase. That's significant.

If you do one thing in a code review, check for instances where you're executing any type of SQL deep inside a series of program loops or many times within one shallower loop. This is absolutely the most important thing you can do to improve performance in application code.

It also has the advantage of giving you a tremendous amount of leverage. By leverage, I mean that you do something once, and the results get multiplied by hundreds or thousands of times. Once a programmer sees you speed up her code one time and sees the results that it brings, you can be certain that she'll go back to her desk and start looking for other places to apply the same code changes. If you want to look like a wizard, do this and then give the credit to the programmers. "Nah, I didn't do anything. I just showed her a couple of tricks and she took it from there." This is the perfect lazy DBA technique. If the programmers can make their queries much more efficient, it will make your management job much easier. The benefits of PREPARE/EXECUTE don't end with queries. Just about any type of SQL statement can benefit from being prepared once and repeatedly executed.

Rational Design

Try to understand the logic flow behind any programs that you are reviewing. Often, the problems have nothing to do with the SQL or with the database for that matter. Check to be sure that the work being done by a program actually makes sense. I have seen instances in which a programmer would SELECT a processing date a million times inside a loop and then do some processing inside the loop using the processing date. The date didn't change between executions of the loop. SELECT the date once, put it in a variable, and use the variable rather than a SELECT statement. Always ask yourself if tasks really need to be done, and if they do, can they be done more efficiently.

Dynamic Queries

Dynamic queries are often used to allow the user to modify WHERE clauses or to request different columns from the database tables. While this is very flexible, it can cause problems when users want to do a query on the last digit of the zip code in a 10 million row table. If the program allows dynamic queries like this, make sure that there are some limitations on what the user can request and make sure that your tables have indexes that can satisfy all the possible queries.

Of course, if you're in a DSS environment, you'll have to make sure that your system is tuned to allow maximum efficiency in handling these types of ad hoc commands.

Concurrency Issues

Often, a program will work well during testing and even during stress testing only to completely fall apart when it goes into a production environment. Many times, the problem will relate to locks and concurrency issues. If you are experiencing inexplicable slowdowns, killed jobs, or system timeouts, look to concurrency issues as the culprit. If the problems only occur under heavy load look to concurrency issues. There are several things that you can do to reduce these concurrency issues:

- Change the table from page-level locking to row-level locking. This reduces the possibility that someone will lock one row on a page and prevent others from accessing any rows on the page.

- Change your isolation level. Dirty reads can occur whether or not a row is locked by someone else.

- SET LOCK MODE to WAIT. This prevents an immediate failure if a row that you want is temporarily locked.

- Build in robust error-checking code. If your error-checking code is good enough, it can detect a concurrency problem, wait a few seconds and then retry the transaction.

- Keep transactions short. Never keep a transaction open for extended periods of time, especially update transactions. They will place all sorts of nasty locks and will affect other users.

Network Considerations

Consider the amount of data that must be transferred between client and server. For example, suppose you have a million-row table and need only a thousand of those rows for your computation. You could query the database for all million rows and let the client application filter out the rows it needs, or you could query the database with a WHERE clause that returns only the thousand desired rows. This may seem like an extreme example of poor programming, but I have seen such code in production systems. You'll see this most often in cases where an existing nondatabase program is converted to use a database and the programmer used the same type of logic in the new code as he saw in the old code.

Use the Database to Do the Work

You may see ported legacy code in which the developer does a SELECT from one table into an array, then a SELECT from another table into another array, and then walks down one array checking data in the second.

This is a holdover from the way the system may have been coded when it was getting its data from ISAM files. The programmer tries to handle the logic in the same way as before. It works, but it is just using the database as a fancy, expensive flat-file storage system. Be on the lookout for places where the programmer is not using the power of the database and is depending upon program code to handle jobs that are best done inside the database.

Stored Procedures and Triggers

Be on the lookout for opportunities to use stored procedures and triggers to accomplish tasks at the engine level that the programmer is trying to accomplish at the program level. Usually it will be more efficient to let the engine do the work.

An example might be a situation in which the programmer is checking for data that has changed. When he detects a change, he goes into a subroutine to update some other tables or to perform some other action. This is a perfect chance to use a trigger at the engine level and to allow the database to do the work and not burden the client or the network with more work that can be done more efficiently by the engine.

Stored procedures can help you achieve some of the same benefits as PREPARES and EXECUTES. The stored procedures are parsed and optimized once and usually perform better than similar queries submitted from the client as straight SQL.

Problem Fixes for Informix Dynamic Server

This chapter is more or less specific to the Informix Dynamic Server (IDS) engine. Much of the data is anecdotal and comes from postings in the comp.databases.informix newsgroup. Absolutely none of this is officially supported by Informix, Informix Press, Prentice Hall, or myself for that matter.

These items are often in conflict with conventional wisdom and are presented to you with a "your mileage may vary" type of disclaimer. These are mostly things that other people have said worked for them. I haven't tried many of them for myself, so if you take any of these suggestions, first of all make sure that you do nothing to harm your database. This means taking adequate backups before beginning and monitoring the status before and after making any modifications. If anything looks suspicious, restore from your archive. It's better to waste a little time now doing a restore than to waste a lot of time later trying to undo the effects. If you have the luxury, test these out on a system that is not business-critical before implementing them on a production system.

BUFWAITS

Problem: Too Many Bufwaits

Excessive number of bufwaits observed in IDS 7.22. What is the cause and what do I need to correct it? Have not seen any ovbuff entries in `onstat -p`.

Solutions: LRUs and Read-Ahead

- Try increasing your LRUS. Sometimes bufwaits can be caused by excessive LRU contention.
- Excessive bufwaits can also be caused by high user activity or excessive number or discarded read-aheads. Try lowering your RA_PAGES and/or RA_THRESHOLD parameters to reduce the number of read-aheads if your `onstat -p` output indicates that you are experiencing lots of discarded read-ahead pages.
- Try increasing the BUFFERS value.
- You may be getting hit by a bug in which certain LRU settings are problematic. Try decreasing or increasing your LRU settings by one and see what happens.

DISK DEVICES

Problem: Wrong Devices

System is using block-special devices rather than character-special devices for database chunks. What kinds of problems can this cause, and what do I need to do to fix it?

Solution: Change the Link

If you have used links for your chunk names, just drop the link to the block-special device and replace it with a link to the character-special device. The disk location is the same; only the data access methods differ between the corresponding block and character devices.

Solution: Mirroring or dd

If you haven't used links, you'll have to physically move the data. The block devices are buffered devices, and UNIX considers that these a write to the buffer for these devices is equivalent to a write to disk. Informix believes that the data is on disk as soon as it does the write and may eliminate some memory structures, believing the data is safely stored. A system crash can cause excessive data loss.

Another problem is that the system may experience frequent lockups during checkpoints when Informix tries to clean all the buffers at once, thus overwhelming the UNIX cache. A quick fix would be to up the UNIX cache numbers, but the real solution is to move the chunks to character-special devices.

There are several possible ways to do this. None of these techniques should be undertaken lightly, and they should not be attempted without having at least one good, recent backup. If possible, test this on another machine first:

- Export your data and reinstall your engine using correct devices, then re-import the data into the new system.

- Use the UNIX dd command to move the data from the block device to the character device, then point the link that you used to identify the device to the character rather than the block device. This is one of the major reasons that you should never use the actual device names when creating chunks. Always use a link. Then you can change the link to point somewhere else if you need to change it due to screwups or due to hardware problems.

- Mirror the chunk in question to another location, even a UNIX file if need be. Mark the primary chunk down. Either delete the primary chunk if it's a UNIX file, or relink it to the proper character-special device. Recover from the mirror to the new primary chunk, which should now be on the correct device. This has the advantage of letting you do the move without bringing the database down.

Problem: Checking a Disk

I think I may have a disk problem in one of my chunks. How can I be sure that a disk device has no bad blocks and can be read. Also, how can I verify that the size of a raw device is what I think it is?

Solution: dd

Use the UNIX dd command. If you are on NT and have the MKS Toolkit, it also has a dd command, so you can do the same thing on NT.

```
dd if=device_name of=/dev/null bs=1024K
```

The system will then attempt to read the device and, if successful, will return with a number of blocks read. In this case, the blocksize is 1 megabyte (1024K), so the number will be the size in megabytes of the device.

You can also check the UNIX system logs to see if UNIX has complained about any disk reads or other hardware errors. See your system administrator for help with this.

You can also do a limited validity check of the actual contents of the disk device by deleting the "of=/dev/null" parameter in dd and piping the output to od -x. Look at the pages and see if you can read the page numbers (first word on each 2K page is the address of the page) and timestamps (second word on the page). The timestamps should match the last word on each page.

Question: How can I Measure Disk Speed

How can I time the speed of the disks that I'm using for IDS?

Answer: Use dd

Use the following dd command:

```
time dd if=/dev/yourchunk of=/dev/null bs=2048 count=5000
```

TABLES

Problem: Table Compression

How do I compress a table in order to reduce the number of extents and restore them to one contiguous chunk?

Solution: Exports, Alters, or Alter Fragment

There are several ways to do this, depending upon which version of the IDS engine your have.

- Export the table to a flatfile, drop and rebuild the table, and import the table back into the newly built table.
- ALTER INDEX TO CLUSTER (requires enough space for a duplicate copy of the table.
- ALTER FRAGMENT ON TABLE tablename INIT in spacename. This works for later versions of IDS and is the fastest, most efficient method.

DETERMINING LOCALES

Problem: Locales

I'm getting errors regarding locales. How do I see what locale my system is set up for?

Solution: sysdblocale

Do a SELECT from sysmaster:sysdbslocale to find your locale setup. The dbs_collate value is the name of the locale you are set up for. You can also run the following query against the database in question:

```
SELECT site from systables where tabname = `` GL_COLLATE"
```

The first character in the tabname is a SPACE, so the tabname is "<SPACE>GL_COLLATE."

DBSPACETEMP AND TEMPORARY SPACES

Problem: Out of Sort Space

I'm trying to do an indexing operation on a large table (500 million rows), and the index continuously fails with an "out of sort space" error. I have my DBTEMPSPACE set to a series of 10 chunks, each with the maximum size of 2 gigabytes. I can watch the temp space usage, and there's no way that I'm using up all of this space. What's happening?

Solution: Build a Big Tempspace

Informix has a 2-gigabyte size limit for chunks, and the way your system is set up is correct for most types of operations. You decided to use 10 separate sort spaces to spread the temp table activity across multiple spindles in the finest tradition of optimizing disk I/O.

When Informix is doing an index, it begins placing temporary tables in each space of your DBTEMPSPACE. As it gets toward the end of the sort, it begins to consolidate these temporary tables into fewer, larger tables. At some point, the table size exceeds the 2 gigabytes size of the chunk. The sort is limited by the size of your smallest dbspace that is used for a tempspace.

The solution is to reboot the engine with no DBSPACETEMP and to drop the dbspaces that were used for temp space. Then re-create it as one very large dbspace having 20 gigabytes, rather than 10 having 2 gigabytes. You'll lose the benefits of multiple spindles, but when the tablesize goes over 2 gigabytes, it will be able to move into the second and subsequent chunks that comprise the large tempspace and the sort will not fail. You can then break the dbspace up into multiple dbspaces if you want to get the I/O benefits, after the index is created.

If you have lots of space in your UNIX filesystem, you could also try setting PSORT_DBTEMP to a large UNIX filesystem and using the PSORT parameters to do parallel sorting outside of the database.

You could also consider creating the index with more fragments. The sort will then generate more sort files but it should distribute them a little more evenly, since the amount of data sorted for each fragment will be less.

Another thing to be concerned about is the size of the dbspaces listed in the DBSPACETEMP variable. Some versions of IDS have a bug (#83745) that occurs during index builds. If IDS finds that the size of the first dbspace listed in DBSPACETEMP was not the same size as all the others, IDS assumes that the total DBSPACETEMP is the size of the first dbspace and restricts itself to using just the space in the first dbspace. This results in a single-threaded, slow index build. It's best to have equal-sized chunks for the dbspaces comprising DBSPACETEMP.

Problem: Out of Space with no Log

When I create a temporary table using "WITH NO LOG," the temporary table seems to be fragmented across all of the dbspaces included in the DBSPACETEMP variable. When I create the temporary table without using the "WITH NO LOG" flag, only one fragment is used. I have several gigabytes of free DBSPACETEMP, and yet when I create a temp table without the "WITH NO LOG" clause, I run out of space. Why?

Solution: Use a Big Temporary Space

The dbspaces detailed in DBSPACETEMP are only used for unlogged temp tables. If you don't use the "WITH NO LOG," implicit temp tables are created in the rootdbs and explicit temp tables are created in the dbspace where the current database resides. Use the "WITH NO LOG," not only for the benefits of no logging, but also to ensure that the temp table is placed in the DBSPACETEMP dbspaces.

Problem: -229 Error

I'm getting a (-229) error when trying to create a temp table. I have plenty of space in DBSPACETEMP and can't create the table. Why?

Solution: Use at Least Two Chunks for each Temporary Dbspace

Sometimes the optimizer will predict a very large number of rows will be returned from a query and will then go out and grab each block of the first chunk of each dbspace in DBSPACETEMP for the result set. When the engine subsequently needs to write to a temporary space for something like a hash join, the query fails, even though not all of the temp space has actually been used. You can avoid this behavior by creating each dbspace listed in DBSPACETEMP with two or more chunks. This avoids the problem because the big query only lays claim to the entire first chunk of each dbspace.

ARCHIVING AND TEMPORARY SPACES

Problem: Temp Space Problems

I'm archiving very large 24 x 7 databases while they are seeing significant amounts of user updates, inserts, and deletes. My archive is failing with temp space errors. Why?

Solution: Use a Big Temporary Space

This is similar to the quandary of one large DBSPACETEMP versus a DBSPACETEMP composed of more, smaller dbspaces. While you want to have multiple smaller DBSPACES comprising your DBSPACETEMP for query performance, IDS versions before 7.3 have some problems with DBSPACETEMP usage.

IDS systems changed their archiving methodology from OnLine. Now, at each checkpoint during an archive, the physical log pages are stored in one of the tempdbspaces listed in DBSPACETEMP before the physical log is cleared and the checkpoint is allowed to complete. When the archive of each dbspace is completed, these temp tables are written out to tape as part of the archive. This is the mechanism that allows IDS to simultaneously archive to tape and to modify pages that may have already been written to tape.

These temp tables are distributed across all of the dbspaces in DBSPACETEMP, but each temp table will not span dbspaces. Thus, under very heavy user activity, a temp dbspace holding the stored physical log spaces can fill up, even though there is plenty of space left in the other temp dbspaces. When this happens, the archive aborts. This is made worse by the fact that versions prior to 7.3 do not clean out these dbspaces after each regular dbspace is archived. This occurs only after the entire archive is completed.

The way to cure this is to configure your DBSPACETEMP as one or two multichunk, large dbspaces rather than as many small dbspaces. This is scheduled to be fixed in 7.3.

UPDATE STATISTICS

Question: When was Update Statistics Last Run?

How can I tell when my last UPDATE STATISTICS was run?

Answer: Query the sysdistrib Table.

If you are using either UPDATE STATISTICS HIGH or UPDATE STATISTICS ME-
DIUM, you can run the following query against the sysmaster database and see when the
last UPDATE STATISTICS was run:

```
select distinct tabname, b.constructed, b.mode
from systables a, sysdistrib b
where a.tabid=b.tabid
order by 1
```

     This does not work with an UPDATE STATISTICS or an UPDATE STATISTICS
LOW, as it depends on the distributions tables.

MULTIPROCESSORS

Question: Do I Run my Two-processor System with MUL-
TIPROCESSOR = 1 or 0?

I have a system with two physical processors. Do I set my system up with the
MULTIPROCESSOR flag set to 0 for no multiprocessors or set to 1 for multiprocessors.
How many CPU-VPs should I set up?

Answer: It depends.

This is a somewhat noncommittal answer. The only way to find out for sure is to test it with
your application on your own server. "Conventional wisdom" for Informix says that the
overhead of handling the processor switching code that is implemented when you run with
MULTIPROCESSOR = 1 eclipses the performance gains with only two processors and that
this flag should only be set when you have four or more processors. There has been some
recent anecdotal evidence that shows that this may no longer be valid. Some users claim that
this is valid with slower processors but not valid with processors over about 200 MHz. With
the rapid increase in processor speed, especially in NT systems, this should be tested rather
than taken for granted.

Question: How many CPU-VPs Should I set up in a Multiprocessor System?

The manual suggests running with a number of CPU-VPs one fewer than the number of physical processors. Is this still true?

Answer: It Depends upon your System and Application.

The manual recommendation is based on leaving one processor always available for non-database operating system activities, thus allocating #CPUs - 1 to the database. Again, with faster processors, this may not be accurate. With systems in which the only application running on the server is the database engine itself, it may pay to go ahead and increase the number of CPU-VPs up to the number of physical CPUs.

On decision support systems that make extensive use of PDQ and parallel index builds and which have multiple, fast processors, some users report up to a 60 percent improvement in index build times by increasing the number of CPU-VPs to one plus the number of processors. I've seen claims that having up to twice the number of CPU-VPs in relation to physical CPUs will increase the speed of the system.

You've got to remember that as systems increase in speed, they become more efficient and can handle such things as thread switching much faster than before. The manuals and even the conventional wisdom from the Internet discussion groups cannot always keep pace with the increase in capability of the technology. You've got to test these things for yourself on your own system.

TUNING

Question: How can I use the Undocumented QSTATS & WSTATS Parameters?

How can I use the statistics collected by either the QSTATS or WSTATS parameters (see `onstat -g wst` and `onstat -g ost`) to find bottlenecks in my system?

Answer: Query the sysseswts Table.

Set WSTAT to 1 in your ONCONFIG file, restart the server, and run the following query at frequent intervals during heavy loads:

```
select sum(cumtime), reason from sysseswts where
reason != "condition" and cumtime > 1000
group by reason
order by 1 desc
```

NETWORK PERFORMANCE

Problem: Poor Network Performance

It's taking my applications an inordinate amount of time to connect to Informix databases and to pull data back from it. When I'm on the server and using a shared memory connection, the data comes back fast, but over I-Net, the speed seems way too slow.

Solution: FET_BUF_SIZE

Explore the FET_BUF_SIZE environment variables on both clients and hosts. The Informix defaults often result in the transmission of lots of empty packets. A good number to start out with is 8192. Also, look at your applications to be sure that they are sending data over the network only when it is actually needed. Do as much filtering as possible with your WHERE clauses on the server rather than sending data over the network only to filter it out by the client. Explore the use of VARCHARs if you have lots of large character variables that may not be totally filled. Look at using stored procedures and PRE-PARED/EXECUTED statements to reduce network traffic during the formulating of SQL statements.

USING THE VIOLATIONS TABLES

Problem: Using During Loads

I'd like to be able to use dbaccess to load from a flatfile, but it may have duplicate records. I know I can use dbload and get around this, but is there any way I can have the "load" command work the same way?

Answer: Start Violations

Beginning with IDS 7.1 you can use the violations table facility to do this. Run the following SQL from `dbaccess`:

```
START VIOLATIONS TABLE FOR tablename;
SET INDEXES, CONSTRAINTS FOR tablename FILTERING WITHOUT ERROR;
LOAD FROM "tablename.unl" INSERT INTO tablename;
STOP VIOLATIONS TABLE FOR tablename;
```

This will create two tables in your database, tablename_vio and tablename_dia. The rows that violate the constraints or indexes will go into tablename_vio, and a line explaining the type of violation will go into tablename_dia.

VARCHARS VERSUS CHAR DATA TYPES

Question: How much Varchars cost in Performance?

I'd like to be able to take advantage of varchars instead of chars to save on disk space, but I'm concerned about a possible performance loss. How much will varchars cost me?

Answer: Somewhat less Performance with Varchars.

This is one of those "your mileage may vary" answers, but in general, varchars are compressed character fields. Your engine knows where the field starts, but it has to make some calculations in order to find out where the field ends. With fixed-length character fields in your table, it is relatively easy for the engine to parse the row into fields. It's a little more CPU-intensive with varchars, as each field depends upon the amount of data in the varchar.

Ad hoc tests have shown INSERT and SELECT statements costing about 5 percent more with varchars. UPDATES can be more expensive, with additional costs up to 20 percent or so depending upon the amount of page reorganization needed. Some studies have show that DELETES are for some reason a little faster with varchars than with chars. (I'll believe it when I see it.)

CONNECTIONS

Problem: Finding the Server Name

How do I find the server name of the system I am connected to?

Solution: Query the systables Table

Run the following query against the system tables:

```
SELECT DBSERVERNAME from systables where tabid = 1;
```

This also demonstrates a method for doing a SELECT for other SQL constants when they are not in a particular table. You can do this by selecting such items as CURRENT or USER in the same manner. The "WHERE tabid = 1" is simply a way of ensuring that you get only one row returned. Another method of doing this is to create a dummy table called "dummy" with only one row and only one column in the table. Then you could

```
SELECT CURRENT from dummy;
```

and get the same type of result.

Problem: How many Users are Connected to a Database?

How can I tell how many users and sessions are connected to a particular database environment?

Solution: syssessions and syssqlstat

Run the following SQL command:

```
DATABASE sysmaster;
SELECT b.sid, b.pid, b.username, a.sqs_dbname, b.tty
FROM syssqlstat a, syssessions b
WHERE a.sqs_sessionid = b.sid
AND a.sqs_dbname = 'your_db_name';
```

SET EXPLAIN

Problem: How can I Embed SET EXPLAINS in Code?

I'd like to be able to imbed diagnostics capabilities into my programs so that I could use an environment variable to turn on and turn off the SET EXPLAIN command at will. How do I do that?

Solution: Use an environment variable.

Before running the code set an environment variable wantexplain = "Y." Early in the code, after the connection to the database is made, include some code similar to this pseudocode:

```
retrieve the environment variable into wantenv
if wantenv == "Y"
EXEC SQL SET EXPLAIN ON;
else
EXEC SQL SET EXPLAIN OFF;
done
```

If you use this technique, be sure that the environment variable is set to "N" by default in your environment, since the output files from SET EXPLAIN can grow very large very quickly.

STORED PROCEDURES

Problem: How to Increase the Cache.

I have a lot of stored procedures and the stored procedure cache is limited to 50. Can I increase it so that more of stored procedures are cached?

Solution: PC_POOLSIZE

Insert the parameter PC_POOLSIZE into the ONCONFIG file and set it to whatever number you like. This parameter is not usually in the ONCONFIG file, but it defaults to 50.

ESQL/C

Problem: How do I Run an "UNLOAD" Command from ESQL/C?

ESQL/C does not support the UNLOAD command. How can I duplicate this functionality in ESQL/C?

Answer: Use an ESQL/C Program to Unload Data

Write an ESQL/C program along the lines of this one:

```
strcpy (select_string, "SELECT field1, field2, ...FROM tablename WHERE ....")
$PREPARE my_statement from select_string;
$DECLARE my_cursor CURSOR for my_statement;

while ()
{
$FETCH my_cursor INTO variable1, variable2....;
if  ( sqlca.sqlcode != 0 )
        {
$CLOSE my_cursor;
$FREE my_cursor;
break;
        }
frprintf (stdout, "%s|%s|%s....\n", variable1, variable2....);
 }
```

Of course, you have to specify the select statement and declare and arrange the variables correctly, but this can allow you to achieve the needed functionality.

TRIGGERS

Question: How can I Disable Triggers Temporarily?

I have tables with update and insert triggers and there are times that I want to work with them for maintenance and not have the triggers fire. Can I do this without dropping and re-creating the triggers?

Answer: Disable the triggers.

You can use a SET TRIGGERS trigger_name DISABLED statement. When you finish your work, run a SET TRIGGERS trigger_name ENABLED command. The system will not attempt to go back and run the triggers, but instead will continue as though all triggers had fired correctly during the manipulations. You are responsible to be sure that any referential integrity that may have been enforced by the triggers is handled manually, so be careful in using this.

ARCHIVES AND LOGS

Question: What can I do to Prevent Logs from Filling up During a Long Transaction?

Answer: Set LBU_PRESERVE = 1.

In earlier versions of the OnLine engine, users occasionally ran into a problem with getting into a long transaction and filling the logfiles when rollback occurred. This would result in the "Informix Death Penalty" in which the only way to recover the system was to restore from archives.

Later IDS engines set the LTXHWM and LTXEHWM to lower defaults of 50 and 60, reducing the likelihood of this happening. There is another setting that can provide a second layer of protection if you want a belt-and-suspenders approach to preventing this. Run your engine with LBU_PRESERVE=1 in the $ONCONFIG file. This prevents the last logfile from being used. If you ever get into a potential "death penalty" situation, shut the engine down and reset LBU_PRESERVE = 0 before restarting. If your logfiles are big enough to handle the rollback records, you'll be able to roll back the transaction using this last logfile.

Problem: Point-in-Time Recovery

On my OnLine (5.X) system, someone deleted a table and I'd like to try to recover it by restoring from an archive and rolling forward the logs to a point in time just before the delete. Is there any way of doing this?

Solution: Desperate Measures

If it is absolutely critical that you do this and you have no other options, there is something that you can try that is dangerous and totally unsupported. First, take a full backup of the system because there is about a 50/50 possibility that you will destroy your database.

Then start the restore with someone standing by the tape ready to eject the tape immediately. Get the PID of the restore so that you can kill it if needed. Do a continuous series of "tbtape -1" (you could also try this with ontape). When you get to a point just before where the delete occurred (you need to have an idea when this happened: use tblog or onlog to find the spot), have the tape watcher eject the tape. Force a checkpoint with tbmode -c, and then bump to the next logfile with tbmode -l. Take the engine down and start it back up. When it's up, run tbcheck -cr and tbcheck -cI and tbcheck -cD on the system. If it comes back up at all, do an immediate dump of the table to a flatfile with "UNLOAD TO." If the database shows any signs of corruption or other problems, go back and restore from your good archive. With any luck, the flatfile will be good enough to restore the table.

Although this is an OnLine trick, there may be instances in which you could do the same thing on an IDS system.

TIME CALCULATIONS

Question: How can I Convert the Connect Time Values in sysessions to a Readable Time?

Answer: Use the l2date Stored Procedure.

IDS systems create a stored procedure called l2date (the first character is a lower-case "L") which will calculate the date only. If you want to get the date in datetime format, run the following SQL statement:

```
SELECT sid,username,hostname,connected,
DATETIME(1970-01-01 00:00:00) YEAR TO SECOND + connected UNITS SECOND
FROM sysmaster:syssessions;
```

This gives you the date and time in GMT (Universal Time) for the connection.

Building Manageable Client/Server Projects

We often look at a client/server integration project as having two separate components, the client and the server. The client side has the user interface and maybe some business logic. The server side contains the database that handles data manipulation and storage. This two-sided view leaves out a critical third section, namely, the administration of the system.

If the administration side of the equation is ignored, you may end up with a beautiful and functional client talking to an industrial-strength server that is an absolute horror to administer. If you develop the project with the system administration and database administration tasks as a consideration from the beginning, you can ensure that the housekeeping functions of your project enjoy the same elegance and utility as the rest of the project.

CLIENT/SERVER APPLICATION DESIGN

An integration project or a software development project typically goes through several phases. The first phase is usually a planning phase and consists of gathering users' needs and preferences. Often, a prototype phase follows. Next comes an initial development phase in which actual coding and software development occurs. This is followed by a testing and acceptance phase in which the user eventually signs off on the phase. Finally the project goes into a production mode in which maintenance and upgrades are the primary function of the integrator/developers.

Often, the development cycle proceeds in phases that consist of iterations of the planning/development/testing/acceptance cycle until the entire project is completed and implemented. Of course, this assumes that the project is eventually completed. In real life, projects tend to go through this development cycle forever. As long as the code can be modified, someone is going to want to modify it.

The administrative and maintenance needs of your project will vary greatly depending upon your position in the development cycle. During the initial planning phase, most of the administrative needs will consist of completing the specs for the project and tracking the changes and updates to the project's specs. During development, you may be concerned more with project management and directing the activities and progress of a team of developers. During testing and acceptance, you'll need to track and eventually clear up the users' lists of objections or problems. Finally, during production, you'll need to be able to provide maintenance and housekeeping functions that allow for the management of day-to-day operations.

During the entire cycle, you'll provide documentation for everything that eventually goes into the system. After the system is in production, you'll be referring to the documentation and history files for purposes of upgrading and debugging.

We're really talking about two distinct types of administrative functions, those that are important in the development phase and those that are important in the production phase. During development, you'll be mostly concerned with tracking and documenting. During production, you'll concerned with troubleshooting and system housekeeping.

When you take a global view of the development process, you will see that the administrative and maintenance needs are interrelated. What happens during testing depends on your specs. You will probably discover needs during testing that will force you to go back to the specs as the users begin to see a real system in action. You'll discover items that need to be included in the housekeeping functions as you go through the development process.

Let's look at the administrative needs for both the development and production phases of your project.

Administration During Development

The first need during the development project is for project management. Project leadership needs to be able to plan and direct the activities of the development team for the duration of the project. This topic has been covered extensively in many places, so we'll assume that you are working with some type of project management system. Take your choice. There are many good project management tools available.

Most of the administrative needs during the development phase of any project will consist of document management. You'll need to be able to generate and track changes in the spec documents. You'll need to develop and track changes in code. You'll have the same need to generate and track testing results and customer "punch list" items during testing. Your best tool here is a an organized approach and a good source code control system.

Project Team Communication

The key to keeping everything organized is keeping it in the same place and available to everyone who needs access to the information. The important factors are communication and access. If your project is big enough to have multiple developers, put everyone on the same UNIX system or the same LAN. Tie everyone together on the system with e-mail. If you have access to groupware, use the groupware as the central point of control for the project. When assigning tasks or requesting information, do it through e-mail or groupware. Much of the accumulated data that piles up during the development phase will be useless in later phases, but some may be critical later in the process. After the project goes into maintenance and upkeep mode, you may be able to use the information contained in old e-mail messages to solve problems long after the original developers are out of the picture. Disk space is cheap. Don't throw anything away. Put it on tape if you have to, but keep it all.

It is important that your project team communications system provide an area to store notes and ideas for later implementation. Things will come up during development that will point you toward tools that will be needed during the production phase. For example, if you find that your developers are constantly having to import and export data from flat files, you may want to consider giving this type of capability to the users as part of your administrative toolset. You may very well end up giving the users a subset of the same tools that you use during development.

Source Code Control

A good source code control system is critical to any project. Don't even think about developing anything nontrivial without some sort of source code control. Source code control should not be limited to source code. Put your specifications under source code control. Put configuration files, batch files, scripts, database schemas, SQL scripts, and system layout information under source code control. Put the system documentation under source code control.

Whoever is managing the development project must consistently and adamantly enforce rules about source code control. Every time someone changes a comma in the code, it should go through the source code control system.

This is important not only during development but during the maintenance and production phase as well. View source code control both as a development tool and as a debugging tool. As you begin to troubleshoot and debug system problems once the system is in production, you may find that you are suddenly having problems with a module. You'll talk to the developer. "Nope, I haven't made any changes in the last month," you'll hear. Later, you'll hear, "Well, I did delete that comment line yesterday. Oops, looks like I deleted a closing quotation too." People tend to remember big changes that they make but they will often forget about the "minor" changes that they make for cosmetic or formatting changes. Religious use of source code control throughout the project will let you catch items such as this without getting an ulcer.

Administration in Production

Once the project goes into production, the administrative functions will probably be turned over to the users. Depending upon the scope of the project, these administrative functions may be split between different users or even between different user departments. In a small project, the administrative requirements may be minimal and may end up being simply an adjunct to one of the user's job functions. In a larger system, there may be a division of labor between system administration, database administration, and application administration. In any case, being able to provide administrative tools that are of the same high quality as the applications you develop is the signature of a professional development effort.

System Administration Functions

Most client/server integration projects involve either UNIX servers with PC clients or a LAN with PC clients and a PC fileserver. Some projects still include mainframes as servers or as sources of data. Usually, the system administration needs will be fairly well defined and similar to the needs of others on the same type of system. In a existing system, the project may be simply added onto other systems, and there may already be system administration functions in place. If your system is a stand-alone system, you will need to integrate system administration tools into your system.

In most cases, it doesn't make sense to write your own tools. See what your operating system or hardware vendor provides and provide menu options to invoke these functions. If necessary, look at third-party system administration tools. Provide documentation and instruction in the use of these tools as part of your documentation package. There are certain things that your system administration tools will need to handle well.

User Management Functions

Adding and deleting users is one of the more common tasks for the system administrator. In addition to providing logins and directories for new users and deleting them for users who leave, the system administration tool should make it easy to assign the proper levels of access and security to new user accounts.

System Backup Functions

Provide a backup plan and schedule based upon the users' needs. Be sure that in addition to the normal day-to-day backups you also make provisions for failure from catastrophic system events such as hard disk failures. Make sure that your backup plan contains off-site storage of at least one set of backup data.

Monitoring Functions

Provide a mechanism to monitor the error logs that your operating system generates. Watching the logs can often give you advance warning of a developing situation. Catching problems in advance is always cheaper and less disruptive than discovering them through a system crash.

Users should also be able to monitor such items as system load, amount of free disk storage, hardware status, and system performance. Unless your user has a dedicated system administrator, you may have to provide simpler, less technical tools to allow for less sophisticated users. Many vendor and third-party tools will allow the administrator to set thresholds that trigger alarms and provide notification of problems. If you are able to incorporate such tools into your project, you will benefit in several ways. First, your system will be more integrated and professional to your users. At least as important is that support costs will be less if you can catch upcoming problems before they become emergencies.

Database Administration Functions

The database administrator faces many of the same challenges that are faced by the system administrator. In many cases, the database administrator *is* the system administrator. Just as there are vendor-provided and third-party tools for system administration, there are excellent tools available for the administration of the database. Identifying these tools is often more difficult than finding their counterparts in the system administration arena because the database administration tools are more specialized. They are often specific to a particular database. The natural place to begin looking for database administration tools is with the database vendor. If the vendor's own tools are not adequate for your needs, they may be able to direct you toward third-party database administration packages that work with their database.

Problems that arise for the developers during the development stage will most likely also arise during production. Let these problems guide you in providing end-user tools to aid in the administration of your database. Production problems may not be exactly the same as the development problems, but you can be certain that they will be similar.

Database Backups

Often, the user is confused about the differences between database backups or archives and the backups done at the operating system level. In some instances, these backups may be one and the same, but most often the database will have its own archiving needs.

Database backups are intrinsically more complicated in a transaction processing environment because of the need to maintain database consistency. If you are using transactions in your database, you certainly do not want to archive the first part of a transaction and not archive the subsequent portions.

Some older database management systems require that the database be off-line before it can be archived in order to ensure that the database is in a consistent state when it is archived. This can be a significant factor for a system that needs to be available to the users on a 24-hour basis.

The amount of data to be backed up can also be a critical factor in database administration. The anticipated amount of data to be backed up and the amount of time required to back up the system should be considered early in the development effort. During the design phase, it is possible to logically partition the data in such a way that not all of it needs to be backed up every day. Making these types of changes in your data structures and layouts may be impossible once you get to the production phase and actually see the effects of trying to back it all up at once.

At best, changing the design at this late stage will be time-consuming and costly.

Logging

Many relational databases provide transactional integrity through some variation of transaction logging. Often, transaction logs will have their own backup and retention requirements. These logs are usually important in case of a catastrophic failure resulting in the need to restore the system from tape.

The restore process often involves restoring first from an archive tape and then applying any transactions that have occurred since the time the archive was done. This has critical implications for downtime in the case of system failure.

Be certain of one thing. The system *will* fail at some time. It'll be hit by a bolt of lightning or the computer room will flood or a programmer will make some sort of mistake and delete all the data. You *will* have to recover from tape in production, and you need to take into account the amount of time that this will take. Make your design decisions accordingly.

Monitoring

Understanding what is actually happening inside a database can be a difficult task even for the best database administrator. UNIX gurus who can recite chapter and verse from the UNIX manpages may be totally at a loss when trying to figure out why the database is behaving as it does. A lot of this is because the database is often considered as a "black box." You give it queries. It gives you data.

Even some simple questions such as "How full is my database?" can often be difficult to answer. Anticipate these questions and build or provide tools to answer them for the administrator. Monitoring what's going on inside the database will make it much easier for support staff when they get emergency calls at three in the morning.

Monitoring tools should allow the administrator to monitor and track items that are unique to the database. The administrator needs to be able to monitor the use and activity of system resources such as database storage and free space. She will also need to be able to monitor items that can cause problems with database operations such as deadlocks, communication timeouts, lock usage, and database checkpoints. Database management systems use different terms for these items, and different systems may use different mechanisms to meet the same functional requirements. That's why database monitoring tools are less generic than system administration tools. If something can happen inside the database that will kill your application or kill its performance, the user must be able to detect and report the problem before it can be fixed. The monitoring tool is the best way to provide this assistance to the user.

There is a growing trend toward database and system management tools that are graphically oriented. These tools are client/server applications in themselves and can provide a simple and understandable presentation of system activities to a relatively unsophisticated audience. The same tools can assist the sophisticated user or support person with understanding the sometimes subtle relationships between various aspects of the system. Such tools can be a valuable addition to an integrated system.

The good part about database monitoring tools is that once you've found or written a good one, it will serve you in subsequent projects using the same database management system. You'll find that the applications may differ, but the general types of problems will remain the same no matter what you're doing.

Application Administration Functions

In your application, you'll face many of the same general types of monitoring and troubleshooting problems that you do at the operating system and database levels. The difference is that you will be more limited in the tools you have available to solve problems at the application level.

If you are integrating a third-party application into your system, you may be limited to the tools that are provided by your application vendor. If you are creating your own application, you will have to also create your own administration and monitoring tools.

If you are using a third-party application, be sure to have access to their table and file layouts. This way, if your vendor does not provide the facility that you may need, you can always create it yourself. If you are dealing with a vendor that will not provide this information or this access, you may need to consider your choice of vendors. This, after all, is the whole idea behind open systems development.

Troubleshooting

Just as you will have hardware failures, you will also have instances in which jobs freeze up or terminate or otherwise behave in a strange or irrational manner. You'll have times when a program suddenly slows down to a crawl and the administrator is called in to solve the problem. These cases increase at an exponential rate as the system load goes up. Systems that work flawlessly with 5 users may go to their knees with 50 users.

Many of these load related-problems will result from contention and locking within the database. As more users enter the system, the possibilities for contention and conflict increase. Deadlocks, system freeze-ups, and poor performance result.

It would be best if the users could solve these problems themselves, but what usually happens is that the support team gets called. Early design decisions can make their job much easier or much harder, depending upon whether these decisions were made with future troubleshooting in mind.

Solving problems in a production environment requires understanding how the application interfaces with the database and with the operating system. Design decisions made for one reason may have serious drawbacks when it comes to supporting the product. For example, if one particular module or program begins to fail in production, the first order of business for the support person will be to find out exactly which processes are failing. If all of the users log in as a single master user, it will be difficult to determine exactly who is doing what. The same thing applies to the database. If all users look alike to the database engine, it will be very difficult to find out what is happening to one particular user. Ease of support should play a part in all design decisions for the system.

Application Error Handling

When developing an application, there are several things you can do to make subsequent debugging and tuning easier. It is essential to provide a robust and well thought out error-logging facility. Spend some time and effort on this and use it for the entire application. This facility should provide ample, descriptive error messages to the user as well as history or trace information that helps support personnel track the problem to its root cause. As a minimum, this should include:

- Time of the error
- Operating system or database error text
- Application name generating the error

- Process ID of the task that failed
- Action taken such as transaction rollback

The problem with trying to chase down problems that occur in database systems is that in many cases all of the evidence is gone by the time support is notified. You may know from database logs that a particular process ID died because of a deadlock or lock contention, but how can you find out which task had that particular process ID? This is where a good error-logging facility can pay off . Another useful technique is providing a logging or history mechanism that tracks when programs were run, who ran them, and the process ID of the program. This can often be included as part of a built-in auditing capability. Not only will it help the auditors, but it will also make program debugging much simpler.

We've covered a lot of ground in this article, ranging from the need for a good source code control system up through the necessity of providing good error logging inside your programs. There's a common thread, though, and understanding it can allow a systems developer or systems integrator to provide a professional and maintainable system to the users. This common thread is the need to consider the support and upkeep needs of the project from the very beginning of the design phase. If you do this, you will end up with a system that is truly integrated and can be supported with minimal effort.

Index

!

!!, 329

$

$$
generates a unique filename, 324

.cshrc, 323

<

<<
used in here documents, 324

2

24x7
full-time operations, 3
24x7 systems, 72

A

Ability of Informix utilities, 65
Access buffer, 186
Access Times, 279
Accounting transactions, 22
ACE program, 328
ACE report, 217, 327, 329
Add button, 162
Addr Address, 269
Addr fields, 271
Address of latch, 242
Address of page cleaner thread, 248
Address of resource, 246
Address of table, 243
Address of threads
    waiter, 252
ADM Runs, 28
Administration arena, 451
Administration functions, 450
Administration needs, 450

D

M

O

U

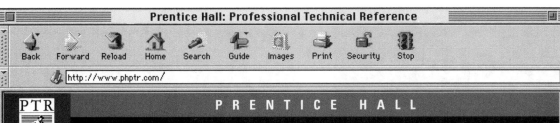

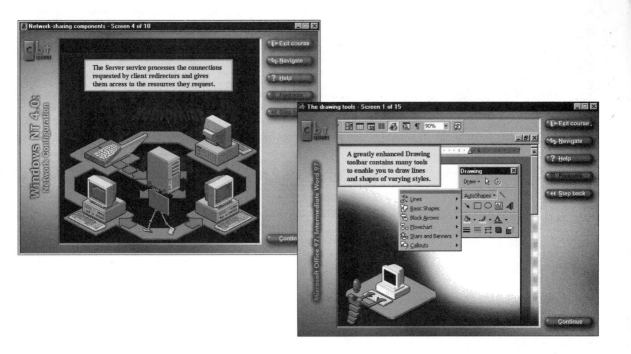

Other curricula available from CBT Systems:

- Cisco
- Informix
- Java
- Marimba
- Microsoft
- Netscape
- Novell

- Oracle
- SAP
- Sybase
- C/C++
- Centura
- Information Technology/
  Core Concepts

- Internet and Intranet
  Skills
- Internetworking
- UNIX

INFORMIX-ONLINE DYNAMIC SERVER HANDBOOK

CARLTON DOE

Hands-on information that will help Informix-OnLine Dynamic Server administrators get their job done as effectively as possible.

- Hands-on techniques and ideas for effective administration.
- Covers the entire process of starting up and running an Informix-OnLine Dynamic Server database environment
- CD-ROM contains a library of administration scripts saving you hundreds of hours.

1997, 496pp., paper, 0-13-605296-7

A BOOK/CD-ROM PACKAGE

PROGRAMMING INFORMIX SQL/4GL:
A Step-By-Step Approach, Second Edition

CATHY KIPP

The most thorough, up-to-date primer on INFORMIX SQL/4GL database design and programming.

- Revised and updated to cover new Informix product features, especially the INFORMIX-4GL Interactive Debugger.
- Includes an overview of relational database design, and step-by-step techniques for building and maintaining databases.
- New CD-ROM includes extensive SQL/4GL software tools.

1998, 512pp, Paper, 0-13-675919-X

A BOOK/CD-ROM PACKAGE

INFORMIX PERFORMANCE TUNING
Second Edition

ELIZABETH SUTO

1997, 192 pp, Cloth,
0-13-239237-2

INFORMIX STORED PROCEDURE PROGRAMMING

MICHAEL L. GONZALES

1996, 200 pp, Paper,
0-13-206723-4

EVOLUTION OF THE HIGH PERFORMANCE DATABASE

INFORMIX SOFTWARE

1997, 432 pp, Cloth,
0-13-594730-8

OPTIMIZING INFORMIX APPLICATIONS

ROBERT SCHNEIDER

1995, 300 pp, Paper,
0-13-149238-1

ADVANCED INFORMIX-4GL PROGRAMMING

ART TAYLOR

1995, 400pp, Paper,
0-13-301318-9

ALSO AVAILABLE...

SELECTED DOCUMENTATION FROM INFORMIX SOFTWARE, INC.

INFORMIX-4GL BY EXAMPLE
0-13-100355-0

INFORMIX GUIDE TO SQL:
Reference • 0-13-100363-1

INFORMIX GUIDE TO SQL:
Tutorial • 0-13-100371-2

PRENTICE HALL PTR

TOMORROW'S
PTR **Solutions** FOR TODAY'S
PH **Professionals.**

CBT SOFTWARE LICENSE AGREEMENT

IF YOU DO NOT AGREE WITH THESE TERMS AND CONDITIONS, DO NOT INSTALL THE SOFTWARE.

This is a legal agreement you and CBT System Ltd. ("Licensor"). The licensor ("Licensor") from whom you have licensed the CBT Group PLC courseware (the "Software"). By installing, copying or otherwise using the Software, you agree to be bound by the terms of this Agreement License Agreement (the "License"). If you do not agree to the terms of this License, the Licensor is unwilling to license the Software to you. In such event, you may not use or copy the Software, and you should promptly contact the Licensor for instructions on the return of the unused Software.

1. Use. Licensor grants to you a non-exclusive, nontransferable license to use Licensor's software product (the "Software") the Software and accompanying documentation in accordance with the terms and conditions of this license agreement ("License") License and as specified in your agreement with Licensor (the "Governing Agreement"). In the event of any conflict between this License and the Governing Agreement, the Governing Agreement shall control.

You may:

a. (if specified as a "personal use" version) install the Software on a single stand-alone computer or a single network node from which node the Software cannot be accessed by another computer, provided that such Software shall be used by only one individual; or

b. (if specified as a "workstation" version) install the Software on a single stand-alone computer or a single network node from which node the Software cannot be accessed by another computer, provided that such Software shall be used by only one individual; or

c. (if specified as a "LAN" version) install the Software on a local area network server that provides access to multiple computers, up to the maximum number of computers or users specified in your Governing Agreement, provided that such Software shall be used only by employees of your organization; or

d. (if specified as an "enterprise" version) install the Software or copies of the Software on multiple local or wide area network servers, intranet servers, stand-alone computers and network nodes (and to make copies of the Software for such purpose) at one or more sites, which servers provide access to a multiple number of users, up to the maximum number of users specified in your Governing Agreement, provided that such Software shall be used only by employees of your organization.

This License is not a sale. Title and copyrights to the Software, accompanying documentation and any copy made by you remain with Licensor or its suppliers or licensors.

2. Intellectual Property. The Software is owned by Licensor or its licensors and is protected by United States and other jurisdictions' copyright laws and international treaty provisions. Therefore, you may not use, copy, or distribute the Software without the express written authorization of CBT Group PLC. This License authorizes you to use the Software for the internal training needs of your employees only, and to make one copy of the Software solely for backup or archival purposes. You may not print copies of any user documentation provided in "online" or electronic form. Licensor retains all rights not expressly granted.

3. Restrictions. You may not transfer, rent, lease, loan or time-share the Software or accompanying documentation. You may not reverse engineer, decompile, or disassemble the Software, except to the extent the foregoing restriction is expressly prohibited by applicable law. You may not modify, or create derivative works based upon the Software in whole or in part.

1. Confidentiality. The Software contains confidential trade secret information belonging to Licensor, and you may use the software only pursuant to the terms of your Governing Agreement, if any, and the license set forth herein. In addition, you may not disclose the Software to any third party.

2. **Limited Liability.** IN NO EVENT WILL THE Licensor's LIABILITY UNDER, ARISING OUT OF OR RELATING TO THIS AGREEMENT EXCEED THE AMOUNT PAID TO LICENSOR FOR THE SOFT-WARE. LICENSOR SHALL NOT BE LIABLE FOR ANY SPECIAL, INCIDENTAL, INDIRECT OR CON-SEQUENTIAL DAMAGES, HOWEVER CAUSED AND ON ANY THEORY OF LIABILITY., REGARDLESS OR WHETHER LICENSOR HAS BEEN ADVISED OF THE POSSIBILITY OF SUCH DAMAGES. WITH-OUT LIMITING THE FOREGOING, LICENSOR WILL NOT BE LIABLE FOR LOST PROFITS, LOSS OF DATA, OR COSTS OF COVER.

3. **Limited Warranty.** LICENSOR WARRANTS THAT SOFTWARE WILL BE FREE FROM DEFECTS IN MATERIALS AND WORKMANSHIP UNDER NORMAL USE FOR A PERIOD OF THIRTY (30) DAYS FROM THE DATE OF RECEIPT. THIS LIMITED WARRANTY IS VOID IF FAILURE OF THE SOFTWARE HAS RESULTED FROM ABUSE OR MISAPPLICATION. ANY REPLACEMENT SOFTWARE WILL BE WARRANTED FOR A PERIOD OF THIRTY (30) DAYS FROM THE DATE OF RECEIPT OF SUCH REPLACEMENT SOFTWARE. THE SOFTWARE AND DOCUMENTATION ARE PROVIDED "AS IS". LICENSOR HEREBY DISCLAIMS ALL OTHER WARRANTIES, EXPRESS, IMPLIED, OR STATUTORY, INCLUDING WITHOUT LIMITATION, THE IMPLIED WARRANTIES OF MERCHANTABILITY AND FITNESS FOR A PARTICULAR PURPOSE.

4. **Exceptions.** SOME STATES DO NOT ALLOW THE LIMITATION OF INCIDENTAL DAMAGES OR LIMITATIONS ON HOW LONG AN IMPLIED WARRANTY LASTS, SO THE ABOVE LIMITATIONS OR EXCLUSIONS MAY NOT APPLY TO YOU. This agreement gives you specific legal rights, and you may also have other rights which vary from state to state.

5. **U.S. Government-Restricted Rights.** The Software and accompanying documentation are deemed to be "commercial computer Software" and "commercial computer Software documenta-tion," respectively, pursuant to FAR Section 227.7202 and FAR Section 12.212, as applicable. Any use, modification, reproduction release, performance, display or disclosure of the Software and accompanying documentation by the U.S. Government shall be governed solely by the terms of this Agreement and shall be prohibited except to the extent expressly permitted by the terms of this Agreement.

6. **Export Restrictions.** You may not download, export, or re-export the Software (a) into, or to a national or resident of, Cuba, Iraq, Libya, Yugoslavia, North Korea, Iran, Syria or any other country to which the United States has embargoed goods, or (b) to anyone on the United States Treasury Department's list of Specially Designated Nations or the U.S. Commerce Department's Table of Deny Orders. By installing or using the Software, you are representing and warranting that you are not located in, under the control of, or a national resident of any such country or on any such list.

7. **General.** This License is governed by the laws of the United States and the State of California, without reference to conflict of laws principles. The parties agree that the United Nations Convention on Contracts for the International Sale of Goods shall not apply to this License. If any provision of this Agreement is held invalid, the remainder of this License shall continue in full force and effect.

8. **More Information.** Should you have any questions concerning this Agreement, or if you desire to contact Licensor for any reason, please contact: CBT Systems USA Ltd., 1005 Hamilton Court, Menlo Park, California 94025, Attn: Chief Legal Officer.

IF YOU DO NOT AGREE WITH THE ABOVE TERMS AND CONDITIONS, SO NOT INSTALL THE SOFTWARE AND RETURN IT TO THE LICENSOR.

LICENSE AGREEMENT AND LIMITED WARRANTY

READ THE FOLLOWING TERMS AND CONDITIONS CAREFULLY BEFORE OPENING THIS DISK PACKAGE. THIS LEGAL DOCUMENT IS AN AGREEMENT BETWEEN YOU AND PRENTICE-HALL, INC. (THE "COMPANY"). BY OPENING THIS SEALED DISK PACKAGE, YOU ARE AGREEING TO BE BOUND BY THESE TERMS AND CONDITIONS. IF YOU DO NOT AGREE WITH THESE TERMS AND CONDITIONS, DO NOT OPEN THE DISK PACKAGE. PROMPTLY RETURN THE UNOPENED DISK PACKAGE AND ALL ACCOMPANYING ITEMS TO THE PLACE YOU OBTAINED THEM FOR A FULL REFUND OF ANY SUMS YOU HAVE PAID.

1. **GRANT OF LICENSE:** In consideration of your payment of the license fee, which is part of the price you paid for this product, and your agreement to abide by the terms and conditions of this Agreement, the Company grants to you a nonexclusive right to use and display the copy of the enclosed software program (hereinafter the "SOFTWARE") on a single computer (i.e., with a single CPU) at a single location so long as you comply with the terms of this Agreement. The Company reserves all rights not expressly granted to you under this Agreement.

2. **OWNERSHIP OF SOFTWARE:** You own only the magnetic or physical media (the enclosed disks) on which the SOFTWARE is recorded or fixed, but the Company retains all the rights, title, and ownership to the SOFTWARE recorded on the original disk copy(ies) and all subsequent copies of the SOFTWARE, regardless of the form or media on which the original or other copies may exist. This license is not a sale of the original SOFTWARE or any copy to you.

3. **COPY RESTRICTIONS:** This SOFTWARE and the accompanying printed materials and user manual (the "Documentation") are the subject of copyright. You may not copy the Documentation or the SOFTWARE, except that you may make a single copy of the SOFTWARE for backup or archival purposes only. You may be held legally responsible for any copying or copyright infringement which is caused or encouraged by your failure to abide by the terms of this restriction.

4. **USE RESTRICTIONS:** You may not network the SOFTWARE or otherwise use it on more than one computer or computer terminal at the same time. You may physically transfer the SOFTWARE from one computer to another provided that the SOFTWARE is used on only one computer at a time. You may not distribute copies of the SOFTWARE or Documentation to others. You may not reverse engineer, disassemble, decompile, modify, adapt, translate, or create derivative works based on the SOFTWARE or the Documentation without the prior written consent of the Company.

5. **TRANSFER RESTRICTIONS:** The enclosed SOFTWARE is licensed only to you and may not be transferred to any one else without the prior written consent of the Company. Any unauthorized transfer of the SOFTWARE shall result in the immediate termination of this Agreement.

6. **TERMINATION:** This license is effective until terminated. This license will terminate automatically without notice from the Company and become null and void if you fail to comply with any provisions or limitations of this license. Upon termination, you shall destroy the Documentation and all copies of the SOFTWARE. All provisions of this Agreement as to warranties, limitation of liability, remedies or damages, and our ownership rights shall survive termination.

7. **MISCELLANEOUS:** This Agreement shall be construed in accordance with the laws of the United States of America and the State of New York and shall benefit the Company, its affiliates, and assignees.

8. **LIMITED WARRANTY AND DISCLAIMER OF WARRANTY:** The Company warrants that the SOFTWARE, when properly used in accordance with the Documentation, will operate

in substantial conformity with the description of the SOFTWARE set forth in the Documentation. The Company does not warrant that the SOFTWARE will meet your requirements or that the operation of the SOFTWARE will be uninterrupted or error-free. The Company warrants that the media on which the SOFTWARE is delivered shall be free from defects in materials and workmanship under normal use for a period of thirty (30) days from the date of your purchase. Your only remedy and the Company's only obligation under these limited warranties is, at the Company's option, return of the warranted item for a refund of any amounts paid by you or replacement of the item. Any replacement of SOFTWARE or media under the warranties shall not extend the original warranty period. The limited warranty set forth above shall not apply to any SOFTWARE which the Company determines in good faith has been subject to misuse, neglect, improper installation, repair, alteration, or damage by you. EXCEPT FOR THE EXPRESSED WARRANTIES SET FORTH ABOVE, THE COMPANY DISCLAIMS ALL WARRANTIES, EXPRESS OR IMPLIED, INCLUDING WITHOUT LIMITATION, THE IMPLIED WARRANTIES OF MERCHANTABILITY AND FITNESS FOR A PARTICULAR PURPOSE. EXCEPT FOR THE EXPRESS WARRANTY SET FORTH ABOVE, THE COMPANY DOES NOT WARRANT, GUARANTEE, OR MAKE ANY REPRESENTATION REGARDING THE USE OR THE RESULTS OF THE USE OF THE SOFTWARE IN TERMS OF ITS CORRECTNESS, ACCURACY, RELIABILITY, CURRENTNESS, OR OTHERWISE.

IN NO EVENT, SHALL THE COMPANY OR ITS EMPLOYEES, AGENTS, SUPPLIERS, OR CONTRACTORS BE LIABLE FOR ANY INCIDENTAL, INDIRECT, SPECIAL, OR CONSEQUENTIAL DAMAGES ARISING OUT OF OR IN CONNECTION WITH THE LICENSE GRANTED UNDER THIS AGREEMENT, OR FOR LOSS OF USE, LOSS OF DATA, LOSS OF INCOME OR PROFIT, OR OTHER LOSSES, SUSTAINED AS A RESULT OF INJURY TO ANY PERSON, OR LOSS OF OR DAMAGE TO PROPERTY, OR CLAIMS OF THIRD PARTIES, EVEN IF THE COMPANY OR AN AUTHORIZED REPRESENTATIVE OF THE COMPANY HAS BEEN ADVISED OF THE POSSIBILITY OF SUCH DAMAGES. IN NO EVENT SHALL LIABILITY OF THE COMPANY FOR DAMAGES WITH RESPECT TO THE SOFTWARE EXCEED THE AMOUNTS ACTUALLY PAID BY YOU, IF ANY, FOR THE SOFTWARE.

SOME JURISDICTIONS DO NOT ALLOW THE LIMITATION OF IMPLIED WARRANTIES OR LIABILITY FOR INCIDENTAL, INDIRECT, SPECIAL, OR CONSEQUENTIAL DAMAGES, SO THE ABOVE LIMITATIONS MAY NOT ALWAYS APPLY. THE WARRANTIES IN THIS AGREEMENT GIVE YOU SPECIFIC LEGAL RIGHTS AND YOU MAY ALSO HAVE OTHER RIGHTS WHICH VARY IN ACCORDANCE WITH LOCAL LAW.

ACKNOWLEDGMENT

YOU ACKNOWLEDGE THAT YOU HAVE READ THIS AGREEMENT, UNDERSTAND IT, AND AGREE TO BE BOUND BY ITS TERMS AND CONDITIONS. YOU ALSO AGREE THAT THIS AGREEMENT IS THE COMPLETE AND EXCLUSIVE STATEMENT OF THE AGREEMENT BETWEEN YOU AND THE COMPANY AND SUPERSEDES ALL PROPOSALS OR PRIOR AGREEMENTS, ORAL, OR WRITTEN, AND ANY OTHER COMMUNICATIONS BETWEEN YOU AND THE COMPANY OR ANY REPRESENTATIVE OF THE COMPANY RELATING TO THE SUBJECT MATTER OF THIS AGREEMENT.

Should you have any questions concerning this Agreement or if you wish to contact the Company for any reason, please contact in writing at the address below.

Robin Short
Prentice Hall PTR
One Lake Street
Upper Saddle River, New Jersey 07458

ABOUT THE CD

The enclosed CD-ROM contains the following computer-based training (CBT) course module from CBT Systems:

MS Exchange Server 5.5: Connectors

The CD can be used on Windows 95/Windows NT

Informix documentation files included on the CD were downloaded from the Informix web site (http://www.informix.com/answers) for the convenience of users, and are subject to the Informix web site terms and conditions. They are available solely for personal, informational and non-commercial purposes; are subject to copyright; and may not be modified, copied, or posted. Check the web site for the most up-to-date versions of these documents.

Technical Support

If you have a problem wiht the CBT software, please contact CBT Technical Support. In the US call 1 (800) 938-3247. If you are outside the US call 3531-283-0380.

Prentice Hall does not offer technical support for this software. However, if there is a problem with the media, you may obtain a replacement copy by e-mailing us with your problem at : disc_exchange@prenhall.com